Employment Relations

A Critical and International Approach

PAULINE DIBBEN, GILTON KLERCK AND GEOFFREY WOOD

Pauline Dibben is Senior Lecturer in Employment Relations at the University of Sheffield.

Gilton Klerck is Associate Professor of Sociology at Rhodes University, South Africa.

Geoffrey Wood is Professor in Human Resource Management at the University of Sheffield.

The Chartered Institute of Personnel and Development is the leading publisher of books and reports for personnel and training professionals, students, and all those concerned with the effective management and development of people at work. For details of all our titles, please contact the publishing department:
tel: 020 8612 6204
e-mail: publish@cipd.co.uk
The catalogue of all CIPD titles can be viewed on the CIPD website:
www.cipd.co.uk/bookstore

Employment Relations

A Critical and International Approach

PAULINE DIBBEN, GILTON KLERCK AND GEOFFREY WOOD

Chartered Institute of Personnel and Development

Published by the Chartered Institute of Personnel and Development,
151, The Broadway, London, SW19 1JQ
This edition first published 2011

Typeset by Fakenham Photosetting Ltd, Norfolk

Printed in Spain by GraphyCems

British Library Cataloguing in Publication Data
A catalogue of this publication is available from the British Library

ISBN 978 1 84398 268 5

The views expressed in this publication are the authors' own and may not necessarily reflect those of
the CIPD.

The CIPD has made every effort to trace and acknowledge copyright holders. If any source has been
overlooked, CIPD Enterprises would be pleased to redress this in future editions.

Chartered Institute of Personnel and Development, CIPD House,
151 The Broadway, London, SW19 1JQ
Tel: 020 8612 6200
E-mail: cipd@cipd.co.uk
Website: www.cipd.co.uk
Incorporated by Royal Charter
Registered Charity No. 1079797

Contents

List of Figures and Tables

Acknowledgements

The authors would like to thank Kirsty Smy, CIPD, for her helpful advice and encouragement, in addition to the time and efforts of anonymous reviewers.

DEDICATION

This text is dedicated to Peter, Alan and Violet Dibben, John and Sandra Smith, Harrison and Spencer Corrin, Lalitha and Denis Naidoo, Millicent, David, Michael and Cameron Klerck, and Vicky, Alice, Robert and Myfanwy Wood.

Preface

THE APPROACH USED WITHIN THE TEXT

The text seeks to emphasise the centrality of employment relations to the study of human resource management. Why do employment relations matter? Firstly, the employment contract lies at the heart of modern economic life – one cannot understand how modern economies and societies function without understanding the basis of the employment relationship. Secondly, there is a close relationship between long-term economic trends and the relative power of employees vis-à-vis employers. Understanding changes in the latter sheds new light on the former, and vice versa. Thirdly, whatever their failings, neo-liberal policies remain the favoured paradigm among political elites in many advanced economies and other societies worldwide. Embedded in such policies appears to be a commitment to rolling back the rights of employees. Quite simply, employment relations are today a site of contestation and change, making their study particularly topical. Finally, employment relationships are bound by both legal and informal rules. Effective people management requires an understanding of how such rules work, and how they constrain – and in some cases enable – managerial actions.

The study of employment relations is relevant to union and non-union, public, private and voluntary sector organisations because, firstly, collective relationships exist. In large firms this might focus particularly on works councils or joint consultative committees. Secondly, employee grievances have to be resolved. Thirdly, negotiation and the management of conflict are important to all organisations. Fourthly, fairness and equity within the workplace are essential. Fifthly, it is important to have good practices, and not be known for bad practices (see Gennard and Judge 2005).

A CRITICAL, ACADEMIC AND INTERNATIONAL APPROACH

This textbook explores a range of aspects of employment relations, taking a critical and international approach to the subject. It is 'critical' in that it does not simply take for granted general assumptions about best practice in employment relations. The chapters set out key developments in employment relations and explain current practices, but also involve in-depth discussion and analysis, questioning current practice. For example, in whose interests do managers make decisions? The state is composed of political parties and conflicting interests. To what extent do these competing interests and tensions influence its role as an employer and legislator? Trade unions have arguably been forced into a defensive role. Why is this? Are they still regarded as the conscience of HR managers, or simply as an irritation? Do they defend the interests of weaker employees? In order to tackle these and other questions, the book is divided into two main parts. The first engages with fundamental academic debates within the field of employment relations, while the second is arguably more practical in orientation, engaging with such issues as voice and engagement, conflict and dispute resolution, discipline and grievance, downsizing and redundancy, discrimination, and pay and reward.

In covering conceptual debates and functional areas, the book takes an academic approach in that it draws on established theories of employment relations in addition to empirical research. Many other textbooks carefully explain employment relations legislation and employment practices but do not draw heavily on academic research. Yet other books do take a 'critical' and 'academic' approach but do not explicitly address CIPD standards, and neglect the practical dimensions of addressing key concerns for HR managers and for employees.

The text is also 'international' in approach. The way in which this is tackled in this volume is three-pronged. Firstly, the coverage of concepts and practices of employment relations is undertaken in a way that is relevant to most societies and understandings rather than purely from a British perspective (which is often the case with employment relations texts published in Britain). Where there are particular differences in other countries, these are highlighted and discussed. Secondly, where employment legislation is relevant to a particular chapter, there is reference to the British context, but it is not taken for granted that this applies in all country contexts. Particular attention is accorded to the British and European context where relevant to the CIPD syllabus, such as in the use of employment tribunals. However, in these sections attempts are made to draw out the broader significance of these examples. In addition, where relevant, examples are provided of legislation in other country contexts. Thirdly, learning features within the text such as 'Applying theory to practice' boxes, 'Legislation in practice' boxes and 'Case studies' cover either or both British and other country examples. Fourthly, particular attention is accorded to the international dimensions of employment relations within chapters such as Chapter 5 (*Local, National and Global Effects*) and Chapter 14 (*The Relevance of Comparative Employment Relations*). More generally, there is an implicit understanding that the employment relationship is essentially universal insofar as it relates to capitalist economies and to formal sector work within emerging economies, but differs in terms of strategic choice and practice and according to context.

The book is pitched at Master's-level students studying CIPD-accredited courses. However, it should also be relevant to postgraduate certificate students who wish to develop their knowledge of academic debates more deeply, and to engage critically with the subject. It might also be used on MBA and Executive MBA courses, where lecturers wish to encourage students carefully to consider the roles of each of the parties involved in the employment relationship. Further to this, the book will be of value to those teaching undergraduate courses in employment relations since these students will require a conceptual underpinning in employment relations but will also benefit from the explanation of functional areas.

MAPPING ONTO CIPD LEARNING OUTCOMES

The text maps onto CIPD learning outcomes as shown in the table below.

CIPD learning outcomes	Chapters within *Employment Relations: A Critical and International Approach*
1 Different theories and perspectives on employment relations	Chapter 1: Introduction Chapter 3: Theories of ER Chapter 4: ER and HRM Chapter 6: Power and authority
2 The impact of local, national and global contexts shaping employment relations climates	Chapter 5: Local, national and global effects on the practice of ER
3 The roles and functions of the different parties that control and manage the employment relationship	Chapter 1: Introduction Chapter 2: The main players in ER: trade unions, employers and the state Chapter 6: Power and authority
4 The importance of organisational-level employment relations processes that support organisational performance, including the design and implementation of policies and practices in the areas of: employee engagement, diversity management, employee communication, involvement and participation, negotiation and bargaining, conflict resolution, and change management and management control	Chapter 6: Power and authority Chapter 7: Voice Chapter 8: Employee engagement Chapter 9: Pay and reward Chapter 10: Discrimination, difference and diversity Chapter 12: Conflict and dispute resolution
5 The importance of employment relations procedures that help mitigate organisational risk, including the design and implementation of policies and practices in the areas of discipline, grievance, dismissal and redundancy	Chapter 11: Discipline and grievance Chapter 13: Downsizing and redundancy
6 The integration of employment relations processes and how they impact on policy, practice and organisational outcomes such as performance and employee engagement	Chapter 8: Employee engagement Chapter 14: Conclusion: the relevance of ER and comparative ER

More specifically, the chapters relate to the CIPD learning outcomes, but also develop certain themes in detail in order to engage critically with the topics covered. An outline of the chapter contents is provided below.

A BRIEF EXPLANATION OF CHAPTER CONTENTS

The text covers theory, context, functions and processes. To enable this, the book is divided into two main sections. The first part covers broader conceptual debates and contextual factors and the second part focuses on management interventions in employment relations. Each chapter includes a range of learning features.

Chapter 1: Introduction begins by examining some of the core concepts of employment relations that are returned to throughout the book. In particular, it addresses the following:

- the *employment relationship*, and definitions of employment relations
- the potential differences between employer and employee expectations
- explanations of the employment contract according to legal, economic and psychological perspectives
- different approaches to managing employment relations in union and non-union organisations
- a consideration of aspects of employment relations in multinationals, small and large, private, public and non-profit-making organisations.

Part One: Conceptual debates and contextual factors

Chapter 2 covers the main 'players' in terms of the state, unions and employers. It maps onto CIPD Learning Outcome 3 and the related indicative content from the CIPD Managing Employment Relations module. Each of the parties to employment relations is analysed in some detail. The individual sections cover the practical nature of each of these dimensions, but also engage with more critical debates about their past, current and future roles. The areas covered include:

- Trade unions
  - Trade unions and other collective employee associations (at national and European levels)
  - Union growth and decline
  - Organising and servicing models
- Employers
  - Employer groups and associations (at national and European levels)
  - Management styles
- The state
  - State institutions
  - The objectives and role of government as employer, economic manager and regulator of employment relations
  - Types and forms of legal intervention and regulations; individual and collective law
  - Voluntarism
- The role of management consultants and NGOs.

Chapter 3 covers the theories of employment relations. It maps onto CIPD Learning Outcome 1 and related indicative content from the CIPD Managing Employment Relations module. The chapter covers each of the well-known theories of employment relations, and incorporates critiques of them. Following this, the chapter investigates further the contested nature of work, referring to the indeterminacy of the labour contract and concepts such as structured antagonism. The areas covered include the following theoretical perspectives:

- Unitarism, pluralism and radical theories
- Labour process theory
- Feminism
- Postmodernism
- Critical management studies.

Chapter 4 conceptualises employment relations and human resource management (HRM). This chapter maps onto CIPD Learning Outcome 1, but provides conceptual debates additional to those outlined in the indicative content of the CIPD Managing Employment Relations module. The chapter takes a historical approach to the development of the subject of employment relations, tracks the relationship between employment relations and HRM, and examines how different perceptions of the HR role have implications for the management of employment relations. The areas covered therefore include:

- The origins of employment relations: an interdisciplinary approach
- From industrial relations to employment relations
- Employment relations and HRM
- The development of HRM.

'Human resource management' has been the dominant term for describing the process of people management since the 1980s, and assumes that people represent the key to organisational competitiveness. It has sometimes been argued that the study of employment relations has, with the decline of unions, become less relevant – that employees are less able to contest the terms and conditions of employment. Yet the underlying issues of the employment relationship – the challenges of operationalising an unclear exchange – are central to understanding work and employment relations. Furthermore, the field of employment relations has strong theoretical underpinnings, enabling a more nuanced and critical understanding of what really happens in the workplace.

Chapter 5 examines the local, national and global effects on the practice of employment relations, and in particular engages with international dimensions. The chapter maps onto CIPD Learning Outcome 2 and the related indicative content from the CIPD Managing Employment Relations module. In addition to addressing the practical influence of a range of factors on employment relations, the chapter also includes a critical evaluation of more recent developments. The areas covered include:

- Market factors impacting on performance, such as customers and competitors, globalisation, technology and demographics (include PESTLE)
- The role of institutions and different varieties of capitalism
- The European Union and European legislation
- International employment relations, multinational corporations and employment relations, the international activities of trade unions
- Labour and product markets, and the effects of different forms of ownership
- Workforce diversity.

Chapter 6 examines power and authority in employment relations. The chapter maps onto CIPD Learning Outcomes 1, 3, 4 and the related indicative content from the CIPD Managing Employment Relations module. The chapter focuses on power and authority, critically evaluating these terms and detailing their relevance to corporate governance, the management of change, and understanding resistance to change initiatives. The areas covered therefore include:

- Co-operation and compliance
- Corporate governance
- Managerial legitimacy
- Change management and managerial control
- Resistance to change and overcoming resistance to change.

The employment relationship is not just about the supply of labour but also about authority. In entering into an employment contract, the employee agrees, during the course of the working day (and sometimes outside it as well), to be subject to the authority of the employer. As with any such relationship, some conflict and contestation is likely, centring on the boundaries of this authority and issues of equity.

Part Two: Management interventions in employment relations

Chapter 7 examines voice. The chapter maps onto CIPD Learning Outcome 4 and the related indicative content from the CIPD Managing Employment Relations module. It covers the subject of voice in some depth due to the centrality of this topic to employment relations. The areas covered include:

- Involvement, participation and industrial democracy
- Communication
- Consultation mechanisms
- Negotiation and persuasion skills
- Collective and individual bargaining
- The nature of voice in non-union firms.

Chapter 8 then moves on to investigate what is meant by the relatively recent term 'employee engagement'. The chapter maps onto CIPD Learning Outcome 4 and the related indicative content from the CIPD Managing Employment Relations module. Within the chapter there is acknowledgement of the multi-faceted and contested nature of this prescriptive toolbox for managing employment relations. The areas covered therefore include:

- Formal and informal employee engagement
- Organisational commitment and job satisfaction
- Employee involvement for the purposes of employee engagement
- Teamworking
- Work–life balance
- Performance and employee engagement
- Emotional labour.

Reference to the construction and organisation of work should help to show that the economic imperative is always to the fore in the way people are organised at work, and therefore how they are seen in the employment relationship.

Chapter 9 examines pay and reward systems. The chapter maps onto CIPD Learning Outcome 4 and the related indicative content from the CIPD Managing Employment Relations module. Pay can be a key area of contention within employment relations. The areas covered include:

- Pay determination
- Approaches to reaching pay awards/settlements
- Incentives and reward
- Individual and collective pay systems
- Pay and equity.

Chapter 10 covers discrimination, difference and diversity. The chapter maps onto CIPD Learning Outcome 4 and the related indicative content from the CIPD Managing Employment Relations module. The topic of discrimination is central to the subject of employment relations due to discrimination's potential damage to the individual employment relationship if it is not properly managed. The areas covered include:

- Theories of justice and fairness
- Forms of discrimination
- Employment law and mitigating risk
- Policies and practices of diversity management
- Moral and business case arguments for addressing discrimination in the workplace.

Chapter 11 examines discipline and grievance. The chapter maps onto CIPD Learning Outcome 5 and the related indicative content from the CIPD Managing

Employment Relations module. Discipline and grievance must be handled effectively in order to secure effective employment relations and to mitigate risk. The areas covered include:

- Discipline and grievance policies and procedures
- Factors that influence effective discipline and grievance-handling
- Dealing with bullying and harassment
- Legal aspects of discipline (including those 'leading to dismissal') and grievance to mitigate organisational risk
- The 'new' self-discipline.

Chapter 12 covers conflict and dispute resolution. The chapter maps onto CIPD Learning Outcome 4 and the related indicative content from the CIPD Managing Employment Relations module. Conflict arises in a range of forms which must be recognised and effectively dealt with in order to manage employment relations successfully. The areas covered include:

- Conflict behaviours and industrial sanctions
- Strikes: causes and trends
- Dispute resolution and dispute-handling
- Third-party conciliation, mediation and arbitration
- Employment tribunals – how to conduct employment tribunal cases
- Managing conflict in non-unions firms.

Chapter 13 covers downsizing and redundancy. The chapter maps onto CIPD Learning Outcome 5 and the related indicative content from the CIPD Managing Employment Relations module. Downsizing and redundancy is a topical issue. The chapter situates the discussion of downsizing and redundancy within the context of flexibility, elucidates practical ways of dealing with dismissal and redundancy, and also critically assesses potential strategies. The areas covered include:

- Flexibility and 'flexicurity'
- Legal aspects of dismissal and redundancy, and the mitigation of risk
- Dismissal and redundancy policies
- Collective redundancy consultation
- Handling redundancy equitably
- Negotiating redundancy agreements
- Managing 'survivor syndrome'.

Chapter 14 concludes the book by considering the integration of employment relations. The chapter maps onto CIPD Learning Outcome 6 and related indicative content from CIPD Managing Employment Relations module. It draws together key themes covered in the book, and also highlights topical themes and future areas of contention, including comparative employment relations. The areas covered include:

- The crisis of employment relations
- The practical and academic relevance of employment relations studies
- The strategic importance of the management of employment relations
- The importance of an international perspective in employment relations
- Comparative employment relations.

THE USE OF SPECIFIC FEATURES WITHIN THE TEXT

A range of features is used within the text in order to provide illustrative examples of concepts, to draw attention to a range of examples from different countries, and to encourage critical thinking. A list of learning outcomes is provided at the beginning of each chapter. This is for ease of reference for both lecturers and students, and will help to show how the book relates directly to the Managing Employment Relations syllabus. Further features are provided in boxes within each of the chapters. One set of features covers 'Applying theory to practice' and 'Applying legislation in practice', and highlights the challenges inherent in applying theory or legislation within the workplace. A second type of feature covers 'Reflection on practice', encouraging students to reflect on their own work experiences, where relevant. A third feature is a 'Critical debate', where attention is drawn to a contentious issue and the reader is encouraged to consider different perspectives on the given topic. A fourth feature is the use of case studies and accompanying questions, including British and international examples, where appropriate. Further case studies are included on the companion website (as outlined below). Each chapter has its own list of references in a dedicated section at the back of the book, but individually ends with a list of further reading sources to encourage more in-depth exploration of core concepts.

WEBSITE

A companion website provides answers to case study questions presented in the text, updates to reading and other source materials, PowerPoint slides, self-test questions for students that can be used for revision, additional case studies with questions, annotated web links, updates including links to new research, and tutor notes for each chapter.

Walkthrough of textbook features and online resources

CHAPTER OVERVIEW

This chapter examines all aspects of employment relations, drawing attention to contentious issues that may impact on the employment relationship. In doing so, the chapter begins by exploring the employment relationship, and then moves on to determine what might be meant by the term 'employment relations'. Taking something of a pluralist perspective (see Chapter 3), the next section investigates the different interests of employers and employees in terms of their expectations of workplace terms and conditions. Later sections focus on different dimensions of the employment contract, including both legal and economic perspectives, and

CHAPTER OVERVIEW

Each chapter opens with an overview outlining the purpose and content of the chapter.

LEARNING OUTCOMES

After studying this chapter you should be able to:

•• critically discuss the concept of the employment relationship

•• define what is understood by the term 'employment relations'

•• explain the potential differences between employer and employee expectations

•• define the employment contract from legal, economic and psychological perspectives

LEARNING OUTCOMES

A bulleted set of learning outcomes summarises what you can expect to learn from the chapter, helping you to track your progress.

CASE STUDY

FORMAL AND INFORMAL RULES IN THE BRITISH POST OFFICE

Postal workers in the UK have traditionally worked on a basis whereby they have considerable discretion over their labour time. They have determined when precisely letters are delivered to individual houses, and how quickly they work. This has allowed them to have longer breaks in return for rapid working. In turn, postal workers are expected to cope with seasonal and unexpected fluctuations in the volume of letters to be delivered, again within broad parameters. This informal agreement – only partly defined in the employment contract – makes for speedy and reliable postal deliveries, but has always been the bane of consultants and managers seeking to 'modernise' the postal service. Modernisation, in these terms, would imply bringing work and employment

with similar skill levels elsewhere in the economy. Understandably, postal workers have interpreted such interventions as challenging or undermining the existing employment contract and have resisted them, a good example being the 2010 Royal Mail dispute.

Questions

Postal workers appear traditionally to have had quite a lot of discretion in how they choose to deliver mail.

How do they feel about the loss of discretion?

What should HR managers do to address their concerns?

What role should trade unions take in this situation?

CASE STUDIES

Case studies from a range of different countries with related questions will help you to place the concepts discussed in each chapter into a real-life context.

CRITICAL DEBATE

Do employees and employers have the same expectations?

Firstly, consider the issue of pay. It could be argued that both employers and employees would prefer that employees are rewarded fairly, and in a way that incentivises employees to maximise their work effort. At the same time, both parties would wish payment to be feasible, given the profits/resources available within the company/to the organisation. Employees within the private sector would not wish their company to go bankrupt; employees within the public sector would not wish to exceed budgetary constraints. However, this is not the end of the story. For example, within all organisations there are a range of stakeholders. Private sector owners may wish to please employees, customers and shareholders. The more money paid to employees, the less

CRITICAL DEBATE

Improve your critical thinking skills by considering these contentious employment relations issues and discussing or reflecting on different perspectives on the issue.

APPLYING THEORY TO PRACTICE

Employee and employer expectations

Do employees and employers have mutual interests?

List the interests that an employee has within the workplace.

Next, list the employer's main interests.

Are they the same?

APPLYING THEORY TO PRACTICE

These boxes highlight real challenges connected to applying employment relations theories in practice and are designed to help you think about practical solutions.

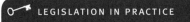

LEGISLATION IN PRACTICE

Contracts in South Africa

Labour law distinguishes 'employees' (who enter into a contract of employment and are protected by labour laws) from 'independent contractors' (who enter into a contract for service and are not covered by labour legislation). The development of new working arrangements has led to an increasing number of workers being excluded from the protection of labour legislation because the terms of their contract do not meet the traditional employment test. These include

REFLECTION ON PRACTICE

The psychological contract

How do you feel about the organisation where you are currently working, or an organisation where you have previously worked? Would you say that you have (or had) a positive psychological contract? If you have not worked for an organisation, you could perhaps apply these questions to your current experience of studying at your particular institution.

EXPLORE FURTHER

Reading

●●Collings, D. and Wood, G. (2008) *Human Resource Management: A critical approach.* London: Routledge

●●Marsden, D. (1999) *A Theory of Employment Systems: Micro-foundations of societal diversity.* Oxford: Oxford University Press

Websites

●●UK Department for Business, Innovation and Skills www.bis.gov.uk

●●The Communication Workers' Union www.cwu.org

●●The South African Government www.gov.za

●●The Health and Safety Executive www.hse.gov.uk

●●European Foundation for the Improvement of Living and Working Conditions

Glossary

Arbitration: a process that involves third-party adjudication in a dispute. The arbitrator actively intervenes in the dispute and makes a decision (in the form of an arbitration award) on the terms of settlement of the dispute. The arbitrator's decision is final and binding on the parties concerned.

LEGISLATION IN PRACTICE

These boxes highlight real challenges connected to applying employment relations legislation in practice and are designed to help you think about practical solutions.

REFLECTION ON PRACTICE

Reflect on your own experiences at work in light of what you have learnt from each chapter.

EXPLORE FURTHER

Explore further boxes contain suggestions for further reading and useful websites, so that you can develop your understanding of the issues and debates raised in each chapter.

GLOSSARY

Key terms and their definitions can be found in the glossary at the end of the book.

ONLINE RESOURCES FOR STUDENTS

- Content updates – including links to new research and an annually updated list of key Acts.
- Self-test questions – test your understanding of key concepts, ideal for revision.
- Annotated web links – access a wealth of useful sources of information in order to develop your understanding of employment relations issues.

Visit **www.cipd.co.uk/sss**

ONLINE RESOURCES FOR TUTORS

- Lecturer's Guide – advice on how to teach using the book and guidance on the questions and issues raised in the book.
- PowerPoint slides – design your programme around these ready-made lectures.
- Additional case studies with questions.

Visit **www.cipd.co.uk/tss**

CHAPTER 1

Introduction

CHAPTER OVERVIEW

This chapter examines all aspects of employment relations, drawing attention to contentious issues that may impact on the employment relationship. In doing so, the chapter begins by exploring the employment relationship, and then moves on to determine what might be meant by the term 'employment relations'. Taking something of a pluralist perspective (see Chapter 3), the next section investigates the different interests of employers and employees in terms of their expectations of workplace terms and conditions. Later sections focus on different dimensions of the employment contract, including both legal and economic perspectives, and – somewhat unusually for an introductory chapter – the psychological contract. As is explained later in the chapter, although the psychological contract is not formalised, it can nevertheless be a key feature of the employment relationship. The final section of the chapter begins to explore the management of employment relations in different contexts. Although much of the chapter assumes the potential involvement of trade unions as a key party to the employment relationship, it is acknowledged that the majority of small firms tend to be non-unionised, and this is particularly the case in developing and emerging economies. We therefore also consider non-unionised firms. Finally, attention is drawn to the differences inherent in the management of employment relations in private, public and non-profit-making organisations, in small firms, and – of particular relevance to a text that covers international dimensions – initial insights are provided of the nature of employment relations within multinationals.

LEARNING OUTCOMES

After studying this chapter you should be able to:

- critically discuss the concept of the employment relationship
- define what is understood by the term 'employment relations'
- explain the potential differences between employer and employee expectations
- define the employment contract from legal, economic and psychological perspectives
- explain different approaches to managing employment relations in unionised and non-union organisations
- compare aspects of employment relations in multinational, small and large, private, public and non-profit-making organisations

THE EMPLOYMENT RELATIONSHIP

Employment relations deal with the individual and collective dimensions of labour and the buying and selling of labour power. However, the fundamental object of inquiry that defines the field of employment relations is not the institutions of trade unions, employers' associations or government agencies or the processes of collective bargaining, but rather the employment relationship. In Chapter 2, the different parties to the employment relationship are considered in some depth. Here, however, it is important to note what defines the employment relationship itself.

As Poole (1986) points out, employment relations are best described as a discipline concerned with the systematic study of all aspects of the employment relationship. This relationship is one in which the employee sells his or her capacity to work in exchange for a wage and other benefits, and the employer hires employees in order that they produce goods or services that can be sold at a profit or – in the case of the public sector and non-governmental organisations (NGOs) – in order that they are productive members of the workforce (see Collings and Wood 2009).

The employment relationship may be defined as 'the set of conditions determining the exchange, use and reproduction of the labour force' (Michon 1992: 224). It is therefore the product of economic, social, political, legal and technological developments as well as the ways in which the various actors interpret and respond to these developments. It is possible to discern, as Blyton and Turnbull (1998: 8) argue, a growing tendency

> to locate the [employment] relationship within the broader nature
> of economic activity; to analyse the structural bases of conflict and

accommodation between employer and employee; to consider the influence of the wider society; and to develop an interdisciplinary approach using concepts and ideas derived from sociology, economics, psychology, history and political science.

In other words, in seeking to understand the employment relationship it is not sufficient simply to consider the relationship between the employer and employee. It is also necessary to consider the potential for disagreement between them, and also to take account of the broader context.

The legal element of the contract of employment is the express promise to perform work in return for a promise to pay wages. However, most contracts of employment do not and cannot specify in detail the work that should be provided. This uncertainty is resolved by creating a standard contractual rule: the employer has the power to direct labour and the employee is under a corresponding obligation to comply with all lawful instructions of his or her employer. In its most basic form, therefore, every employment relationship is an economic exchange (an agreement to exchange wages for work) *and* a power relation (the employee 'agrees' to submit to the authority of the employer). The employment relationship is linked, on the one hand, to the position of employers and employees in the product and labour market, and on the other hand, to the division of labour within the workplace and to the control systems (such as a performance management system) which govern their behaviour (Bryson *et al* 2006). In some instances, the market-determined aspects of the employment relationship may dominate the relationship – for example, where an employee is hired on a temporary basis to perform a specified task. Here the employment relationship is essentially a cash nexus. In other instances, the organisation-determined side of the exchange may be predominant – for example, where the employee is appointed to a permanent, full-time job. Thus, there is more to the employment relationship than the simple sale of an amount of labour power: it involves issues such as power and managing expectations. Much of modern HRM and employment relations is really concerned with an attempt to resolve these issues.

THE EVOLUTION OF THE EMPLOYMENT RELATIONSHIP

The employment relationship, as we understand it today, is a comparatively novel phenomenon. In most industrialised and industrialising countries, as recently as the late nineteenth and early twentieth century, other ways of organising the sale of labour services predominated, the most common being some variant of the labour contract system. Historically, managers sought to evade responsibility for the control and direction of labour through using intermediaries such as labour brokers and subcontractors. Research by Littler (1982: 46) demonstrates that early capitalist industrialisation was 'based on the *avoidance* of direct employer/ employee relationships and the reliance on existing patterns of subordination'. The employment relationship is one of the great innovations behind the rise of the modern business enterprise. It revolutionised the organisation of work, providing managers and workers with a very flexible method of coordination and a basis for investing in skills.

THE ADAPTABILITY OF THE EMPLOYMENT RELATIONSHIP

The employment relationship is adaptable, enabling management to decide detailed work assignments *after* workers have been hired. Given the enormous difficulty in anticipating all of the problems that may arise in providing customers (or citizens) with the goods and services they desire, the flexibility of the employment relationship – which builds on workers' agreement to be available to undertake certain types of work as and when their employer directs – is a great advantage. However, few employees would agree to giving their employers unlimited powers over work assignments. The rise of the employment relationship owes much to 'the development of job rules that square the apparent circle of providing employers with flexible job allocations and employees with limited liability to follow their employer's instructions' (Marsden 1999: 3–4). For the employment relationship to provide a stable framework for collaboration in the workplace, it must protect against opportunism (whereby the employer may try to exploit the worker in the short term) and satisfy both the employer's need for flexibility and the employee's need for security. The employment relationship therefore reflects the struggle over the degree of employer control and the nature and extent of autonomy under which people work.

Defining the limits within which management may determine the tasks to be assigned is problematic. If we assume that employer and employee are pursuing their own (partly divergent) goals, that information is asymmetrically distributed, and that both employers and workers find it costly to find alternative labour and jobs respectively, then we must accept that the conditions for opportunism are ripe (Marsden 1999: 12). Managerial authority is therefore likely to be problematic both in its application by managers and in its subsequent acceptance by workers. Opportunism can be restrained by factors such as loyalty and commitment, but they are inherently unstable and never given once-and-for-all. In a context of high replacement (such as recruitment) costs, individual workers or firms may have to tolerate quite wide margins in co-operation before quitting or firing becomes a viable option, especially for workers with extensive experience and company-specific skills (Grimshaw *et al* 2001).

The problems of opportunism are intensified by a lack of clear definition of the range of tasks over which the employer's authority extends, and the tasks on which the employee will agree to work (Bryson *et al* 2006). Such problems can potentially undermine the advantages of the employment relationship. Faced with a restrictive attitude from employees, the employer might lose the inherent flexibility of the employment relationship; faced with demands for flexibility beyond the bounds of agreement, employees may prefer the additional bargaining power that they would acquire when they can quit easily (Marsden 1999: 13). The resulting conflict is likely to reduce the gains to either party from combining work tasks into a single transaction – namely, the employment relationship. The stability and durability of the employment relationship are therefore dependent on effective regulation.

REFLECTION ON PRACTICE

Managerial opportunism

The text refers to 'managerial opportunism'. Have you have worked within an organisation, or are you currently working within an organisation?

If you have or you are, to what extent would you say that managers are opportunistic? In other words, have you been aware of managers attempting to encourage employees to work beyond their contracted hours, or to engage in job roles that should be seen as outside their remit?

An example here might be of a waitress working in a small café in France. Her usual duties might include taking orders, serving customers and wiping tables. However, placed outside the café are small round tables and chairs. Litter has been dropped under the tables and has also blown along the street from the café. The manager asks the waitress to collect the litter from under the tables and to take a brush and sweep along the street. Is this part of her job role? Should she agree to sweep the streets?

THE CONTEXT FOR THE EMPLOYMENT RELATIONSHIP

Employment relations do not operate in a vacuum. The nature of work organisation, the character of product markets, the composition of the workforce, government policies and many other contextual aspects influence employment relations policies and practices. Orthodox approaches to industrial relations tend to treat employment as a largely self-contained sphere of social activity that leads to a clearly bounded set of 'labour problems' (Hyman 1994b: 121). In reality, however, the employment relationship is dependent on a set of social structures and practices (such as the law, government policy, collective bargaining, social security, behavioural norms, and education and training systems) to mitigate the contradictions inherent in capitalist accumulation, whereby the employer seeks to extract profits from the employee's labour power.

At the basis of the employment relationship, according to Peck (1996), are three sets of social processes. Firstly, the processes of production and the structuring of labour demand. In other words, what is made and how, including the use of technology, how much labour is needed, and the type of skills that are required. Secondly, the processes of social reproduction and the structuring of labour supply – the processes that ensure that job seekers are available in areas of demand, and the process through which job seekers gain relevant skills. The third social process is related to the forces of regulation – formal rules underpinned by legislation and informal rules regarding what is socially acceptable within a particular context. Here it is important to note the wide variation in country context, depending on factors such as whether the country is an advanced or emerging economy, and a democratic or perhaps socialist economy. The employment relationship within an advanced economy is most often formalised through an employment contract. In a developing or emerging economy, as much as 75% of the workforce might be employed outside the formal economy in either informal sector work (otherwise referred to as 'undeclared work' or 'the shadow economy'). In the feature below, insights are given into the employment relationship within Mozambique, an emerging economy within Africa (see Dibben 2010).

APPLYING THEORY TO PRACTICE

The employment relationship within an emerging economy

Mozambique is an emerging economy with a difficult past. Indeed, 'Mozambique has moved from a colonial past through socialism, then liberalisation, rapid privatisation and industrial restructuring, to a lightly regulated capitalist economic system and a democratic government' (Dibben 2010: 2). Moreover, only 8% of workers are in the formal sector, and many of these are in casual work. The remaining workforce are either officially unemployed (17%), working in the informal sector or engaged in agricultural work (AfDB/OECD 2008).

In countries such as Mozambique, a number of factors impact on the employment relationship that may differ from what is considered to be 'normal' within advanced economies. Firstly, jobs in the formal sector are insecure and very few. The small proportion of workers within the formal economy (the public and private sector) may have a formal contract. However, jobs are few and potential workers are many. Secondly, a large proportion of work is within the informal sector (undeclared work) with no obvious employer and difficult working conditions, particularly in areas such as health and safety. Those who work in the informal sector might either be self-employed or have a verbal contract with employers, but are unlikely to have a written contract and are not covered by employment regulation. Thirdly, much of the population lives in rural areas and is engaged in peasant subsistence-level agriculture, either working for a family member or simply producing enough to survive.

Thus, labour supply and demand have a significant impact on the employment relationship. Specific forms of organisational structure, specific sets of tasks and specific types of technology will theoretically require particular amounts of labour and skill sets. However, there may either be a surplus of workers wishing to obtain formal sector work (as is the case in countries such as Mozambique) or labour may not be immediately available, meaning that the firm has to adjust operations. These adjustments may include increases in wage levels, changes in the use of technology to reduce the need for skills, or investments in training. Conversely, if there is a surplus of labour (high levels of unemployment) with desirable skill sets, firms may wish to cut wages because labour is easily substitutable. The nature of the production process and the structures of the labour market are therefore primary determinants of the specific forms that employment relations assume at a particular time and place. Chapter 5 examines these factors in more detail.

It is also important to note that the way in which firms act is not simply a matter of raising or cutting pay. It is likely that existing employees will resist cuts, even if apparently similar labour can be secured externally. Moreover, any costing of labour based purely on a reading of external labour market conditions assumes that the accumulated knowledge of existing employees can be readily quantified. Few organisations automatically raise pay should the general wages in the sector rise; some will count on the loyalty and inertia of existing employees, whereas others may adopt a more strategic view and accord particularly high increases in those jobs where employee turnover is high.

DEFINING EMPLOYMENT RELATIONS

Central to social life is the making of things and the provision of services. Individuals may work independently. However, when there is an organisation – in other words, more than one person working together in order to attain a goal – there are likely to be power imbalances. As organisations grow, such imbalances are likely to become more pronounced, and lines of authority more formal. Within modern societies, the employment relationship is an exchange relationship: the employee exchanges her/his physical and/or intellectual labour power in exchange for a cash wage. The employment contract – the actual deal – may be written or verbal, but is likely to cover: the broad duration of labour time expected, the nature of work, and expected outcomes. It should also clarify lines of authority and the rights of both parties.

There are several ways in which employment relations has been defined. Essentially, employment relations represent both the study of the employment relationship within the individual firm and the regulation of employment in the wider social context. They are sometimes referred to as 'employee relations', given that the primary focus of study is the person who is employed, not the owner of the enterprise that employs her/him (Collings and Wood 2009). They are also sometimes referred to as 'industrial relations', which is not only a legacy of an industrial past but also a term describing a proud intellectual tradition (studying the employment relationship from the perspective of the employee and within the context of social inequality). In Chapter 3 the term 'industrial relations' is therefore used.

An analysis of the employment relationship and the ways in which it is controlled and reproduced has long been a central concern of social scientists. The study of employment relations can be traced back to the 1890s. The early pioneers – Sidney and Beatrice Webb (in Britain) and John Commons (in the United States) – were primarily concerned with the role of trade unions, and attempted to convince the government and employers of the positive functions of collective bargaining. The first studies in the subject area were in response to the growing concern of the British upper classes with what they saw as the 'labour problem'. There were two aspects to this 'problem':

- the rapid spread of trade unionism and an upsurge in militant, industrial conflict in the 1880s – ie a problem of *social order*, and

- the depth of poverty and related deprivation suffered by a large section of the working class – ie a problem of *social welfare* (Hyman 1989).

The origins of institutionalised employment relations lie in a public policy commitment to achieve and maintain a balance between the problems of social welfare and social control in industry. The purpose of employment relations, as Edwards (1995) points out, is the control, adaptation and adjustment or 'regulation' of the employment relationship. 'Regulation' in this context means the provision of basic rules of conduct, binding both parties. By the 1930s, the problem of social order had become so great in much of Europe that it had led to civil war. In Britain, the USA, South Africa, Australia, New Zealand and Canada there had been challenges to the basis of the existing socio-political order. Post-World War II social settlements in Europe – and, indeed, labour law reforms in much of the English-speaking world in the 1930s – sought to limit the unbridled power of employers. Today, much of what is included within employment relations concerns rules, their interpretation and evolution.

Employment relations is therefore 'a set of phenomena, both within and outside the workplace, concerned with determining and regulating the employment relationship' (Salamon 1998: 3). There are three levels of regulation involved in negotiating order in the workplace (Hyman 1994a; cf Charlwood 2006). First, the individual contract of employment between employer and employee consists of an exchange involving work performance and pay. Second, collective bargaining between unions and employers results in the exchange of standardised improvements in the terms of employment. This leads to predictability and regularity in workplace employment relations. Third, political exchange involves the government making concessions to trade unions in return for union support for social order and legitimacy. The section below discusses in more detail the importance of the regulation of the employment contract.

REGULATION AND THE EMPLOYMENT CONTRACT

The employment contract is not simply an objective reality. It also implies a relationship between the employer and the employee. However, maintaining that relationship is complicated since employers and employees may have different expectations of what is required.

APPLYING THEORY TO PRACTICE

Employee and employer expectations

Do employees and employers have mutual interests?

List the interests that an employee has within the workplace.

Next, list the employer's main interests.

Are they the same?

BALANCING EMPLOYER AND EMPLOYEE EXPECTATIONS

The employment contract is a means of regulating the employment relationship, and is itself subject to external regulation. As noted earlier, the modern employment relationship is an uncertain exchange between a difficult-to-quantify amount of effort and immediately quantifiable wages. There is therefore an underlying tension. Firms will naturally seek to maximise the effort exerted by their employees and keep wages to the minimum; employees will have the opposite agenda. Consequently, it is necessary for the parties to exercise control over their relationship. This control is problematic and necessitates the development of regulatory processes. Mechanisms of labour regulation tend to endure insofar as they find a sustainable compromise between two conflicting demands: enhancing competitiveness (considerations of efficiency) and avoiding the excesses that stem from unconstrained competition (considerations of equity). As such, the preconditions for 'good' employment relations include:

- satisfying the needs and aspirations of both employers and employees
- operating without undue industrial conflict
- determining wages, working conditions and working practices that are consistent with national economic and social needs, and
- facilitating the organisational and technological change that is essential to a competitive economy, while at the same time ensuring that the costs and rewards of adjustment are shared equitably.

In summary, the regulation of employment can be defined as the means by which people are encouraged to behave in a 'regular' fashion, or according to rules of behaviour (Picciotto 2002: 1). As noted earlier, the regulation of work can be established through either (or both) formal or (and) informal rules and conventions. The feature below provides insights into the way in which both formal and informal understandings affect the employment relationship.

CASE STUDY

FORMAL AND INFORMAL RULES IN THE BRITISH POST OFFICE

Postal workers in the UK have traditionally worked on a basis whereby they have considerable discretion over their labour time. They have determined when precisely letters are delivered to individual houses, and how quickly they work. This has allowed them to have longer breaks in return for rapid working. In turn, postal workers are expected to cope with seasonal and unexpected fluctuations in the volume of letters to be delivered, again within broad parameters. This informal agreement – only partly defined in the employment contract – makes for speedy and reliable postal deliveries, but has always been the bane of consultants and managers seeking to 'modernise' the postal service. Modernisation, in these terms, would imply bringing work and employment relations closer to that encountered in jobs with similar skill levels elsewhere in the economy. Understandably, postal workers have interpreted such interventions as challenging or undermining the existing employment contract and have resisted them, a good example being the 2010 Royal Mail dispute.

Questions

Postal workers appear traditionally to have had quite a lot of discretion in how they choose to deliver mail.

How do they feel about the loss of discretion?

What should HR managers do to address their concerns?

What role should trade unions take in this situation?

REGULATION OF THE EMPLOYMENT RELATIONSHIP AND SOCIAL STABILITY

Regulation can be characterised as a way of ensuring social stability in broader social life, particularly the regulation of property rights, and also lends stability to the working relationship. In the area of property rights, regulation constrains the comparative ability of owners to control the actions of managers, who are, after all (other than in the case of owner-managers), employees (or agents of the owner) themselves. Do worker rights dilute the rights of owners? On the one hand, it could be argued that gains for one party will necessarily weaken the other. On the other hand, it could be argued that when both have significant rights, they are forced to work together, or co-operate better. The regulation of the employment relationship can thus also help to ensure stability. However, as noted above, the contract of employment does not (and cannot) specify precisely the amount of effort to be expended and the degree of initiative to be displayed by the employee (Hyman 1989). The employer's requirements are rarely predictable in detail and benefit from retaining a wide margin of discretion. This indeterminacy of the employment contract may be explained in terms of the distinction between 'labour' and 'labour power' (see Figure 1.1). The employer purchases labour power (the capacity to work) and not labour itself (the performance of work). Every workplace must therefore solve an implacable dilemma at the heart of the employment relationship – namely, the conversion of labour power (the time of individual employees and their capacity) into actual labour.

Figure 1.1 Labour versus labour power

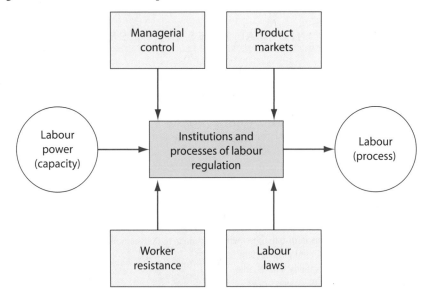

The way in which each of the aspects within Figure 1.1. link together is subject to ongoing and usually tacit negotiation. This implies that the employment relationship is essentially a power relationship, qualitatively different from a 'pure'

exchange relationship. In fact, labour power is a fictitious commodity – it is a lot harder to quantify than most other resources and does not behave in the same way. Since it is not a true commodity, the self-regulating mechanisms associated with conventional commodity (product) markets cannot be expected to regulate labour. According to Polanyi (1957: 73):

> the alleged commodity 'labour power' cannot be shoved about, used indiscriminately, or even left unused, without affecting also the human individual who happens to be the bearer of this peculiar commodity … Robbed of the protective covering of cultural institutions, human beings would die as the victims of acute social dislocation through vice, perversion, crime, and starvation.

The question of whether workers should be treated as just another commodity is an important point, and central to much of the discussion of employment relations.

Due to the issues around the commodification of labour, the employment relationship cannot 'work' without regulation. There is a need for a complex network of regulatory processes that generate the social rules and conventions essential for the employment relationship's durability. Any form of stability that does arise in employment relations is therefore socially constructed (due to interactions within the workplace), politically mediated (through government intervention) and institutionally embedded (reproduced according to commonly understood norms and rules of behaviour).

DOES LABOUR REGULATION ONLY PROTECT WORKERS?

Labour regulation should not be equated solely with protective and redistributive interventions: it is not just about protecting the rights of workers or rebalancing power in the favour of workers. It may assist one vulnerable group at the expense of others, but it may also sanction or reinforce forms of discrimination and disadvantage. For example, in British common law the employment relationship was traditionally seen as one between 'masters' and 'servants': the latter had few rights but many obligations. We should also not assume that regulation always has a redistributive effect, even if that is the stated aim. In many countries, social inequality has worsened since the late 1970s, despite an increase in the body of legislation governing the employment relationship.

More generally, labour regulation serves a number of functions that include:

- protection against oppression and discrimination
- attributing responsibility
- enhancing productive efficiency
- expanding social security and welfare
- consolidating a sustainable distribution of the costs and benefits flowing from capitalist economic development
- legitimating the production and distribution of economic and other resources

- decreasing transaction costs through a reduction in employer and employee opportunism
- encouraging specific behavioural patterns (that is, encouraging employers and employees to engage in certain behaviours) through the imposition of costs and rewards.

Even if having to comply with the law imposes costs on firms, greater regulation imparts a greater predictability, which firms may benefit from themselves. When employers have overwhelming formal power, employees may seek to respond through withdrawing their discretionary co-operation, and, indeed, retaliate in a wide range of hidden (eg theft of company property) and overt (eg mass desertions, striking, mass protests) ways. In this sense it could be argued that much employment law 'saves employers from themselves', and this was certainly a major reason why governments enacted labour protection in the first place.

THE THREE FORMS OF EMPLOYMENT REGULATION

There are three forms of employment regulation. First, *statutory* regulation (or regulation under the law) is often regarded as the prime source of rules in the employment relationship. As Kahn-Freund observes, law is a technique for the regulation of social power – power being the capacity to direct the behaviour of others (cited in Bellace 1994: 35). Standing (1999: 41) lists a number of potential advantages associated with statutory regulation:

- It is in principle predictable, transparent and equitable. Transparency assists in the structuring of the wage–effort bargain since those entering an employment relationship have reasonable information on the terms of the bargain.
- It decreases the insecurity associated with participation in the labour market.
- It provides clear monitoring mechanisms that are justified as a corrective for market failure, especially due to a lack of information among employees.
- It may discourage short-term profit maximisation, but encourages longer-term efficiency. Such trade-offs often can be secured only by statutory means.
- It may prevent forms of discrimination, such as racism and sexism, which would not otherwise disappear.

However, Standing also identifies potential disadvantages of statutory regulation, including:

- There is an inherent tendency towards rigidity, in that no law or administrative regulation can cover every contingency; towards excessive legalism that may intensify the disadvantages of those incapable of operating in this sphere; and towards increasing complexity because of the numerous situations that have to be covered in any regulatory framework.
- The efficacy of legal regulation presupposes an administrative apparatus (government departments) with the capacity to manage and enforce it efficiently, but the resulting bureaucratic apparatus absorbs substantial resources and may develop its own vested interests. According to public choice

theory, managers of government departments can be inclined to seek to extend their responsibilities in order to gain prestige.

- It may encourage an instrumental compliance (only complying because it is required, rather than through desire).

Second, regulation can also include *social* regulation – the management of the employment relationship through a process of (explicit or implicit) bargaining between the representatives of business and labour. To be effective, collective regulation requires some balance in the bargaining power of the parties. Social regulation has several advantages that include:

- reducing the extent of unilateral managerial control
- facilitating dynamic efficiency
- achieving some measure of distributive justice by limiting the scope for competitiveness purely on a cost basis
- encouraging investment in skills development
- making it harder for management to ignore or sideline the grievances of employees
- introducing an element of reciprocity into the employment relationship, whereby there is a feeling of give-and-take between employees and employers
- generating a more legitimate and hence sustainable balance between efficiency and equity
- reducing both excesses of market regulation (here referring to the labour market) and rigidities.

However, it also has disadvantages, including:

- It is time-consuming and prone to power plays between unions and employers.
- It has a tendency for coordination failure, such as an unequal distribution of information leading to a breakdown in negotiations.
- It intensifies labour market inequalities and insecurity when the institutions of collective regulation exclude, as they inevitably do, the interests of more vulnerable and disadvantaged groups.
- In the current climate of rising levels of global competition, collective regulation is increasingly hard pressed to balance representativeness with responsiveness.

Collective bargaining is a key feature of the collective employment relationship: more detail is provided on the nature of collective bargaining in Chapter 7.

Third, *market* regulation occurs where legislation and other regulatory mechanisms are geared towards maximum reliance on market forces (the 'laws' of supply and demand). The rights of employers to use and dispose of the labour power of employees increase with the developments of markets. Accordingly, market regulation allows for greater employment flexibility, involves less costly administration than statutory regulation, and lowers the transaction costs of most economic activities. However, it also:

- encourages short-term perspectives since there is no compulsion to be locked into a stable employment relationship
- promotes and rewards risk-taking
- allows decision-makers to absolve themselves from responsibility for environmental degradation, the oppression of women, rising unemployment, and so on
- decreases the obligations of employers towards their employees
- encourages opportunism as a result of the modest monitoring capacity
- increases social inequalities by rewarding those with resources and penalising those who lack resources.

As we have seen, labour is not just another resource or commodity. We cannot simply presume that the market for labour will 'work' in the same way that other markets work. Consequently, markets are dependent on extensive regulation by political, social and other institutions.

THE EVOLUTION OF THE EMPLOYMENT CONTRACT

Many of the advantages of the employment relationship contributed towards the gradual displacement of alternative forms of transaction as the modern firm evolved (Streeck 1992; Marsden 1999). At one extreme was 'inside contracting', whereby the entrepreneur provided tools, materials and money, and an autonomous supervisor-contractor dealt with labour and arranged to deliver the product or service at a specified time and cost. Here, the firm existed primarily as a business rather than an organisation. Today, this system is uncommon outside the building trade. At the other extreme was a collective contract by which groups of skilled workers contracted directly with the entrepreneur. In a diluted form of the labour contract system – the so-called 'drive system' – the foremen retained many of the powers of contractors, notably hiring, firing, pay-fixing and the organisation of specific areas of work, but their income was derived from a salary rather than being constituted by the surplus of the contract price over the money paid to their helpers (Marsden 1999: 24; Streeck 1992). In other words, they themselves were subject to a regular employment relationship.

Although the labour contract system gradually declined in significance relative to the employment relationship, it was efficient in its context. The advantages of subcontracting include the fact that the system was flexible in that it enabled rapid labour force adjustments to cope with fluctuating markets, and alleviated skill shortages. It was efficient in providing the contractor with incentives for effective supervision, thereby externalising the managerial problem of control. It was also a mechanism for distributing commercial risk between the entrepreneur (financial risk) and the subcontractor (production risks), and provided an element of certainty in costing (Marsden 1999: 25). However, developments in the size, scale and complexity of production eroded many of these advantages and created new disadvantages.

The reasons for the decline of the contract system reflect some of the advantages of an employment relationship over subcontracting. In particular, problems of predictability and quality of labour supply assumed increasing importance with the changing nature of industrialisation in the twentieth century. Marsden (1999: 25–7) identifies four major disadvantages or failings of the subcontracting system.

- It proved incapable of ensuring the availability of labour when employers needed it. Problems of labour turnover, absenteeism and general instability were common, especially during periods of strong labour demand.

- It lacked incentives to develop skills in response to the needs of individual employers. There were powerful incentives for the subcontractor to withhold information about production methods and the extent of improvements from the firm.

- It led to difficulties in controlling opportunism, notably among contractors who would typically spend little on maintenance and undermine quality standards in an effort to maximise short-term output. This became a greater obstacle as the level of capital intensity and demands for quality increased.

- It raised a problem of social order. Haphazard earnings differentials among workers, hard bargaining by contractors or foremen, unstable and short-term employment, and frequent interruptions in earnings meant that resentment and conflict were endemic.

It is advantageous for the employer to offer an employment contract if, at the time of agreement, it is not known precisely which tasks will be required. Here the employment relationship has an inherent flexibility: a single contract is substituted for a series of contracts related to each operation. In modern times, the use of contracts varies between different countries. Whereas in many advanced countries the permanent employment contract is the more common form of contract, in others, subcontracting is a predominant form. The *Legislation in practice* box below provides insights into the situation in South Africa, an emerging economy that has industrialised significantly in recent years, yet that in many aspects – such as the high degree of absolute poverty in rural areas – can still be regarded as within the developing world.

⚷ LEGISLATION IN PRACTICE

Contracts in South Africa

Labour law distinguishes 'employees' (who enter into a contract of employment and are protected by labour laws) from 'independent contractors' (who enter into a contract for service and are not covered by labour legislation). The development of new working arrangements has led to an increasing number of workers being excluded from the protection of labour legislation because the terms of their contract do not meet the traditional employment test. These include part-time employees, temporary employees, employees on fixed-term contracts, employees supplied by employment agencies, casual employees, home-workers and workers engaged under a range of subcontracting relationships. Many of these employees are particularly vulnerable to exploitation because they are unskilled and work in sectors with little or no trade union organisation or little or no coverage by collective bargaining. A high proportion of these employees are women. Frequently, they have less favourable terms of employment than other employees performing the same work, and have less security of employment. These employees therefore depend on statutory employment standards for basic working conditions.

In South Africa, the Basic Conditions of Employment Act of 1997 recognises that some employers have attempted to bypass statutory protections by persuading their employees to sign contracts which designate them as 'independent contractors', although their employment relationship has remained essentially unchanged. The Act empowers the Minister of Labour to deem any category of persons to be employees. To this end, the Act introduces a list of factors that indicate who should legally be regarded as an 'employee' and therefore eligible for protection. Where a particular factor is present in the relationship between a worker and the person for whom he or she works, the worker is presumed to be an employee unless the employer proves the opposite. A person who works for, or provides services for, another person is presumed to be an employee if:

- his or her manner or hours of work are subject to control or direction

- he or she forms part of the employer's organisation

- he or she has worked for the other person for at least 40 hours per month over the previous three months

- he or she is economically dependent on the other person

- he or she is provided with his or her tools or work equipment

- he or she only works for, or renders service to, one person.

The aim of these provisions is to prevent employers from developing work arrangements in a manner designed to deny certain persons the rights accorded to 'employees' in labour legislation.

In common with South Africa, in many countries there has been considerable debate as to how an employee is defined, as to the relative rights to be accorded to agency workers, and as to who, indeed, is an agency worker. In some countries, the outcome has been to strengthen the rights of agency workers. In others, governments have actively sought to cut back on the rights of individual employees and shift their position to one more akin with that commonly associated with agency workers. A good example of the latter would be the efforts of the 1996–2007 Howard government in Australia to promote 'Australian contracts', which, in turn, directly contributed to its electoral defeat.

A further dimension of employment relations is the informal understandings underpinned by what has been termed the 'psychological contract'. Although not formalised, these understandings can impact on the expectations of the employer and the employee, and the endurability of trust and loyalty between the two parties. The next section investigates what is meant by the concept of the psychological contract and considers the causes and consequences of changes to that contract, beginning with its relationship to equity.

FAIRNESS AND THE PSYCHOLOGICAL CONTRACT

So far we have talked a great deal about the employment relationship, regulation and the employment contract. Yet also relevant are questions of equity. No organisation can sustain itself through constant recourse to the law. This means that employers will seek to ensure that at least part of what they do is accepted by employees as legitimate and fair, and, indeed, that there are some basic principles of equity between employees (for example, to treat those with similar skills in similar jobs in broadly the same way, naturally taking account of objective differences in performance). Employees themselves, based on their previous life experience and their expectations of work, will have their own expectations of what is fair and reasonable. The two sides are likely to seek consensus in this area because it makes their everyday dealings more predictable and less subject to constant renegotiation. This consensus might be achieved through a psychological contract that is understood by both the employer and employee.

THE PSYCHOLOGICAL CONTRACT

The psychological contract relies on mutual expectations of employers and employees being fulfilled. It therefore consists of 'a set of reciprocal or two-way obligations and promises between the worker and the employer (or representatives of the employer such as the immediate boss and section manager)' (Guest and Conway 2002: 1). These psychological factors guide and characterise the relationship between employees and employers. For this reason it is the perceived obligations, rather than the actual terms of the employment contract, that must be studied in order to understand workplace attitudes and behaviour. The terms or obligations described by psychological contracts differ according to the extent to which they are *transactional* (impersonal obligations concerning economic exchange with little emphasis on extended relationships between the parties) or *relational* (personal obligations rooted in an ongoing relationship with fewer defined terms and characterised by attributes such as trust and commitment) in nature. These two aspects exist on a continuum: a psychological contract that is high on one type of obligation will be low on the other. The state of the psychological contract thus relies on whether the obligations and promises have been met, if they are considered to be fair, and whether both parties trust that they will be kept in the future (Guest and Conway 2002). Essentially, it contains three kinds of unwritten expectations (Daniels 2006):

- the need to be treated fairly
- a level of security and certainty in return for giving loyalty to the employer
- a need for fulfilment, satisfaction and progression – employees want to know that organisations place value on their contributions, successes and relationships.

Guest and Conway (2002: 2) present a model of the causes and consequences of the state of the psychological contract (Figure 1.2).

Figure 1.2 Causes and consequences of the psychological contract

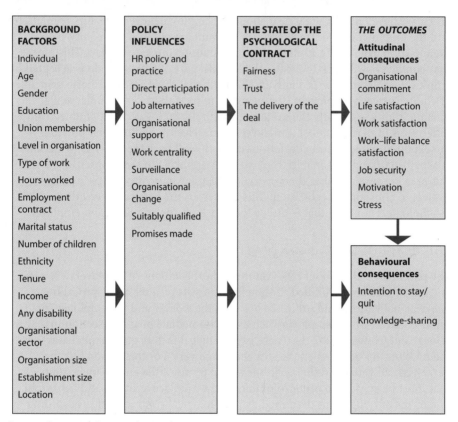

Source: Guest and Conway (2002: 2)

The framework shown in Figure 1.2 implies causality, but the various elements should be regarded as associational. The framework is sufficiently general as to be relevant to many country contexts, and yet is specific enough to be useful for informing the development of questionnaires that might be used to 'test' the nature of the psychological contract within large and small organisations, and to compare the situation across countries.

Although not as comprehensive as the Figure 1.2 framework, the questions in the *Reflection on practice* box below might be used to develop a snapshot of perceptions, which can, in turn, be used to indicate the state of an individual's psychological contract.

An important point to remember about the psychological contract is that it is unwritten. Assumptions are therefore made on both the employer's and the employee's side as to what is expected. This could be problematic if both sides have different interpretations of expectations. Where an employee feels that an employer has not kept to its side of the bargain, it may be referred to as a violation of the psychological contract (Guest and Conway 2002). An example of this might be where an employee anticipates job security but the employer starts to talk about the possibility of compulsory redundancies without prior consultation with employees or a trade union. Perceived violations of the psychological contract may negatively affect work attitudes and behaviour.

One area in which the psychological contract might be violated is with regard to expectations about pay for a given amount of effort, and another might be the area of health and safety. Earlier in this chapter we considered the potentially different expectations of employees and employers. Elsewhere in this book we consider circumstances when these expectations may not be met.

pay, employees will wish to increase it. Both sides might have the same goals but might have different expectations regarding the concessions that the other side is likely to make.

Secondly, consider the area of health and safety. Is this an area in which both employers and employees will have the same attitudes?

List the reasons why employers and employees might agree on the importance of health and safety and then consider reasons why there might be differences of opinion. In doing this, you might wish to consider whether employers and employees will have the same attitudes towards factors such as costs and risk.

As explained above, the psychological contract implies certain expectations. In some respects these expectations will relate to positive HR practices such as training and pay. However, the psychological contract is also relevant to disciplinary action, since employee handbooks should set out employer expectations for employee behaviour. (More detail is provided on grievances and discipline within Chapter 11.)

The role of employment relations (ER) specialists and line managers is crucial in establishing and ensuring the continuance of a positive psychological contract. In addition, the nature of the interaction between these two parties is also vital to the employment relationship since the former are often required to inform/police/advise the latter, who may or may not be sufficiently receptive/ competent/knowledgeable in HR policies and practices. The respective roles and responsibilities of HR and ER specialists and line managers are returned to in many later chapters.

MANAGING EMPLOYMENT RELATIONS IN DIVERSE ORGANISATIONS

The nature of employments relations varies according to the political, economic, social and regulatory context and the nature and role of institutions within a particular society (factors returned to in Chapter 5). In addition, it varies in different types of organisations. The sections below consider, in turn, some general points regarding employment relations in non-unionised organisations, public and non-profit-making organisations, and multinationals.

EMPLOYMENT RELATIONS IN UNIONISED AND NON-UNIONISED ORGANISATIONS

The global decline in union membership (see Chapter 2 for more detail on this) has meant that in many industries – even within advanced societies – employment relationships without unions are the norm rather than the exception. In other words, employees deal with employers directly as individuals or as members of informally constituted groups, rather than via a trade union. Where they are represented by a trade union, the union represents employee interests to management, rather than employees having to do it themselves. Typically, in the case of unionised organisations, a significant proportion of the workforce comprises members. The union then bargains with management on the behalf of workers ('collective bargaining') and intervenes in the case of disputes between employees and the employer. Of course, this does not necessarily prevent the organisation from also engaging with workers directly, and firms often choose to do so. Organisations may either supplement or build on what is agreed via collective bargaining or, indeed, constrain the scope of agreements. This behaviour may result in tensions between the process of collective bargaining and the union representatives who engage in it. In many national contexts, a union that is representative of the workforce (typically representing 50% or more of the workforce) has rights to collective bargaining under the law; these rights cannot be diluted through other forms of engagement.

What sets employment relations in non-union firms apart from those in firms that are unionised? In unionised firms, employees join the union so that it may represent their interests to management. Such contact between employees and management is 'indirect', in that the union seeks to voice the actual concerns and interests of employees to management. How accurately the union does this depends on how democratic it is, and the extent to which union officials and leaders may be prone to pressures from management or external players such as politicians. The union's 'third-party' role may seem to be less effective than managers and employees directly talking to each other; conservative managers may seek to dismiss the union as 'troublemakers' intervening in a freely negotiated contractual relationship between willing parties. However, from an employee perspective, the intervening role of the union allows employees to express important concerns that management may be unwilling to hear, and shields individual employees from victimisation. In addition, unions often enjoy formal rights under the law, and, because they represent many members, they are harder for management to ignore than a single employee who voices concerns. Finally, unions are likely to have considerably more accumulated financial resources and expertise than a simple grouping of employees.

Should unions be absent, managers may seek to impart information, consult, and/or negotiate with employees in a plethora of different ways. Talks can range from one-on-one informal discussion to meetings, to specially constituted bodies convened to deal with a specific brief (eg health and safety) (Budd *et al* 2009). Of course, in a unionised firm, employers can and, indeed, often do, engage with workers through all of these methods (see Taras and Kaufman 2006; Gollan 2009). What sets unionised firms apart is that the role of the union means that management may be legally bound to take such procedures more seriously, and the union can back up its position in collective bargaining with the threat of collective action.

EMPLOYMENT RELATIONS IN SMALL, PRIVATE, PUBLIC AND NON-PROFIT-MAKING ORGANISATIONS

Employment relations are likely to differ according to the type of organisation. Let us first look at organisational size. Very small organisations are difficult for trade unions to organise in because unions have limited resources, and it is a lot more difficult to organise workers in many small establishments than within one large one. This means that smaller organisations are less likely to be unionised. Secondly, in smaller organisations the owner-manager model is more common, and consequently the issue of managers being 'agents' or employees themselves does not emerge. Thirdly, in smaller organisations there is less need for formal rules and bureaucratic procedures; this is likely to result in greater inconsistency in employment relations. Fourthly, larger organisations are likely to be higher-profile, and any breaches of labour law are more likely to be noticed by employers. In contrast, law enforcement in small organisations is likely to be more difficult.

At this point we need to consider what the organisation does. Non-profit organisations tend to be less concerned with short-term returns and more concerned with sustainability. This means that employees may enjoy longer-term job security and be less compelled to operate according to the demands of profitability. On the other hand, many charitable or voluntary organisations expect employees to have a high degree of personal commitment to the organisation's goals, and may assume that employees are prepared to put in more than what is formally stated in the contract and work for lower wages than would be the norm for similar jobs in conventional private and public sector organisations.

This raises the question of differences between employment relations in the public and private sectors. The state is, of course, a major – and in most national contexts, the largest and most important – employer in its own right. A consideration of countries within Europe helps to identify trends in public sector employment relations. In terms of the size of public sector employment, during the 2000s, some countries experienced a reduction both in central government and public sector employment (Austria, Hungary, Malta and the Netherlands). A larger group of countries saw a rise in overall employment (Belgium, Cyprus, Greece, Ireland, Lithuania, Luxembourg, Norway, Slovenia and the UK), while a third group of countries experienced a decline in central government employment but a rise in other areas of public sector employment (Denmark, Finland, France, Spain and Italy). A fourth group of countries, most of which were formerly communist, saw a reverse trend (Latvia, Estonia, Poland, the Czech Republic, Slovakia, Bulgaria, Romania), as did Germany (Eurofound 2007). The proportion of women in public sector employment tends to be higher than in the economy as a whole, and has been increasing in many countries in Europe since the mid-1990s. But the number of fixed-term workers has tended in the past, and still now tends, to be lower than in the private sector. Union density has generally been higher in the public than in the private sector, but with marked variations – from around 75% in Denmark and Norway to 30% in Portugal and 15% in France (Eurofound 2007).

However, there have been changes over time. In the past, civil servants and public sector employees had special status, but in recent decades there has been extended collective bargaining, decentralisation of bargaining, individualisation of pay, more flexible recruitment practices, the extension of fixed-term contracts, a reduction in pension privileges, weakened job protection and consolidated dismissal procedures. These changes have been made in order to achieve cost effectiveness and efficiency and to respond to local market conditions (Eurofound 2007).

Governments may seek to promote employee-friendly practices either as a way of setting an example/enticing private sector employers to follow suit, and/or because public sector workers are themselves voters to be placated (Dibben *et al* 2007). On the other hand, a commitment to neo-liberal ideologies may result in conflict between the state and public sector workers, with the aim of undermining a large component of the labour movement or in order to encourage practices seen as more generally desirable. In countries such as Britain, public sector reforms have been quite dramatic. In others, such as Canada, the changes were later, but still illustrate how employment relations have altered, resulting in a significant impact on the role of trade unions and working practices. Some of these changes are outlined in the case study below.

CASE STUDY

PUBLIC SECTOR EMPLOYMENT RELATIONS IN CANADA

Research undertaken in Canada by Lonti and Verma (2004) has drawn attention to changes in both individual and collective employment relationships, and the nature of work. Dramatic public sector reforms have been undertaken in a range of countries over recent years. Often, the stated aim has been to increase efficiency, and the justification has been couched in neo-liberal terms. In Canada, the reforms undertaken during the 1990s were primarily due to the need to reduce government deficits. This was achieved in a variety of ways, including cutting wages and introducing wage freezes, reducing the headcount by cutting jobs, and reorganising work, leading to work intensification. At the same time there was increased use of performance indicators and new technology. All of these changes were designed to achieve savings. Yet they have also resulted in 'increased employee burnout, fatigues, and low morale' (Lonti and Verma 2004: 153).

The changes for individual workers were accompanied by legislation that altered collective relationships, removing rights from trade unions and favouring individualised relationships.

Questions

How would you define relations between management and unions in Canada?

How would you describe the state of the psychological contract?

What should HR managers do in this situation? Which policies and practices could they use to improve matters?

The Canadian budget cutbacks were intended to be a temporary measure, and, to a significant extent, this was the case. In contrast, the 2010 budget cutbacks in the United Kingdom were promoted as being long-term, raising the question whether the impact on public sector morale and capabilities would be greater than that experienced in the Canadian case.

As noted above, public sector organisations can employ a large proportion of the workforce within a given country, and consequently the consideration of employment relations within the public sector is important. However, it is also necessary to pay particular attention to employment relations within multinational corporations, particularly in the light of globalisation.

EMPLOYMENT RELATIONS IN MULTINATIONAL CORPORATIONS

Multinational corporations (MNCs) are companies whose headquarters are based in one country but other sites are located in one or more different countries. Employment relations may therefore differ according to country locale. This, however, depends on the strategy followed by the corporation in question. According to Perlmutter (1969), such strategies can be described as ethnocentric, polycentric or geocentric. Ethnocentric behaviour means that the firm is highly centralised – the majority of managers are recruited from the home country and employment relations policies will follow their lead. Those taking a polycentric approach may employ more decentralised practices. For example, local nationals will be employed in host countries and HR practice may vary according to the country of operations. A geocentric approach aims to transcend the limits of a focus on either the home or host country.

It is also important to consider that – as noted in Chapter 5 – multinationals can be very powerful, and indeed, in some cases more powerful than nation states. From 1980 to 2004 the number of MNCs increased by more than eight times. By 2004 there were over 61,000 MNCs that had ownership in over 900,000 foreign-affiliated operations around the world, and these MNCs accounted for around 10% of gross domestic product worldwide and employed more than 54 million employees (see Morley *et al* 2006). This means that they may be in a position to be able to relocate to where there are the best incentives, such as areas where there are fewer labour rights. The lack of employment rights may relate to the minimum wage, equal opportunities legislation or health and safety enforcement. Such behaviour can be described as 'social dumping'. MNCs can lobby government and employer organisations to change employment policy and legislation. In order to counterbalance MNCs' power over nation states, there is a need for trade unions to engage with them through international institutions (see Collings 2007).

SUMMARY

This chapter has explored the nature of the employment relationship in a range of sectors and highlighted variables impacting on the employment contract, both in a formal sense and in terms of the psychological contract. In doing so, some comparisons have been drawn between country settings and organisational types. Of particular note is the difference between advanced and emerging economies, and trends over time. In terms of historical developments, it is evident from the discussion above that the employment contract is not a static concept. Moreover, the nature of employment relations has changed within countries and within sectors. Although the public sector is often held up as a model employer, public sector reforms have fundamentally altered the nature of employment relationships.

The employment relationship lies at the heart of modern economic and social life. It embodies many dimensions: commercial exchange and promises, power and subordination, co-operation and confrontation, authority and assumptions of equity in treatment. This volume aims not only to provide the fundamentals of this essential area but also to provide the critical theoretical and applied understanding necessary for effective people management, for careers in trade unions and NGOs, and for further postgraduate study.

EXPLORE FURTHER

Reading

- Collings, D. and Wood, G. (eds)(2009) *Human Resource Management: A critical approach*. London: Routledge

- Marsden, D. (1999) *A Theory of Employment Systems: Micro-foundations of societal diversity*. Oxford: Oxford University Press

Websites

- UK Department for Business, Innovation and Skills www.bis.gov.uk

- The Communication Workers' Union www.cwu.org

- The South African Government www.gov.za

- The Health and Safety Executive www.hse.gov.uk

- European Foundation for the Improvement of Living and Working Conditions (Eurofound) www.eurofound.eu.int

PART ONE

Conceptual Debates and Contextual Factors

CHAPTER 2

The Main Players in Employment Relations: Trade unions, employers and the state

CHAPTER OVERVIEW

The introductory chapter examined the nature of the employment contract and began exploring the employment relationship, which concerns the two parties to the employment contract (the employee and the employer), and also the state and potentially other actors: collective representatives of employees (ie unions), employer associations, community organisations, NGOs and external consultants. Each of these parties to the employment relationship is analysed in this chapter. The individual sections cover the practical nature of each of these dimensions, but also engage with more critical debates about their past, current and future roles.

Firstly, the chapter examines the role of trade unions, their organisation, structure and function, and then turns to consider the various factors that might influence union growth and decline. A focus on trade unions is appropriate, since their role has traditionally been a central feature of employment relations. The second part of this chapter examines labour management theory and employer management styles. Thereafter, attention turns to the role of the third party in employment relations – the state – scrutinising its activity as legislator and employer. Finally, some consideration is paid to the role of other parties to the employment relationship such as management consultants and NGOs. These focal areas are represented in Figure 2.1.

LEARNING OUTCOMES

After studying this chapter you should be able to:

- analyse the role of trade unions and their organisation, structure and functions
- determine the factors that influence union growth and decline
- critically evaluate the role of employers (and employer associations) in the employment relationship and explain various management styles
- evaluate the role of the state as legislator, regulator, conciliator and employer
- explain notions of liberalism, corporatism and voluntarism
- outline the role of management consultants and NGOs in employment relations

Figure 2.1 The main parties in the employment relationship

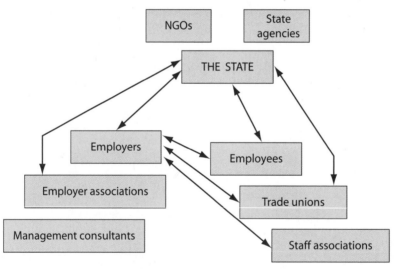

The two-way arrows indicate interrelationships between the various parties to employment relations.

THE ROLE OF TRADE UNIONS IN THE EMPLOYMENT RELATIONSHIP

Trade unions are normally depicted either in terms of their functions or by reference to a statutory definition. In 1902, Sidney and Beatrice Webb defined a trade union as 'a continuous association of wage-earners for the purpose of improving the conditions of their working lives' (cited in Burchill 1997: 35–6). Subsequent studies have sought to refine this definition. More recently, Salamon (1998: 85) has suggested the following definition:

> any organisation, whose membership consists of employees, which seeks to organise and represent their interests both in the workplace and society and, in particular, seeks to regulate their employment relationship through the direct process of collective bargaining with management.

Here, the emphasis is on regulation, and also captures the broader role of a trade union with regard to improving society beyond the workplace.

The subsections below outline the structure, organisation and functions of trade unions.

TRADE UNION STRUCTURE: CRAFT UNIONS, GENERAL UNIONS, INDUSTRIAL UNIONS AND FEDERATIONS

Trade union structure refers to the classification of unions by their recruitment patterns or the occupational orientation of their membership (Salamon 1998: 130). Trade unions may be characterised by a variety of structures. Craft unionism is characterised by its exercise of control over entry into a trade and its concern for the skill basis of that trade (Bendix 2000: 168; Grossett and Venter 1998: 76). These unions seek to represent all workers performing a particular type of skilled labour irrespective of the industry or area in which the work is performed. Craft unions also routinely develop rules that specify appropriate levels of output in an effort to control the work intensity of their members. In addition to the functions of wage and job regulation, craft unions have traditionally performed a number of insurance and welfare functions for their members (such as strike, unemployment, injury, retirement and funeral benefits). By contributing to these benefit funds, individuals are tied to the union since a loss of membership would entail a loss of benefits as well as the contributions made. Craft unions are not now common in liberal market economies, although craft- or trade-based associations remain very influential in countries such as Germany.

General unions are the earliest forms of trade unionism among less skilled workers. The development of these unions stems from a politically inspired goal to organise all workers into one big union (Bendix 2000: 169; Grossett and Venter 1998: 77). General unions organise workers from a variety of different industries and occupations. Because general unions are incapable of asserting meaningful control over the supply of labour, their ability to influence wages lies in a capacity to impose a threat of mass strike. However, again, general unions are not common. They typically emerge in contexts where workers are in an extremely weak position, and where activists adopt the strategy of signing on members regardless of the sector in which they are employed, with the aim of rapidly increasing membership and influence. A particularly ambitious example includes the Industrial Workers of the World (IWW, otherwise known as 'the Wobblies') that is open to all workers regardless of national locale. In practice, this is primarily a US-based union, represented in a relatively limited number of workplaces (and, indeed, is recognised by a small number of employers). At its peak in the 1920s, it had over 100,000 members. The problems experienced by the IWW mirror those experienced by general unions in many other settings. Firstly, an organising strategy aimed at uniting all workers is particularly likely to attract the repressive attentions of authorities – by their nature, general unions represent a far greater threat to existing employment practices than unions focused on particular sectors. Secondly, general unions aim to unite very diverse sections of the workforce, which may lead to divisions and conflict. Thirdly, an open approach to membership makes it difficult to service the needs of individual members: it is much easier to service the needs of members who are concentrated in particular industries and locales.

Industrial unions attempt to establish national collective bargaining structures to regulate employment conditions in the industry as a whole. The emphasis is on strong shopfloor organisation and industry-wide collective bargaining. There are four major advantages associated with industrial unionism (Bendix 2000: 170; Grossett and Venter 1998: 76):

- It strengthens the unity of trade union membership by removing competition between unions and spreading the bargaining strength of strong groups (eg skilled workers) across all unions.

- It simplifies collective bargaining by making union structures correspond to those of employers' associations and integrates the industrial and organisational levels of bargaining.

- It deepens the union officials' understanding of a particular industry and increases the union's power base through its ability to launch industry-wide strikes.

- It facilitates the process of economic planning by creating closer links between the trade union and the industry it represents.

Because the industrial system cannot be neatly divided into distinct industries with clear boundaries, the industrial base of a union always reflects trade-offs. 'Pure' industrial unionism is difficult to sustain since industries do not always clearly correspond to boundaries set by the unions and industry-wide regulation is never possible in any absolute sense. For instance, where does the engineering industry begin and end? Furthermore, many large (often multinational) corporations straddle several industries and deal with several industrial unions. The wider concept of 'sectoral unionism' refers to unions 'which are by historical origin or "principle" of organisation, concentrated in a particular section of the economy, but prone to take an "open" approach to the definition of that sector and ready to extend into "allied" fields' (Hughes, cited in Salamon 1998: 150).

Industrial unionism is the dominant form of trade union organisation in many countries within Western Europe, and in countries such as South Africa, Australia, New Zealand and Canada.

Most unions are affiliated to a federation to allow for greater co-operation and coordination of their activities. Trade union federations consist of a grouping of organisations rather than individuals and have no direct role in collective bargaining. According to Taylor (1989: 30), the national centre of the trade union movement has two roles:

- internal movement coordination (eg regulation of inter-union conflict, formulating and implementing policies, providing services, research and advice)
- external political coordination (eg representing the interests of their members as a pressure group).

These roles invariably raise questions about the balance of power between the federation and its individual constituent unions. The federation's authority is constrained by the autonomy that each affiliated union enjoys in advancing and protecting the interests of its members. However, the federation retains considerable influence over the policies of affiliated members and plays a vital role in shaping the government's socio-economic policies.

In Britain, the union federation is the Trades Union Congress (TUC), established in 1868. It acts as the collective voice of the UK trade union movement to governments and international trade union bodies, and also influences the behaviour of its affiliates. It intervenes in: industrial disputes, inter-union disputes and the conduct of affiliates. However, it does not intervene when there is a dispute between an affiliate and an employer unless the affiliate asks it to do so (Gennard and Judge 2010). At a broader level, bodies include the European Trade Union Confederation (ETUC), which was set up in 1973 and lobbies the European Union. This body represents around 60 million members (see www.etuc.org). In addition, the International Trade Union Confederation (ITUC) lobbies the International Labour Office (ILO), a United Nations Agency, to obtain minimum labour standards on a global scale. It represents around 166 million workers within 156 countries and territories. Its main areas of activity include trade union and human rights, economy, society and the workplace, equality and non-discrimination, and international solidarity (see the ITUC website for further details).

TRADE UNION ORGANISATION

Trade union 'organisation' refers to the institutions and processes that form a union's internal administrative, representative and authority systems. Although each union's organisation is unique in terms of the relationship between union officials and union members and the lines of accountability, all unions tend to adopt a similar institutional pattern. This pattern is reflected in Figure 2.2.

Figure 2.2 Trade union organisation

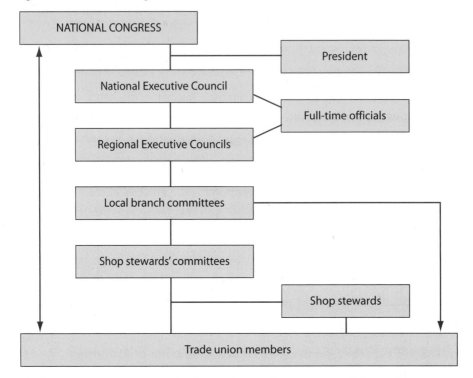

The local branch constitutes the forum for regular meetings of the trade union membership and facilitates the democratic process by allowing the members to convey their views on union policy, elect delegates to union committees and draft resolutions on union strategy and tactics. The branch also allows for report-backs and the dissemination of union policy from the executive councils. Full-time officials such as a general secretary and organisers constitute the 'employees' of the union. Other functionaries that deal with matters such as legislation, occupational health and safety, gender, finances and administration support these officials in the day-to-day running of the organisation. As the unions develop in both size and the scope of their activities, officials are increasingly compelled to acquire an in-depth understanding of social and labour legislation, government policies, administrative procedures and negotiation tactics.

A national congress, which consists of delegates nominated from the various regions in proportion to the number of members in a region, represents the ultimate authority of the membership over the union officials. The major issues raised at a congress can be divided into constitutional, policy and collective bargaining matters. The national executive council is charged with the responsibility of administering and managing the union between national congresses and carrying out the resolutions adopted by congress. In reality, however, the distinction between policy formulation and implementation is not clear-cut. The national executive council is compelled to engage in some degree of policy formulation in an effort to interpret and apply what are often generally worded policies and respond to developments that occur between congresses.

A shop steward is a lay official who works alongside the union members who elected him or her to represent their interests at a particular workplace and in the union structures. The trade union's constitution sets out the election procedures and terms of office for shop stewards. The role of the shop steward has an administrative and a representative dimension. Stewards carry out several essential functions such as:

- recruiting new union members
- holding regular meetings with the membership
- taking up the grievances of members with management
- defending members in disciplinary hearings
- negotiating terms and conditions of employment
- representing members in the union structures
- ensuring that management sticks to collective agreements
- taking a leadership role in local union structures
- educating the members through formal and informal learning, noticeboards and newsletters
- ensuring that members are informed about trade union policies and campaigns.

However, there are disparate demands placed on the shop steward, and potentially conflicting interests of the union, the membership and management (Darlington 1994: 33). In his or her relationship to the trade union, the role of the shop steward is influenced by the formal expectations expressed in the official documents of the union and the informal expectations derived from full-time officials. The informal expectations are often more influential than the formal ones in shaping the actual behaviour of the steward because they are more direct and constantly reinforced through interaction.

The relationship between the steward and union officials can range from almost total dependence to almost total independence (Salamon 1998: 200–2). The shop steward's primary role – protecting and advancing the interests of the members in their relationship with management – contains an inherent tension. Although the shop steward is the elected representative of the union members at the workplace, the official status of the role depends on accreditation by the union and recognition by management.

In their relationship to the rank-and-file members, shop stewards can exercise a leadership role only through argument and persuasion since they have no sanctions that may be applied against the members collectively. A shop steward does not work as an individual but forms part of a shop stewards' committee that directs and coordinates the work of all shop stewards at the workplace, and the only power he or she possesses is that which the members have explicitly mandated. Stewards are directly accountable to the members who elected them, in the sense that they can be removed from office if the members who elected them are not happy with their performance and they must be re-elected on a regular basis.

In his or her relationship to management, the shop steward has to balance resistance and accommodation. On the one hand, by accommodating the views and interests of management, the steward may be perceived by the union members as taking on a managerial role. On the other hand, by continuously confronting management, he or she may jeopardise the bargaining relationship. The shop steward may be able to satisfy the interests and needs of the union members only by antagonising management. Worse, failing to antagonise management in these circumstances may be perceived by union members as a dereliction of responsibility.

◖◉▷ REFLECTION ON PRACTICE

The role of shop stewards

Shop stewards can face a number of conflicting demands.

Is a trade union recognised in your organisation, or within an organisation where you have worked or studied?

In his or her relationship to *management*, does the shop steward appear to have to balance resistance and accommodation?

Does the shop steward seem to find it difficult to balance the different interests of rank-and-file *members*?

TRADE UNION FUNCTIONS

Salamon (1998: 103) defines an organisation's function as 'the role or task it is required to perform and the means employed to carry it out'. Although the overall objective of a trade union is the representation of the needs and interests of its members, trade unions also have a range of other functions (Bendix 2000: 171–5; Salamon 1998: 103–17).

A trade union is, first and foremost, 'an agency and a medium of power' (Hyman 1975: 64). As an individual, the employee is at a serious disadvantage in relation to the employer, lacking the knowledge and power to negotiate his or her terms and conditions of employment on an equal footing. Moreover, management can also more easily substitute the individual as a source of labour than he or she can substitute the employer as a source of income. By enabling workers to act collectively, trade unions frustrate management's attempts at treating employees as individuals.

Secondly, trade unions are involved in *economic regulation*. Most union members tend to regard the collective negotiation of wages and other monetary terms of employment as the primary function of a trade union.

Thirdly, trade unions are concerned with *job regulation* – protecting and enhancing the position of members in the employment relationship, which is supported by legislation covering issues such as training, health and safety, the handling of grievances, discipline and dismissals.

The fourth function is *social change*. Most trade unions seek, through their policies and actions, to attain a more egalitarian society.

Fifthly, trade unions provide member services such as mutual insurance benefits to cover the loss of income during a strike, unemployment, sickness, injury or death. During the course of the twentieth century these benefits have become a less important sphere of the unions' activities as the state has taken over many aspects of this function. Even so, services such as financial advice, insurance, personal loans and legal assistance remain an important function of professional and white-collar unions. The individual basis of these services, however, may detract from the fundamental nature of trade unionism. As Salamon (1998: 113) points out, the unions that emphasise member services may attract members who are more concerned with their own self-interest than the more traditional militant, collective and consolidatory goals of a trade union. Yet the latter are precisely what make the economic and job regulation functions of a union possible and effective.

Blackburn and Prandy (cited in Farnham and Pimlott, 1983: 74) put forward several characteristics by which to judge the extent to which an organisation is a whole-hearted trade union that identifies with the labour movement, encapsulating their independence from management and both their workplace and political role:

- It regards collective bargaining and the protection of its members' interests, as employees, as its major functions.
- It is independent from any influence by employers, particularly in relation to collective bargaining.
- It is prepared to be militant and to use industrial action.
- It declares itself to be a 'trade union'.
- It is registered as a trade union.
- It is affiliated to a trade union federation and to a social-democratic or labour party.

ECONOMIC AND POLITICAL ANALYSES OF TRADE UNIONS

In taking an independent role from employers, trade unions may focus on economic issues or adopt an overtly political role. Each of these dimensions is discussed, in turn, below.

Economic analyses of trade unions

Trade unions clearly play a vital economic role in negotiating the wages of their members. Orthodox economic theory regards unions as utility-maximising agents with clearly defined goals and preferences. According to this theory, trade unions establish a monopoly over the supply of labour and are therefore an obstacle to the 'free' operation of the laws of supply and demand (Burchill 1997: 12–18). Unions are assumed to be concerned with unilaterally setting a wage rate at the highest level possible for their members. By using their control over labour supply, unions are able to raise wages above competitive levels and reduce employment levels. For orthodox economists, therefore, unions have a perverse influence on the operation of labour markets. By operating solely for the benefit of their members and themselves as organisations, unions operate to the detriment of society as a whole.

This simple model of union influence has several shortcomings. Firstly, the capacity of unions to exercise labour market power in the manner suggested by orthodox theories presupposes the existence of profit levels over and above what would exist if product markets were competitive. However, the existence of a surplus level of profit by itself does not guarantee union influence over wage outcomes. Unions need to exercise power (through industrial action) to impose costs on employers who are unwilling to accept their wage demands.

Secondly, orthodox theories assume the pursuit of rational self-interest, accordingly explaining the defining characteristic of trade union activity – collective behaviour – in individual terms.

Thirdly, there is an emphasis on the trade union pursuit of higher wages. However, employees combine and co-operate with each other not only to bargain over wages and working conditions but also to influence or control the pace of work, to protect themselves from overworking, and to eliminate unpaid work, in addition to seeking 'fair' allocation of work effort and greater job satisfaction and security. Unions provide workers both with protection against arbitrary management decisions and with a voice at the workplace level and in the political arena (Freeman and Medoff 1984: 3–4).

A further problem with the orthodox economic model is the assumption of a narrow pursuit of its members' economic self-interests as the primary objective of a trade union. This assumption ignores the pursuing of divergent goals by union members. One of the most difficult political tasks of any union leader – the reconciliation of conflicting group interests within the union – is thus effectively excluded from analysis. In an attempt to protect their theory against numerous counter-instances, orthodox economists put forward a number of 'imperfections' that supposedly account for these empirical anomalies, or suggest that there is collusion between the employer and the union on setting higher wages than those determined by a 'free' market.

Political analyses of trade unions

Trade unions can also be considered from a political perspective. Historically, trade unions have responded to the structured power imbalance between capital and labour through their involvement in the political process. The rationales for this involvement, as Gahan (2006: 268) points out, include influencing law and public policy decisions and acting as a democratic counterbalance to the inherently authoritarian influence of business interests.

Participation in electoral politics and the process of policy formulation can be seen as essentially a defensive reaction by the trade unions. Forging links with political parties to benefit their members means that unions have to engage in a process of 'political exchange' whereby government concessions are granted in return for concessions from the unions. The unions generally support parties who make workers' concerns central to their appeal. Most trade unions established links with political parties from the trade union's inception. Establishing close links with a political party gave the trade unions a voice in Parliament and facilitated the development of policies that furthered the interests of union members. The need to establish links with a party stems largely from the political weakness of trade unions. Political action can complement the gains achieved through collective bargaining. The surest way to generalise the gains of highly organised workers (for example, through fewer hours of work and improved health and safety) is to pass laws that enforce them. The electoral weight and organisational capacity of the labour movement is a valuable asset for any political party. Both the trade union and the political party therefore stand to gain from close co-operation or affiliation.

Not all union movements are equally effective in securing a meaningful place in the processes of policy formulation and implementation. Unions have few sanctions at their disposal. If they assert their dominance, the party will lose electoral support. If they withdraw from the alliance, workers would be without a political voice. 'Separate but interdependent' best describes the relationship between trade unions and political parties. However, it is possible to distinguish between three contemporary political systems:

- integration – unions are part of the governing structures (Sweden)

- inclusion – unions have a representational status and are regularly consulted, but are excluded from effective decision-making (Germany and Britain)

- marginalisation – unions achieve representational status but are kept at the margins of the political process (Japan and the USA).

The political programme of the ruling party, in particular, can have an important bearing on the balance between the autonomy and subordination of the unions, as illustrated in the *Applying theory to practice* box below.

APPLYING THEORY TO PRACTICE

Taiwanese unions and political involvement

In Taiwan, trade unions have tended to work closely with the government, and have been regarded as 'auxiliary institutions and administrative arms' (Chen *et al* 2003: 315). The role of trade unions has been viewed positively, since their co-operation has led to industrial peace, and helped in securing economic growth (Frenkel *et al* 1993, in Chen *et al* 2003).

In 1987, however, martial law ended, and the climate for industrial relations also changed. New 'unofficial' workplace-based unions were created by labour activists and anti-government leaders. Later, in 2000, further developments in industrial relations were anticipated when the Kuomintang (KMT) party was removed from power by the Democratic Progressive Party (DPP). However, the unions have been disappointed by a lack of legislation in their favour. Moreover, they have been negatively affected by the privatisation of state-owned assets (Chen *et al* 2003).

How has the role of trade unions changed over the past two decades?

Are you aware of other countries where trade unions have changed their role as a result of political change?

What might trade unions in Taiwan do in order to achieve greater influence?

A further dimension of political analyses of trade unions is related to trade unions and internal democracy (see Harcourt and Wood 2004). Trade union leaders are often criticised for having 'too much' power when they call for industrial action and for having 'too little' power when the membership pushes for industrial action. This quandary reflects the fact that trade unions, as organisations, seek to represent their members and develop an efficient administrative system capable of carrying out their functions effectively (rationality of administration). However, there is an inherent tension between these two dimensions. The demands of efficiency require a standardisation of operations, accountability of the members and speed in decision-making. The demands of democracy require extensive flexibility, accountability of the leaders, the maximum possible debate and widespread canvassing of opinions.

A key criticism of trade unions' ability to establish internal democracy comes from Michels (1966), according to whom all voluntary democratic organisations will, by virtue of the need to develop an effective system of internal administration, tend towards an oligarchical system of government involving a hierarchical bureaucracy with power and influence concentrated in the hands of formal office-bearers. Following this line of argument, the establishment of trade unions led to the formation of a privileged elite of working-class leaders who used unions to further their own sectional interests. As this elite became entrenched in the union bureaucracy, its material and social conditions became progressively distanced from those of ordinary workers.

Michels (1966) asserts that trade unions are subject to an 'iron law of oligarchy', which means that the leadership invariably acquires dominance over the membership through its control of administration (organisational), its monopoly on expertise (technical), and the exercise of 'charismatic authority' (psychological). The effects of this 'iron law' undermine the commitment of union leaders to the radical goals of the labour movement. The union bureaucracy develops interests separate from those of the members, leading to conflict over goals and methods. In this clash, according to Michels (1966), the demands of administrative efficiency will always override the requirements of democratic representation. His arguments have inspired conservative criticisms of trade unions: an undemocratic, militant and politically motivated leadership forcing ordinary members to accept radical policies that they do not really support. These criticisms, in turn, have been deployed to justify legislative intervention in the internal functioning of trade unions.

In practice, most unions attempt to find some balance between the demands of representation and those of administration, rather than emphasise one at the expense of the other. There is no point in having a perfectly democratic organisation that never succeeds in implementing any policies. Conversely, workers do not need a perfectly efficient organisation that ignores their interests. Michels' argument (1966) implies that trade unions can maximise their administration to the absolute detriment of representation, assuming passive workers who allow their interests to be undermined. In reality, union leaders are subject to a range of different checks and balances such as the influence of shop steward structures, the diffusion of organisational power, and the need to prevent union members from voting with their feet. The simple model of union politics based on the division between officials and members should be jettisoned in favour of a more complex analysis, which recognises competing interests both within and between the ranks of the officials and the membership (Harcourt and Wood 2004; Wood and Dibben 2008).

SERVICING AND ORGANISING MODELS

Another way in which trade unions have been viewed is in relation to the strategies used in engaging their membership. As Blyton and Turnbull (1998) outline, with the servicing model, the union is an external body that relies on workplace access and employer co-operation. Moreover, there is a strong reliance on services and insurance protection. Full-time officials recruit members and also determine how members should solve problems, but there tends to be friction between officials and members, with members not regularly attending meetings or participating in organising. Moreover, in relation to management, the union tends to take a reactive stance. In contrast, under the organising model members identify issues and solve them together, are empowered through education and support, participate in union affairs, and help to build the union through active recruitment and organising. The union takes a more proactive stance towards engagement with management.

Underpinning the idea of the organising model is that militancy has proved to be an effective guarantor of a union's survival, autonomy and capacity for resistance. Moderation, by contrast, has brought unions only meagre returns and has subjected the union to greater dependence on the 'goodwill' of the employer (Blyton and Turnbull 1998: 136). This is the inherent danger of a 'servicing' relationship between the union and its members rather than an 'organising' model based on a participatory relationship. The members of a servicing union are likely to ask 'What can the union do for me?', whereas those of an organising union will tend to ask 'What can we achieve with the union?'

TRADE UNIONS AND LABOUR MARKET SEGMENTATION

A further important aspect of trade unionism – particularly given the growth in non-standard work and the division between the formal and informal economy in emerging economies – is labour market segmentation. Several studies identify a 'crisis of representation' stemming from the difficulties that the unions face in finding a common strategy for an increasingly heterogeneous workforce, aggregating the growing diversity in employee values and interests, and representing workers in precarious jobs whose interests differ from or even conflict with those of employees in stable jobs. A characteristic shared by the various forms of 'non-standard' or 'atypical' (part-time, temporary, casual or fixed-term) employment is that they are invariably unorganised and commonly excluded from the structures of representation in the workplace. These employees are rarely in a job long enough 'to earn entitlement to occupational welfare, social security, or even privatised benefits, let alone long enough to develop the confidence to join or form unions' (Standing 1993: 433). An almost inevitable result of this lack of collective influence on terms and conditions of employment is that these workers tend to remain in non-standard employment.

The people in non-standard jobs are widely dispersed across the labour market; concentrated in jobs and sectors that have historically proved difficult to organise; denied access to established industrial relations procedures; and less likely to perceive themselves as sharing common interests with organised employees, participate in trade union activities, and identify with the labour movement. The heterogeneity of this workforce has also compounded the problems of interest representation faced by the unions. Despite some efforts at organising non-standard workers in countries such as Germany, Canada, France, Korea, Chile and South Africa, no meaningful gains have yet been made in this regard. The fact that the standard versus non-standard employment divide is largely conterminous with that between organised and unorganised employees raises the question of trade union complicity in labour market segmentation. Despite rhetoric to the contrary, trade union practice seems primarily oriented towards defending 'the relative advantages of the stronger sections of the working class against possible encroachment by the weaker (whether unionised or not), rather than challenging the system on behalf of the class as a whole' (Hyman 1996: 68). As a result, the consequences of excessive wage demands (such as job losses) have to be accommodated by a buffer of disadvantaged (often non-standard) workers.

The strategies and tactics of unions reflect the complex interaction between the two 'faces' of trade unionism (Flanders 1968). The 'vested interest' face is characterised by a narrow, defensive preoccupation with the economic concerns of organised employees in the workplace, whereas the 'sword of justice' face involves a broader, socio-political role normally pursued nationally to influence the government. Advantages secured by powerful groups may be at the absolute or relative expense of weaker groups (Peck 1996).

Working-class fragmentation is not a new phenomenon. Although it may assume different forms, the perennial tension between unity and division within the union movement is rarely, if ever, resolved decisively in favour of an unremitting solidarity. Hyman (1992) outlines an inverted U-curve of unionisation that reflects variations in employment status and labour market position. Employees with professional qualifications or high levels of technical expertise may perceive little need for trade union support, while the growing number of workers in precarious forms of employment lack the resources and cohesion for collective organisation. Unions have historically been strongest among intermediate categories of employment such as semi-skilled manufacturing workers. Despite the many seemingly insurmountable obstacles, successful organisation among non-standard workers is of great political significance, especially in countries with a post-colonial experience such as many within Africa that still face inherited divisions and social exclusions (Dibben 2010).

TRADE UNIONISM IN EMERGING ECONOMIES

Whereas the development of trade unions in the industrialised countries may be viewed as a social response to the advent of industrial capitalism, in the industrialising countries this process took place later and over a much shorter period. Furthermore, as Salamon (1998: 86–7) points out, the development of trade unions in the industrialising countries was subject to different influences:

- Low levels of industrialisation and the extensive use of migrant labour in the primary producing sectors during the colonial period limited the development of trade unionism.

- Trade unions played a significant role in the struggle for independence, which generated more of an 'anti-colonial' or political rather than an 'anti-capitalist' or industrial ideology.

- The extensive role of post-independence governments in economic development encouraged a tendency to subordinate and direct the trade union movement towards the objectives of national economic development as defined by the ruling elite.

Despite these influences, however, an integral part of trade union development is the struggle to secure a 'fair' share of economic gains for labour. The case study below illustrates the role of trade unions in South Africa, an emerging economy that has a challenging political and economic history.

CASE STUDY

TRADE UNIONS IN SOUTH AFRICA

Trade union density in South Africa amounts to about 30% of the economically active labour force employed in the formal sector. High levels of unemployment, an extensive informal sector, and extremely low levels of unionisation in sectors such agriculture and in occupations such as domestic work account for this comparatively low figure.

Drawing on Hyman's typology of union identities, the history of South African trade unions can be analysed in terms of the shifts from (1) guild or craft unionism, predominantly representing white craft workers; to (2) populist unionism, with the idea of one large union for all workers (from the 1920s); to (3) political unionism, established on the principles of equality and the unity of all workers in the struggle against class exploitation and national oppression, and an alliance with the struggle for national liberation, led by the African National Congress (ANC) from the 1950s; to (4) rank-and-file unionism, concerned with establishing a strong workplace presence from the early 1970s; to (5) social-movement unionism. In the words of Webster (1988: 176):

unions have two faces, each of which leads to a different view of the institution. One, the economic dimension, is that of a union trying to win increases and improvements in living conditions; the other is that of a voice institution – ie a social and political institution. Where, as in South Africa, the majority does not have a meaningful voice within the political system, unions will inevitably begin to play a central role within the political system. However, it was the decline in living standards accompanying the economic recession that brought the two faces of unionism together. It is this fusing of the economic with the political ... that I call social-movement unionism.

Social-movement unionism can be distinguished from 'orthodox' unionism (focus on workplace issues at the expense of politics) and 'populist' unionism (focus on wider political struggles at the expense of workplace issues). Social-movement unionism is comprised of both an economic and a political dimension.

In response to the demands of reconstruction and development following the transition to democracy, the possibility emerged for South African trade unions to amend their social-movement role to strategic unionism (Baskin 1995). Strategic unionism incorporates a labour-driven process of strategic change and involves an ongoing commitment to structural reform based on independent labour and popular organisation. This commitment depends on the building of alliances between different trade unions, and on forming coalitions with mass-based community organisations. According to Von Holdt (1992), strategic unionism has three key areas of action: redistribution (industry and societal level), economic growth (job creation, job security, training, productivity, industrial restructuring) and economic democracy (workplace, labour market, centralised bargaining). Moreover, strategic unionism involves the amalgamation of two different types of union activity: a type of 'grassroots' unionism which seeks to establish and consolidate effective and democratic shopfloor structures, and an 'institutionalised' unionism which has established organisational structures that facilitate policy formulation at the highest levels of the economy (Von Holdt 1992).

Questions

What are the advantages of strategic unionism, given the political and economic context of South Africa, particularly its colonial past and the legacy of *apartheid*?

What are the challenges associated with strategic unionism?

For additional, detailed accounts of trade union transition within South Africa, see, for example, Brookes *et al* (2004); Wood and Dibben (2008); Dibben (2004, 2007). More literature on trade union strategies is also included within *Explore further* at the end of this chapter. In addition to – and indeed, influential in – determining trade union strategies is the role of unions and union federations at the regional and global level, and detailed discussion of these issues is provided in Chapter 5. Yet another important consideration, especially in the light of the changing fortunes of trade unions over the years, is the issue of the factors that cause a rise and/or a decline in membership levels. A number of possible determinants are assessed in the following section.

UNION GROWTH AND DECLINE

In most national cases, unions have had to contend with declining membership over the past four decades. A variety of explanations have been put forward for this decline, ranging from increasingly hardline policies by neo-liberal governments and the law (see Godard 2006) through to economic long waves (Kelly 1998), to changes in the outlook of workers (Goldthorpe *et al* 1968). There is little doubt that many national governments – and employers – have taken increasingly hardline approaches towards unions since the 1970s, in line with the dominance of neo-liberal ideologies. Examples include the Thatcher government in Britain in the 1980s, the Reagan administration in the USA in the same decade, the Bolger government in New Zealand in the 1990s, and the Howard government in Australia in the 2000s. In all of these cases, however, it would have been more difficult to mount offensives against unions if unemployment had not been quite so high, and if specific heavily unionised industries had not faced real crises of competitiveness. This suggests that there is some merit to arguments that link union decline to the onset of periods of mediocre growth and recession – employers are likely to use such periods to reverse earlier gains (Kelly 1998). However, there is little doubt that changes in social attitudes also have an impact. With increased leisure time and the rise of greater consumerism, many employees adopt an instrumental attitude to work (Goldthorpe *et al* 1968). If working life becomes less central to existence, or at least to fulfilment, then bodies concerned with work are likely also to lose influence.

A further potential cause of the decline in union membership has been associated with labour market trends. These trends are discussed in more detail above, and also in Chapter 5. However, here it is worth noting that unions have struggled to organise workers from ethnic minorities and, in particular, immigrant workers. In some cases this has been due to the illegality of such workers, whereas in others it has been argued that unions have not paid adequate attention to workers that are outside their traditional membership.

Additional explanations for the fall in trade union membership have included the strategies that unions have undertaken (including the use of servicing rather than organising models of unionism, or business unionism rather than social-movement unionism), as described in some detail in the sections above.

EMPLOYERS

The second party to the employment relationship that is analysed in some depth in this chapter is employers. Employers do not represent a unified grouping, and fall into many different categories. Firstly, there is the state and private sector. Governments are concerned with ensuring that the employment relations policies adopted in the public sector result in the efficient and cost-effective delivery of public services, and with promoting best practices, which may encourage other employers to follow suit. The adoption of best practice reflects the fact that in a democracy, public sector workers also represent voters, and/or that the public sector represents a good vehicle to promote particular ideologies, ranging from social democracy (and a commitment to fairer work and greater equity) to neo-liberalism (and a commitment to freeing up labour markets and removing barriers such as unions). Secondly, there are variations according to sector. In

Chapter 12 it is explained how the nature of technology adopted in particular industries may result in higher or lower levels of industrial conflict. Other variations can include the relative skills base of employees within a particular sector (and, hence, the amount of leverage that they can bring to bear against employers), and the relative prosperity and competitiveness of the industry in question (and, hence, the ability of employers to grant concessions to employees).

In order to promote the ability to present a unified voice in discussion with governments or in bargaining with trade unions, employers have formed employer groups and associations.

EMPLOYER GROUPS AND ASSOCIATIONS

An employers' organisation is a formal, voluntary grouping of employers set up to advise, defend or represent their interests in dealings with organised labour, the public and the government. It is important to note that employers' organisations are associations of corporate bodies rather than individuals, and therefore reflect, rather than establish, the bargaining power of the affiliated organisations. Compared to trade unions, employers' organisations conduct their affairs in a low-key manner, preferring 'to run their internal affairs and to advance the interests of their members privately rather than publicly, confidentially rather than openly' (Farnham and Pimlott 1983: 171).

Trade unions seeking more stable and uniform bargaining relationships provided a stimulus for the establishment of employers' organisations in the early 1900s. In particular, industrial action by trade unions was a major historical factor in the development of collective organisations by employers (Farnham and Pimlott 1983: 164). The primary objective of these pioneering employers' organisations was to protect the managerial prerogative and resist the development of trade unionism (Salamon 1998: 250). However, as trade unions became permanent organisations, so did employers' organisations, and as trade unions moved from being locally based to nationally based, so did employers' organisations (Burchill 1997: 77). These organisations generally owe their establishment to attempts by employers to achieve certain goals in pursuit of their collective interests. Their interests revolve around regulating matters of trade and competition by mutual agreement, and include:

- seeking statutory protection in matters of trade
- establishing joint marketing arrangements
- preventing wage-cutting among competing employers
- providing services in industrial relations and personnel administration
- establishing a united front in dealing with trade unions
- contesting the passage of social and labour legislation that is deemed to be inimical to the interests of employers.

Most employers' organisations were initially formed at the local level and then expanded to regional and national levels.

As is the case with the structure of trade unions, collective bargaining has a significant impact on the structure of employers' organisations (Jackson 1991: 130–3). In a decentralised system of collective bargaining, where negotiations on terms and conditions of employment occur exclusively at the workplace level, employers' organisations are largely redundant. Centralised negotiations, by contrast, presuppose the existence of employers' organisations that seek, on behalf of their members, to conclude collective agreements with trade unions at industry level. By ensuring that as many employers as possible are members of the employers' organisation, the threat of non-affiliated employers paying lower wages and thereby undercutting prices is reduced. The expansion of employers' organisations provides trade unions with the means to extend the coverage of collective agreements and establish a common rate for the whole industry.

The role of employers' organisations in the negotiation of terms and conditions of employment varies by industry depending on the nature and scope of collective agreements. Sisson (1983: 126) identifies three main types of agreement:

- minimum agreements – setting minimum rates and allowing individual employers to negotiate higher rates with their employees at the workplace level. These agreements are normally regarded as a 'safety net', make no provision for relative wage rates, and have little impact on conditions of employment other than pay

- comprehensive agreements – setting actual rates of pay, making detailed provision for relative levels of pay and providing a range of employment conditions other than pay (eg training schemes and pension plans)

- partial agreements – setting minimum rates that are often supplemented by additional payments, making fairly detailed provision for relative levels of pay, and providing some coverage of employment conditions other than pay which allow a degree of discretion.

In addition to the historical evolution of bargaining and the balance of power between employers and trade unions, the structure of the industry concerned is a significant factor in explaining differences in multi-employer agreements (Sisson 1983: 127). Industries such as engineering and chemicals are extremely heterogeneous: there are significant differences in the size of firms, technology and products. These make the negotiation of comprehensive agreements difficult and impractical. In industries such as construction and shipping, the product or service is more homogeneous, and technology and jobs are very similar. This homogeneity lends itself to standardised rates of pay and conditions. Moreover, given the fact that firms in these industries tend to be small, they can derive significant economies of scale in using an employers' organisation as a bargaining agent.

In general, the governing structures of an employers' organisation are composed of four levels:

- an assembly
- a general council
- an executive committee
- a presiding officer.

In theory, ultimate authority in an employers' organisation lies with a general meeting of the members (an assembly). In practice, real power resides in the executive committee since it is small in number, meets regularly, and usually includes representatives of the most important industries and regions. Key decisions such as top staff appointments, bargaining positions, budgets, strike or lockout strategies and the like are usually within the committee's area of competence. Decision-making in employers' organisations is therefore largely a centralised matter, far removed from individual firms. This concentration of authority reveals that, different from in trade unions, participatory forms of democracy are not a characteristic feature of decision-making processes in employers' organisations. In addition, the need to maintain consensus among members with often widely diverging industrial relations policies and practices means that the decisions of employers' organisations have to be founded on the lowest common denominator that will unite the membership.

In the sphere of employment relations, employers' organisations have generally favoured a restricted role for the government as an 'impartial' rule-making authority, endorsed 'free' collective bargaining and the managerial prerogative, and called for curbs on union powers deemed to be 'excessive'. Attitudes towards trade unions vary considerably. For some employers' organisations the aim has been to ensure a balance of power in favour of employers. Other employers' organisations have been hostile to trade unions from the outset, and focused their policies on union suppression and/or avoidance.

At a European level, multinational firms are represented via the Federation of European Employers (FedEE). The latter seeks to help firms to comply with the law and operate effectively in a range of European settings, to promote best practices, and to help firms benefit from the process of EU expansion. There are few truly international employers' associations. One notable example is the World Shipping Council (WSC). The WSC seeks to promote greater openness in access to national ports (which may have the effect of undermining efforts by national governments directly or indirectly to regulate the use of labour in ships calling into their ports) and maritime security (which may be difficult to attain if labour use is totally unregulated).

LABOUR MANAGEMENT THEORY

The origins of modern theories of labour management can be traced back to the classic theorists – Marx, Durkheim and Weber – who were all concerned with the changes in production and employment associated with the historical transition from feudalism to capitalism. Despite their different theoretical influences and orientations, the writings of the classic theorists reflect a deep sense of concern over the nature of work and the living conditions of workers in industrialising societies.

Marx (1967) characterised the relationship between the employer and employee as a 'cash nexus'. In other words, employers had no obligation towards their employees other than the payment of wages in return for work done, while employees merely sold their effort for an agreed price. He argued that the historical evolution of capitalist production corresponds to a shift from 'formal' to 'real' subordination. When the labour process was first brought under the control of the capitalist, the nature of work was not very different from independent craft or domestic production. The capitalists merely brought the existing skills and organisation of work under their control, and made the product of labour their property and not that of the producer. Marx classified this stage of industrialisation as the formal subordination of labour. The inability of the capitalists to increase production through technology led them to resort to methods such as increasing the length of the working day. The shift towards the 'real' subordination of labour could only be secured on the basis of the introduction of science and technology into large-scale production. This allowed capitalists to increase the intensity of work as opposed to merely extending its duration.

❓ CRITICAL DEBATE

Management theory and workplace conditions

As stated above, Marx (1967) characterised the relationship between the employer and employee as a 'cash nexus'. Employers had no obligation towards their employees other than the payment of wages in return for work done, while employees merely sold their effort for an agreed price.

To what extent is this the case in workplaces now?

Do employers and workers merely see the employment relationship as a 'cash nexus'?

If your answer is yes, does this apply equally to all types of workplace?

If your answer is no, explain the other elements of the relationship that a focus on the economic exchange might tend to ignore.

Unlike Marx, Durkheim (1969) argued that the increasing differentiation of the division of labour was a source not of instability and conflict but of stability and social solidarity. Prior to the industrial revolution, society consisted largely of small, isolated communities with little division of labour. In the constant struggle for survival, people engaged collectively in a relatively small variety of tasks. Since people were involved in similar occupations, the social system was based on what they shared in common. This Durkheim referred to as 'mechanical solidarity' – in other words, a more or less 'organised totality of beliefs and sentiments' common to all members of the group. For Durkheim (1969), the growing division of labour under capitalism laid the foundation for increasing co-operation and functional interdependence, which he referred to as 'organic solidarity'. Achieving societal cohesion in the face of increasing differentiation, he argued, involved the institutions performing the same role of binding individuals to society in complex societies as the kinship group performed in simple societies. Durkheim (1969) suggested that a 'community of interests' (developed through occupational associations) replaced the 'community of blood' (developed through kinship structures) to preserve the overarching ethical and moral principles of society.

This emphasis on social cohesion was contradicted by the widespread conflict, displacement and disintegration associated with industrialisation. In order to account for such contrary evidence, Durkheim (1969) devised two models of 'abnormal' divisions of labour.

- an 'anomic' division of labour
  He argued that '*anomie*' is the result of a state of normlessness in which society no longer provides a common moral reference point for individual action. Industrial strife and meaningless work is the result of the organisation of work developing too fast for the establishment of an effective body of moral rules. Solidarity in an organisation is undermined, according to Durkheim (1969), when there is insufficient coordination between workers' activities. However, he regarded these conditions merely as temporary effects of a lack of suitable institutional and organisational controls. Greater coordination between workers could be developed through work organisation, worker involvement and increased skills.

- a 'forced' division of labour
  This occurs when the existing patterns of inequality fail to reflect the 'normal' or 'inevitable' distribution of social and personal inequalities which exist between the old and the young, men and women, and so on. For example, he argued that the 'natural' functions of women are domestic responsibilities and the 'natural' intellect of men destines them for skilled work. In his study of abnormal forms of division of labour, Durkheim was as concerned with the human effects of capitalism as Marx or Weber. However, he did not clearly specify how solidarity is maintained in the face of potentially anomic factors.

Weber argued that an important trend in relation to modern, large-scale organisations was the development and application of bureaucratic techniques (cited in Gerth and Mills 1977). Bureaucracies contain an over-arching rational-legal value system that is embodied in company rules, is internalised as the orientation of its members, and provides the norms of effective work performance and the legitimation of managerial authority. To understand the organisation of a modern workplace, we must understand the development of industrial bureaucracy. The key elements of bureaucracy – hierarchy, specialisation, impersonality and formalised rules – all reflect its control function since they appear neutral and therefore legitimate. Weber regarded bureaucratisation as an inherent feature of the development of economic enterprises (cited in Gerth and Mills 1977). The growth of bureaucracies was necessitated by an increase in enterprise size, growing specialisation and mechanisation, and an increase in the size and functions of management. Three important consequences flow from the process of bureaucratisation:

- the development of strict work discipline and job fragmentation

- the imposition of uniformity and calculability of performance

- the impersonal and seemingly rational nature of control.

Weber analysed managerial power through examining how legitimation converts power into authority. Unlike Marx, Weber's theory of domination did not depend largely on economic mechanisms of control. For him, the compliance of subordinates rests on their perceptions of the legitimacy of the control relationship (cited in Gerth and Mills 1977). The orders of superiors are obeyed because subordinates regard them as reflecting acceptable rational-legal norms. Weber did not argue that the legitimation of authority through bureaucratic administration is, by itself, sufficient to control subordinates (cited in Gerth and Mills 1977). Like Marx, he assumed that industrial control in market economies demands an essential degree of economic need and normative acceptance of a work ethic and bureaucratic authority.

Weber did not view bureaucracy simply as 'efficient' and acknowledged that bureaucracies could be dysfunctional in the sense of being inefficient or irrational. For example, he recognised that increasing technological rationalisation may undermine individual freedom due to the increasing bureaucratisation of all aspects of society (cited in Gerth and Mills 1977). Moreover, his notion of the 'dictatorship of the official' has strong links with Marx's notion of 'alienation'.

MANAGEMENT STYLES

The managerial prerogative (the ability of managers to determine what happens within the workplace) depends in large part on the particular management 'style' that is adopted. Purcell (1987: 535) defines 'management style' as

> the existence of a distinctive set of guiding principles, written or otherwise, which set parameters to and signposts for management action in the way employees are treated and particular events handled.

On the one hand, management may seek to maintain unilateral control of the firm by maintaining its prerogative and sustaining the widest possible freedom and discretion. On the other hand, management may include workers and their representatives in the organisation's decision-making processes and accept joint regulation of terms and conditions of employment. This distinction in management ideology mirrors the unitarist and pluralist approaches that are later outlined in more detail in Chapter 3. In practice, however, most managers regard unitarism as a 'natural' position to adopt because (Purcell and Sisson 1983: 113):

> Unitary values have been strongly inculcated in their own training and development, they are uncomplicated in their implications, and they are self-reassuring.

According to Purcell (1987), management style can be described firstly in terms of an individualism dimension relating to how an individual worker is treated and the extent to which his or her feelings and capabilities are considered. This has a bearing on issues such as advancement, personal fulfilment and opportunity for self-expression. There are three stages along the individualism dimension:

- commodity status – the employee is regarded as a unit of production to be hired and fired in accordance with demand and therefore has little job security; management's focus is on direct control and profit maximisation

- paternalism – the employee is regarded as subordinate and in need of the guidance and welfare of a benevolent employer. The emphasis is on 'caring for' rather than 'developing' human resources

- resource status – the employee is regarded as a potential resource to be developed, trained and rewarded in terms of performance; management's focus is on communication, worker involvement and stable employment.

The second, collectivism dimension refers to the extent to which management policies aim at encouraging or inhibiting the development of collective representation by workers. Accordingly, this dimension revolves around the degree of legitimacy afforded the collective by management. There are three stages along the collectivism dimension:

- unitary – management opposes all forms of collective regulation and challenges the legitimacy of collective arrangements that normally applies to non-union firms

- adversarial – management's focus is on stability, control and the institutionalisation of conflict, and collective bargaining is characterised by reluctance to compromise and narrowly defined areas of collective decision-making

- co-operative – the managerial focus is on building a constructive relationship that goes beyond bargaining over terms and conditions of employment; employees and their representatives are incorporated into the firm and managers are more willing to compromise.

Purcell (1987) argues that the relationship between these two dimensions within managerial style is complex and non-zero-sum. That is, the individualism and collectivism dimensions can both develop at the same time and an organisation may alter its styles along both dimensions simultaneously. For example, management may strengthen its relations with the union on some issues while encouraging the involvement of individual employees in others. In fact, most managers remain committed to unitarist values in spite of recognising and bargaining with trade unions.

Using Purcell's grid, we can identify four different management styles: autocratic unitarism (low individualism and low collectivism); sophisticated human relations (high individualism and low collectivism); constitutional pluralism (low individualism and high collectivism); and consultative pluralism (high individualism and high collectivism).

Although Salamon (1998) broadly accepts Purcell's model of management styles, he stresses that the lowering of labour costs and increasing profits remain a crucial goal of management in all the stages identified by Purcell. The dimensions outlined by Purcell are confined to a spectrum of managerial styles that limits the scope of challenges by individual employees and restricts collective regulation. In order to accommodate a participatory management style that integrates 'employee development' individualism with 'independent' collectivism, Salamon (1998: 225) suggests a third dimension – namely, management's attitude towards the underlying employment relationship. This may range from 'employee subordination', where the maintenance of the managerial prerogative is the overriding concern, through a 'limited acceptance' of the right of the employee to engage in some degree of joint decision-making on operational matters, to 'genuine partnership', where all organisational decisions are open to employee participation and influence.

The typologies of managerial strategies in industrial relations based on ideal types are rarely, if ever, observed in practice in their 'pure' form. In other words, most organisations do not fit neatly into a single ideal type of managerial style. Moreover, when mapping changes in management styles it is important to distinguish between managerial rhetoric and the actual practice of industrial relations. Many of the recent changes introduced by firms do not constitute a dramatic shift in managerial style as defined by Purcell. A good number of these initiatives, according to Purcell (1987: 546), are 'like the seeds on stony ground', having only 'a short life because there is no underlying accepted standard of treatment for employees beyond pure short-run commercial logic'. This is particularly pertinent to the currently fashionable emphasis on 'flexibility' – a concept that is critiqued in Chapter 13.

THE STATE

The state may be defined as 'the politically based and controlled institutions of government and regulation within an organised society' (Salamon 1998: 268). The elected government is the most active and important element within the state, determining the direction, policies and actions of the state machinery. The latter encompasses institutions such as Parliament, the executive, the judiciary, the public service, public enterprises, the police, the armed forces and local government authorities. The government is the third party to the employment relationship. The importance of its role in industrial relations stems from the fact that it is 'the only actor in the situation which can change the rules of the system' by virtue of its law-making function (Crouch 1982: 146). In addition, government policies and actions play a crucial role in shaping the socio-economic context within which employers and employees conduct the employment relationship. In fact, the diversity in national industrial relations regimes can be explained in large measure by the differences in the degree, method and content of government intervention.

The political party that runs the government may change on a regular basis, but the state as the continuous process of governance is more durable. The state machinery and the law continue to exercise social control with some degree of independence from the ruling party and its particular approach to industrial relations.

LIBERALISM AND CORPORATISM

Differences between countries with regard to the rules governing labour market behaviour revolve largely around the relative weight attached to government regulation (corporatism) versus market regulation (liberalism). Liberalism and corporatism are associated not only with divergent political ideologies but also with opposing economic theories. Typical liberal policy prescriptions include reducing company taxes, deregulating the economy and the labour market, and minimising the government's and organised labour's ability to intervene in the economy. Corporatist policy prescriptions follow a different line of reasoning. Government intervention is regarded as vital in promoting the expansion of local demand and increasing employment, with strategies including active labour market and industrial policies, the provision of social welfare programmes, and increasing exports through carefully managed integration into the world economy. Corporatism is generally characterised by trade unions agreeing to restrain the pursuit of their members' sectional interests in order to further the 'national interest'. In return for their co-operation, the unions accept concessions from the government.

Crouch (1982: 213) describes this model as one in which 'the government interposes itself between the unions and their normal bargaining partner, the employer, but in so doing becomes itself their bargaining partner – and the government is able to offer several things which cannot be achieved in bargaining … such as social policy reforms, workers' rights, changes in economic and fiscal policy'. However, it is possible to distinguish between countries such as Sweden, where trade unions are firmly integrated into the government's policy-making machinery and countries such as Germany, where the unions are merely included in regular consultations with the government.

'Corporatism' has operated under different historical and socio-economic conditions and assumed different forms: consultative corporatism, bargained corporatism, social corporatism and state corporatism.

Consultative corporatism or tripartism (where the government, employers and trade unions work closely together) is restricted to consultation and does not necessarily involve any formalised outcome or joint decision-making.

Bargained corporatism involves an institutionalised arrangement whereby capital, labour and the government jointly formulate labour market and economic policies, implying in principle, if not in practice, that the three parties have an equal say in decision-making. But there are potential dangers of elitism with bargained corporatism: it excludes a range of social interests and only takes place at the leadership level (Bean 1985: 124). In terms of economic policy-formation, however, it may be the only way of ensuring the consent of the major role-players. A further danger is that pressures at the workplace level may lead to the withdrawal of union support for tripartite structures and powerful unions may not continue consensual relations with the government and employers over the long term. Some form of bargained corporatism is usually introduced in these circumstances, whereby the government may be compelled to make concessions on items such as working hours, pensions, tax reductions, price controls and subsidies as well as introduce social policy reforms and job creation schemes.

Social corporatism involves the inclusion of a broader range of interests in civil society (such as the voluntary sector or those representing business). However, Von Holdt (1995) warns the organised labour movement of dangers posed by social corporatism, including a growing divide between leadership and membership, unrelenting pressure on unions to accept the economic perspectives of business, and a 'stakeholder' capitalism that may rule out a radical transformation of society.

State corporatism is found in several developing countries, especially in Latin America and Africa. With independence, many African governments sought to establish conditions that were conducive to industrial growth and rural development. This explains, in part, why trade unions in most African countries have been limited to economic or 'bread-and-butter' issues (mainly focusing on improving wages) since independence, in sharp contrast to their explicit political role during the struggle for independence.

Within the broad organising scheme or framework of 'corporatism', there are thus many variations. However, the classifying of 'ideal types' outlined above can result in an oversimplification, and reality can be influenced by powerful social groupings, the strategic orientation of labour, capital and government, and the broader global context in which the processes of political exchange take place.

For example, in Japan, Germany and Sweden, governments have become committed to running their labour markets in the interests of economic development. Typically, employers, bankers and trade unions co-operate with the government in order to run the labour market in a way that will aid the 'right' kind of social and economic development. This approach places a premium on social welfare and is based on the conviction that labour markets work better if they are institutionally regulated. Demand-side economists (stimulating demand for goods in the economy) argue that such intervention is necessary to ensure that economic growth enriches employers and also improves employees' living conditions. To this end, they encourage the establishment of 'growth compromises' between capital, labour and the government and protective frameworks to shield employees and consumers from the worst effects of the market. Other countries appear to be less convinced of the merits of intervention and planning, and during the 1980s the governments of the USA and the UK engaged in extensive deregulation of the labour market, preventing or limiting 'interference' by governments, employers, trade unions or anyone else in the 'free' play of market forces.

The following case study illustrates the complexities of state intervention and reveals how both corporatism and liberalism can be dominant within one country at different time periods.

CORPORATISM AND NEO-LIBERALISM IN A LIBERAL MARKET ECONOMY

The two contrasting approaches of neo-liberalism and corporatism are clearly illustrated by government strategies in Britain during the 1970s and 1980s. As Salamon argues, in the 1970s, the Labour government favoured a 'corporatist ideology'. This involved support for trade unions and for collective bargaining, using conciliation and arbitration processes for dispute resolution, regulating incomes and job security. Conversely, from 1970 the Conservative government's strategy was informed by a 'liberalist/*laissez-faire* ideology', and appeared to be aimed at restoring the power balance in favour of management. Moreover, it promoted 'responsible' trade unionism and labour flexibility, involving the deregulation of employment (Salamon 1998: 276).

Thus, different strategies may be used within the same country by governments in different time periods, or indeed at the same time. An example of the latter would be the case of contemporary South Africa, where essentially neo-liberal macro-economic policies are combined with relatively progressive labour legislation. An example of the former would be Australia, where the increasingly hardline anti-union policies of the Howard (Liberal) government from 1996 to 2007 were replaced with more progressive policies by the incoming Labour government.

Questions

Think of the country with which you are most familiar. This might be Britain or another country.

What is the government's apparent attitude toward trade unions?

How do trade unions influence government? Through being incorporated into decision-making? Through lobbying government? Through other means?

Would you describe government policies as illustrating neo-liberalism or corporatism, or do neither of these concepts seem to apply to the country in question?

VOLUNTARISM

The conduct of employment relations is governed not only by the law but by the various players. Proponents of neo-liberalism have suggested that external players impede the effective operation of labour markets and the operationalisation of the employment contract. Liberal market economies such as the United Kingdom and the United States retain strong elements of voluntarism – individual employers have considerable room to choose the strategies that they adopt toward unions. In contrast, many continental West European economies are far more closely regulated, the bargaining being centralised in many industries. This forces employers in such industries to engage with unions whether they want to or not. The centralisation and decentralisation of collective bargaining is discussed in more detail in Chapter 7, where the implications of these two types of bargaining for trade unions are outlined.

THE GOVERNMENT AS LEGISLATOR

The government sets the general framework and basic rules that govern industrial relations, establishing minimum conditions of employment including health and safety, wages and working hours. Legislation on individual rights compensates for the lack of protection against exploitation and ill-treatment afforded in some countries by common law. In the sphere of collective rights, the government establishes rules for the registration of trade unions and employers' organisations, protects the freedom to strike, sets up statutory collective bargaining machinery, and entrenches the right of employees to participate in decision-making at the workplace. Bean (1985: 102) argues that government relations with the labour movement have undergone a historical evolution from

> an initial phase of suppression of workers' organisations and collective action at the onset of industrialisation, moving to one of toleration and encouragement, to be followed by a later period of greater detailed regulation.

However, given the significant differences in both socio-economic conditions and the nature of industrialisation, this evolutionary process has taken distinctive forms in different countries (Bellace 1994). As well as significant variations in legislation on the procedural aspects of collective bargaining, there are also marked differences in the extent to which governments provide statutory regulation of the substantive terms of the employment relationship.

In order to consider the role of government as legislator, the following *Legislation in practice* box summarises the role of the government in India, and how the nature of its legislative role impacts on the economy.

⊶ LEGISLATION IN PRACTICE

Labour legislation in India

Indian labour legislation is extremely complex, with a plethora of overlapping laws. This has led to accusations that it constrains employers, discourages investment, has created an excessive regulatory bureaucracy and works against the efficient operation of labour markets (Bhattacharjea 2006). Yet in practice India is a fast-growing economy with many highly competitive firms across a wide range of sectors. There are two reasons for this seeming contradiction. First, the enforcement of the law is at best uneven (*ibid*); in all contexts there is a considerable difference between the letter of the law and actual firm-level practice. Second, there is the issue of complementarity: firms devise ways of compensating for any inefficiencies through building on the specific strengths of the system.

THE GOVERNMENT AS REGULATOR

The need for government regulation of the economy through legislation and policy stems from the inability of market forces to ensure that the risks and rewards of growth are equitably distributed. Whereas the proponents of 'deregulation' view government intervention in the labour market as a source of distortion in market forces, the supporters of regulation regard government intervention as a necessary feature of economic governance. The role of the government as market regulator is particularly evident in relation to the levels of wages, employment and unemployment. Governments that subscribe to a market individualist (or liberal) approach will combat unemployment by reducing social security and welfare benefits, abolishing wage policies, encouraging greater wage dispersal, and placing the responsibility for training on individual employers. Corporatist governments, by contrast, are more likely to take responsibility for training schemes, encourage job sharing, a reduction in working hours and higher premiums on overtime work, and protect living standards by maintaining social security and welfare systems.

In terms of the levels of income and their potential impact on price stability and competitiveness, the development of an incomes policy constitutes a vital component of a government's role in managing the economy. An incomes policy involves the use of measures to moderate the rate of price inflation through agreeing wage increases with trade employers and trade unions.

APPLYING THEORY TO PRACTICE

The regulation of the economy in South Africa

After 1994, the South African government had to confront the legacy of *apartheid* in the labour market: mass unemployment and poverty, discrimination and inequality, intense conflict at the workplace, low levels of productivity, and a marked absence of the managerial and technical skills required to drive the economy in an increasingly open and competitive international market. A balance had to be found between the creation of sustainable employment opportunities and the maintenance of acceptable standards of employment. To this end, the post-*apartheid* government pursued an active labour market policy geared towards maximising the quality of employment and minimising unemployment while at the same time seeking to improve efficiency, equity, growth and social justice. This included job-creation programmes (for example, the Working for Water programme) and legislation aimed at promoting more equitable representation on ethnic and gender lines across job categories. In addition, the creative redeployment of tariff barriers stimulated a major upsurge in the export of motor cars and motor car components. In practice, these initiatives have had significant but limited impact, which has been somewhat dulled by a broader commitment to neo-liberal policies, including public sector reforms.

THE GOVERNMENT AS ADJUDICATOR

The government plays a vital role in establishing the rules that govern the employment relationship through the establishment and management of a judicial system. However, trade unionists argue that frequent resort to the courts encourages a tradition of 'legalism', which is counter-productive because it relocates the site of workers' struggles from the workplace to the courtroom. This prevents workers from developing the necessary confidence and degree of organisation to win their own struggles. Turning to the court involves sacrificing trade union control of the dispute and relying on a disinterested outsider who may understand the law but is not swayed by the politics of the workplace.

THE GOVERNMENT AS EMPLOYER

The government is a direct and primary participant in industrial relations through its role as an employer in the public sector. Bean (1985: 100–1) suggests that the greater the importance of the government as an employer, the more pervasive its influence is likely to be on collective bargaining since it may then influence the pattern of industrial relations by its own behaviour and example. By ensuring that public sector wages conform to the government's income policies, a benchmark is set for private sector wage increases. Although there is great diversity across the public sector in terms of the nature of work, occupational structures and so on, some common industrial relations practices can be identified (Blyton and Turnbull 1998: 167):

- a formal separation of political and operational control such that managers are responsible for day-to-day administration while government ministers are empowered to provide general direction

- an 'obligation' to be a 'model employer', setting a 'good example' for the private sector with respect to matters such as health and safety, trade union recognition and job security

- formalised and centralised collective bargaining procedures

- high levels of trade union membership with negotiated industrial relations procedures

- hierarchical and bureaucratic management structures with internal promotion, a uniform approach to industrial relations, and an emphasis on service delivery.

However, in recent years there has been some critique of the government role as a model employer. Although in many countries within both advanced and emerging economies government work still offers job security and equity, there has been a greater tendency over time towards individualised pay and the use of non-standard work (Dibben *et al* 2007).

THE GOVERNMENT AS CONCILIATOR

Collective regulation of terms and conditions of employment presupposes the possibility of disagreement and, by extension, of disputes. A well-established government function in many countries is the provision of mechanisms for conciliation, mediation and arbitration designed to facilitate the settlement of disputes and to minimise industrial action. A government's dispute resolution function is examined in detail in Chapter 12.

OTHER PARTIES TO EMPLOYMENT RELATIONS: THE ROLE OF MANAGEMENT CONSULTANTS AND NGOS

Other parties to employment relations include consultants and NGOs. Many governments have encouraged the widescale use of management consultants to introduce more modern working practices into the public sector. In practice, consultants do not always deliver value for money – for example, obsessions with measuring performance may deliver superficial improvements but may undermine long-term staff morale and commitment. In addition, high consultancy fees may mean that the state ends up spending far more than was clawed back from workers through greater efficiency. NGOs (non-governmental organisations) may supplement the activities of unions, reaching out to marginalised categories of labour, such as women and those working in the informal sector. However, NGOs are not always accountable to those whom they are meant to be serving, and those running NGOs may not always have a real understanding of the needs of workers and the community. In some cases, therefore, it appears to be better for unions to work with NGOs since together they can achieve broad representation, and the trade unions – as recognised and established institutions – can have a voice in the government, and can therefore hope to influence legislation and policy at a higher level (see, for example, Dibben and Nadin 2010).

SUMMARY

There are three main parties to employment relations: employers, employees and the state. However, as explained above, the situation is much more complicated than this since both employees and employers have bodies representing their interests. In the case of employees, this chapter has been particularly concerned with the role of trade unions. Their role has developed over different time periods, and has been problematised in different ways, with particular attention paid to their economic and political operations. Although their essential structure and functions might remain the same, the strategic choices that unions make are dependent on a broad range of variables. Moreover, in considering employers it is not sufficient to refer to them as a homogeneous group. The sections focusing on employers and management behaviour drew attention to the different frameworks that have been employed to conceptualise behaviour, covering, for example, variations in management styles. Here, it is important to remember that the idealised forms presented may be more nuanced in practice. The role of the state was the focus of attention in the third main part of this chapter. Variation was noted both over time and within different country contexts, particularly in terms of the state's role as a 'model employer' and in terms of its relationship to trade unions.

EXPLORE FURTHER

Reading

- Bean, R. (1985) *Comparative Industrial Relations: An introduction to cross-national perspectives.* London: Croom Helm

- Crouch, C. (1982) *Trade Unions: The logic of collective action.* London: Fontana

- Harcourt, M. and Wood, G. (eds) (2004) *Trade Unions and Democracy: Strategies and perspectives.* Manchester: Manchester University Press

- Kelly, J. (1998) *Rethinking Industrial Relations: Mobilization, collectivism and long waves.* London: Routledge

- Purcell, J. (1987) 'Mapping management styles in employment relations', *Journal of Management Studies*, Vol.24, No.5: 533–48.

Websites

- Trades Union Congress www.tuc.org

- European Trade Union Confederation www.etuc.org

- Confederation of British Industry www.cbi.org.uk

- Union Network International www.union-network.org

CHAPTER 3

Theories of Employment Relations

CHAPTER OVERVIEW

As noted in the introductory chapter, the study of employment relations concerns the employment contract and the unclear exchange between fixed wages and anticipated amounts of labour power. The analysis of 'labour problems' and of related issues has attracted the attention of scholars in a variety of different disciplines. Employment relations as a field of study is a continuation of the industrial relations discipline, renamed to encompass employment relations in sectors other than industry. In this chapter, however, we retain the term 'industrial relations' because this is the one most commonly used in the theoretical literature.

The chapter covers a range of theories including unitarist, pluralist and radical theories, systems theory, social action theory, labour process theory, feminism and postmodernism. More aspects of theory are covered in greater detail in other chapters. For example, the work of Marx, Durkheim and Weber was explained in Chapter 2.

LEARNING OUTCOMES

After studying this chapter you should be able to:

- critically evaluate unitarist, pluralist and radical theories
- explain approaches to employment relations: HRM, systems theory, social action theory, labour process theory
- identify broad theories related to feminism, and the main strands of postmodernism
- describe what is understood by 'critical management studies'
- appreciate the indeterminate nature of the employment contract and structured antagonism

THE DISCIPLINARY UNDERPINNING OF 'INDUSTRIAL RELATIONS'

Industrial relations is a field of inquiry in which different academic disciplines apply their own approaches by using employment-related phenomena to address debates internal to each discipline. Hyman (1994: 3) refers to theories *in* industrial relations as opposed to theories *of* industrial relations because he does not regard industrial relations as a distinct discipline with its own conceptual and theoretical apparatus, but rather as 'a field of study in which a variety of disciplinary perspectives can be applied, integrated and tested'. Likewise, Edwards (2003: 338–9) observes that industrial relations is 'a field of study rather than an academic discipline ... [that contains] some distinctive perceptions which are more than the sum total of individual disciplines'. The multiplicity and diversity of factors that have an impact on the employment relationship have frustrated attempts by the various academic disciplines to appropriate industrial relations as their own.

Sociology brings a distinct set of concepts and orientations to this endeavour (see Roberts 2003). In contrast to other academic disciplines, it brings a critical yet sympathetic understanding to bear on the 'problems' of labour. As Allen (1971: 16–17) points out:

> People who are antipathetic towards the aims of organised labour, who do not sympathise with the conditions in which so many working people find themselves, are not likely to get very far with their investigations ... I am not suggesting that those who engage in the sociology of industrial relations should adopt a partisan approach. I am suggesting that they should be motivated by an element of social purpose.

Other academic traditions have also sought to conceptualise industrial relations. Most influential of these has been economics (see Rubery and Grimshaw 2003). Within orthodox economics, the central idea is that of 'economic man', with the assumption that society is composed of rational profit-maximising individuals. From this starting point it is assumed that, if lightly regulated – as is the case with any other market – labour markets will function efficiently. Firms will compete for suitable labour, forcing up wages in areas where skills are scarce. In turn, this will incentivise job seekers to obtain the needed skills or move location to areas where their skills are scarce. In other words, labour is a readily substitutable commodity. However, the idea of rationality assumes that individual actors are possessed of perfect information. In fact, there may be great imbalances in terms of knowledge and understanding as to real skills and what specific jobs really entail and require. Mainstream (neo-liberal) economics further assumes that the two contractors to the employment relationship – the firm and the individual – are inherently equal parties; it discounts the view that the employment contract is generally one of inequality, and that termination generally imposes a far greater cost on the employee than the employer (Harcourt *et al* 2004). Traditional economic approaches often pay too little attention to the transaction costs associated with the hiring and firing of labour. The employee cannot change jobs too often, whereas high turnover rates impose additional formal and informal induction and development costs on the firm, which are often discounted.

◉ REFLECTION ON PRACTICE

Rational behaviour?

Do you think that all managers behave *rationally* when they make decisions?

If you are currently working in an organisation, or have had work experience, think of a time when your manager made a 'rational' decision, drawing on all available evidence before deciding on the action to take. Then think of a time when the manager did not appear to act 'rationally'. Why was this the case?

However, economics offers useful tools for the study of industrial relations. The quantitative tools of econometrics enable the researcher to explore the relationship between different numerical indices (for example, those derived from relative employee rights under the law and staff turnover rates at the firm level) on a sophisticated basis, and have done much to advance understanding of what is likely to occur when and where, and to provide benchmarks for comparison. In addition, writers within the economics tradition are taking increasing account of the effects of institutions and collectives, albeit primarily as providers of incentives to rational actors. One could argue that key strands of economics are becoming more sociological.

A further discipline that contributes to the study of industrial relations is psychology (see Brotherton 2003). At the level of the individual, psychologists have explored work and employment dynamics for many years, examining, for example, attitudes towards job satisfaction and determinants of stress. However, critics have charged that many of these endeavours have been aimed at promoting a better fit between the individual and the organisation, filtering out the potentially deviant, and exploring ways of moulding the individual to fit the managerial agenda (see Thompon and McHugh 2009). More recent work in the psychological tradition has moved beyond this, taking account of the effects of associations, key writers promoting a more progressive agenda, exploring issues such as the psychological contract and its violation by firms.

Although both economics and psychology have an important role to play, sociological starting points tend to be dominant in the field of industrial relations, and particularly the concern with the social relations between individuals and groupings, and an interest in the relationship between embedded rules and practice. However, econometric tools and techniques are dominant in the most prominent journals of the field.

To some extent, as Kelly (1998: 18) notes, industrial relations remains oriented towards fact-finding and describing institutions. A theoretical framework is nonetheless important since it informs the questions we pose, the structure of our analysis, the inferences we draw, and the conclusions we reach. While descriptive measures such as aggregate patterns and trends of trade union membership, the number of strikes, and so forth, are useful and significant, they cannot *explain* the social relations between individuals and groups of individuals that generate these phenomena. Theories of industrial relations function as ideologies, justifying particular worldviews and providing a coherent framework for understanding and explaining industrial relations.

APPROACHES TO ORGANISATIONS: UNITARISM, PLURALISM AND RADICAL THEORIES

There are three broad approaches to organisations: unitarist, pluralist and radical or class conflict (Batstone 1988: 218–39). With the exception of radical theories, these are analytical categories, rather than theories, in that they do not seek to explain or predict but to describe and summarise, or, in some instances, to express a desired state rather than actual reality. Nonetheless, unitarism finds theoretical support within more conservative strands of Parsonian sociology (named after Talcott Parsons and implying a view of society and institutions that views organisations and relationships as part of a functioning system). The unitarist perspective assumes that working societies function as a coherent whole, and draws on economic theories that see the employment contract as an essentially equal and fair one. Pluralism finds theoretical justification in the sociological work of Emile Durkheim and in theories that derive value in economic activity from the factors of production. The class conflict approach draws on the Marxist tradition which views value as the product of human labour. Each of these theories is explained in more detail below.

UNITARISM

At the heart of a unitarist conception of industrial relations lies the idea that the workplace is an integrated and harmonious entity. This approach is managerially oriented in its assumptions and application (Salamon 1998: 5–7). In his evidence to a commission on industrial relations, the managing director of the Portland Cement Company in England (cited in Farnham and Pimlott 1983: 52) captures many of the key elements of unitarism:

> An employee, at whatever level, must be made to feel that he is not merely a number on a payroll but a recognised member of a team ... We reject the idea that amongst the employees of a company there are 'two sides', meaning the executive directors and managers on the one hand and the weekly-paid employees on the other. Executive directors are just as much employees of the company as anyone else. We are all on the same side, members of the same team ... We recognise that the tone of any organisation depends primarily on one man [sic] – on the executive head of it: on his philosophy, on his outlook, on the standards which he sets, on his example – in short, on his leadership. Leadership ... must embrace, *inter alia* ... [the] maintenance of strict discipline.

Thus, all employees – no matter what their role – work together as a functioning team with one set of goals. As Fox (1966) points out, managers identify with the unitarist perspective because it provides them with reassurance in their roles as organisational decision-makers and legitimates their authority over employees. Unitarism is particularly prevalent in small businesses and in some cases has been associated with overt control. Not surprisingly, this has led in some instances to employee dissatisfaction, labour turnover, absenteeism and industrial action. The central assumptions of unitarist approaches include:

- that work organisations have a unitary structure with a common purpose and value system

- that management and labour share a common set of interests and operate as a 'harmonious team'

- that since management 'knows best' and acts in the best interests of all, employees need not be actively involved in the decision-making processes in the workplace

- that the employer's disciplinary powers are necessary and legitimate

- that collective bargaining and trade unions promote distrust and disunity and are therefore unnecessary and unwarranted

- that industrial conflict is an aberration and invariably the result of bad communication, stupidity or simply the work of 'agitators'.

According to Farnham and Pimlott (1983: 54–5), the extent to which unitarism represents a consistent and compatible viewpoint depends on (a) the internal social structure of the organisation, and (b) whether the predominant value system of the organisation is accepted by the personnel that it employs. Different individuals and groups have different perceptions of what is 'good' or 'bad', 'right' or 'wrong', and what constitutes a 'legitimate' use of power. These differing perspectives provide the underlying dynamic tension within industrial relations. Industrial relations are precisely concerned with subjective value-judgements about concepts such as fairness, power, rights and trust (Salamon 1998: 67–80). Those taking a unitarist perspective might therefore be mistaken in assuming that the parties to the employment relationship share a common value system and that conflict is somehow pathological. Moreover, unitarism may be logically inconsistent: it stresses the common interests of the parties while, at the same time, justifying the substantial inequalities in income, status and power between managers and workers.

PLURALISM

Pluralism is associated with a view that society has moved on from the inequalities of the nineteenth century. Societies have become more democratic; authority and property are more widely distributed (many workers are shareholders, directly and/or via their pensions); there is a division of ownership and management, an institutional separation of political and industrial conflict, and a commitment to the institutionalisation of conflict (Farnham and Pimlott 1983: 55–8; Salamon 1998: 7–8). It is held that in advanced societies there is a plurality of interests; this will naturally make for conflict, but is best dealt with via compromise. The existence of third-party representation ameliorates individual self-interest, and provides the basis for co-operative actions (Durkheim 1957).

Pluralism characterises the industrial relations practices of many large work organisations. It is also the most widely adopted framework in research and forms the bedrock of the industrial relations policies of most governments and international agencies (such as the International Labour Organisation). However, pluralism is far from being a homogeneous framework of analysis with uniform prescriptions: its development reflects varied disciplinary roots, diverse conceptual and interpretative frameworks, and the impact of assorted ideological forces. Accordingly, pluralism should be regarded as 'a loose and incomplete set of ideas, beliefs and values which acquire coherence only when complemented by background assumptions which are rarely articulated by pluralist writers themselves' (Hyman 1989: 55). These assumptions include:

- that just as society consists of different interest groups, so work organisations contain different pressure groups. 'The essence of pluralism', Hyman (1989: 66) argues, 'is that employees should not be regarded as a single coherent group (let alone a *class*) but as fragmented among a multiplicity of sectional grouplets'

- that society is 'a coalition of plural interest groups held together in some sort of balance or equilibrium by the agency of the state' (Farnham and Pimlott 1983: 57). All interest groups in society have a more or less equal influence on state policies

- that the state is the impartial servant or referee of society as a whole

- that the enterprise, like society in general, consists of individuals and groups with conflicting interests and goals

- that trade unions are legitimate and necessary vehicles for protecting and promoting the interests of employees. Unions do not, in themselves, cause conflict within the organisation but 'simply provide a highly organised and continuous form of expression for sectional interests which would exist anyway' (Fox 1966: 8)

- that industrial conflict is the inevitable result of the different interest groups pursuing their own objectives

- that given the interdependence of employers and employees, both parties agree that destructive conflict should be avoided, principally through institutionalised collective bargaining

- that although conflict in the workplace is accepted as both inevitable and legitimate, the dominant concern of pluralists is with the establishment of structures and procedures within which the legitimate conflicts of interest can be contained and prevented from undermining the interests of all, leading to 'negotiated order'

- that the 'institutionalisation' of industrial conflict is a primary function of industrial relations

- that pluralism is the 'ideal' state towards which all industrial relations systems are tending. Departures from this ideal-typical model (eg *apartheid*, dictatorships) are merely temporary aberrations.

More recent work in the pluralist tradition has lamented the visible decline of social solidarity within advanced societies – most notably the literature emerging from lightly regulated liberal markets, such as the USA and the UK (Etzioni 1995; Kalleberg 2009). A lack of collective identity and expression can result in self-seeking individuals and disempowered workers.

It is worth noting that pluralist approaches have come under attack from resurgent neo-liberal economists. A concern within much of the economics and finance literature in recent years has been with exploring ways of solving the agency problem, whereby professional managers have interests different from those of owners (expanding and sustaining the firm, rather than returning profits to owners). Solutions centre on incentivising managers through appealing to their individual profit motives (eg linking rewards to share prices) and through weakening the pull of other interest groupings such as unions (cf La Porta *et al* 2000).

RADICAL OR CLASS CONFLICT APPROACHES

These approaches endorse the Marxist view of capitalist societies as divided into antagonistic class forces. Accordingly, class conflict is unavoidable, rooted in the structures of society itself and not just an industrial phenomenon (Farnham and Pimlott 1983; Salamon 1998). Industrial relations can therefore be understood only as part of a broader analysis of capitalist society in general, and the social relations of production, class struggle and the dynamics of capitalist accumulation in particular (Blyton and Turnbull 1998). In other words, it is not possible to separate what happens at work from what is happening outside the workplace, where there will inevitably be differences of opinion between those with money and property and those without, especially since those with property (or owners of industry) try to obtain profits from their workers.

The central assumptions of class conflict approaches include:

- that capitalist societies are characterised by private property, production for profit and class struggle. While pluralists assume that the joint regulation of industrial relations is in the interests of both parties, Marxists view the normative structures (in simple terms, the accepted way of doing things) and institutionalised forms (the established organisations, rules and behaviours) of industrial relations as the outcome of a power struggle between capital and labour

- that a capitalist society is characterised by great material inequalities and a highly unequal distribution of power. The individual worker is far more dependent on his or her employer as a source of income than the other way around

- that the asymmetry of power relations in the workplace is derived mainly from the ownership of the means of production (eg some people own factories while others simply work for those owners). Ownership leads to power and control: it grants employers the 'right' to hire and fire employees as well as the 'right' to direct their labour

- that association in trade unions for the purpose of collective representation of interests reflects an attempt by wage labourers to overcome the power imbalances they experience as individuals in the workplace

- that although trade unions can assume a certain protective function with regard to their membership (for example, representing them in cases of discrimination), their influence on industrial relations and the capitalist system in general is overestimated. Unions only normally challenge the roots of 'ownership, inequality, hierarchy, and privilege' at the margins (Fox 1974: 276)

- that at best, industrial relations can only alter marginal issues and power (such as the relative distribution of wages) rather than fundamental issues (such as the distribution of wealth in society). That is, trade unions and collective bargaining have become an established, accepted and supportive part of the capitalist system rather than a challenge to it

- that the trade-off between profits and wages is a zero-sum process (one wins while the other loses). The lower the wages paid by the capitalist, the greater are his or her profits; the higher the wages that workers receive, the lower are the profits of the employer

- that the wage–effort bargain which underlies the employment relationship is a contested terrain, and is a 'compromise unsatisfactory to both parties' (Hyman 1975: 26).

Some versions of the class conflict approach have been rightly criticised for offering a simplistic vision of the workplace in which managers control workers, who either accommodate or resist, and in which any reform is merely a means to assert greater managerial control (Edwards 1986). The proponents of the 'radical' approach also have an image of management as unduly unified and rational (being able to know all possible options before making decisions and not influenced by emotions). Ironically, they share this view with the unitarist claim that it is possible to produce rules that are in the interests of all. They also tend to regard workers as simply recalcitrant, whereas the unitarist view tends to regard them as simply obedient. However, not all criticisms of this approach are justified. For instance, it is often argued that because capitalist societies have not been overthrown and replaced with socialism, this in itself is sufficient grounds for dismissing Marxism. Such arguments conflate an essential distinction between Marxism as an analysis of capitalism (theoretical movement) with a prescription for socialism (political movement). The major contribution of Marxists, according to Hyman (1989: 128),

> has been as much in the questions asked as in the answers given or the methods of their attainment. It is the framework of what is taken for granted or what is regarded as problematic that most clearly differentiates Marxists from conventional 'industrial relations' analysts.

Marxism as a theoretical movement is unparalleled in terms of its ability to uncover the inner workings of a capitalist economy. In this regard it constitutes a significant challenge to other theoretical frameworks. Even scholars who are committed to pluralism acknowledge that it needs to incorporate 'the endemic nature of class conflict in plural societies which is highlighted by Marxist theory' (Farnham and Pimlott 1983: 67). Marxism went out of fashion in the 1990s, following the implosion of the ostensibly Marxist Soviet Union. In recent years it has come back into vogue as a result of persistent economic crises, and rising social inequality within liberal market economies.

In the case study below, attention is drawn to an area of conflict between employers and workers.

CASE STUDY

WORKING CONDITIONS IN CHINA

A range of protests have been made about working conditions within a large Taiwanese manufacturer, Foxconn, operating within China (Brannigan 2010). According to Brannigan (2010), the company employs around 900,000 people. Around a third of these people are employed in a plant in Shenzhen where particular concerns have been raised about the length of working hours, low pay and monotonous work. In certain cases the outcome appears to have been extreme – at least nine workers have apparently committed suicide as a result of having to endure such conditions.

The company has attempted to address problems in a number of ways. Firstly, it has installed safety nets around buildings. Secondly, it has provided a counselling service for employees. Thirdly, it has begun playing music on production lines in order to alleviate the monotony felt by employees.

However, campaigners argue that the company has not gone far enough. In addition to changes in working practices and conditions, they are also arguing for independent voice mechanisms for workers.

Why should the company change its practices? Company sources refer to a huge flood of applicants whenever vacancies are announced, so does the company need to change?

Question

Which theory/set of theories would best explain the occurrences at Foxconn, and why?

In answering this question consider the relationship between the employer and employees and the nature of the 'conflict'.

The case study above shows workplace situations where conflict might appear, drawing attention to the plight of workers who do not have secure positions in the workforce, and to health and safety issues. In some countries, such as the UK, health and safety is covered by legislation, and a range of regulations have been brought into force in order to protect workers (www.hse.gov.uk). However, even in the UK legislation is not always applied in practice, particularly within small manufacturing firms. The situation can be exacerbated in emerging economies where governments lack the resources for the adequate inspection of workplaces.

A SYNTHESIS?

Is it possible to combine theories? The divergence that does exist, according to Clegg (1979: 455), is to be found 'mainly in their attitudes'. However, in his attempt to downplay the differences between pluralism and Marxism, Clegg overlooks the significant discrepancies between their basic political and theoretical assumptions. Understating the differences between the various theoretical approaches to industrial relations encourages a tendency to combine them in an *ad hoc* and eclectic manner, which leads to theoretical incoherence and a lack of clarity.

Given the different presuppositions that inform these two approaches, the challenges confronting an attempt at synthesis are daunting, especially as unitarism, and to an extent pluralism, are not coherent theoretical traditions at all. This becomes starkly evident when we consider a basic Marxist critique of pluralist industrial relations.

- Pluralists tend to ignore the crucial decision-making powers that lie beyond collective bargaining, and the effects of persistent inequalities in material resources.

  A simple idea of power cannot reveal the extent to which power relationships have already shaped the agenda of collective negotiations. Radical theorists also point out that power is not only about being able to secure certain decisions in your favour, but is also about the ability to prevent certain matters from becoming issues for discussion in the first place.

- Pluralists tend to place an undue emphasis on consensus and integration.

  The focus of pluralists tends to be on how conflict is resolved rather than on what causes it, minimising 'the material basis of this conflict' (Hyman 1989: 82). Class divisions mean that class conflict is a permanent feature of industrial relations.

- Pluralists tend to assume that there is a balance of power in industrial relations.

  With their emphasis on the role of collective bargaining, pluralists assume that negotiations can reach a compromise suitable to both employers and employees. However, the ability to reach a compromise assumes (implicitly, if not explicitly) that there is an approximate balance of power between business and organised labour, with the state acting as neutral referee.

- There is a tension in pluralism between its commitment to the idea of 'voluntarism' and the reality of extensive government intervention in industrial relations.

  The government is regarded as the more or less impartial or neutral guardian of the 'public interest' and as not subject to excessive influence from economically powerful groups. However, the government for a capitalist safeguards the capitalist state (Schienstock 1981: 183) and can be influenced by powerful employers.

- Pluralists tend to accept it as natural and inevitable that trade unions should pursue narrow and readily negotiable objectives in collective bargaining.

  However, it will not necessarily be the case that both parties will reach a consensus. By adopting a restricted view of the legitimate interests of workers and their organisations, compromises in negotiations are seen as easily attainable.

Two further arguments are worth considering here.

Firstly, although unions have declined in much of the developed world over the past 40 years, many employers have found themselves in a weak position (Kelly 1998). It would be a mistake to assume that because workers have become weak, employers have necessarily become stronger. Rather, the structural imbalances within the global economy have led to a protracted period of volatile and uneven growth interspersed with recession, with entire sectors within specific nations (for example, manufacturing in liberal markets) in long-term decline. Finance capital (or *rentiers*) may have made great gains at the expense of ordinary employees, but this is at the cost of other segments of capital (eg manufacturing) (Krippner 2005).

Secondly, it is often assumed that as societies progress, they become more civilised. Yet the force that the police have used against striking miners and anti-war protestors, and indeed, the shift of US foreign policy towards a greater use of war and coercion at least partly in response to its relative economic decline, underscores the extent to which governments may make use of violence when their economic interests are under threat (Kelly 1998; Harvey 2003).

APPLYING THEORY TO PRACTICE

The relevance of different theoretical perspectives

Think of a workplace that you are familiar with, either from your work experience or from the media. What form did employment relations assume: pluralist, conflictual or unitarist? Give reasons for your answer.

APPROACHES TO EMPLOYMENT RELATIONS

The approaches to organisations outlined above inspired distinct orientations towards industrial relations. Most influential have been systems approaches (drawing on Durkheim and Parsons), approaches looking at social action and choices (within the tradition of Max Weber), Marxist approaches (expressed via the radical approach outlined above), and postmodernism. These are outlined in Figure 3.1.

Within pluralist industrial relations we can discern a basic contrast between systems approaches that reflect the needs of an economy (context determines strategies), which are associated with the work of Dunlop (1958), and behavioural theories (strategies determine context) that focus on bargaining strategies, which are reflected in the work of authors such as Walton and McKersie (1965).

The 'structuralist' dimension of systems theories emphasises the ways in which the regulation of industrial relations is influenced by the wider context.

Figure 3.1 Approaches to organisations and industrial relations

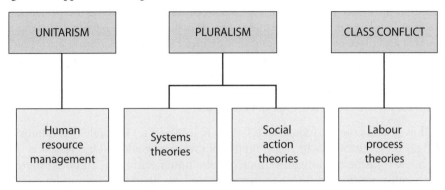

However, these insights often seem to assume *determinism* (the inability to change what is happening) and fail to appreciate the active role of human agency in sustaining and transforming the system itself. Action theory approaches, as reflected in the current emphasis on 'strategic choice', instead examine ways in which the different parties to industrial relations are positioned to realise their respective objectives within the framework of the collective regulation of work.

THE INDUSTRIAL RELATIONS SYSTEM

Dunlop (1958) developed a theoretical approach based on the 'systems' approach and its core concern with how the elements of society interact to produce social continuity. He argued that the central task of a theory of industrial relations is 'to explain why particular rules are established in particular industrial relations systems, and how and why they change in response to changes affecting the system' (Dunlop 1958: viii–ix). This implies that it is rule-making, rather than the totality of worker–management–government interaction, that is central to the industrial relations system. Dunlop focuses on the manner in which outcomes (the rules formulated by the parties) reflect the needs imposed by objective (economic, technical, political) constraints in the environment of labour–management relations. Systems theories draw from the basic organic analogy used by Durkheim in which social systems have to adapt to their environment if they are to survive. This functionalist theory regards social systems as self-regulating bodies, tending towards a state of equilibrium and order. Dunlop (1958: 7) suggests that the industrial relations system is comprised of four interrelated elements: actors, contexts, an ideology which binds the industrial relations system together, and a body of rules. This network of rules consists of procedures for establishing the rules, the substantive rules themselves and the procedures for deciding their application to particular situations. The actors include a hierarchy of management and their representatives, a hierarchy of workers and their representatives, and third-party bodies such as governmental agencies (see Salamon 1998: 14). The environmental context that shapes the decisions and actions of the parties includes technology, the characteristics of the workforce, market or budgetary constraints, and the locus and distribution of power in the wider society (Dunlop 1958: 9). Interaction between the parties is governed, in large measure, by an ideology or common set of beliefs that 'defines the role and place of each actor and that defines the ideas which each actor holds towards the place and function of others in the system' (1958: 16). Dunlop's view of ideology as 'binding the system together' echoes Parsons' emphasis on the vital social role of a 'common value system' – all people essentially have the same attitudes towards accepted ways of behaviour.

Within systems theory, industrial relations is seen as a set of stable institutions and processes through which the 'inputs' of divergent goals and interests are routinely transformed into an 'output' of rules underwriting the smooth progress of capitalist production. These arguments were later developed into an input–output model (Figure 3.2) that regards industrial relations primarily as a process of converting conflict into regulation.

Figure 3.2 The input–output model of industrial relations

A range of objections has been raised against Dunlop's systems approach. According to Marsden (1982: 239), systems analysis is at best a description of industrial relations rather than a theory. The character of an industrial relations 'system' is simply attributed to the nature of its environment. Moreover, Dunlop locates the concept of power at the societal level (ie national industrial relations systems) rather than at more micro levels (ie the industry or workplace). This results in an inability to explore:

- the possibility of a conflict between rules
- the dynamics and sources of rule-breaking
- the legitimacy of power at lower levels
- the relative bargaining power between the parties (Wood *et al* 1975: 302).

Moreover, system theorists' overriding concern with the 'problem of order' diverted attention away from the structures of power in the workplace and beyond. For instance, in his emphasis on the 'regulatory' functions of industrial relations, Dunlop assumes that the parties to collective bargaining have an essential interest in the stability of their relations and share a common set of priorities and values. However, it could be argued that Dunlop was wrong to regard conflict and change as aberrations from, rather than central characteristics of, the employment relationship. According to Shalev (1980: 26), he was also mistaken in implying that the context of industrial relations is a given and that it plays a more or less determinate role in the production of system outcomes. Consequently, Dunlop's systems methodology precludes an adequate treatment of conflict and change.

Over time, there has been a shift from general systems theory to a theory of 'open systems' in which industrial relations are viewed as 'cybernetic systems'. Although subsequent expositions of systems theory have considerably expanded and refined Dunlop's original schema, functionalist assumptions of order and stability remain. Moreover, there is a continued neglect of informal workgroup relations and unofficial custom and practice. However, informal and loosely structured relationships in the workplace can tend to subvert the decisions taken within the official or formal institutions.

SOCIAL ACTION AND STRATEGIC CHOICE

In contrast to Dunlop's approach, which emphasises the role of structures, 'social action' theories emphasise the processes through which people construct social reality – the way in which they interpret what is happening (Thompson and McHugh 1990: 36). An emphasis on the importance of choices and strategies in the development of industrial relations is a key element in these theories. In common with organisational behaviour approaches, action theories highlight the ways in which the parties adapt to and exploit their operating environments.

In social action approaches, the relationship between the employer and the union, involving dimensions such as trust and co-operation, is a key element of industrial relations strategy. Fells (1989: 484) points toward a range of arenas for strategic choice, and indicates the parties involved:

- organisational – focusing on the individual futures of employers and unions
- institutional – focusing on the nature of the industrial relations system
- relationship – centring on the relationships between employer and unions
- dispute-handling – whereby both employer and union seek to achieve maximum gains from a dispute.

Although, in common with the systems approach, action theories place the collective regulation of industrial labour at the centre of analysis, they are more sceptical about the stability of institutions (Kelly 1998). Moreover, they emphasise the role of human action and interpretation. Managers may devote time and resources to attempts at altering the behavioural expectations of employees, while in turn employees need to recognise the constraints managers operate under, and forge realistic compromises. The strategic choice model makes specific assumptions in this regard: employers and employees act within a framework that can best be described as a 'coalition relationship'. Although the parties may differ in the relative weight they attach to the problems of common concern (eg wages, work design) and may also favour different solutions, the conflict is not viewed as irresolvable. Conflict between the parties is not the product of antagonistic (different and conflicting) interests. Instead, it is argued, the parties have an interest in co-operating to resolve disputes and in preventing conflict from threatening the survival of the enterprise.

Critics have charged that the strategic choice model does little more than list the parties to industrial relations and their interactions, and provides little insight into the relations of conflict and dependence that bind the parties together (Edwards 1995). The strategic choice model also discounts the extent to which structural factors limit the choice of action. Action-oriented approaches generally make no reference to wider structural determinations and can be criticised for failing to acknowledge that which takes place beyond the bargaining table. For instance, the strategic choice model says very little about the role of the government. Governmental policies, however, constitute 'one key element of a national regime of labour regulation – that is, the means through which the interests of capital, labour and the state are organised and represented' (Edwards 1995: 21). Explaining the variations in the role of the government is therefore vital for a proper understanding of the differences between the various regimes. Moreover, in reality, managerial choice is plagued by complexities, tensions, uncertainties and conflict.

CONTROL OF THE LABOUR PROCESS

After a long period in which the sphere of production (in simple terms, what happens within the workplace) received little attention from social scientists, the work of Braverman (1974) paved the way for a flood of writings on the 'labour process', which can be defined (Thompson 1989: 15) as:

> the means by which raw materials are transformed by human labour, acting on the objects with tools and machinery, first into products for use and, under capitalism, into commodities to be exchanged on the market.

Like Marx, Braverman regards the transformation of labour power into actual labour as the central dynamic of the labour process. This poses a problem for management: profitable labour must be extracted from employees. Consequently, employers are compelled to enforce managerial control mechanisms on a continuous basis in order to achieve profits.

The development of labour process theories arose from the inadequacies of existing approaches, the dramatic increase in industrial conflict in most industrialised societies from the late 1960s onwards, advances in technological development, and the growing diversity of the workforce. Unlike many of the approaches that preceded his work, Braverman (1974) downplays consensus and assumes that employees have to be coerced into realising their labour power potential, and this results in a constant class struggle at the point of production. In short, the amount of work achieved depends on the extent of coercion. According to Braverman (1974), technological innovations in the workplace are not directed primarily at enhancing 'efficiency' but rather at securing greater control over the workforce. For Braverman, it therefore became essential for the capitalist that control over the labour process pass from the hands of the worker to those of management. He also argued that in order to control work and justify low wages, jobs were broken up into their simplest component parts – a process that was facilitated through the selective use of machinery. The outcome for workers was the deskilling and degradation of their work. Following Marx, Braverman (1974: 120–1) argues that

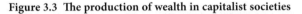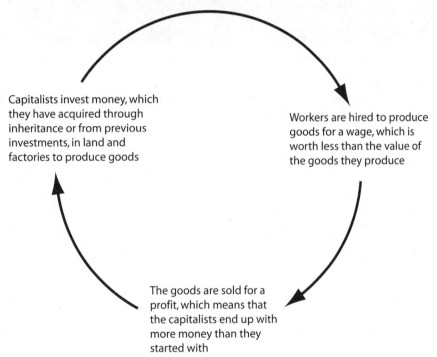

as craft declined, the worker would sink to the level of general and undifferentiated labour power, adaptable to a wide range of tasks, while as science grew, it would be concentrated in the hands of management.

The divisions of labour in production included the separation of the labour process into its constituent elements, and the allocation of the separated constituent elements of work to different workers. These developments laid the basis for the creation of the 'detailed worker'. This 'detailisation' increases productivity and managerial control and cheapens the cost of labour by reducing the time skilled workers must devote to job elements that do not require skill and recreating those elements as jobs for the unskilled.

Figure 3.3 The production of wealth in capitalist societies

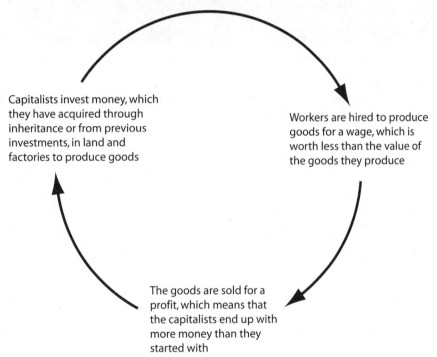

Capitalists invest money, which they have acquired through inheritance or from previous investments, in land and factories to produce goods

Workers are hired to produce goods for a wage, which is worth less than the value of the goods they produce

The goods are sold for a profit, which means that the capitalists end up with more money than they started with

Science and technology are thus employed to strengthen the trends towards deskilling and task fragmentation – and nowhere was this clearer than with the introduction of the assembly line and the unskilled assembly worker. This form of production is labelled 'Fordism' or mass production. The methods of control are sometimes referred to as 'Taylorism', after F. W. 'Speedy' Taylor, a shift boss turned early efficiency expert, who advocated time-and-motion studies to determine how long it would take to perform each job component, keeping tasks separate and distinct to facilitate monitoring, and linking pay to output. According to Beynon (1984), Fordism achieved the necessary extension of Taylorism in the labour process. By 1914, work had been reorganised with the introduction of a conveyor belt on which car assemblies were carried past fixed stations where workers performed simple operations. This innovation cut assembly time for a car by nine-tenths, greatly increasing productivity. However, the increase in productivity was the result of both the reorganisation of work and management control over the pace of assembly and the rate at which operations had to be performed. Fordism pushed job fragmentation and task-cycle times to an extreme by granting management direct control over the pace of work. The trends towards increased mechanisation and deskilling were not limited to the manufacturing sector. Braverman held that the computer would be to office workers what the assembly line was to manual employees. The rise of the call centre industry has since been associated with highly deskilled, electronically controlled and monitored, and routinised work.

◀◉▶ REFLECTION ON PRACTICE

Braverman, the labour process and current workplaces

To what extent is Braverman's work relevant today?

Are the work processes organised in a way that enables managers to exert maximum control over workers?

In addition to control, management has also had to seek workers' active co-operation and consent. Considerable refinement of the conceptual tools used by Braverman has occurred subsequently, and the focus of the labour process approach has moved well beyond his original concerns (see Knights *et al* 1985; Knights and Willmott 1988; Sturdy *et al* 1992).

The central criticisms levelled against Braverman's work revolve around his neglect of worker resistance – workers are seen as passive subjects rather than active agents. Further limitations are his overemphasis on the impact of Taylorism as a strategy of managerial control, his neglect of the varied conditions under which Taylorism was implemented, the effects of worker resistance, and the obstacles to increased profitability that this presented. Moreover, rising levels of resistance have forced management to seek the co-operation of workers by instituting forms of control that departed from Taylorism with consent being prioritised rather than coercion (Burawoy 1985).

None of these criticisms diminishes the importance of Braverman's seminal work. Much of the persuasiveness of Braverman's arguments stems from its broad sweep and its success in incorporating a number of seemingly unrelated developments within one overall framework. Debates around the labour process remain a vibrant area of enquiry, with an excellent series of books, the Critical Perspectives on Work and Employment (or the 'Labour Process' series, published initially by Routledge, and later by Palgrave) regularly updating issues and debates. Recent debates have sought to impart an international and comparative perspective, and to encompass new areas (eg work–life balance, creative work, knowledge and management) (Thompson and Smith 2010). In the 1990s, labour process writing diverged between new wave postmodern accounts and more traditional approaches. More recently, there has been greater dialogue between these two points of view, and a greater attempt at synthesis (*ibid*: 4).

FEMINISM

In both nineteenth-century and contemporary sweatshops an often visible feature is the disproportionate use of women. Moreover, within many organisations, women tend to be clustered within certain occupations – 'women's work' – such as secretarial and administrative positions, often paid less than men doing similar work. Yet management and politics are professions that are both dominated by men. Why is this the case? There are two possible explanations for horizontal segregation.

The first is an essentially liberal argument. As suggested by neo-liberal economic theory, labour markets should function efficiently. In other words, over time, women and men should be equally distributed in occupations across an economy. Any factor that impedes the progress of women can be seen as a market distortion, a dysfunctional product of past prejudices, or meddling by governments or vested interests. Greater equality can be promoted through legislation centring on individual rights, and through raising awareness of the inefficiencies of discrimination (firms are not using talent to its fullest potential).

A second argument is a more radical one – gender inequality is an inherent feature of capitalism. Child-bearing roles and patriarchal roles in the family complement discrimination at the workplace. Women constitute an inherently flexible 'reserve army of labour'; their services can be called on when needed, and readily disposed of when not. A large floating male workforce would present the possibility of social unrest.

❓ CRITICAL DEBATE

Reasons for women's position in the workplace

As outlined above, the liberal argument is that any factor that impedes women's recruitment or promotion is a result of a market distortion, a dysfunctional product of past prejudices, meddling by governments, or vested interests. Greater equality can be promoted through legislation centring on individual rights and through raising awareness about the inefficiencies of discrimination. A more radical argument is that gender inequality is a result of capitalism. Women are essentially a 'reserve army of labour'; their services can be called on when needed, and readily disposed of when not.

Do you think that if employers were persuaded that promoting women to the highest levels would lead to greater efficiency, more women would hold a higher proportion of top positions?

If your answer is yes, then explain how employers might be persuaded that this is the case.

If your answer is no, outline why simply persuading employers of the economic benefits of promoting women would not lead to change.

We further explore debates on why organisations tend to systematically discriminate against women and other categories of labour in Chapter 10.

POSTMODERNISM

Postmodernism is a very broad concept, and encompasses disciplines ranging from management studies to literature studies, workplace practice to art. It is neither appropriate nor feasible to provide a full account of all the different variations of postmodernism here. However, there are three strands of postmodern thought that have been particularly influential in terms of industrial relations debates.

Firstly, there was the argument that most advanced societies had fundamentally changed in the 1980s away from manufacturing-based ones to service-based ones. Post-modernity was inherently post-industrial, the remaining industry being forced to adopt more participative and democratic principles in order to make the most effective use of new technologies (Hirst and Zeitlin 2001: 506). With these fundamental changes, employees became empowered, and old class divisions eroded. Similarly, social relations and ties became more fluid (*ibid*: 506). A limitation of this view is that the promised changes did not result in good, empowered jobs driving out 'bad' ones; rather, new technology allowed for the expansion of traditional Taylorist methods into large areas of service work (*ibid*). Within liberal market economies, industrial decline was not replaced by sustainable work in the service sector, while many of the old mistakes and problems – lack of commitment to employees, lack of emphasis in skills and technology, and ignorance of the genuine potential of technological advances – persisted (*ibid*). Meanwhile, a number of prominent advanced coordinated markets – for example, Japan and Germany – remain as highly successful export-oriented manufacturing-based economies. Nevertheless, assumptions of post-industrialism permeated a large body of postmodern writing in the 1970s and 1980s (see Poster 1984).

A second strand of postmodern thinking draws heavily on the tradition of Michel Foucault. Foucault argued that – contrary to traditional modernist assumptions – there was no inherent reason underlying social progression, or a single dominant set of tensions (eg between workers and employers). Rather, the story of history is one of power struggles. Nobody has a monopoly on power – for example, even the slave may resist in subtle ways (which explains why slave-based production was so inefficient). Although some may have more power than others, any exertion of power will encourage responses. Related to the uneven concentration of power is the question of knowledge: those with access to more information will invariably have more power, and knowledge is used as a mechanism of control (Foucault 1988). Foucault argued that, for example, the modern profession of psychology was more geared towards normalising and controlling the deviant (those who challenge existing ways of doing things) than genuinely helping those who are mentally 'unwell' (Foucault 1988). Foucault associated the rise of modern psychology with a long-term trend towards more subtle surveillance and control.

The emphasis on power and knowledge has some relevance to understanding employment and work relations. There has been a huge rise in the surveillance of people both within and beyond the workplace, with the explicit aim of identifying the deviant, the 'socially useless' and the shirker. The only limitation is that a sheer proliferation of information may, in fact, be precluding the authorities from using the information in such a manner that genuinely can be defined as knowledge or intelligence.

THE SURVEILLANCE OF WORKING PRACTICES

CASE STUDY

Margaret had woken up early that morning, and had left the house before 7am. She rushed to the bus stop and just managed to catch the 7.15am bus. While on the bus, she checked her emails using her iphone. Her manager, Cerise, had already emailed her. She must have started work early that morning! She was asking whether Margaret had written up the minutes for the previous day's meeting. 'No, not yet. I will work on them as soon as I get into the office,' Margaret replied. Margaret could have ignored the email, waited until she reached the office, written the minutes up quickly, and circulated them, but she knew that her manager wanted a response immediately.

An hour later, having stepped off the bus and rushed up the road to the office, Margaret was inserting her unique number into the keypad. As she did so, she wondered if this was just a security measure or whether the data would be sent to a central place where records could be kept of the times that people entered and left the building. She called, 'Hello' to the receptionist on her way in. The receptionist, Marcus, replied, 'Good morning, Margaret,' without looking up from his desk. He had already noted Margaret's arrival when he had glanced at the screen next to

the reception desk two minutes before, showing the doorstep outside the front of the building.

Margaret took the lift up to her office on the fourth floor. She wondered why it was necessary to have a camera in the lift. What did people do in lifts that required them to be watched? Arriving at the fourth floor, she walked briskly to her office, put her bag down on the floor, sat down on her chair, and turned on the computer. Eight-thirty already! She entered her username and password and found the file within which she had placed the draft minutes. Just a few changes to make, and then she could circulate the minutes before reviewing her list of 'things to do' for the day.

Questions

How many times was Margaret monitored between 7am and 9am?

Is this a 'normal' experience for workers? In answering this question, try to consider three different types of work and three different country contexts.

Is the surveillance of workers a necessary feature of modern life or an unnecessary invasion of privacy?

The postmodernist viewpoint outlined above may help to reveal the dynamics of working life. However, a problem with this viewpoint is that it dismisses worker organisation. Any collective involves power, inequality and subordination, and, by implication, trade unions will ultimately not improve the lot of their members (Sheridan 1990). In addition, even though employees are subordinate, they may still possess knowledge and understanding, and have real resources at their disposal to resist (Thompson and Smith 2010: 19). Indeed, even in highly

Taylorist settings, workers can and do find a vast range of ways of resisting. Postmodern accounts suggest that the identities workers may assume are multiple and fragile, incorporating work and non-work influences (Jaros 2010: 75).

A third influential strand of postmodernism centres on culture – it assumes that contemporary postmodern societies are 'hyperreal' (Baudrillard 1990). In other words, the boundaries of what is real and what is constructed become blurred. There seems to be some truth to this argument. At a time when personal ties of family and friendship are being eroded, individuals, aided by the popular media, construct delusions of intimate familiarity with 'celebrities', people who are famous simply through the virtue of being famous. In each case, the individual closely follows their progress, expressing genuine personal grief at their setbacks, triumph at their successes, or in some regrettable instances, the converse.

A criticism of postmodernism is that there is insufficient attention paid to the manner in which identities may be, and indeed often are, manipulated to suit the interests of the economically powerful. In Britain, some sections of the media are remarkably adept at rechannelling genuine anger at rising inequality and downward social mobility towards vulnerable people such as single mothers and foreigners, and in promoting the idea that anyone may become rich and famous, and if one does not, it is a personal failing rather than that of the system. Marx described the manipulation of identity and outlook over a century ago as the engendering of 'false consciousness'. It is thus hardly surprising that, within present scholarly debates, a concern with the multiple facets of identity and world-view is not the exclusive preserve of postmodernists (Jaros 2010: 75).

CRITICAL MANAGEMENT STUDIES

Critical management studies represent a heterogeneous camp. Indeed, so much is this so, that in a recent informal scholarly debate, one of the authors of this volume was confronted by the argument that since all industrial relations is in some manner critical, industrial relations as a field of enquiry forms part and parcel of critical management studies. In fact, critical management studies can be loosely defined as studying management and what occurs within the organisation from a starting point rooted in the Frankfurt tradition, its postmodern developments and extensions, and other strands of radical (eg deep green, anarchist, etc) thinking. This analysis places the individual and social action at the centre of the analysis (even if, as some postmodernists suggest, actions are increasingly devoid of the possibilities of meaning). More specifically, the classical Frankfurt tradition concerned itself with the relationship between the individual and the object of perception, and the extent to which the former has the capacity to draw a distinction between essence and appearance (Parekh 1982: 75). Domination occurs when some use others to suit their own needs. This occurs when society is structured in such a way as primarily to serve an elite, and when others lack the capacity for resistance (*ibid*: 82). Class-based societies (eg contemporary capitalism) are based on inequalities in material resources, which in turn necessitate ideological domination (*ibid*: 82). In other words, as workers are being exploited under capitalism, their allegiance has to be secured through ideological indoctrination and the engendering of false consciousness, as alluded to above (*ibid*: 82). Writers in the classic Frankfurt tradition, such as Marcuse, concerned themselves with the conditions and processes that would make resistance possible. The stability of Western capitalism – and genuine improvements in the conditions of the working class in the West – in the 1950s and 1960s led to something of a crisis within this tradition. Writers diverged around issues such as ways of promoting social change and desirable outcomes.

Critical management studies follows in this tradition through its focus on the position and choices open to the individual, and the manner in which identities are constructed. As can be seen, there is not necessarily a vast divide between the concept of hyperreality and false consciousness, a key difference being that the latter is seen as deliberately constructed and inherently functional for the capitalist system. A criticism that may be levied against critical management studies is that in focusing on the negative – oppression, power and domination – it is unclear what is actually desired (Jaros 2010). In addition, critical management studies is somewhat divided over the possibilities of resistance, which may be variously seen as hopeless, inevitable and potentially transformative, or somewhere in between.

INDETERMINACY OF THE LABOUR CONTRACT AND STRUCTURED ANTAGONISM

In this text we have attempted to move beyond the common practice in industrial relations textbooks of simply noting that both conflict and co-operation are important. The key point about the indeterminacy of the labour contract and strategies of labour control is that (Edwards 1995: 15):

> managers and workers are locked into a relationship that is contradictory and antagonistic ... There is thus a relation of 'structured antagonism' between employer and worker. This term is used to stress that the antagonism is built into the basis of the relationship, even though on a day-to-day level co-operation is also important.

A structured antagonism must be distinguished from a simple conflict of interests. The latter implies that the fundamental interests of capital and labour are opposed, and hence that any shift towards greater co-operation merely reinforces capital's interests in new ways. However, both employees and employers may have several different interests. The idea of structured antagonism also takes account of rules within the workplace as well as the sanctions that accompany their breach. These rules and sanctions are part of the wider relations of conflict and control within the workplace. The successful application of rules reflects organisational imperatives and the demands and interests of different groups within management, as well as the reactions of workers on the shopfloor (Hyman 1987).

APPLYING THEORY TO PRACTICE

Theoretical approaches and common assumptions

Theory seeks to help us understand and predict the social world around us. It goes beyond a specific set of descriptions. As a practitioner, one may use theory to help make sense of real-world situations, and make some projections about likely outcomes. Although the choice of theory is likely to reflect one's personal orientations and ideologies, it is important to keep an open mind, and be aware of the compatibility of what really goes on with what one expects to be the case. It can be argued that a great deal of the 2008 financial crisis was predicated on the wholehearted adoption of neo-liberal conceptualisations of economic man, and the broad economic benefits of a mass of individual profit-seeking. A general failure to spot the crisis reflected an inability to see beyond theoretical preconceptions, and a willingness to reinterpret facts according to what was supposed, rather than what was really happening. For the HR practitioner, curiosity, a willingness to be proved wrong and to move forward is likely to yield far better results than wishful thinking based on what should be the case.

SUMMARY

Although the study of employment relations has tended to be dominated by practical issues and concerns, there are indeed many different ways of describing and theoretically conceptualising the employment relationship. This chapter has covered three main theories of industrial relations – unitarism, pluralism and radical theories – in addition to more recent developments.

An interesting feature of the most recent debates has been the willingness among those adhering to different perspectives to engage in dialogue, and to search for new syntheses. It would not be correct to describe employment relations as a discipline devoid of theory – most accounts start with some or other theoretical or ideological preconceptions. At the same time, there is considerable room for more rigorous theory-building, taking fuller account of the foundations of different traditions rather than eclectic blends of ideas, whatever their origins.

EXPLORE FURTHER

Reading

- Ackers, P. and Wilkinson, A. (eds) (2003) *Understanding Work and Employment: Industrial relations in transition*. Oxford: Oxford University Press

- Bendix, S. (2004) *Industrial Relations in South Africa*, 4th edition. Cape Town: Juta

- Edwards, P. (ed) (2003) *Industrial Relations: Theory and practice*, 2nd edition. Oxford: Blackwell

- Kelly, J. (1998) *Rethinking Industrial Relations: Mobilization, collectivism and long waves*. London: Routledge

Websites

- Health and Safety Executive www.hse.gov.uk

- *The Guardian article* www.guardian.co.uk/world/2010/may/25/foxconn-ninth-worker-death-fall-china

CHAPTER 4

Employment Relations and Human Resource Management

CHAPTER OVERVIEW

In developing some of the themes that were raised in the introductory chapter and in Chapter 3, this chapter critically evaluates the concepts of employment relations and human resource management, seeking to identify the differences, similarities and complementarities between these two fields of study. In doing so, it highlights the contribution of employment relations to both theoretical development and practice, and explains how employment relations arguably has analytical dominance over HRM.

The chapter begins by exploring the origins of employment relations, which have been informed by a range of disciplines, each of which contributes to the ability of employment relations studies to evaluate and explain practice. It then traces the development of industrial relations to become employment relations, and outlines what is commonly understood by the two terms. The chapter moves on to compare and contrast employment relations and HRM. To what extent are these distinct subject areas? How does the study of employment relations contribute dimensions that are missing from HRM? Finally, it critically evaluates the development of HRM.

LEARNING OUTCOMES

After studying this chapter you should be able to:

- explain the origins of employment relations, and the usefulness of taking an interdisciplinary approach
- trace the development of industrial relations to employment relations
- compare and contrast employment relations and HRM
- critically evaluate the development of HRM

THE ORIGINS OF INDUSTRIAL RELATIONS

An understanding of work and the ways in which it is managed has long been a central concern of social scientists. As explained in Chapter 1, the study of industrial relations can be traced back to the nineteenth century and the work of Sidney and Beatrice Webb and John Commons, and a policy commitment to maintain a balance between the problems of social welfare and social control.

However, a survey of the literature reveals a surprising lack of consensus among scholars concerning the central object of study in industrial relations. Conceptions of the subject of industrial relations range from broad definitions that encompass all aspects of employment to narrow definitions that confine it to a study of collective bargaining. Indeed, Bain and Clegg (1974: 95) defined industrial relations as the study of all aspects of job regulation – the making and administering of the rules which regulate employment relationships – regardless of whether these are seen as being formal or informal, structured or unstructured.

With some notable exceptions, however, modern industrial relations research can be located within a much narrower definition of the field than the one identified by Bain and Clegg. The 'original' industrial relations paradigm centred on the employment relationship and included both union and non-union sectors as well as personnel management and labour–management relations. This paradigm went into decline from the 1930s and was largely replaced, in the period following World War II, by a narrowly constructed paradigm focusing on the unionised sector and related topics, such as collective bargaining and strikes. This overly restricted and union-centric perspective was a significant factor in the widely noted 'crisis' of industrial relations (Kaufman 2004). Having tied its fortunes so closely to that of trade unions, modern industrial relations was bound to face a crisis of relevance with the precipitous decline of trade unionism in most developed countries over the last two or three decades.

Narrow approaches to industrial relations tended to place almost exclusive emphasis on the collective regulation of employment conditions by management and trade unions. Common features of collective workplace relations include a history of mutual antagonism between union and management, strong shopfloor organisation that relies on traditional patterns of negotiation underwritten by a formal framework of procedural agreements, the existence of few or no consultative mechanisms, and constant disagreements about union rights and management style (Kelly 1998). Today, the processes of collective bargaining are outside the experiences of a growing proportion of workers. Moreover, collective bargaining is seldom capable of decisively influencing the production, investment and location decisions of capitalist enterprises. The day-to-day management of labour is conducted through different forms of regulation from those involved in wage determination. In particular, collective bargaining is not geared towards or designed for managing the organisation of work. The complexity of daily production issues are incapable of regulation by collective agreements given the contingencies, emergencies, and so on, that invariably arise. As Bélanger (1994: 62) puts it:

even in the context of a unionised workplace and once a collective agreement has been struck, shopfloor management and employees still have to make arrangements on the contours and the nature of the numerous tasks to be included in a given job, as well as the volume and quality of actual work to be performed on every shift.

In other words, union-centric approaches to industrial relations are not only increasingly out of touch with changes in the workplace but also fail to account for much of the day-to-day interaction between employers and employees.

◉ REFLECTION ON PRACTICE

Unions as a focal point of industrial relations

It was argued above that the study of industrial relations/employment relations has sometimes tended to focus almost entirely on the role of trade unions.

To what extent does your current module on Employment Relations focus on the role of trade unions?

FROM INDUSTRIAL RELATIONS TO EMPLOYMENT RELATIONS

The revitalisation of the industrial relations field demanded a fundamental reorientation of its analytical focus and conceptual framework. In particular, industrial relations scholars could no longer stake a claim to relevance by confining their research to a narrow and shrinking sector of the labour market. Nor could they continue emphasising the collective and formal dimensions of work to the exclusion of its individual and informal dimensions. Fortunately, since the mid-1990s, it has been possible to discern a growing tendency (Blyton and Turnbull 1998: 28):

> to focus on and define the distinctive characteristics of the employment relationship; to locate that relationship within the broader nature of economic activity; to analyse the structural bases of conflict and accommodation between employer and employee; to consider the influence of the wider society; and to develop an interdisciplinary approach using concepts and ideas derived from sociology, economics, psychology, history and political science.

The purpose of industrial relations, as Edwards (1995) points out, is the control, adaptation and adjustment or 'regulation' of the employment relationship. Likewise, Salamon (1998: 3) regards industrial relations as 'a set of phenomena, both within and outside the workplace, concerned with determining and regulating the employment relationship'. The fundamental object of enquiry that defines the field of industrial relations is therefore not the institutions of trade unions and employers' associations or the processes of collective bargaining, but rather the employment relationship. Given the centrality of the employment relationship to the study of industrial relations, 'the name of the field could thus be more accurately called *employment relations*' (Kaufman 2004: 45). The core of the subject is the buying, selling and deployment of labour power.

However, according to Poole (1986), employment relations should incorporate all aspects of the employment relationship. This might include the relationship with the employer (and colleagues) and also the context within which this takes place (including the economic, social, political, legal and technological environment). Because employment relations do not operate in a vacuum, it is vital to acknowledge the influence of the wider society on the employment relationship. The nature of work organisation, the character of product markets, the composition of the workforce, government policies, and many other contextual aspects influence employment relations policies and practices. These aspects are covered in more detail in Chapter 5.

The industrial relations tradition of focusing almost exclusively on trade union–management relations in the workplace led to a neglect of competition between organisations and labour supply (Rubery and Grimshaw 2003: 48–9). In their attempts to locate the employment relationship within the context of economic activity, employment relations scholars are increasingly drawing on economics to develop their analysis. As Hyman (1994: 177) notes, it is impossible to understand employment relations in the last three decades without 'giving central attention to the impact of intensified global competition, the restructuring of capital and employment, the eclipse of Keynesianism in one country and the consequent pressures on governments to curb public expenditure'. However, if focusing only on the union–management relationship, employment relations scholars are unlikely to contribute to our understanding of changes in production and paths of economic development and their implications for employees (Rubery and Grimshaw 2003). Conversely, a wholesale adoption of economic theories and assumptions is likely to undermine many of the key insights of employment relations. The integration of economic perspectives into employment relations is therefore both necessary and fraught with risks.

More generally, employment relations scholars now tend to recognise the advantages of an interdisciplinary approach. By drawing on several disciplines, according to Strauss and Whitfield (2008: 176), employment relations may be enriched in the sense that 'each discipline can provide its own insights and so reduce the likelihood of narrow, single-dimensional perspectives on complex, multidimensional problems'. In reality, however, employment relations scholars have rarely managed to reap the benefits of interdisciplinary research. Although employment relations research has largely remained discipline-bound, there is increasing evidence of cross-fertilisation between disciplines. Kelly's (1998) analysis of trade union behaviour, which draws on sociological theories of collective action, is a good example of the benefits that may be derived from crossing entrenched disciplinary divides. Obstacles to interdisciplinary research are significant and include the fact that scholars from different disciplines draw on different conceptual and methodological frameworks. Even when they are investigating similar phenomena, employment relations researchers from different disciplines may fail to communicate with each other because they use different concepts, draw on different assumptions and utilise different criteria to evaluate research findings. Moreover, insofar as employment relations constitutes an area of study with a range of disciplinary inputs, theoretical shifts that occur in these disciplines can have profound implications for the conduct of research into employment relations matters.

APPLYING THEORY TO PRACTICE

The interdisciplinary foundations of employment relations

Employment relations draws on a range of fields of study, including economics, sociology, psychology and social policy.

Try to think of particular topics that each of these disciplines inform. In other words, think of the type of research that could be conducted in employment relations from each perspective.

For example, if considering sociology, one of the areas of study could be the nature of interactions between miners on a picket line and those employees who wish to work and break the picket line.

Many of the articles found in the leading industrial and employment relations journals are highly quantitative and engage with large datasets either through firm-level surveys or through national-level statistics. On the one hand, such articles allow a general understanding of what is likely to take place where and when, enabling national variations to be systematically explored and long-term trends evaluated. On the other hand, the advanced statistical tools employed may be not readily comprehensible to the uninitiated. It could be argued that scholars and students of industrial relations need to do more to make such important work more accessible to a wider audience, especially given the default policy position of many governments to greater deregulation, and the determination of some to avoid contrary factual evidence.

CHALLENGES TO THE STUDY OF EMPLOYMENT RELATIONS: CHANGES IN THE EMPLOYMENT CONTEXT AND EMPLOYMENT RELATIONSHIP

A central feature of the standard employment relationship is the growing collectivisation and institutionalisation of employment relations. Employees were originally bound to the enterprise through the development of internal labour markets that led to greater job security, favourable career prospects, regular working hours, comprehensive protections against dismissal, rights to collective representation, and increasing rewards for seniority. However, with the growth in neo-liberalism, the utility, efficiency and adaptability of this employment pattern have been increasingly questioned. It was argued that what was required is a shift from a dominant pattern in which internal labour markets shielded workers from market forces, to a 'new' employment relationship where pressures from product and labour markets are internalised within the enterprise. This is evident in the mass redundancies associated with industrial restructuring; a generalised decline in job security, stable jobs and career prospects; the polarisation of the workforce into 'insiders' and 'outsiders' associated with the outsourcing of 'non-core' activities; increasing pressure on core employees to intensify effort levels; attacks on traditional job demarcations and skill boundaries; the growing variability of earnings as wages are linked more closely to individual performance; and the consolidation of 'flexible' wage systems tied to the decentralisation of collective bargaining and the dilution of basic employment conditions (Barker and Christensen 1998; Crompton *et al* 1996; Felstead and Jewson 1999; Gallie *et al* 1998; Heery and Salmon 2000).

From the 1980s on, the standard employment relationship came under increasing pressure as institutionalised employment relations faced unparallelled challenges and drastic changes unfolded in the regulatory framework of the labour market. As Hakim (1990: 167) states in her review of workforce restructuring, strategies varied from one country to the next and followed different paths, 'but all pointed in the same general direction of increasing ... segmentation of the labour market and exploring new forms of differentiating wage/labour relations'. The rise of non-standard employment relationships (with subcontracting and a growth in temporary work) is therefore part of a wider process of fragmentation in employment relations. Far from simply being a rational response to changing economic imperatives, the decisions concerning the restructuring of the employment relationship are political in origin and outcome. The redistributive effects of these decisions involve a diversion of the costs of restructuring on to the least politically and economically entrenched groups in society.

By the 1990s, the employment relationship increasingly manifested the signs of the growing internationalisation and volatility of economic activity. Changes in the way that production is organised altered the types of skills and aptitudes required, changing the bargaining power of the parties. It also led to (Streeck 1992: 66–7):

> a polarization in two opposite directions ... within national societies between industries, within industries between enterprises, and within enterprises between groups of employees, with the emergence of 'good' – that is, status-secured – jobs coinciding with growing disparities with a secondary labour market for 'poor', marginal and uncertain employment relationships.

APPLYING THEORY TO PRACTICE

Core and periphery workers and employment relations

It was argued above that the workforce now tends to be divided into those in core jobs with good benefits and high job security and others on the periphery that have poor job security.

To what extent is this division common in the following industries?

- retail
- manufacturing

- construction

- public transport provision

In answering this question, draw on your knowledge of (or consider empirical research on) both an advanced economy (such as Britain, France or Germany) and a transitional or emerging economy (such as a country within Eastern Europe or Africa).

The standard employment relationship was not only rooted in the employment relations regimes of post-war Europe and North America but was also closely linked to the Taylorist–Fordist organisation of production that prevailed during this period, with standardised products and close supervision of workers. However, the shift from economies of scale (mass production) to economies of scope (flexible production) necessitated a greater emphasis on employee co-operation, multi-skilling and a de-layering of the managerial hierarchy. The concerted efforts by employers to circumvent shop stewards as a channel of representation and deal directly with the workforce through individualised forms of 'direct' participation generated informal assumptions and modes of behaviour. The establishment of quality circles, just-in-time inventories, semi-autonomous work groups, and so on, are presented as a move away from the alienating and deskilled employment associated with Fordism towards new forms of employee involvement and high-trust relations in the workplace.

In summary, recent managerial approaches (Salamon 1998: 220–2) increasingly

> emphasise individualism (rather than collectivism), unitarism (rather than pluralism), consultation (rather than negotiation and agreement), flexibility (rather than uniformity), employee commitment (rather than simple compliance) and empowerment and 'responsible' autonomy (rather than direct control). This can be seen as a reassertion of managerial prerogative … particularly in so far as employees are expected to be committed to management's organisational objectives … and the process of regulation emphasises consultation which provides greater management freedom to 'set the agenda' and make decisions.

DEFINING HUMAN RESOURCE MANAGEMENT

The term 'human resource management' (HRM) became increasingly popular from the 1980s onwards although its roots can be found in the human relations approach of the 1950s and 1960s. HRM shares with the human relations approach a concern for the internal dynamics of the workgroup, a desire to create social cohesion and value consensus through an emphasis on the 'corporate culture', an attempt to integrate personnel issues within the overall business strategy, and an effort to generate higher levels of employee commitment and involvement.

The importance of HRM to employment relations, according to Salamon (1998: 19), lies in its association with 'a strategic, integrated and highly distinctive managerial approach to the management of people'. It is closely tied to managerial interests, has strong unitarist overtones in its approach to employees as a collective, and rejects a pluralist understanding of the employment relationship (see Chapter 3 for an explanation of these two perspectives).

Insofar as HRM represents a distinctive approach to labour management, it relies primarily on direct communication with employees rather than indirect communication through collective bargaining with trade unions. In terms of their conceptions of employees employment relations is associated with a sociological and collective approach, whereas HRM relies on a psychological and individualistic orientation (Bacon 2003: 74). In fact, Storey (1989: 9) suggests that HRM

> eschews the joint regulative approach, … places emphasis on utilising labour to its full capacity or potential … [and] is therefore about … exploiting the labour resource more fully.

Fowler (cited in Salamon 1998: 19) goes even further and questions whether supporters of HRM are

> genuinely concerned with creating a new, equal partnership between employer and employed, or are they really offering a covert form of employee manipulation dressed up as mutuality?

A significant obstacle in the way of providing a coherent assessment of HRM is the sheer number of alternative and conflicting definitions of the subject (Kaufman 2004: 322–6). HRM, as Storey (1992: 24–5) points out, has a variety of different meanings along a continuum:

- it is used merely as a synonym for personnel management (emphasising employee welfare)

- it conveys the idea that the various techniques of personnel management are or ought to be used in a more integrated manner (implying that HRM is strategic)

- it represents a more business-oriented approach to the management of labour that places employees alongside the other factors of production such technology and materials (seeing workers as resources)

- it signals not only a greater integration and business orientation but a qualitatively different intervention that seeks more than mere compliance by actively pursuing qualities as such employee 'commitment'.

◖◑ REFLECTION ON PRACTICE

Employee involvement and employee commitment

If you are currently working in an organisation, or have previously worked in an organisation, to what extent did HR managers or line managers seem to encourage the above practices?

To what extent did managers seem to encourage employee involvement, using mechanisms such as employee suggestion schemes?

To what extent did managers seem to be aiming for employee commitment to the organisation? And how would employees demonstrate their commitment?

According to Sisson (1990), HRM is associated with four main characteristics. In common with Storey, Sisson refers to integrating human resource policies with each other and the organisation's business strategy and a focus on high commitment and employee involvement. However, he also points to a greater role for line managers in labour management and a non-union approach. Yet in practice it is rare to find an integrated approach to HRM which incorporates all these aspects.

In addition to the characteristics identified above, a common way of conceptualising HRM is by using two broad perspectives (Storey 1992: 26). A *hard* version stresses the idea of 'resource' and suggests that the services of employees should be used dispassionately and in a formally rational manner, whereas a *soft* version emphasises the term 'human' and suggests that the potential of employees should be released through communication, motivation and leadership.

However, this distinction has been criticised. In the face of the growing levels of competition associated with globalisation, it has been argued that firms that are unable to achieve continuous improvement in product and service quality as dictated by the 'soft' version tend to resort to the 'hard' version of HRM (Newell 2000). In fact, the 'hard' version shares many of the key elements of the 'soft' version, including using workers as a resource, seeing the management of HR as a strategic issue and central to the core performance of the business, clear communication, the evaluation of performance, and a carefully thought-out reward system (Storey 1992: 26–8).

In common with the study of employment relations, conceptions of HRM range from those with a broad scope (all forms of labour management are included within the broader study of HRM) to a narrow one (HRM is contrasted to other forms of labour management) (Storey 2001: 5). Whereas the former accepts the continued relevance of employment relations as a study of the collective aspects of employee relations, the latter points to the eclipse of employment relations (Guest 1987: 503):

> HRM comprises a set of policies designed to maximise organizational integration, employee commitment, flexibility and quality of work. Within this model, collective industrial relations have, at best, only a minor role.

Exclusive definitions clearly constitute a greater challenge to the continued relevance of employment relations.

In addition, in considering concepts such as 'hard' or 'soft' HRM, one should bear in mind that these represent archetypes. Although many organisations are more readily associated with one than the other, no organisation practises either pure 'hard' or 'soft' HRM – many mix and match practices, some of which are hard and others soft.

EMPLOYMENT RELATIONS, HRM AND PERSONNEL MANAGEMENT

Several attempts have been made to distinguish HRM from personnel management and employment relations (Bacon 2003; Legge 1995; Storey 1992). Edwards (2003: 341) suggests that several possible connections between HRM and employment relations can be identified:

- HRM and employment relations can be regarded as co-equal, employment relations handling collective bargaining and HRM dealing with personnel administration.

- HRM can be regarded as the generic term, employment relations being a subordinate and possibly waning sub-set.

- HRM can challenge employment relations by claiming to be more proactive and even strategic.

- Employment relations can retain analytical dominance, HRM then being regarded as one particular technique to manage the inherent contradictions of the employment relationship.

There are also two contrasting sets of perspectives on the relationship between HRM and personnel management. Taking the first perspective, there are no meaningful differences between personnel management and HRM. The second regards personnel management and HRM as largely distinctive approaches to labour management. Whereas the former view amounts to all continuity and no change, the latter amounts to all change and no continuity.

Further distinctions have been drawn by Storey (1992). Whereas 'personnel management' implies a pluralist approach, a focus on procedures and piecemeal initiatives, HRM is underpinned by a unitarist approach, with a focus on business needs and integrated and strategic initiatives. Meanwhile, personnel managers tend to see their role as monitoring and dealing with collective agreements, whereas HR managers see it as nurturing and determining individual contracts.

In the following *Critical debate*, some of these features are investigated in more detail.

CRITICAL DEBATE

HRM and personnel management

Some people would argue that there has not been a movement towards HRM in practice, and that those in 'HR' positions are confined to a traditional 'personnel' role. In other words, they do not engage with business strategy, and tend to spend their time merely checking employment contracts and helping line managers out in providing welfare advice or information on legislation.

Think about your workplace, somewhere you have worked, or an organisation where a member of your family or one of your friends has worked. If you are unable to do this, review articles within CIPD publications such as *People Management*.

What do HR staff tend to do in practice? Would you characterise their role in terms of 'personnel management' or 'business strategy'?

The examination of the use of 'personnel' or 'HR' practices is interesting in its own right. However, it is also important to consider these developments in their broader context.

HRM AND PERSONNEL MANAGEMENT IN CONTEXT

As with employment relations, the development and diffusion of HRM practices must be situated within the context of social, economic and political conditions. Unprecedented competitive challenges have made the survival of most enterprises dependent on drastic cost-cutting rationalisation. Consequently, there is less room in which to accommodate a militant, defensive trade unionism. This explains, in part, the concerted efforts by employers to circumvent collective channels of representation and deal with employees through individualised forms of direct participation. The growing preference of employers for one-way communications between junior managers and their subordinates is more consistent with attempts by employers to reassert their authority than it is with genuine attempts at involving and empowering employees. A vital part of HRM is a concerted attempt to avoid, remove or minimise employment relations practices, such as negotiations with trade unions, in an effort to shift the balance between individualism and collectivism (Storey and Sisson 1993). Many, if not all, of the personnel practices associated with HRM (eg psychological testing, appraisal, performance-related pay, quality circles and teamwork) are designed to shape employees' beliefs and attitudes, and to emphasise individualism. These strategies have struck a sympathetic chord with employers given the context of rising economic instability and uncertainty. When cost-cutting is prioritised, the scope for compromise is reduced, and the unions are generally on the defensive.

THE DEVELOPMENT OF HRM AND HRM PRACTICES

The subsections below examine whether HR has really developed over time, and also question the impact of any changes.

HRM AND THE 'NEW' HIGH-COMMITMENT MANAGEMENT PRACTICES

A range of new concepts and practices has emerged, reflecting views about what employers are doing or should be doing to improve their performance in the management of human resources. A common theme in the literature is the idea that an increasingly competitive economic climate necessitates a greater emphasis on employee co-operation, multi-skilling, quality control, teamwork and a de-layering of the managerial hierarchy. The establishment of quality circles, just-in-time inventories, semi-autonomous work groups, and so on are presented as a decisive move away from the alienating and deskilled employment associated with Fordism towards new forms of employee participation and high-trust relations in the workplace. HRM acquired much-needed empirical validation as research findings emerged that seemed to link 'high-commitment management' practices to superior levels of organisational performance (see Frost 2008; Procter 2008). These findings provided some theoretical coherence for the HRM agenda and identified a set of practices that define the HRM approach. Although there is still no consensus on the precise nature of these high-commitment management practices, the list popularised by Pfeffer is typical and contains the following: employment security, selective hiring of new personnel, self-managed teams, comparatively high compensation linked to organisational performance, extensive training, reduced status distinctions, and extensive sharing of information (cited in Bacon 2003: 78). Conspicuous in their absence from this list are traditional employment relations issues such as collective bargaining and dispute resolution. In fact, the high-commitment management debate downplays the role of employment relations issues (as compared to HRM policies) in the attainment of increased organisational performance.

HAS HRM REALLY CHANGED?

Although recent developments in the theory and practice of HRM have led to a more sophisticated and coherent agenda, many of the core assumptions of the original model remain largely unchallenged. It is to these that our attention now turns. First, the assumption that we are witnessing some kind of qualitative shift in the organisation of work has been the subject of considerable debate. HRM is closely associated with the transition towards a distinct phase of development based on different economic, social and political institutions and values. The decline of industrial labour, the rise of the 'service economy', the central importance of knowledge and information, the 'hollowing out' of the national state (transferring public sector jobs to the private sector), the increasing prominence attached to individualism, and the waning of collective identities are all presented as decisive proof of the demise of the post-war model of Fordist production. On this view, the traditional methods for managing employees were undermined in the 1980s, and HRM constituted (Storey 2001: 6)

> an attempted articulation of an alternative to the Fordist-IR model of labour management which aimed to secure compliance through temporary truces based on negotiated settlements.

Many of these arguments tend, however, to underestimate the multiple ways in which organisations have not changed. The efficacy of organisations lies entirely in the stability of their internal rules, but these allow them limited scope to respond to changes in their environment. Likewise, the compromises between interest groups within the organisation need stability in order to endure. There is also a tendency to exaggerate the coherence of the changes that are unfolding. Evidence to support the notion of a single successor to Fordism is far from convincing.

If we wish to make sense of emergent trends, we need to identity the directions of change. The constant change in the economy and in workplaces, however, implies the incomplete and uneven nature of changes. At best, therefore, we can only specify the broad directions or lines of change, or alternatively seek to analyse the diversity in contemporary workplace restructuring and not take to grand theorising.

IS HRM REALLY STRATEGIC?

The proponents of HRM tend to view management as the most important strategic actor in employment relations (Bacon 2003: 76–7). Managers are regarded not as members of an interlocking system functioning in accordance with its own internal logic, but rather as 'agents' who shape the environment in which they operate. Management is seen as a strategic actor in two senses: its actions are regarded as critical not only in determining the main changes taking place in employment relations, but also in the choice of business strategy that is pursued. This model has been criticised for assuming that strategy formulation is a straightforward process and that managers in fact have the degree of choice with which they are credited. Even firms with sophisticated HRM policies rely on negotiation to establish what workplace rules actually mean, and managers depend on workers to interpret their instructions intelligently (Marsden 1999).

To warrant the label 'strategic', managerial actions must be deliberate, coherent, ubiquitous, integrative, proactive, consistent and long-term. There is strong evidence for the absence of any coherent, let alone strategic, approach towards the management of labour. Instead, research shows that management practices are generally 'opportunistic, habitual, tactical, reactive, frenetic, *ad hoc*, brief, fragmented and concerned with fixing' (Thompson and McHugh, 1990: 137). Workplace restructuring is usually characterised by slow and cautious changes on a trial-and-error basis, a limited and discontinuous search for new employment strategies, a *status quo* bias in the need to maintain worker commitment and legitimate managerial authority, and an *ad hoc* and piecemeal renewal of policies in response to specific pressures (Gallie and White 1994: 107). Moreover, management's labour strategies 'are not calculated; they are struggled over', and these struggles mobilise particular political resources and capacities, are constrained by different sets of political and economic forces, and are regulated in contrasting ways (Peck 1996: 138).

In short, strategy is a problematic concept and choices are not made in a vacuum. Even practices that are said to be at the centre of an HR strategy, such as new staffing policies, are seldom part of a long-term, coherent and strategic plan on the part of employers. For instance, Hunter *et al* (1993: 401) found 'an absence of strategy for labour use, and much more concern about survival and opportunistic cost-saving'. Their research suggests that managerial decisions about employment contracts, staffing levels and recruitment are largely *ad hoc*, tentative and based on the perceived benefits and drawbacks of each type of employment. No matter what strategy it pursues, management's basic objective remains a stable, predictable and cost-effective workforce.

Moreover, environmental constraints place limits on the strategic choices available to management. In the workplace, managerial practices find a number of distinct compromises depending on the differences between and within established national work systems and their associated regulatory institutions (Whitley and Kristensen 1997). The wider societal and cultural milieu in which employment relations systems are embedded is so varied that a search for universal models of management is destined to end in disappointment.

Implicit in much of the thinking underlying HRM is the fallacy that there exists 'one best way' in which to manage human resources. This conception of managerial strategy tends to neglect the complex and contingent ways in which order is actually negotiated under specific conditions. That is (Spencer 2000: 555):

> labour management issues are dealt with under conditions of deep uncertainty, creating an important gap between intent and outcome in actual managerial practice. In this sense, labour management is an on-going process, involving frequent surprise and disappointment. Thus, it cannot always be assumed that the actions taken by capitalist employers are in any meaningful sense the 'best' ones, or more importantly, will yield the same results, regardless of when and where they are taken.

A further problem with the idea of HR's being strategic is that in order to pursue policies it is necessary to elicit active co-operation from employees. However, employee collaboration is never guaranteed or unconditional. This underlying contradiction inherent in management's control over labour decisively qualifies management's capacity for strategic action. In other words, managerial strategies are often compromise solutions reached between groups with competing values, policies and interests.

CASE STUDY

HR STRATEGY IN MAINLAND CHINA, HONG KONG, KOREA AND JAPAN

A study by Morris et al (2009: 368) revealed that HR strategy in manufacturing organisations in China and the practices undertaken in commodity chains in Chinese, Japanese and Korean plants varied: 'In a number of cases in our study, therefore, the same organisation was pursuing different HRM strategies at different points in the commodity chain and at different locations.'

Plants in Chinese firms tended to follow a cost-reduction strategy. They were staffed by expatriates, and the parent company supplied materials and production equipment. Moreover, output and quality were closely monitored. Employees were made to undertake simple tasks, and limited resources were provided for recruitment and training, while wage levels were low compared to parent company plants. In terms of voice mechanisms used, these tended to be dominated by top-down information provision. In contrast, in Japanese, Korean and Hong Kong-based plants the HRM strategies sought to achieve quality and innovation, and the practices used included high levels of participation and extensive training and development, while workers benefited from high job security.

Questions

How can you explain the difference in practices between mainland Chinese, Hong Kong, Japanese and Korean-based plants?

Referring back to Chapter 1, consider the nature of the psychological contract for workers in each plant.

What would you anticipate to be the long-term implications of this HR strategy?

There are many other examples where employment relations practices differ significantly between neighbouring countries. For example, unions remain somewhat stronger, with employees enjoying greater legal rights and social protection, in Canada than in the United States. Again, in Ireland, employers, the union and the state negotiate national-level agreements on a broad range of issues, a practice not encountered in the contemporary United Kingdom. In both cases, this will make for differences in employment relations practices at firm level.

TO WHAT EXTENT DO HR PRACTICES RESULT IN POSITIVE OUTCOMES?

A significant shortcoming in much of the literature on HRM has been a failure to canvas the views of employees. As Bacon (2003: 81) points out, the attention paid to the impact of HRM on organisational performance overshadowed the attention paid to its effects on employees. Consequently, the bulk of the research on the impact of new working practices on employees has been carried out by (more critical) employment relations scholars. For instance, a study of the British automobile sector found that most workers perceived the changes associated with new managerial practices as 'concrete mechanisms of labour subordination' (Danford 1997: 19). Case studies of 'transformed' workplaces have also revealed that workers are subjected to intense managerial scrutiny, a vigorous pace of work, and strong pressures to conform to the corporate culture (see, for example, Fucini and Fucini 1990). Similarly, Elger (1990: 90) argues that the dominant feature of work reorganisation is 'the mobilization of productivity through stress, for the moment underpinned by a compelling ethos of competitive teamworking'. Quality circles and teamworking contain a strong control function aimed at disciplining employees – namely, 'management through blame' (Delbridge and Turnbull 1992). For workers, teamworking often amounted to little more than the redistribution of extra tasks among fewer workers. Teamworking, as Garrahan and Stewart (1992: 106) point out,

> is a process in which workers control one another's actions. It is this which gives to the autocratic internal regime a spurious air of employee participation and control in work.

In many cases, new work arrangements could only be established through a more aggressive and hostile managerial style (Stewart 1997). The superficial nature of co-operation and empowerment underlying HRM means that the actual experiences of workers will reinforce existing low trust and adversarial employment relations. Kelly and Kelly (1991) noted that the methodologically strongest studies of employee perceptions of new management strategies all revealed that there has been no change in the underlying 'them–us' attitudes of employees. They conclude (1991: 43–4) that

> there is little or no evidence to suggest that a variety of new industrial relations practices has altered workers' largely negative views of management in general ... In reality, managements on both sides of the Atlantic have sought to guard their own authority, prerogatives and

privileges against encroachment from below; they have claimed the lion's share of the gains; and they have been prepared to ditch schemes that no longer suited their purpose or were failing to deliver the goods.

Furthermore, the ideology of 'employee involvement' is circumscribed by the real imperative of HRM – namely, getting employees to work harder. Human resource managers would do well to heed the following warning: many of the changes introduced into the workplace are 'like the seeds on stony ground', having only 'a short life because there is no underlying accepted standard of treatment for employees beyond pure short-run commercial logic' (Purcell, 1987: 546). Achieving a sustainable trade-off between employers' needs for efficiency and employees' needs for security involves a complex process of social and political mediation. However, a proliferation of quality circles and other direct forms of representation means that company-specific employment relations systems have attained greater prominence than union representation. This can have the effect of diluting the power of the trade unions and hampering the development and implementation of coordinated human resource strategies.

HRM IS SILENT ON POWER

HRM also tends to lack 'not only a theory of bargaining power but a theory of power and as such it cannot address the question of who gets what' (Bacon 2003: 80). In this regard, employment relations has much to offer as a field of study. We should acknowledge the limitations of both worker autonomy and managerial control within the employment relationship. Even employee involvement schemes, which seek to encourage employee voice, may not challenge power relations. Managers are often more interested in consultative participation to tap the knowledge of employees and increase their motivation to work than to extend their decision-making powers (Cressey *et al* 1985: 81; Milkman 1997: 140). Consequently, employee involvement may increase the scope of employee input into some managerial decisions without altering the underlying structures of power in the workplace. Accordingly, the various forms of task participation associated with HRM do not spell a contraction in managerial authority but rather signal its reconstitution. Hence the paradox: 'as workers were given more autonomy, they were increasingly coming under tighter managerial control' (Geary 1994: 648).

LIMITATIONS TO THE ADOPTION OF THE HRM MODEL

Empirical evidence suggests that despite considerable employer innovation, the HRM model has diffused relatively slowly in developed countries (Bacon 2003). In practice, workplace changes linked to the implementation of HRM practices are often limited in scope and only partly realised. The emphasis on 'strategic choice' within HRM perspectives has encouraged a disregard for the wider context in which particular managerial strategies are most likely to succeed. The proponents of HRM have been quick to generalise their findings across occupations, industries and regions, thereby ignoring the constraints and opportunities created by specific forms of mechanisation and labour market structures. By contrast, employment relations scholars have always insisted that it is essential to investigate the constraints on new managerial strategies imposed by existing institutional arrangements as well as sectoral and occupational dynamics. For example, case studies reveal that employee involvement schemes are as much affected by the prevailing organisational culture and environment as they are a source of change (Marchington *et al* 1994). Research by Geary (1994) shows that new employment practices are most likely to succeed under specific conditions – namely, in companies that have been successful in retaining a significant market share and are highly profitable, and where management is committed to the implementation of the practices and workforce opposition to them is low or non-existent. Establishing a co-operative and integrative form of labour management is a contingent process dependent on experimentation and chance discoveries.

LINKS BETWEEN HRM PRACTICES AND PERFORMANCE

Finally, it has been widely noted that studies linking new managerial strategies to enhanced organisational performance are plagued by methodological difficulties. For example, since workplaces with a majority of high-commitment human resource practices in England also recognise trade unions, it is not possible to attribute a performance effect to either HRM practices or union presence (Bacon 2003: 79). In an extensive overview of the impact of new managerial practices, Kelley and Harrison (1992: 248–9) suggest that there is no statistically significant evidence that employee involvement *per se* has any effect on levels of productivity. Aggregating the sheer variety of inputs into the production of goods or delivery of services has proved to be an intractable obstacle to an adequate conceptualisation of comparative productivity measures over time and space (Nolan and Marginson 1990: 235). The claim that there is an unequivocal link between HRM practices and superior organisational performance is simplistic to the extent of being misleading. That is (Brown and Nolan 1988: 353),

> there is no simple relationship between the extent to which a change improves productivity, the extent to which it impinges upon an employee's work experience, and the extent to which the employee will require compensation for its acceptance ... [The] success with which labour is managed depends less upon the relatively simple task of meeting employees' comparative wage aspirations than on the endlessly demanding one of creating and maintaining the institutional forms that will maximise their willingness to work efficiently.

The introduction of HRM practices may be more significant in removing obstacles to further productivity growth and enabling more efficient working practices than in providing a direct and unmediated contribution to the levels of output.

Through employee involvement in managerial decision-making – according to the proponents of HRM – the efficiency of the firm is enhanced by an increase in the flow of information. Management, in turn, will encourage informed decisions and tap the skills and insights of workers. Hence it is not participation *per se* that translates into enhanced economic performance but rather the ability of management to obtain better knowledge of the production process and thereby avoid mistakes. Several of the managerial practices associated with HRM are designed to obtain systematic access to the knowledge accumulated on the shopfloor. Clearly, the success of such endeavours depends on a whole range of factors such as the time and resources management is prepared to commit to consultation procedures, the willingness and ability of employee representatives to volunteer information, the impact of product market conditions, and levels of conflict and co-operation in the workplace. Moreover, the introduction of participatory structures such as teamwork contains not only opportunities for management but also significant threats. For instance, the productive capacity of work performed collectively by skilled teams cannot be measured by a common yardstick that specifies the contribution of each individual separately. However, a single lapse by a team member can have severely disruptive consequences for production processes that are highly vulnerable to breakdowns or accidents.

EMPLOYMENT RELATIONS, HRM AND NON-UNION FIRMS

The main reason why employers initially engaged with unions through collective bargaining was to reach deals on the terms and conditions of the employment contract and how it is regulated. In contrast, whether unionised or not, employers may engage directly or indirectly with workers on a range of other issues encompassing work organisation, skills and quality (Bryson *et al* 2006). What sets non-union firms apart is that employment relations are less likely to be a subject of renegotiation on a regular basis – the main site of negotiation between employer and employee in this area is likely to be at the point of recruitment (see Budd *et al* 2009). In other words, although employers and employees may engage with each other in a wide range of different ways, in non-union firms such engagement is likely to be more circumscribed, in that the employment contract and the rules governing it are much less likely to be regularly reviewed and renegotiated by employers and employees.

SUMMARY

There seems to be a growing consensus that rather than being opposed, HRM and employment relations have much to learn from each other. Employment relations scholars need to acknowledge that the break-up of wage scales and the individualisation of career paths have encouraged greater variation in employment standards. A problem that HRM fails to address relates to the emphasis by employment relations researchers on the fact that management's capacity for strategic action is constrained by the fact there are definite limits and risks involved in the extent of autonomy that management can concede to any sector of the workforce. Employment relations research has consistently emphasised the conflict, uncertainty and opposition associated with the managerial function. As Edwards (2003: 339) points out:

the management of labour entails the two principles of control and consent. In particular, any concrete 'industrial relation' will have elements of both, and these elements are necessarily in contradiction.

The so-called 'crisis' of industrial relations is merely a crisis of a particular conception of the employment relationship – one that is narrowly focused on mass production and revolves largely around the experiences of organised, permanent (typically male) workers. In contrast to such a restricted view, an employment relations approach has been applied effectively to account for non-traditional industrial relations issues such as non-union firms, non-standard employment, quality circles and networked organisations (Davies and Ryner 2006; Peck 1996).

The idea that employment relations is a study of the ways in which the employment relationship is regulated is a welcome departure from the voluntaristic overtones of HRM approaches, which tend to treat structures in the workplace as the product of conscious human activities. In practice, employment relations is a dialectical and continuous process of challenge and response, co-operation and conflict, control and autonomy. HRM is simply one way of managing these contradictions – not a means to evade or eliminate them.

EXPLORE FURTHER

Reading

- Gallie, D., White, M., Cheng, Y. and Tomlinson, M. (1998) *Restructuring the Employment Relationship*. Oxford: Clarendon Press

- Legge, K. (1995) *Human Resource Management: Rhetoric and realities*. London: Macmillan

- Rubery, J. and Grimshaw, D. (2003) *The Organization of Employment: An international perspective*. Basingstoke: Palgrave Macmillan

Website

- Chartered Institute of Personnel and Development www.cipd.co.uk

CHAPTER 5

Local, National and Global Effects on the Practice of Employment Relations

CHAPTER OVERVIEW

This chapter examines the context for the practice of employment relations, covering local, national and global effects. Whereas some texts focus on the national-level features of a particular country, due to the international approach taken in this text, this chapter concentrates on international influences. Within the literature on employment relations there has been growing awareness of the effects of context on practice, in terms of firm diversity versus the tendency of firms and employees within particular industries and regions to do similar things (Marsden 1999). In addition to addressing the practical influence of factors on employment relations, the chapter also includes a critical evaluation of more recent developments.

The chapter begins with a case study which highlights some of the key factors covered in this chapter. It then moves on to examine what is meant by the term 'globalisation', a term that has commonly been used to imply a wide range of trends and processes. The second section covers 'PESTLE' – factors associated with politics, economics, social trends, technology, legislation and the environment. Attention then turns to the varieties of capitalism literature used to analyse firm behaviours and institutions within different country contexts. The next sections cover broader issues of labour markets and migration, and subsequent sections engage with a range of international issues – the role of the EU and EU legislation, the role of international institutions, and international employment relations. This chapter therefore sets the context for a further exploration of international dimensions and empirical evidence within later chapters.

LEARNING OUTCOMES

After studying this chapter you should be able to:

- define 'globalisation' and assess its impact on employment

- outline the potential effects of politics, economics, society, technology, legislation, and the environment on employment relations, and the important influence of changing demographics

- describe, giving examples, what is meant by varieties of capitalism

- assess the role of the European Union and EU legislation

- explain the role of the international institutions the World Bank, the International Monetary Fund, the World Trade Organisation and the International Labour Organisation

- evaluate the role of international trade union bodies

The case study below highlights some of the key issues covered in this chapter – the power of multinationals, the relationship between a range of factors (politics, economics and consumers), and also the challenges that trade unions can face in fighting for workers' rights.

CASE STUDY

THE RESPONSIBILITIES OF MULTINATIONALS: A GLOBAL CONCERN

Evidence reported in the *Guardian* newspaper (the *Guardian*, Thursday 24 July 2003) has highlighted the way in which large multinationals can intimidate workers who actively engage in trade unions. It was alleged that a bottling plant partner in Colombia contracted illegal paramilitary groups to 'intimidate, threaten and kill its workers' and that Coca-Cola was indirectly responsible. Indeed, it was claimed that nine union members of the food and drink union Sinaltrainal had been killed at Colombian bottling plants in the previous 13 years. Frustrated with the courts' delays in dealing with the deaths of the workers, Sinaltrainal sought international support from other unions. In response to the claims, trade unions in the UK, USA,

Germany, Italy and Australia campaigned for consumers to stop buying Coke and other Coca-Cola products. However, the local media was silent on the issue, for fear of reprisals.

Questions

Do you think that Coca-Cola has any responsibility for situations such as that described above?

How do you think the company should respond to such situations?

Is a consumer boycott likely to be the most effective response by the global labour movement to victimisation of union members? In what other ways could the global labour movement respond?

This case study assesses the role of a major multinational corporation, and its conduct of global operations. The next section examines the broader concept of globalisation.

GLOBALISATION AND ITS IMPACT ON EMPLOYMENT

The concept of 'globalisation' has received much attention relating to its definition, its implications for convergence and integration, and its positive and negative outcomes on human resource management and employment relations.

DEFINING 'GLOBALISATION'

It has been argued that 'Globalisation is one of the most used, but also one of the most *mis*used and one of the most *conf*used, words around today' (ILO 2004, cited in Dicken 2007: 3). Similarly, Edwards and Rees (2006: 4) suggest that it is a 'very slippery concept'. A partial reason for the confusion is the negative and positive connotations that have been associated with globalisation. However, another reason for the difficulty in defining the term is that it has been used to define a range of changes that have occurred over the last hundred years. Indeed, Strange has argued that globalisation 'is a term which can refer to anything from the Internet to the hamburger' (Strange 1996, cited in Bisley 2007). In referring to the Internet, this statement reflects the idea that globalisation has often implied changes in technology that have been disseminated throughout many parts of the world, and the connectedness of people as a result of these changes. Reference to the hamburger can be seen as either positive or negative, but acknowledges the tendency for social trends to have converged, including similarities in eating patterns, in addition to the changes in human resource management associated with the growth of multinationals such as McDonalds that have spread to very many countries in the world. The reference to the hamburger also speaks to concerns relating to the nature of the jobs that are associated with fast-food production, an issue referred to in more detail in a later section of this chapter.

There are, moreover, two other definitions that are arguably very helpful in understanding the scope of globalisation. The first is by Seger (2003: 13):

> Globalisation refers to a multidimensional set of social processes that create, multiply, stretch and intensify worldwide social interdependencies and exchanges while at the same time fostering in people a growing awareness of deepening connections between the local and the distant.

This quote usefully emphasises the idea that there have been growing connections between nations, and also that there are 'interdependencies'. In other words, people are increasingly relying on each other for support. Some might argue that a number of countries such as the USA and the UK have, conversely, become more individualistic and independent. However, evidence also suggests growing interdependencies, as illustrated by the growth in the power and scope of the European Union and its members.

Another quote that is helpful in defining globalisation comes from Bisley (2007: 6):

> [Globalisation] is the set of social consequences which derive from the increasing rate and speed of interactions of knowledge, people, goods and capital between states and societies.

This quote draws attention to the speed of connections, facilitated by the Internet and by greater movement of people through improved transport infrastructure. In addition, there is reference to 'social consequences', highlighting both the economic impacts of globalisation and its wider implications. It is also worth noting that globalisation can be used to describe political, cultural, social, technological, environmental and economic changes, and both dynamic processes and static conditions. The *Applying theory to practice* box below draws attention to one of the above elements: the spread of technology, and its effects.

APPLYING THEORY TO PRACTICE

Technological changes and working relationships

What are the main technological changes that you have been aware of over recent years?

Have these technological changes meant closer connections to people in other countries?

How have these technological changes facilitated closer working relationships?

GLOBALISATION: IS THERE INCREASING INTERNATIONAL INTEGRATION?

We can think about globalisation in terms of three layers (Dicken 2007). The first layer is that of macro-structures, including institutions of the capitalist market system such as the IMF, the WTO and the World Bank, and G8 or G20 meetings. Each of these institutions might arguably result in greater integration between nations. The second layer is that of actor-centred networks – for example, transnational corporations (TNCs), states, firms, labour unions and civil society organisations. In defining a TNC, Dicken (2007) suggests that a TNC is 'a firm that has the power to coordinate and control operations in more than one country, even it does not own them' (Dicken 2007: 16). The third layer is the geographical distribution of goods and services. The term 'goods' is here broadly defined to include employment opportunities, incomes and access to consumer products. Conversely, 'bads' might include unemployment, poverty, resource depletion and pollution. The interconnections might result in a different distribution of 'goods' and 'bads' for different countries.

◀◯▶   REFLECTION ON PRACTICE

Distribution of the 'goods' and 'bads' of globalisation

Dicken (2007) suggests that there has been an uneven distribution of 'goods' and 'bads', involving winners and losers from the process of globalisation.

Based on your personal and work experience, who are the winners and the losers in terms of the 'goods' and 'bads' outlined above?

In addition to implying a redistribution of 'goods' and 'bads', globalisation can also imply a greater level of integration between countries. Rubery and Grimshaw (2003) consider integration by referring to four major trends and developments which they argue provide evidence of increasing international integration:

- the growth of foreign trade

- increasing flows of investment funds

- the development of ICT, facilitating globally integrated production and distribution systems

- the presence and power of multinational corporations (MNCs).

A further issue in relation to globalisation is whether it is new and is far-reaching. It can be argued that the current international economy is no more open now than in the 1800s in areas such as migration and cross-border trade. In addition, foreign direct investment (FDI: investment by one country in another) is heavily concentrated in advanced industrial nations, and although there may have been increased investment into and from emerging economies, it still does not equal that in advanced nations.

Thirdly, it could be argued that transnational firms are relatively rare. Most firms are based nationally and trade multinationally. Fourthly, global economic flows are minor compared to domestic flows (Edwards and Rees 2006). It could therefore be argued that globalisation is not bringing about a fundamental transformation, but is changing the relative influence, behaviours and strategies of states and people. Bisley (2007: 8), moreover, argues that globalisation is a 'deeply political process'; and is 'not a singular homogenising force – rather, it has a deeply uneven, contradictory and unpredictable character'.

POSITIVE AND NEGATIVE PERSPECTIVES OF GLOBALISATION

From a neo-liberal perspective, globalisation will bring the greatest benefit to the greatest number. The market is a self-regulating mechanism tending towards equilibrium of supply and demand, and globalisation will produce the most benefits if companies and consumers are left to their own devices. Moreover, since it is self-regulating, it appears that nobody is (or should be) responsible for globalisation. Globalisation is also, arguably, inevitable and irreversible.

Conversely, critics of globalisation argue against the acceptance that globalisation is an unstoppable juggernaut. There are two main branches of criticism, coming from a perspective of either *particularist protectionism* or *universalist protectionism* (Seger 2003). Particularist protectionism involves concern about the loss of national self-determination. Indeed, it could be argued that with globalisation, the nation state no longer matters. Those coming from a particularist protectionist perspective are also more concerned about the well-being of their own citizens than with a more equitable international order. On the other hand, universalist protectionism is progressive, and dedicated to establishing a more equitable relationship between countries in the north of the world and the south. People coming from this perspective tend to be concerned with the environment, fair trade, labour rights, women's issues and human rights.

From a critical perspective, markets create inequalities and the globalisation of markets increases the scale and extent of inequality (Dicken 2007). Globalisation leads to a reduced role for government and has implications for safety nets, while corporate finance often requires labour market deregulation (Perkins and Shortland 2006). Indeed, Meiksins Wood (1997) argues that:

> There is one major reason why we need to be so careful about how we use the term 'globalisation'. We have to guard against treating the trends that go under that name as if they were natural, inevitable processes, instead of historically specific capitalist processes, the capitalist exploitation of human beings and natural resources, aided and abetted by a direct collaboration between the state and capital.

⊶ LEGISLATION IN PRACTICE

Regulation for equality

The above statement by Meiksins Wood (1997) implies that markets should be regulated.

Assuming that this argument is accepted, how should this happen? Should nation states take the lead in regulating markets? Is it the responsibility of international institutions? Or is this the role of civil society, through anti-globalisation movements (see, for example, Worth and Kuhling 2004).

HOW IS GLOBALISATION RELEVANT TO HUMAN RESOURCE STUDIES AND EMPLOYMENT RELATIONS?

Globalisation is relevant to human resource studies in a range of ways. Firstly, human resources are often seen as a main source of competitive advantage (Porter 1990, cited in Rubery and Grimshaw 2003). There are a range of approaches within the literature that explain how HR contributes towards company performance. One approach assigns value to human intellectual capital, and attempts are made to leverage this asset to produce higher-value products – essentially captured by the resource-based view. Another approach relates to the bundle of HR practices referred to as high-performance practices (eg involvement, training, teamwork and performance-related pay) (Brewster *et al* 2003: 32). A third way in which globalisation is relevant to HR is due to the movement of global capital wherever it is cost-effective to move, impacting on different groups of workers. Fourthly, globalisation may have different impacts on different types of jobs (Reich 1991, cited in Rubery and Grimshaw 2003). Routinised jobs in production and services can be transferred elsewhere, whereas in-person service jobs such as hairdressing are localised. A further group of jobs – symbolic analysts – involve knowledge work or problem-solving and can be local or virtual, or can be relocated.

A fifth way in which globalisation is relevant to human resource studies is in the trends toward 'lean production' and 'the flexible firm', where lean production implies reducing costs, and the flexible firm assumes numerical flexibility of workers. In other words, the choices that firms make in their production regimes will have an impact on the number of workers employed, the types of workers and the labour process. Labour process research in the 1990s drew attention to the 'dark side' of lean production regimes (Thompson and Smith 2010: 16). Lean production can therefore not be seen in a totally objective way but might be viewed as contributing towards the control of workers and changes to their subjective experiences.

A further trend has been toward high-performance management. This is discussed in more detail in Chapter 8, where the relationship between employee engagement and performance is examined. However, here it is worth noting that there has been considerable debate over the move towards the use of high-performance (or high-commitment) practices such as involvement, teamworking, skill development and performance-related pay. Large firms have arguably benefited from the use of such practices. However, again, there has been some debate about whether this has been to the mutual benefit of individual employees (Thompson and Smith 2010).

In summary, since the 1980s there has been growing attention paid to the process of 'globalisation', the unification of markets, a general trend towards reduced regulation, the increased global mobility of investor capital and ideas, and a gradual homogenisation of consumer taste (see Morrissey and Filatotchev 2000). These processes have impacted on employment and employment relationships. However, it is now apparent that any process of globalisation is uneven and contested; there is no uniform process of homogenisation at work, and the impacts of globalisation have also been varied and are contestable.

'PESTLE' AND EMPLOYMENT RELATIONS

The way in which firms interact with their employees depends to a great extent on the broader context. Influences can be grouped into **p**olitical, **e**conomic, **s**ocial, **t**echnological, **l**egal and **e**nvironmental factors (CIPD 2010). Although it is important that firms take the effects of contexts seriously, such approaches represent little more than a 'shopping list' – they discount the extent to which component factors (eg political and economic) may impact on each other and be interrelated.

POLITICAL FACTORS

In Chapter 2, the role of the state was examined in some detail, with reference made to the degree of intervention by the state in employment relations. A lack of intervention can be termed as 'voluntarism', whereby the government allows the market to influence employment relations and does not attempt to manage relationships between employers and their employees (or employee representatives). As mentioned before, other approaches include corporatism and liberalism. Corporatism implies that government intervention is vital in promoting demand and increasing employment, and therefore the government engages in active labour market and industrial policies, providing social welfare, and increasing exports. Conversely, liberalism implies the reduction of company taxes, the deregulation of the economy and the labour market, and minimising trade union influence.

The government can influence employment relations directly through its role as employer. In advanced economies, the government has historically been seen as a 'model employer' (Dibben *et al* 2007), while in emerging economies, secure public sector employment can be relied on in helping to facilitate a sustainable economy, particularly in rural areas where formal sector jobs are scarce. The government is also responsible for legislation, including that relating to taxation, through which it can promote the interests of capital and take disproportionately from poorer members of society (regressive forms) or take a higher proportion from the wealthy and reduce inequality (progressive forms). As noted in Chapter 2, it has an important role in setting incomes policies in difficult times, while in the field of employment regulation the government can emphasise individual rights and/or collective rights.

ECONOMIC FACTORS

Economic factors impacting on employment relations can be related to government intervention. For example, public expenditure cuts (such as those seen in recent years in many parts of Europe) impact on the number of jobs in the public sector and the ability of consumers to purchase goods. In turn, this impacts on the growth of the private sector.

On an international basis, competition between firms also impacts on employment. New competitors may emerge, and old ones may disappear. The long-term decline of manufacturing industry in Britain and the USA does not represent the result of reduced demand for steel, motor cars, or any other set of products. The terms 'rust bucket' or 'sunset' industry are in fact somewhat lazy terms, as industries that are regularly condemned as such are in fact vibrant; it is just that firms producing specific goods in particular places are battling to compete. Since the 1970s there has been a proliferation of new players, largely, but not exclusively, from the Far East. This has meant that established producers have faced renewed competition on both cost and quality grounds. The result has been a shifting of the composition of the jobs market – most new jobs in Britain and the USA are now in the service sector.

Consumer markets are also subject to rapid change. In their classic work *The Second Industrial Divide*, Piore and Sabel (1984) argued that markets were breaking up – in other words, consumers were demanding a greater differentiation of products. In response, companies have to face the challenge of balancing a more diverse product range with economies of scale. Certain manufacturers (eg Volkswagen) have been more successful than others in meeting this challenge (eg General Motors).

SOCIAL FACTORS INCLUDING DEMOGRAPHICS

Social factors include the degree of inequality in society, and attitudes towards poorer groupings. For example, Levitas (1999) examines the different discourses that have emerged around social exclusion, emphasising either a redistributive discourse, a social integrationist discourse (encouraging people to work), and a moral underclass discourse, the latter of which sees the poor as responsible for their own situation.

Within most Western societies, an ageing population poses challenges of its own. Firstly, firms can no longer afford to treat older workers as a readily disposable asset – the pool of younger job seekers is getting progressively smaller. Secondly, the increased political clout of the elderly makes discrimination more risky (Wood *et al* 2008). Thirdly, the increased number of pensioners has placed a great strain on company pension schemes. Where companies have reneged on their implicit commitments, this has greatly undermined the basis of trust and co-operation in the workplace. In addition to changes relating to older workers, additional changes have taken place, such as the increased proportion of women who now work, earning primary rather than secondary incomes. A further change has been the increased diversity within the workforce as a consequence of migration, referred to in more detail in a later section of this chapter. The changes to the composition of the labour market have had far-reaching effects and have resulted in changes to legislation. At the same time it could be argued that legislation (including that related to discrimination) has itself contributed toward workplace changes. This topic is covered in more depth in Chapter 10.

TECHNOLOGY

Technology has a major impact in terms of the process of production and markets for goods. For example, new advances in information technology have greatly facilitated productivity and also enabled closer monitoring and control of employees (Hall 2010: 163):

> the effects of technology are various and depend on struggle and contestation at different levels: workplace, enterprise, organisation, sector, economy and society.

More generally, new technological advances may render some products obsolete and create new product markets. For example, the traditional market for film-based cameras has largely imploded, leading to the demise of a number of established brands, while there has been a rise of digital cameras, and more recently, multi-purpose devices combining cameras with media players, communication, and other IT applications. Within the workplace, new technology has included numerous updates to computer software, presenting opportunities for company growth and employee development.

LEGISLATION AND ENVIRONMENTAL FACTORS

As mentioned above, legislation impacts on firm behaviour and employment relations. However, it is important to note both the coverage of employment regulation and the degree to which it is enforced, particularly when considering the practices evident in developing and emerging economies. Further examination of employment legislation is undertaken in later chapters.

With regard to the environment, sustainability of the environment will necessarily impact on firm sustainability. Moreover, in recent times discussion has ensued about the prioritisation of green practices within organisations. Although these factors may not impact directly on employment relations, they nevertheless present future challenges for organisations' strategic choices and employment decisions.

DIFFERENT VARIETIES OF CAPITALISM

The 'varieties of capitalism' literature has grown over recent years. Essentially, it is used to distinguish between different types of capitalist society, and in particular the differences between the existence, nature, functioning and interrelationships of institutions. According to North (1990: 3), institutions are

> a set of rules, formal or informal, that actors generally follow, whether for normative, cognitive, or material reasons, and organisations as durable entities with formally recognised members, whose rules also contribute to the institutions of the political economy.

DICHOTOMOUS MODELS

The uneven consequences of globalisation have led to increased interest in the effects of institutions. At the ending of the Cold War, a number of commentators argued that all economies would converge towards a liberal market model, with, by implication, employment relations policies and practices following suit (Fukuyama 1992). However, the persistence of differences led to an increased awareness that a number of alternative viable national models could persist (Hall and Soskice 2001). More specifically, it was recognised that there were key differences between lightly regulated liberal market economies (eg the UK and the USA) and more regulated coordinated markets (eg Germany, the

Scandinavian countries and Japan) (Hall and Soskice 2001; Dore 2000). In terms of employment relations, liberal markets were characterised by weak vocational training, relatively insecure job tenure, a reluctance of firms to invest in training and development, weaker employee voice and generally more adversarial relations (*ibid*). Meanwhile, coordinated markets are characterised by greater security of tenure, stronger vocational training and in-firm development, stronger employee voice, and a generally greater emphasis on trust and co-operation (*ibid*). This distinction reflected differences in institutions (embedded clusters or frameworks of practices bound by formal and informal rules to act with a specific purpose), such as education or finance (Sorokin 1966: 38–9) and the webs of social relations that surround them. In practice liberal markets are associated with relatively weak ties, and coordinated markets with stronger ties between associations, such as employers and unions.

ADDITIONAL VARIETIES OF CAPITALISM

Although highly influential, this initial 'varieties of capitalism' approach faced a series of criticisms. Firstly, the use of only two archetypes (liberal and coordinated) meant that there were a number of other types of economy (eg Mediterranean/South European) that were difficult to categorise. In addition, the existing categories were somewhat broad – there are many differences between Germany and Scandinavia, for example. This has led to a number of attempts to identify further capitalist archetypes (see, for example, Whitley 1999; Amable 2003; Wood and Frynas 2006). In particular, the earlier discussions tended to ignore emerging economies. This has been regarded by some as a major omission. Consequently, more recent work has sought to explore the extension of the literature to other country types (Wood and Frynas 2006; Wood *et al* 2010).

Secondly, the initial work in this area accorded only a limited amount of attention to issues of change. Although change may often be slow and incremental, systems can and do reinvent themselves (Lane and Wood 2009).

OWNER RIGHTS AND LEGAL TRADITIONS

A somewhat different approach to institutions has emerged in the economics and finance literatures. Based on the account of North (1990), it has been argued that the primary effect of institutions is in terms of private property rights – some contexts are better at ensuring them than others. Where property rights are stronger, firms are more likely to direct resources to ensuring returns to shareholders, and where they are weaker, other stakeholder groupings (eg employees) will more effectively contest for firm resources (La Porta *et al* 1998, 2000). Implicit in this literature is that countries with stronger owner rights (eg the USA) are likely to perform better than those with weaker ones (eg Germany, Japan), although the empirical evidence for this is very mixed. Particularly influential have been approaches that look at the effects of legal tradition – common law countries (eg the USA, the UK) giving owners stronger rights and workers weaker ones. The converse is true with civil law countries (eg France, Germany) (*ibid*). These approaches tend to assume that worker and owner rights are a zero-sum game: if one side gains, the other must lose (Goergen *et al* 2009). In contrast, the 'varieties of capitalism' literature holds out the possibilities for compromises, complementarities and synergies, allowing for win/win situations (Hall and Soskice 2001).

Legal rights vary across countries. The questions in the *Legislation in practice* box below probe into the relationship between investment decisions and employment rights.

○━⚷ LEGISLATION IN PRACTICE

Employment rights and investment choices

The World Bank's Doing Business Index (www.doingbusiness.org) suggests that countries which give employees greater job security under the law are less favourable environments for doing business, and, by implication should be shunned by investors.

Do you think that investors should avoid countries where legislation helps to provide workers with greater job security?

What are the positive effects of job security for employers and employees?

LABOUR MARKETS AND THE EFFECTS OF DIFFERENT FORMS OF OWNERSHIP

Where unemployment is high, and where there is weaker job protection under the law, firms can force down wage costs and readily rid themselves of those who under-perform. Does this mean that firms do better in such contexts? Unfortunately, the more that firms have access to cheap labour, the more is required. Moreover, there can be a default tendency to throw cheap labour at any problem that arises, rather than planning and using labour intelligently. In contrast, where labour markets are more regulated, and/or where labour is scarcer, firms have to take greater care in selection and recruitment, ensuring that employees have optimal skill sets through training and actively promoting the development of human capital. Employers use labour more efficiently and therefore increase labour productivity in a context of higher wages. In such a context, unprofitable, inefficient enterprises are not subsidised by poorly paid workers. In other words, low wages in effect subsidise labour inefficiency by making it easy for employers to use workers inefficiently. By forcing enterprises to compete by increasing efficiency rather than by reducing labour standards, resources will be shifted to more efficient uses and human resources will be protected and developed.

The nature of firm ownership may also impact on practices. An owner-manager is more likely to have sunk emotional capital in the firm, and to take a longer-term view. In contrast, listed firms (ie firms owned by shareholders) are likely to face market pressures to optimise returns. In recent years, private equity – meaning investment in unquoted companies that includes early-stage venture capital and later-stage buyouts – has become a more common feature (Wood and Wright 2009). Early-stage venture capital is generally seen as having a beneficial social and economic impact (in supporting new startups and innovation), but the role of manifestations of private equity has been more controversial. Indeed, it has been argued that private equity invariably loads companies with excessive debt and is highly detrimental to employees in terms of jobs, wages and working conditions. However, recent work has pointed to the very diverse effects of private equity. In general, management buy-outs (MBOs, where managers are involved in buying the company from outside shareholders) appear to have more positive effects than management buy-ins (MBIs – that is, the replacement of managers by a new managerial team) (Wood and Wright 2009).

WORKFORCE DIVERSITY AND MIGRATION

Irrespective of ownership, as a result of the mobility of people, firms have to deal with an increasingly diverse workforce. Line managers need to deal sensitively with a growing diversity of subordinates, and HR managers need to provide training in order that this is achieved (Brewster *et al* 2003).

With rapid technological changes, more open markets and great demographic imbalances, national competitiveness depends at least in part on having access to sufficient labour possessing relevant skills. Even within Europe, despite a single market, the workforce has, until relatively recently, not been very mobile. Most European countries have rapidly ageing workforces, increasing the need for labour from abroad. Although internal migrants in Europe have tended to be skilled or professional, there has been also a significant movement of unskilled workers both across and from outside Europe. This does not mean to say that all skilled workers moving across national boundaries find skilled jobs in their target country – semi-skilled workers and women tend to experience significant drops in occupational status when they move. Moreover, skills are not always portable: those that seek to migrate are often forced into low-status jobs.

MIGRATION WITHIN THE EUROPEAN UNION

The enlargement of the European Union has increased internal migration. With this questions of discrimination have emerged. For example, there is evidence that incoming Romanian workers are widely discriminated against in countries such as Britain. This is particularly ironic given that older Britons moving abroad do not always have a good reputation for fitting into their chosen country, instead forming small closed expatriate communities, often not bothering to befriend locals or even to learn the local language.

In recent years there has been a major expansion of the European Union. The biggest set of country accessions was in 2004, increasing the Union's population by 75 million, and the size of the European economy to approximately the size of the USA (Euractiv 2004). In theory this should have meant that all the new citizens should have free movement across the Union. In practice, many countries initially kept some restrictions in place. In the UK, it led to an influx of a relatively large number of workers, most notably from Poland. Many, however, chose to return to Poland following the onset of the 2008 financial crisis and the resulting evaporation of large numbers of jobs in the UK construction sector. In 2007, Romania and Bulgaria joined the EU. Because Romania has a relatively large population, this reopened questions about mobility, especially given the large number of Poles moving westward after that country's accession. On the far right, racists took the opportunity to draw attention to the large ethnic Roma/gypsy population in Romania. In practice, all but two European states (Finland and Sweden) initially limited inward migration from these countries. However, all committed to free movement of people by 2014. Other future EU member states, such as Macedonia and Croatia, have relatively small populations, making their cases less contentious. It should not be assumed that the flow is only one-way; small but significant numbers of highly skilled workers have chosen to move eastward, attracted by the economic opportunities opened up by rapid change, more affordable standards of living and often better-quality housing.

MIGRATION FROM OUTSIDE THE EUROPEAN UNION

In addition to migration within the EU, there are also interesting trends in migration from outside the EU. In some advanced countries there are bogus claims that foreign migrants are primarily seeking to live off state benefits, while in less advanced economies the emphasis can tend to be on job replacement. However, the reasons for migration might not correspond to either of these perceptions. Because most immigrants are relatively young but of working age, they need far fewer state services (eg education and health care), and are more likely (when they are legal) to pay taxes. Those migrating when they are adults have had their education paid for by their country of origin – and deploy their skills elsewhere. Hence, for example, the migration of nurses from tropical Africa to Western Europe involves, in effect, a subsidy by the former to the latter.

Heavily deregulated labour markets (ie with fewer restrictions on hiring and firing) such as the UK afford many opportunities in poorly paid, flexible jobs with low job security. Marina Lewycka's humorous novel *Two Tractors* provides an alarmingly accurate depiction of the nature of unskilled migrant work in the UK. Moreover, in the UK there is very lax enforcement of laws precluding illegal immigrants from seeking employment. Crackdowns on illegal labour have accorded disproportionate attention to smaller ethnic-owned business, as adverse to big employers in the agriculture and food processing industry. This reflects the fact that large areas of agriculture and the food industry are, in fact, heavily dependent on cheap unskilled workers, who are not in a position to insist on either their legal rights regarding working conditions and health and safety, or decent pay. Ironically, restrictions on migration may thus serve as a mechanism for labour coercion, rather than protecting the interests of local job seekers. Interestingly, although the media have tended to focus on the problems associated with those seeking to enter the country legally, they are curiously silent on the large-scale exploitation of illegal migrants. Many other European countries

– such as Italy and Greece – have large underground economies, again with large numbers of illegal workers employed under coercive conditions.

Another reason for the pull of Europe reflects the legacies of formal colonial empires: Britain [India, Pakistan, East Africa, etc], Belgium [DR Congo], France [North and West Africa], Netherlands [Indonesia], Italy [Libya, Eritrea, Ethiopia], etc. It also reflects geography – eg those seeking to migrate by open boats via Senegal and Mauritania go to the Canary Islands, and those travelling via Libya initially end up in Malta and Italy. Once in Europe, the lack of opportunities means that unskilled migrants may then drift across the continent.

Controversial in its own right, encouraging the movement of Europeans across Europe does reduce demand for Asian and African labour, and indeed, has been promoted as such an alternative. Increasing xenophobia – and racism – has led to the prioritisation of other measures to respond to increased migration, such as increasing the participation of older workers and women in the workforce *or* encouraging greater migration within Europe. Yet greater migration within and into Europe or other advanced economies is arguably a fact of life that can no more be prevented than the movement of people from country to town in the nineteenth century.

THE EUROPEAN UNION AND EU LEGISLATION

The Europeanisation process has had varying effects on employers and employees. It has served both as a driver of liberal market reforms and a promoter of a common European social model.

THE EUROPEAN UNION AND EMPLOYMENT RELATIONS

The European Commission has extensive powers to implement measures governing employment relations. Countries that refuse to implement Directives may face legal action, although there have been instances of countries negotiating rights for individual employees to opt out of aspects of specific agreements. EU Directives have had implications for both the rights of individual employees and collectives. Individual rights include those that encompass measures against discrimination, for equal pay, and rights for younger, agency and pregnant workers, and working time (CIPD 2009). Collective rights include the rights of workers in the case of collective dismissals and measures to implement European Works Councils (CIPD 2009). Space precludes a full review of European employment legislation, and the following sections concentrate on four examples: working time and the rights of agency workers (individual rights), European Works Councils (collective rights), and measures aimed at promoting competition (corporate governance).

EUROPEAN DIRECTIVES

The 2008 Temporary and Agency Workers Directive builds on similar Directives governing part-time and fixed-term workers, and accords agency workers equal rights to full-time employees. However, these rights only apply to basic working conditions and terms of employment (for example, equal pay, similar working time, parental leave). These regulations do not restrict the use of temporary or contingent workers *per se*. In terms of the 2008 agreement between unions, government and employers in the UK, a 'derogation period' of 12 weeks applies – workers do not have rights until this period ends. Neither do the self-employed, or those employed by 'managed service (limited company) contracts'.

The 1993 Working Time Directive restricts maximum working time to 48 hours per week, with daily minimum rest periods of 11 hours, and a right to paid leave up until a specific duration. Within the UK there is a right to agree an opt-out of the 48-hour clause. However, given the power imbalances between individual workers and employers it is not clear how effective an employee would be in resisting a determined employer set on implementing longer working hours. Attempts in 2009 to negotiate a removal of the opt-out clause failed.

Of the Directives associated with multinationals, one of the more contentious work Directives has been the Seventh (Vredeling) Directive. This Directive was concerned with the requirement of disclosure of company information to trade unions. It met with strong opposition led by the British government, who argued that disclosure of information should be voluntary (Brewster *et al* 2003). This Directive was followed more recently by the 1994 European Works Council Directive that compels firms with more than 1,000 employees, and with a presence of at least 150 employees in more than one European country, to have a European Works Council (EWC). EWCs are, however, very different from the type of works council found in many European states at national level. The latter in many instances (eg in Germany) gives workers a legal right to have a say over changes in the process of production (Murakami 1999). In contrast, the role of EWCs is primarily that of a consultative body: they are more geared to ensuring that employees have access to information on changes in firm policy and practice than any formal negotiating rights, even if they may serve to facilitate greater contact and co-operation between employees working in different locales within the firm.

COMPETITION LAW

In many coordinated European markets, there has been a legacy of strong inter-firm relations (Hall and Soskice 2001). The European Court of Justice and the Commission banned certain practices, such as cartels, at European level, forcing a gradual adaption to European law at national level (Quack and Djelic 2005: 272). By 1983, the European Court of Justice ruled that provisions on competition agreed by treaty were to be followed nationally (*ibid*: 274). The Merger Regulation passed in 1989 restricted takeovers where competition is significantly impeded. Meanwhile, there has been a trend towards the increased scrutiny of state aid at national level, with an application of competition law to state-owned enterprises (*ibid*: 271). What this means in practice is that there has been a slow infusion of elements of US competition law, constraining the consolidation of specific industries, and active state industrial policy. This is not to suggest that active state policy has been totally precluded, however, and there are many instances at both transnational and national level within the EU where governments have intervened to support key sectors and firms. Yet even where jobs may be expanded or protected through state support and/or greater inter-industry co-operation, there is little doubt that the actions of governments have been considerably more impeded than in the past.

INTERNATIONAL INSTITUTIONS

THE IMF, WORLD BANK AND WORLD TRADE ORGANISATION

At Bretton Woods in 1944 there was the creation of three international institutions: the International Monetary Fund, the International Bank for Reconstruction and Development (now called the World Bank), and the General Agreement on Tariffs and Trade (GATT), now renamed the World Trade Organisation (WTO) and providing a forum for trade negotiations.

The primary objective of the Bretton Woods system was to stabilise and regulate international financial transactions between nations on the basis of fixed currency exchange rates, in which the US dollar played the central role. But this broke down in the 1970s (see Dicken 2007).

The IMF's primary purpose was to encourage international monetary co-operation among nations through a set of rules for world payments and currencies. Each nation contributes a quota to the fund, and voting rights are proportional to the size of a nation's quota. A major function of the IMF has been to aid member states in temporary balance of payments difficulties, but a condition of such aid is IMF supervision or advice on the necessary corrective policies – known as 'conditionality requirements'. In 2006 an agreement was reached giving the IMF a surveillance role over global trade imbalances, with the hope of stimulating more balanced growth.

The World Bank's role was originally to facilitate development through capital investment. It focused on Europe in the immediate post-war period, but has since shifted attention to developing economies. In the 1980s it moved beyond lending for projects such as roads and dams to providing structural adjustment loans, but only when the IMF gave its approval. The World Bank and IMF are heavily influenced by G8 countries (the USA, Japan, Germany, Canada, Italy, France, the UK and Russia). In the 1980s, the IMF and the World Bank reached a consensus with the US Treasury about the right policies for developing countries, which emphasised rapid trade liberalisation, capital markets liberalisation and privatisation. However, some have criticised these policies and suggested that not enough attention was paid to different cultural and historical contexts (see Stiglitz 2002). Indeed, it has been argued (Dicken 2007: 531–2) that

> By imposing massive financial stringency – including raising domestic interest rates, insisting on increasing openness of the domestic economy,

reducing social spending, and the like – conditionality makes it extremely difficult for countries to help themselves out of debt.

At the G8 summit in 2005 it was agreed to write off debt for 18 of the world's poorest countries, and that of a further nine countries within a year and a half. However, in common with individuals, countries can be tempted to then take out more debt (as has been the case in countries such as Mozambique).

INTERNATIONAL LABOUR STANDARDS AND THE ILO

Why are international labour standards necessary? There are a number of factors that are influential (see Rubery and Grimshaw 2003). Firstly, international regulation becomes more important as capital becomes mobile, and labour costs and labour standards influence the location of companies and subsidiaries. Without international regulation, individual nation states may offer multinational corporations (MNCs) low labour costs in order to secure investment. To protect against this, each nation state should respect at least a minimum set of international labour standards. Moreover, efficient and productive labour market systems require protection from destructive competition, and international labour standards are necessary in order to defend social justice and human rights. One point for debate, however, is whether human rights should be protected irrespective of economic affordability, or whether 'social justice' should take account of context and affordability.

There are four main types of labour standards (Portes 1994, cited in Rubery and Grimshaw 2003: 245). These are outlined in Table 5.1.

Table 5.1 Labour standards

Basic rights	Survival rights	Security rights	Civic rights
Against the use of child labour	Living wage	Against arbitrary dismissal	Free association
Against involuntary servitude	Accident compensation	Retirement compensation	Collective representation
Against physical coercion	Limited working week	Survivors' compensation	Free expression of grievances

Basic rights are similar to the notion of universal rights, with a fairly high degree of international consensus, while civic rights tend to be accepted by democratic societies. However, survival and security rights tend to be defined according to local conditions.

APPLYING THEORY TO PRACTICE

The variation in human and employment rights between countries

Is it ethical for human and employment rights to be defined according to local conditions such as economic affordability?

Which rights are accepted in your home country?

The International Labour Organisation (ILO) was founded in 1919 in order to protect labour rights at an international level. It is a tripartite organisation of governments, employer organisations and trade unions. It passes conventions on labour standards, and the member states then choose whether or not to ratify them. However, very few have been ratified by all members, and even the abolition of child labour has only been ratified by around two-thirds of member countries.

The ILO also pushes for the implementation of basic labour standards through a declaration on fundamental principles and rights at work. In 1944 it adopted the Declaration of Philadelphia – the right of all human beings 'to pursue both their material well-being and their spiritual development in conditions of freedom and dignity, of economic security and equal opportunity'. This is often enshrined in labour law (see, for example, Mozambique's Labour Law, 2007). Then in 1998 it adopted the Declaration on Fundamental Principles and Rights at Work, which entailed the freedom of association and the effective recognition of the right to collective bargaining, the elimination of all forms of forced or compulsory labour, the abolition of child labour, and the elimination of discrimination in respect of employment and occupation. However, there is not universal enforcement of these. In addition, some developing nations argue that these principles act as a form of protectionism. In other words, emerging economies are not able to afford the enforcement of these rights, and by avoiding them, labour costs are lower and firms are more competitive.

INTERNATIONAL EMPLOYMENT RELATIONS

International employment relations can refer to the comparison of employment relations practices between national contexts, and to employment relations within multinational corporations (MNCs).

COMPARATIVE EMPLOYMENT RELATIONS

The comparison of employment relations practices between nations is covered within the recent literature on institutional effects. However, there is also a significant body of applied empirical research which primarily seeks to compare differences in key indicators between countries. For example, Visser and Ebbinghaus (2000) compare differences in trends in union membership within Western Europe. A host of comparative statistics may be found on the ILO (www.ilo.org) and the OECD (www.oecd.org) websites. Such comparisons are very valuable in that they can provide quick insights into what really defines industrial relations in different settings. Further discussion of comparative employment relations is covered within the *Conclusion* to this book.

MULTINATIONAL CORPORATIONS AND EMPLOYMENT RELATIONS

In this section, the focus is primarily on local employees (almost always, the bulk of employees) within the country of operation, while the following section examines the use of expatriates.

The effect of multinational corporations (MNCs) on employment relations is a mixed one. For example, they may vigorously fend off unionisation efforts, an example being the fast-food chain, McDonald's. Workers in the sector are traditionally poorly paid. However, not only has the chain proved willing to resort to litigation to fend off unionisation efforts but there have also allegedly been cases of where groupings of McDonald's workers on low wages have managed to hire expensive lawyers to undermine unionisation efforts (Featherstone 1998; see also Royle 2006). A union representative (Gallin 2010) has charged that:

> I think it's worse than the others because they've systemised it and they've refined it to the level of a system which they impose everywhere. I can't think of any other company does that. To some degree other fast-food companies have followed their lead, but again they're not as singleminded and consistent in exploiting their workers. … They have an infrastructure devoted to their ideology, a hamburger university where they teach staff to do things the McDonald's way … If McDonald's had a more humane and normal policy of dealing with its employees I think the whole atmosphere in the fast-food industry could change.

This does not mean that the fast-food chain has been able to fend off all unionisation drives. Whereas it has generally been successful in the USA, it has faced bitter and protracted challenges in Canada, and has been legally obliged to engage with unions in several European countries. However, critics have charged that the chain continues to mount challenges to unions even when they are established (Gallin 2010). Significantly, the *Oxford English Dictionary* defines a 'McJob' as 'a low-paid job with few prospects' (*Oxford English Dictionary* 2010).

Other MNCs have attempted to engage with unions, as outlined in the case study below.

CASE STUDY

MULTINATIONALS AND TRADE UNIONS

The mining company Anglo-American has engaged with the ICEM (the International Confederation of Chemical, Energy, Mine and General Workers' Unions), offsetting any costs from revived collective bargaining in one national setting with gains from increased worker legitimacy, and participation in an anti-HIV/AIDS programme in another (Croucher and Cotton 2009: 111).

Anglo-American was a company reconciled to dealing with unions many years ago, and indeed, had experience of leveraging its co-operative relations with unions to reduce costs and enhance productivity (*ibid*: 111). Nonetheless, its willingness and ability to engage with unions in Colombia is of particular importance given the general anti-union environment in that country.

Questions

Why does a large company such as Anglo-American choose to engage with an international federation of trade unions?

Can you think of other multinational corporations that apparently maintain a consistent attitude toward unions across a range of countries in which they operate?

Some MNCs have taken a different attitude towards unions. Many MNCs have shifted – and often outsourced – production to very low-wage countries in the Far East. In 2007, Nike was faced with a major strike at the plant of one of its Vietnamese suppliers. Significantly, the firm's official response was to call for managers and workers to resolve their differences, rather than simply finding ways of supporting the former (BBC 2007). Since then, there has been a wave of strikes at plants manufacturing goods for Western MNCs in China. It is evident that many traditionally low-cost countries are no longer automatically associated with quiescent workforces.

MNCs only employ a small proportion – about 1% – of the global workforce (Croucher and Cotton 2009: 16). However, they do wield extensive power. On the one hand, they often pay more than their local counterparts. On the other hand, many have engaged not only in union-busting but also in aggressively campaigning for local labour legislation to be relaxed and/or special dispensation for their activities. The activities of private equity and other more aggressive types of investor place strong pressure on firms, which may lead to a weakening of labour standards (Clark 2009), as does the rising use of agency workers worldwide.

MULTINATIONAL CORPORATIONS AND THE USE OF EXPATRIATES

Within MNCs, many employees are nationals of the country of operation. However, they also typically make use of expatriates, often in managerial positions, because

- skills may not be available locally
- transaction costs will be lower because parent-country nationals are likely to be more familiar with the firm and what working for it entails (see Marsden 1999)
- experienced expatriates may facilitate in the diffusion of the dominant organisational culture.

However, there are a number of costs entailed with the use of expatriates. Firstly, they may not be fully aware of the local culture and ways of doing business. This may raise the transaction costs in the case of any dealings with locals. Expatriates may choose to isolate themselves in gated compounds or communities, interact largely with their fellow expatriates, and remain determinedly ignorant of local politics and society. Secondly, there is the question of equity. To attract parent-country nationals to work abroad often requires a wage premium, which may cause resentment by local employees, particularly if they perceive that the presence of a large number of expatriates is creating a 'glass ceiling' against their own advancement. Thirdly, expatriates are costly in terms of relocation and repatriation costs, and long-term separations from partners for reasons of work may lead to family breakdown. Finally, the use of expatriates in certain jobs may fall foul of local laws governing non-discrimination and/or affirmative action in respect of historically disadvantaged groupings. Nonetheless, the use of expatriates remains popular among multinationals. Within tropical Africa, some players (most notably Chinese construction firms and US oil and gas firms) have chosen within some countries to import parent-country nationals even into menial jobs. In this context, the role of unions (and their ability to forge international links) becomes very important. This issue is covered in the next section.

INTERNATIONAL ACTIVITIES OF TRADE UNIONS

As Croucher and Cotton (2009: 4) note, unions are still the largest membership organisations in the world, and are often far more democratic than the NGO sector. International union groupings have an important role to play in alleviating power imbalances, in assisting local unions, and in helping to mitigate great imbalances in knowledge, power and resources between organised labour and employers (*ibid*). There are two key organising mechanisms uniting unions across national boundaries. Firstly, there are the global union federations (GUFs) – sectorally based bodies, uniting national unions organising a specific sector. Secondly, there are international union federations, or in other words, super-federations of national level unions. These aim to provide a united voice for unions worldwide. In the Cold War era, the international labour movement was essentially split between pro-Western and pro-Soviet unions. The ending of the Cold War saw renewed moves to unity under the aegis of the International Trade Union Confederation, by far the largest of such bodies. The core of the latter was the old pro-Western International Confederation of Free Trade Unions.

The role of global union bodies is often misunderstood, reflecting both hostility from conservative sections of the media and the problems of organising in repressive environments. A further problem is that although global union outreach initiatives can play a very important role in improving the conditions of workers, their activities at times have been hijacked, most notoriously by the CIA (Southall 1995). Within 1950s and 1960s *apartheid* South Africa, US unions, aided and abetted by the CIA, backed minority splinter unions against the progressive mainstream union movement (Southall 1995). Although this role was later abandoned, it did much to poison relations between progressive South African and Western unions for many years.

In recent times, the American Federation of Labor-Congress of Industrial Organizations' (AFL-CIO's) Solidarity Center has co-operated with the National Endowment for Democracy (NED) (a controversial US governmental body that has a history of backing right-wing political candidates and groupings outside the USA) in support of the conservative CTV union federation against the elected government of Venezuela. Little support for the much larger progressive union movement has been forthcoming.

In short, the role of international union bodies is varied, complex and sometimes controversial. Even those activities that genuinely support workers in the developing world may sometimes lack transparency (Southall 1995). In addition, they still do not cover the bulk of workers in the world – those in the informal sector and peasant-based agriculture. Croucher and Cotton (2009: 79) argue that perhaps the most viable way forward is through small-group work, and a focus on education and developing the skills of union activists. However, because many unions based in the developing world lack resources, they often lack the ability to roll out training even in basic areas of union activity, let alone provide education on the international labour movement and ways of promoting sustainable co-operation. It could thus be argued that rather than large-scale initiatives – such as efforts to promote international collective bargaining – union internationals should devote their attention to building the capacity of local unions in order that they may engage more effectively with multinationals (Croucher and Cotton 2009: 79).

CRITICAL DEBATE

The international activities of trade unions

Is it worthwhile for unions to engage in international solidarity efforts with unions operating in other countries?

If your answer is yes, what challenges might they face in doing so?

If your answer is no, *why* is it not worthwhile for them to do so? List the reasons inhibiting such activity and consider what should be done in order for them to interact effectively.

SUMMARY

This chapter has covered a broad range of contextual influences on employment relations, including those that are evident at a local or national level and others that are international in scope. The chapter began by exploring what was meant by the term 'globalisation' and revealed the varied interpretations of the term, and the implications of such understandings for the treatment of both advanced and emerging economies. An overview of factors grouped under the term 'PESTLE' drew attention to diverse influences on firm behaviour. This was followed by more theoretical consideration of institutions affecting firms and an examination of the impact on employment relations of labour markets, diversity and migration. As the chapter progressed, it became clearer that there are both national and international influences on employment relations, each of which has implications for the rights of workers and their relationships with employers. Although the power of multinationals is evident, there appears to be little evidence of employment relations becoming more similar in developing and developed world countries. Finally, it is worth adding that in order to understand employment relations, it is vitally important to take account of the broader context including structural features (eg the law and institutions), societal and environmental changes (eg demographic shifts) and what is taking place in countries across the world.

EXPLORE FURTHER

Reading

- Amable, B. (2003) *The Diversity of Modern Capitalism*. Oxford: Oxford University Press

- Brewster, C., Sparrow, P. and Vernon, G. (2007) *International Human Resource Management*. London: CIPD

- Croucher, R. and Cotton, E. (2009) *Global Unions, Global Business*. London: Middlesex University Press

- Dicken, P. (2007) *Global Shift: Mapping the contours of the world economy,* 3rd edition. London: Sage

- Hall, P. and Soskice, D. (2001) *Varieties of Capitalism: The institutional basis of competitive advantage.* Oxford: Oxford University Press

- Harzing, A. and Van Ruysseveldt, J. (2004) *International Human Resource Management,* 2nd edition. London: Sage

Websites

- International Monetary Fund www.imf.org

- Organisation for Economic Co-operation and Development www.oecd.org

- International Labour Organisation www.ilo.org

CHAPTER 6

Power and Authority

CHAPTER OVERVIEW

The employment relationship is not just about the supply of labour but also about authority. When entering into an employment contract, the employee agrees, during the course of the working day (and sometimes outside it as well), to be subject to the authority of the employer. As with any such relationship, some conflict and dispute is likely, centring on the boundaries of this authority, what is fair and what is not. This chapter draws on literature from a range of disciplines including political science, organisational behaviour and labour process studies.

The chapter begins by exploring the concept of power and then the balance of power between employers and employees. It then moves on to examine how managers might exert their power through co-operation and compliance in the individual employment relationship. The chapter thereafter considers the issue of corporate governance through analysing the degree to which stakeholders and shareholders are able to exert power, the role of directors, and the way in which financial imperatives and corporate social responsibility (CSR) can impact on the treatment of employees. The next section explores the concept of managerial legitimacy, and outlines the mechanisms used by managers to exert legitimacy, while the last section investigates how change management can be used as a way in which to exert power over employees, and how resistance tends to be overcome.

LEARNING OUTCOMES

After studying this chapter you should be able to:

- explain the importance of power and authority to the employment relationship
- determine how co-operation and compliance might impact on the individual employment contract
- define the term 'corporate governance' and explain the various elements associated with it
- critically evaluate the notion of managerial legitimacy
- critically discuss the issue of change management, resistance to change, and the strategies used to overcome resistance to change

POWER AND AUTHORITY

In its most basic form, every employment relationship is an economic exchange (an agreement to exchange wages for work) *and* a power relation (the employee 'agrees' to submit to the authority of the employer). Freedland (1995: 24–6) distinguishes between two levels at which contracting takes place within the employment relationship. At the first level the concern is with the exchange of services for remuneration. Here collective and associative considerations (such as the relationship between an employee and the union) are marginalised. At the second level the focus is on the creation of obligations relating to the security of expectations such as the security of income or employment and commitments beyond the rendering of particular services. It is the second, relational, level of contracting that generates most concerns. As was mentioned in Chapter 1, no employment contract can specify precisely the amount of effort to be expended or the degree of initiative that should be displayed by employees. Meanwhile, the employer's requirements are rarely predictable in great detail and retain a wide margin of discretion. The wage–effort bargain that underlies the employment contract is subject to ongoing and usually tacit negotiation. This implies a model of the employment relationship as essentially a power relationship, qualitatively different from a 'pure' exchange relationship.

DIFFERENT CONCEPTS OF POWER

The concepts of 'power' and 'authority' are central to a proper understanding of the individual and collective aspects of employment relations. In practice, as Salamon (1998: 69) points out, the two concepts are inextricably linked: authority is achieved through power, and vice versa. Although there is no universally accepted definition of power, Salamon (1998: 70) suggests that it is useful to differentiate between power as the ability to control or impose and power as the capacity to direct the behaviour and decisions of others. Power has various dimensions. The elements of power include:

- the power users or power-builders
- the channels and resources through which power is exercised
- the goals towards which power is geared
- the structure or configuration of power.

An analytical distinction may be drawn between the process of management (its functions) and the structure of authority within the organisation (the forms that authority might take). If we ignore this distinction, management would be viewed as a purely technical or formal process. This would tell us nothing about the context within which the management of employment relations is conducted. Management is therefore best conceptualised as a social relation rather than a person or a thing in itself. In other words, the power that a manager wields in the workplace does not adhere to him or her as a person but rather emanates from his or her position in the social relations of production. This becomes evident when we consider the principles of power, which include:

- Power is always relative and never belongs totally to one party.

- Power can be real or false.
- Power can be exercised without action.
- Power is legitimated to the extent that it is accepted.
- The exercise of power always involves costs and risks.
- The balance of power is never static.
- The exertion of power depends on the ability to apply sanctions should there be no compliance.
- Power always refers to a social relationship between people.

The employment relationship is therefore inherently a power/authority relationship.

In order to exert power, management requires a number of abilities and resources. French and Raven (cited in Salamon 1998: 70) identify five major interrelated sources of power within an organisation:

- reward – based on the ability to control strategic resources to reward others, the strength of this power increasing with the importance of the reward
- coercion – the ability to force an agreement on the other party
- legitimacy – deriving from the situation in which one group of people have internalised the belief that they are subordinate to another group
- deferment – having the personal attributes that lead others to defer in their decisions or opinions
- expertise – the relative amounts of information available to the parties.

Authority is usually defined as the legitimate use of power. The legitimation of power occurs through a range of mechanisms and at various levels. At the wider societal level, processes of socialisation (including the way in which children are brought up by parents and educators) inculcate notions of obedience, respect for superiors and deference to authority. At the organisational level, acceptance of management's 'right to manage' by employees means that managers can control the behaviour of their subordinates without continuously resorting to coercive or punitive measures.

The notion of power being legitimated through authority, according to Salamon (1998: 72–3), has three important implications for employment relations. First, the use of power is likely to be perceived as unacceptable or wrong, whereas the exercise of authority is likely to be regarded as acceptable or right. This is particularly relevant in cases where power is used to further narrow, sectional interests of certain members of the workforce at the expense of the wider, social interests of the organisation. Second, there is a potential conflict of loyalty between the individual's role as an employee and as a trade union member. The extent of this conflict varies depending on the degree of legitimacy accorded to the power of trade unions within both society and the organisation. As was explained in Chapter 2, the power of trade unions may vary depending on the country context, the ideology espoused by government and the legislation that has been imposed. Third, the rights or entitlements of employees are closely linked to the manner in which power and authority are exercised. For example, management's capacity to determine terms and conditions of employment is limited by the power of trade unions to negotiate wages and other aspects of the employment relationship. Likewise, management's ability to treat employees as they see fit is limited by protection against unfair dismissal, discrimination and so on contained in labour legislation. As detailed in Chapter 10, although most countries have brought in anti-discrimination law, the nature of the legislation varies between countries. The scope of the protection contained in the laws of a country is also, in turn, partly a product of the influence of labour over the government.

APPLYING THEORY TO PRACTICE

The way in which power is exerted within the workplace

There is considerable theoretical debate over what really constitutes power. However, in practical terms there are two important dimensions. The first is the power that comes from resources. For example, employers typically have considerably greater financial and logistical resources, enabling them to secure better legal and other expertise than employees are typically able to access, greatly strengthening their hand in any dealings with the latter. All but the smallest firms have more than one employee, whereas most employees have only one employer. The second is that power is an action, and involves issues such as knowledge. Although employees may have more intimate knowledge of the process of production, employers are likely to have better general knowledge of the overall condition of the firm. This means that the latter will be in a more powerful position, but also that the former are not totally powerless.

THE BALANCE OF POWER BETWEEN EMPLOYERS AND EMPLOYEES

Scholars of employment relations differ significantly in their assessment of the balance of power between employers and employees. These differences are rooted in opposing conceptions of the basic structures of society and the nature of organisations (see Chapter 3). Pluralist approaches, for instance, assume that societies are composed of a variety of group interests, adopt an empirical conception of power at the organisational level, and develop a restricted definition of workers' interests that concentrates largely on collective bargaining. Class conflict (or radical) approaches, by contrast, assume that societies are structured by broader class forces, emphasise the underlying structures of social power, and link trade union objectives to the wider distribution of power and rewards in society. Consequently, pluralist approaches tend to assume that there is a rough parity of power between employers and employees as a collective, whereas class conflict approaches suggest that the power relations between management and trade unions are inherently asymmetrical. Pluralists tend to infer that a balance of power will result from a shared interest in survival, which forces the parties to work together. As a result, they confuse mutual dependence (both employers and employees depending on each other to some extent) with equal dependence.

Finding a stable and durable balance of power between employers and employees requires collective and political regulation of the employment relationship. However, the role of trade unions and the state in employment relations is a hotly contested topic. According to the neo-liberal perspective that has gained momentum over the last three decades, governments should (a) allow market forces to balance competitive interests; (b) deregulate markets, especially the labour market; (c) allow unemployment to rise in order to contain inflation and union power; and (d) emphasise the individual rather than the collective as the guiding principle of social organisation (Blyton and Turnbull 1998: 155). The role of the government is largely passive, although it actively protects property rights and circumscribes the power of trade unions. Since the laws of supply and demand (ie market forces) are regarded as the best means of coordinating conflicting interests, there is no need for labour laws or trade unions to protect the employee. The individual contract of employment is viewed as the most efficient and effective regulator of the relationship between employer and employee.

For pluralists, the organisation of employees into trade unions is a necessary part of redressing the power imbalances in the workplace. Organised associations are seen as crucial intermediary power centres between the government and the individual. The recognition of conflicting interest groups involves an acceptance of autonomous trade unions that represent, bargain and reconcile conflicting interests with management through the collective bargaining process. However, this process also ensures that the dominant interests of management are protected by maintaining a division between those issues that are determined by managerial prerogative and those that are determined through negotiation. The government's role is primarily one of providing the framework to reconcile the interests of management and workers. As such, policies that enhance the rights of employees (as a means of accommodating some of the interests of employees) exist alongside coercive measures that ensure the perpetuation of employer dominance. Meanwhile, class conflict (or radical) approaches stress the inability of market forces to define a specific system of employment relations, and the limited protection available for workers.

Conceptions of employment relations systems (such as Dunlop's approach, outlined in Chapter 3) are also influenced by (often implicit) notions of power. Dunlop (1958) locates the concept of power at the societal level (ie national industrial relations systems) rather than at more micro levels (ie the industry or workplace). This means that he does not explore the possibility of conflict between rules, the dynamics and sources of rule-breaking, the legitimacy of power at lower levels, and the relative bargaining power between the parties (Wood *et al* 1975: 302). Systems theorists' overriding concern with the 'problem of order' has, then, diverted attention away from the structures of power in the workplace.

Trade unions and collective bargaining are the principal mechanisms through which employees exert their power as a collective. Collective bargaining is not only a market mechanism shaping the sale of labour but also a political mechanism regulating the power relations between management and the union.

Terms and conditions of employment are therefore not only an outcome of the laws of supply and demand in the labour market but are also a product of the power struggles between the parties. The primary reason why an employer negotiates with a trade union is to institutionalise conflict. This involves recognising the power of employees and accepting that it could be used in a disruptive manner in the absence of negotiated settlements. Collectively negotiated rules are likely to be more legitimate than those unilaterally imposed by management. Collective bargaining thus protects employees from arbitrary action by management and brings a measure of democracy to working life, giving employees some say in matters that affect their working lives. However, as Sisson (1987: 12) points out, in exchange for subjecting certain rules to joint regulation, employers require the unions to recognise their right to make other rules unilaterally. That is, collective bargaining also has an inherent control dimension – it represents (Blyton and Turnbull 1998: 193):

> a potential source of managerial control in the way in which it institutionalises conflict by channelling the power of organised labour into a mechanism which, while acknowledging that power, at the same time circumscribes it and gives it a greater predictability.

However, collective bargaining will not be possible in situations where a union is not recognised. Moreover, even where a union is recognised, management can treat unions as an inferior party and ignore worker rights.

The case study below illustrates how the balance of power can be firmly in favour of management, and reveals the impacts of this for workers and trade unions.

CASE STUDY

THE BALANCE OF POWER BETWEEN EMPLOYER AND EMPLOYEES: THE CASE OF WAL-MART

A report in the *Guardian* newspaper (*Guardian* 2007) revealed that the large retail corporation then known as Wal-Mart had allegedly discriminated against older workers, forced workers to engage in unpaid overtime, and had attempted to prevent workers from organising through trade unions.

In order to prevent staff from participating in union activities, the company had allegedly undertaken a range of measures. These included pointing security cameras at areas where staff tended to gather, and providing managers with a manual that outlined how to avoid trade union organisation, including phoning a particular number if they suspected

staff of participating in union activities. Where unions appeared to be making some inroads, teams of 'union-busters' were apparently sent from Wal-Mart's headquarters to convince workers of the dangers of unionisation.

Questions

What does the above case tell you about power relations at Wal-Mart?

How might the labour movement redress the power imbalance between management and employees?

Should the government take action to change how Wal-Mart treats its employees? If so, what action should it take?

It should be noted that although Walmart (as it is currently spelled) is generally known for hardline HR practices, its UK subsidiary has adopted somewhat softer HR policies and practices. This will, in part, reflect the greater rights employees enjoy under UK law. However, it also reflects informal norms and rules – employees enter jobs in the UK with a different range of understandings and expectations from their US counterparts.

The next section examines in more detail how co-operation and compliance can be used to ensure managerial authority.

CO-OPERATION AND COMPLIANCE

The expectations and values of employees have to be accommodated to some extent if management wishes to avoid the costs associated with disruptions and high levels of labour turnover. The active co-operation of employees – as opposed to mere instrumental compliance – is essential for efficiency in the workplace and has to be sustained on a continuous basis. Although employers and employees have conflicting interests, they also co-operate. Conflict and co-operation constitute interconnected and mutually conditioning aspects of employment relations. Whether the parties engage in co-operative or conflictual behaviour depends on a calculation of the comparative benefits and losses of each approach. The latter, in turn, are dependent on the balance of power between employers and employees in both the workplace and the wider society. A key reason for co-operation in the workplace is that it 'can assist the functioning of an enterprise and thus help its managers and workers secure their own interests' (Edwards *et al* 2006: 126). This is a recurrent theme in the literature on employment relations. The *Applying theory to practice* box below considers the use of 'compliance' measures within the workplace and questions its sustainability over the longer term.

APPLYING THEORY TO PRACTICE

Using the appraisal system to ensure compliance

Many US firms have adopted approaches to performance appraisals whereby the proportion of workforce receiving the lowest appraisals (typically 10 to 20%) are simply fired.

What are the benefits and costs to firms of taking this approach?

How sustainable would you think that such models are?

As is the case with general HR policies, what firms can do in terms of dismissals is greatly dependent on context. The policies practised in the USA would be illegal in many European countries. However, in other countries employers may enjoy even more rights than in the USA. In contexts such as Colombia employers can resort – and, indeed, in some notable instances have resorted – to death squads in order to have recalcitrant employees tortured or murdered, with apparent legal impunity.

THE INDIVIDUAL EMPLOYMENT RELATIONSHIP AND THE EMPLOYMENT CONTRACT

The individual employment relationship is formally governed by the law of contract. A contract of employment is a voluntary agreement between two equal parties, with reciprocal rights and duties. One party (the employee) undertakes to place his or her personal services at the disposal of the other party (the employer) for an indefinite or determined period in exchange for a fixed wage. At the same time, the employer is entitled to define the employee's duties and to control the manner in which the employee discharges them. The contract of employment has three defining elements: an agreement to make personal services available, the payment of remuneration, and the subordination of the employee.

The employment relationship, however, is not a contractual relationship in the normal sense. A contract that grants broad powers of decision to one party and establishes the subordination of another is hardly an ordinary contract. Where market power is as unequal as it is between an employer and an employee, contractual arrangements are 'contracts only in form; in reality they are commands' (Streeck 1992: 41). As Kahn-Freund notes (cited in Davies and Freeland 1983: 17), the relation between an employer and an individual employee

> is typically a relation between a bearer of power and one who is not a bearer of power. In its inception it is an act of submission, in its operation it is a condition of subordination, however much the submission and the subordination may be concealed by that indispensable figment of the legal mind known as the 'contract of employment'.

The notion of a 'freely bargained' agreement hides the fact that the employee is subordinated to his or her employer (Fox 1974). The view of the employment relationship as a contractual relation between equals, according to Salamon (1998: 271–2), is based on three assumptions that are not sustainable: employment contracts are usually not between individuals, but rather between an individual and an organisation; the contract of employment is not simply an economic exchange, but also a means of subordinating the individual to the authority and control of the organisation; and there is an imbalance in the mutual dependence of employer and employee – that is, an employee depends far more on an employer for his or her livelihood than an employer depends on an individual employee as a source of income. Labour legislation and collective bargaining were introduced precisely to assuage this domination of the employee.

A contractual model of employment relations is ill-suited to the task of protecting employment rights since it is too uncertain, too committed to favouring the interests of employers, too exclusive of important categories of workers (such as those in informal work within emerging economies), and too concerned with individuals rather than collectives. It is also difficult to enshrine trust or co-operative and quality commitments in a contract, and contract performance is not always easily monitored. An employer's need for the co-operation of its employees thus cannot be secured by contract alone and has to be achieved in large measure through systems of bureaucratic control. If employers had to rely exclusively on contractual terms to govern the production of goods or services, they would face the impossible task of providing for every contingency and negotiating every change in the workplace. In fact, a largely open-ended employment relationship amounts to an employment contract with conditions that are almost infinitely variable on a daily basis. In practical terms, this means that no employment contract can ever be complete. It also means that much of what takes place at the workplace is due to informal agreements and conventions.

CORPORATE GOVERNANCE

Corporate governance concerns the manner in which a firm is governed, which in turn reflects the relative power of shareholders and other stakeholders, and regulation at both the formal and informal level. This will impact on a firm's strategies, the relative autonomy of management, and, of course, employment relations strategies. We saw earlier that institutions mediate the actions of firms and other social actors, and accordingly have a profound effect on how the firm is governed.

As Chandler (2005) notes, the historical emergence of the modern firm saw the rise of a professional managerial class and the increased systematisation of the managerial function. Critics argued that this led to professional managers diverging from the interests of owners. For example, managers would have a natural tendency to empire-build, and collude with employees (and even unions) in this agenda for reasons of power and prestige (La Porta *et al* 2002). The economic crisis of the 1970s forced a rethink on how firms did business. In practical terms, it led to a renewed emphasis on short-term returns, with legal reforms in many countries making it easier for shareholders to rein in managers and redirect them to the short-term pursuit of profit (Lazonick and O'Sullivan 2000). This has been achieved, at least partly, through incentives aimed at linking reward to share prices (see Chapter 9). It has been argued that such a link has had perverse effects. Managers are now less likely to act in the interests of the organisation and more likely to engage in destructive short-term measures to manipulate share prices (Boyer 2009).

SHAREHOLDERS AND STAKEHOLDERS

There are a number of ways in which the relationship between shareholders and other stakeholders (such as employees) may be seen. Firstly, it may be conceived as a zero-sum game – if, for example, employees gain new benefits, shareholders must lose. Anything that enhances employee rights is thus bad for business (La Porta *et al* 2002). Secondly, it may be conceived in the context of complementarity (that is, some practices may work better than an analysis of their component parts may suggest) (Brewster *et al* 2010). For example, decent pay and job security may encourage employees to increase their commitment and to develop organisation-specific skills, enhancing productivity and quality to a greater extent than would otherwise be the case. Dore (2000) argues that in some national contexts, such as the USA and the UK, shareholder rights are particularly strong; in others, such as Germany and Japan, stakeholders are vested with greater power.

> ### ? CRITICAL DEBATE
>
> **Stakeholder and shareholder power**
>
> It could be argued that where firms emphasise the role of shareholders over stakeholders they may emphasise short-term profits over long-term investment. This might be to the detriment of employees.
>
> Do you think that firms should prioritise shareholders over employees? Or should they prioritise the needs of employees over the concerns of shareholders?
>
> Give reasons for your answers.

CORPORATE GOVERNANCE AND EXECUTIVE/NON-EXECUTIVE DIRECTORS

Boards of directors have the function of overseeing the governance of a firm and ensuring that the interests of owners are served. This does not mean that owners are always interested in profits. For example, in Volkswagen, a major shareholder is the Lower Saxony regional government in Germany, which of course would be concerned with issues such as employment creation and regional development. Similarly, the French government retains a significant stake in the former state-owned car-maker Renault, and would have a similar agenda.

Executive directors are involved in the day-to-day running of the firm – in other words, they serve as both managers and directors. Non-executive directors may be:

- major shareholders
- worker representatives – In some countries, such as Germany, this is legally obligatory for all companies of a certain size. Such workers have to serve two interests: those of the rank-and-file workforce and of the firm as a whole, which may lead to contradictory pressures
- independent experts – In practice, these have often proved powerless to rein in excessive managerial pay or, indeed, to ensure that strategies are sustainable and are not likely to damage the long-term health of the organisation.

CORPORATE GOVERNANCE AND FINANCE

As Lazonick and O'Sullivan (2000) note, investors have, since the 1970s, become increasingly short-termist in their orientation. Critics have charged that this represents a process of 'financialisation' – financial intermediaries and investment fund managers have become considerably more proactive in securing short-term returns. This has led to collusions with management to maximise the release of value, to the detriment of employees and, indeed, long-term investors (Froud *et al* 2006). Although in reality financialisation may not genuinely represent such a coherent phenomenon, there is no doubt that finance and the workings of finance play a crucial role in the remaking of employment relations. The principal sources of firm finance, and how it is regulated, vary greatly between national contexts. Within liberal market economies, investors are more likely to be proactive and pursue short-term returns, rather than aim for the long-term stability of a firm and an industry. Within such national settings, new categories of investor, such as private equity, have become increasingly prominent.

CORPORATE SOCIAL RESPONSIBILITY

Continued economic volatility and high-profile organisational failures (such as Enron and Lehman Brothers) have together raised questions about the extent to which corruption may be systemically embedded. They have also led to calls for organisations to be more 'responsible' in the future and, indeed, to an increased emphasis on the teaching of corporate social responsibility and ethics in management schools. Yet corporate social responsibility may be conceived of in a range of different ways. It could be argued that adopting co-operative forms of people management may result in win/win situations (in other words, be good for both people and profits), so that there is a sound business case for acting responsibly towards employees. This argument is implicit in much of the HR literature. Alternatively, it could be argued that any decisions that are primarily prompted by short-term profitability concerns are devoid of moral worth. In any event, there is considerable evidence that firms can make money as easily from labour repression as good conduct (at least in the short term). Any business case arguments to act responsibly are therefore unlikely to be fully convincing.

MANAGERIAL LEGITIMACY

In the light of the open-ended and indeterminate nature of the wage–effort bargain, organisations structure work in ways that tend to reinforce and reproduce management's control over labour. By virtue of its ownership of the means of production, capital has the 'right' to control both the physical and human elements of the production process. However, a labour process can rarely, if ever, be designed to eliminate the need for initiative and co-operation from employees. This means that control has to be (Keenoy, cited in Blyton and Turnbull 1998: 77):

> constructed in a fashion which also 'manufactures' consent ...
> [H]owever imbalanced the distribution of power, the controlled always have some leverage on the terms of the exchange. No matter how extensive the controls, in the final analysis management is reliant on employee co-operation.

The managerial control necessary to regulate the employment relationship and to establish order in the workplace creates a force over and against the employees. Control may compel a subject to carry out a specific task, raise the costs of doing or not doing something, preventing an agent from doing something that he or she might prefer to do, or penalise an agent for doing or failing to do something. Control is not always or necessarily coterminous with subordination. Social agents may see control as 'inevitable' or 'natural', and it may induce accommodation, deference, fear, resistance, flight, acquiescence and/ or resignation (Standing 1999: 35). Moreover, there are practical limits to how far the employer can subordinate the employee, as well as definite disadvantages in the form of potentially reduced levels of worker creativity and co-operation. A system of employment relations reflects the specific compromise made between control and consent and highlights the need to maintain an institutional framework capable of sustaining that compromise. The construction of discipline over workers depends on a day-to-day negotiation of order. There are often genuine efforts to sustain an implicit bargain, with managers being careful to maintain certain standards of 'fairness'. Punitive and autocratic disciplinary measures simply have too many adverse effects on morale and efficiency. Consequently, management usually strives to underpin its power with consent and reciprocity.

HOW DO MANAGERS ENSURE THAT THEY ARE SEEN AS LEGITIMATE 'RULERS'?

According to Weber's analysis, bureaucracies contain an over-arching rational-legal value system that is embodied in the company rules, internalised as the orientation of its members, and provides both the norms of effective work performance and the legitimation of managerial authority (Gerth and Mills 1977). To understand the organisation of a modern workplace, according to Weber, we need to understand the development of industrial bureaucracy. The key elements of bureaucracy – hierarchy, specialisation, impersonality and formalised rules – all reflect its control function. This primacy of the control function of bureaucracies requires that they appear impartial and therefore as legitimate. Weber regarded bureaucratisation as an inherent feature of the development of economic enterprises. The growth of bureaucracies was necessitated by an increase in the size of the enterprise, growing specialisation and mechanisation, and an increase in the size and functions of management.

Bureaucracies are distinctive for their use of direct, detailed and specific control, represented in elaborate rules and procedures. When they first emerged, bureaucratic forms of organisation were based on entirely new forms of authority. They were seen as rational in the sense of consisting of systems of calculable, quantifiable and explicit procedures and rules. That is, bureaucratisation reflects attempts at imposing a network of rules, regulations and hence predictability on employees. Weber emphasised that bureaucracies are the clearest example of rational authority and were structured in accordance with rational principles of free contract and fixed salaries (cited in Gerth and Mills 1977). Three important consequences flow from the process of bureaucratisation: the development of strict work discipline and job fragmentation, the imposition of uniformity and calculability of performance, and the impersonal and seemingly rational nature of control.

Weber analyses managerial power in terms of the manner in which legitimation converts power into authority. Unlike Marx, Weber's theory of domination did not depend largely on economic mechanisms of control. For him, the compliance of subordinates rested on their attitudes towards and perceptions of the legitimacy of the control relationship (cited in Gerth and Mills 1977). The orders of superiors are obeyed because they are regarded by subordinates as reflecting acceptable rational-legal norms. Weber did not argue that the legitimation of authority through bureaucratic administration is, by itself, sufficient to control subordinates. Like Marx, he assumed that industrial control in market economies demanded an essential degree of economic need and normative acceptance of a work ethic and bureaucratic authority.

It is often pointed out that legitimacy is never total and is never granted unconditionally. Managerial authority and worker obedience are always fluid and open to renegotiation. The Weberian theory of domination is therefore criticised for being incomplete (Storey 1983; Thompson 1989). The day-to-day compliance of workers has little to do with legitimation and can best be described as consent or compliance. The consent of workers to managerial authority depends crucially on material incentives, and legitimacy may be too wide a concept to explain all instances of co-operation by employees. Furthermore, worker consent to managerial authority is not tied only to formal organisational procedures but is also sustained by other socio-economic and political institutions (such as markets and governments).

With the development of large-scale industries, it was soon realised that if no effort was made to create some cohesion between management and labour, workers were unlikely to pursue the interests of management or accept the legitimacy of managerial power. The arguments of Burawoy (1985) are particularly important in this regard. He supports the idea that there has been a move towards bureaucratic forms of control, which rest more on rules and procedures than on coercion. According to Burawoy (1985), bureaucratic control is more efficient in generating the consent of workers than Taylorism or Fordism because (a) control is not experienced as emanating from the discretionary power of the manager or from the technology of production but is institutionalised and appears to flow from the formal structures of the organisation; and (b) the proper functioning of bureaucratic control rests on the institutionalisation of positive incentives for the employee to become a 'good' worker, whereas Taylorism and Fordism rely almost exclusively on negative sanctions to prod recalcitrant workers into efficient action. Burawoy (1985) shows that (a) workers do not always need to be overtly controlled and may effectively 'control' themselves, especially if they are in skilled and white-collar jobs; (b) the imposition of hegemonic forms of control and the creation of informal rules allow workers to adapt and transform the labour process as a means of coming to terms with their working lives – in other words, managerial control is related to the subjective consent of workers; and (c) it is impossible to arrive at an adequate understanding of the labour process without taking account of broader political, ideological and socio-economic relations.

By allowing employees a certain degree of autonomy and by emphasising co-operation, management hopes to obscure the conflicting interests of capital and labour. One critical aspect of this form of control is the institutionalisation of various kinds of procedural safeguards in the workplace. Under despotic forms of control, employers use coercion and threats. With hegemonic control (the ideas of management being accepted by workers), by contrast, workers' efforts are based on consent and are not the response to direct surveillance and threats. However, according to Burawoy (1978) coercion is still needed to control deviant employees. Whereas Taylorism and Fordism had the tendency to unite the workforce, hegemonic control attempts to segment and stratify the workforce by encouraging competition between workers inside the workplace. Hegemonic control, however, does not involve a complete break with earlier forms of control. The impact of Taylorism, for example, is still evident in the fact that the content of jobs remains highly routinised, standardised, fragmented, and defined in detail by management.

APPLYING THEORY TO PRACTICE

Taylorism today

To what extent do you agree that the content of jobs remains highly routinised, standardised, fragmented, and defined in detail by management?

In answering this question you might wish to think about jobs in manufacturing, jobs in retail, and jobs in call centres.

CHANGE MANAGEMENT AND MANAGERIAL CONTROL

The processes of workplace restructuring that have unfolded since the 1980s are conceptualised in different ways: flexible specialisation, the Japanisation of work, new production concepts, manufacturing excellence, high-performance management and lean production. Each of these has formed the focus of change management programmes. Which of these ideal types will consolidate or combine in the future remains an open and vexed question. A general assumption is the notion that changes in the workplace involve a fundamental departure from the employment patterns and mechanisms of control associated with the Taylorist and Fordist organisation of mass production. However, these recent developments, which seem to offer a cycle of growth, seriously underestimate the deep-seated constraints on changes in work and employment arrangements. Ultimately, the restructuring of the employment relationship involves reasserting the priorities of management. Because it does, change management is about reconfiguring managerial authority in an effort to retain control.

CHANGE MANAGEMENT PROGRAMMES

Much of the practice of employment relations is about continuity. Yet both employers and unions can, and do, make real strategic choices. This may concern organisational structures, new priorities, the use of technologies, and the relative importance attached to the short versus the medium and long term. In the case of the employer, changes that impact on the employment contract (for example, reducing the size of the firm) are likely to have legal implications. Similarly, choices as to what types of employment contract to offer in the future (such as a greater use of temporary labour, and different terms and conditions of service) may require some negotiation with unions. Key issues in change management include:

- managerial fads – many firms fall victim to following ever-changing managerial fads

- the implications for staff morale – firms must be realistic about the reasons why employees may not be enthusiastic about change, and must also be aware of the importance of making the benefits more transparent

- the challenges of securing buy-in – top-down change initiatives may be difficult to operationalise in practice

- re-establishing continuity in the aftermath of change – a climate of ongoing 'creative destruction' is likely to prove pathological.

CHANGE MANAGEMENT PROGRAMMES USED AS AN INSTRUMENT OF MANAGERIAL CONTROL

The 'problem' of motivation dominates modern management theory and has forced managers to turn to social scientists and their ideas on 'job enrichment', the 'quality of working life' and 'employee participation'. While these techniques are a conscious managerial attempt at integrating the workforce and securing employee consent, they often do not depart significantly from Taylorism and Fordism and are therefore unable to overcome alienation, discontent and resistance. Managers want involved and co-operative workers – but only within limits, for they do not want to lose control. For instance, some management theorists have warned against employee participation schemes since there is no telling where, once such a scheme is set in motion, it might lead. A survey of British managers by Poole and Mansfield (cited in Blyton and Turnbull 1994: 212) found that they appear to:

> support most employee involvement practices so long as these do not radically affect their control function within the firm. In other words, they tend to prefer a unitary rather than a pluralist approach to employee participation in decision-making.

Boyer (1988) draws a broad distinction between defensive and offensive forms of flexibility. Whereas the former is associated with the establishment of more individualised employment relations and rising inequality, the latter represents a more organised, regulated and collectivised labour setting. On the one hand, management may seek to maintain unilateral control of the workplace by maintaining its prerogative and sustaining the widest possible freedom and discretion to act as it sees fit. On the other hand, management may include workers and their representatives in the organisation's decision-making processes and accept joint regulation of terms and conditions of employment. The essential contrast is therefore between (a) low-discretion, low-trust, rule-bound and hierarchical forms of control, and (b) high-discretion, low-specificity, high-trust and decentralised forms of control. Most change management programmes are associated with the latter. However, often managerial strategies fall between these extremes. As Legge (1995: 14) explains, the fact that

> personnel specialists oscillate between the 'personnel' and 'management', between 'caring' and 'control' aspects of the function, can be attributed to their role in mediating a major contradiction embedded in capitalist systems: the need to achieve both the control *and* consent of employees.

Much of the literature on management's role in changing employment relations can be crudely divided in terms of whether the emphasis is on control *or* coordination. As Hyman (1975) points out, while most orthodox literature on business strategy ignores or marginalises the conflict between capital and labour, most Marxist literature perceives nothing else. A growing consensus is emerging which suggests that such either/or dichotomies are inappropriate and misleading: the real task is to understand the relationship between control and coordination. In capitalist societies, management has evolved as a specialised institution with two dimensions: (a) coordination to ensure the productive use of machinery, raw materials, and so on; and (b) the exercise of authority over the performance of employees through the imposition of a hierarchy of powers and rewards.

Change management often involves a restructuring of managerial relations (power-centred) and a redesign of jobs (task-centred). The distinction between 'hard' production-oriented and 'soft' employee-oriented elements in the managerial process reflects the fact that participatory schemes may increase the scope of employee input into managerial decisions without altering the underlying structures of the workplace. As Geary's (1994: 650) survey of participatory schemes shows: 'management has at once become enabling and restraining'. Given the tension in the very purpose of managerial control – namely, that managers require workers to be 'both dependable and disposable' (Hyman, 1987: 43) – it is hardly surprising that the management of employment relations is marked by contradiction and vacillation.

REFLECTION ON PRACTICE

Change management in practice

Think of a time when the organisation that you were working in wanted to make an important change.

How was that change communicated to employees?

Did the change result in a 'restructuring of managerial relations' – a redistribution of power from some people to others?

Did the change result in a redesign of jobs?

RESISTANCE TO CHANGE

Class conflict approaches to employment relations do not assume a concurrence between the needs of employees and those of the employer. As a result, there is a broader understanding of industrial conflict that starts from the structured antagonism between capital and labour. The workplace is a contested terrain: employers attempt to extract the maximum effort from employees, while employees necessarily resist such impositions (Edwards 1979). As a result, the construction of discipline in the workplace depends on a day-to-day negotiation of order. The need to expand profits and retain overall control of the enterprise means that there is a constant pressure within management to resist any extension of collective regulation and to restore unilateral regulation whenever possible. However, the maintenance of an extensive managerial prerogative often leads to confrontation and cannot provide the basis for a long-term co-operative relationship between management and workers.

Management have a range of possible tactics that they can use to overcome resistance to change, including giving workers more discretion over tasks if they work with management. The degree of discretion conceded to workers will be dependent on the levels of worker resistance and competitive market pressures. Management and labour are involved in a give-and-take situation, with a changing balance of power. The limits of managerial authority and employee obedience are imprecise and always open to renegotiation. Worker autonomy, however, is always conditional in that it cannot be allowed to obstruct managerial goals of productivity and profitability if the enterprise is to survive.

Insofar as change management programmes involve an attempt at reasserting managerial control over the production of goods and services, they are likely to be opposed and challenged by employees in a range of different ways. These variations have been found to result in significant differences, not only in the degree of control that management is able to exert over a particular segment of the workforce but also in the means by which management attempts to exert its control. However, change management programmes tend to enhance the security of some employees while increasing the precariousness of others. This is particularly evident in the association between change management and the proliferation of vulnerable and precarious forms of non-standard employment. Moreover, where unions have succeeded in turning new production techniques into gains for their members, it has often been at the expense of non-standard workers.

Management can use voice mechanisms to promote change. Management-sponsored forms of employee participation usually mean that workers are expected to adopt the interests of the enterprise (eg quality and efficiency) as their own. However, this does not mean that the labour movement has to buy in to a consensual approach. On the assumption that 'successful militancy' demonstrates union effectiveness and therefore encourages the expansion or consolidation of union density, 'then in principle a strategy of militancy through collective bargaining and political action could prove to be at least as effective as co-operation' (Kelly 1996: 54). But this argument tends to underestimate the impact of divisions in the labour market. For workers who do not perceive a serious conflict of interests with their employer, or alternatively are so fearful of losing their job that they dare not challenge management's authority, appeals to militancy are not likely to prove an effective recruitment tactic (Hyman 1996: 77). Militant trade unionism has historically been based on semi-skilled workers in manual occupations, excluding highly paid skilled workers and poorly paid unskilled or temporary employees.

Union militancy has often encouraged employers to seek out less adversarial and less powerful channels of worker representation. Indeed, the level of trade union interest in workers' control and industrial democracy via extended collective bargaining is normally matched by employer interest in rival schemes of 'employee involvement' (Kelly 1996: 60). By involving employees with the aim of their obtaining a better understanding of challenges facing the enterprise, employers hope that they will accept managerial decisions. The 'social partnership' ideology inscribed in new managerial strategies may well undermine the (viable and serious) alternative of militant trade unionism that has been so effective in the past in South Africa, Brazil, the Scandinavian countries, Canada and elsewhere.

◀◉▶ REFLECTION ON PRACTICE

Overcoming resistance to change

Think again of a time (as explored in the previous *Reflection on practice*) when management wanted to implement change in the organisation.

Was there any resistance to change? In other words, did employees like the idea of change? If they did not, how did they try to stop that change from happening?

If you have not worked in an organisation where you were aware of significant changes happening, consider instead how employees working in the housing section of a local authority (responsible for building housing for local people who might be living in poverty) might react if they were told that they were going to move to open-plan offices.

How might they try to resist that change?

OVERCOMING RESISTANCE TO CHANGE

There is little to be gained – and much to be lost – by abandoning the principle of co-operation in employment relations. Meaningful co-operation in the workplace cannot be premised on a denial of the existence of conflict between management and labour, but rather relies on a commitment to manage this conflict through negotiation and compromise. A durable balance between flexibility and security is best achieved through collective agreements between employers and employee representatives. To increase productivity both management and labour must be ready and willing to adapt to new forms of workplace organisation. This is best achieved through consultations between the relevant stakeholders. Periods of rapid and deep-seated economic restructuring demand high levels of flexibility and are associated with high levels of labour market insecurity. The efficacy and dynamism of the processes of workplace restructuring are vitally dependent on regulated participation by the social partners.

The nature of collective employment relations has a profound impact on the levels of co-operation that are possible or feasible in a given workplace. Change management tends to be most effective in a context where employers and trade unions regulate workers' participatory demands in a way that prevents any threat to either collective bargaining or co-operation in the workplace. The value of an institutionalised system of collective employee voice is often overlooked by the proponents of direct forms of employee representation such as quality circles. There is a basic contrast between, on the one hand, making no attempt to become involved in the management process but endeavouring to bargain over it, and on the other hand, becoming a part of the decision-making processes. Despite implying different routes to change management, both approaches accentuate the significance of the links between the workplace and the wider union. A participatory approach to change management is thus more likely to succeed where there is a tradition of collaboration and co-operation in the workplace. Such a tradition is difficult to generate in the context of weak unions and widespread mistrust.

POWER AND AUTHORITY IN NON-UNION FIRMS

In non-union firms, the relative power of employees is likely to be weaker. However, as we have seen, no employee is totally powerless. Employees possess considerable knowledge of the actual process of production and are repositories of accumulated organisation-specific knowledge and wisdom. This means that employers will still seek to find ways of securing the co-operation of employees beyond the narrow terms and conditions of the employment contract (Charlwood 2006). It may be on a coercive basis (ie through implicit threats of marginalisation or dismissal for not 'going the extra mile') or on a more positive basis, through additional incentives (eg bonuses), through participative mechanisms aimed at giving employees a greater say, or through team-building.

SUMMARY

Power and authority are central aspects of the employment relationship, and management asserts its power through a range of mechanisms. However, change management programmes require co-operation which demands more than simply a change in the attitudes or values of the parties. The real challenge is to establish an institutional framework within the workplace that allows interests to be represented and that is also capable of striking a sustainable balance between efficiency and equity and between flexibility and security. If employees regard change management programmes as attempts to achieve efficiency and flexibility at the expense of equity and security, managers are unlikely to secure the co-operation and compliance necessary to realise the objectives of their programmes. Providing employees with security is not simply a political imperative in a democratic society, it is also an effective economic strategy. For example, where employers and the government demonstrate a commitment to ensuring meaningful employment security, employees are far more likely to accept a significant degree of work process and wage flexibility. The success of many of the rapidly growing East Asian economies was based on a combination of security and flexibility, the former being used to secure the latter.

EXPLORE FURTHER

Reading

- Brewster, C., Goergen, M. and Wood, G. (2010) 'Corporate governance systems and employment relations', in A. Wilkinson and M. Townsend (eds) *The Future of Employment Relations: New paradigms, new developments*. Basingstoke: Palgrave Macmillan

- Edwards, P., Bélanger, J. and Wright, M. (2006) 'The bases of compromise in the workplace', *British Journal of Industrial Relations*, Vol.44, No.1: 125–45

- Storey, J. (1983) *Managerial Prerogative and the Question of Control*. London: Routledge & Kegan Paul

Website

- The Partnership Institute www.partnership-institute.co.uk

CHAPTER 7

Voice

CHAPTER OVERVIEW

Earlier in this volume we noted the centrality of the concepts of 'voice' and 'exit' in the employment relationship (see Chapter 1). Voice concerns the process by which – and the structures and procedures whereby – employees communicate with management, with a view to improving the terms and conditions of work and/or employment. Renegotiating the terms and conditions of employment may often challenge the managerial agenda, but altering work relations might be of benefit to both managers and employees. For example, changes in work organisation may make production more efficient and more pleasant. Of course, employers may have an interest in greater control, but they may also have, for example, an interest in offloading some of the supervisory responsibility onto workers themselves. The issue of voice thus concerns both potential conflict and co-operation. It may reflect irreconcilable differences or hold out the prospect of new compromises and complementarities.

LEARNING OUTCOMES

After studying this chapter you should be able to:

- understand the importance of effective communication within the workplace, and discuss a variety of consultation mechanisms
- define what is meant by 'involvement', 'participation' and 'industrial democracy'
- explain the constraints, opportunities and limits of participation
- understand the dynamics of collective and individual bargaining
- describe effective negotiation and persuasion skills
- describe the nature of voice in non-union firms
- outline the critical role of employment relations specialists and line managers

COMMUNICATION

Does communication matter? Early forms of industrial organisation concentrated on control, or, in some instances, focused on giving incentives based on the work performed. However, a great range of writers – ranging from Karl Marx, Max Weber and Emile Durkheim to Adam Smith – recognised that the workplace represents a social context, and that social ties and co-operation between workers in the same position are of great importance in making production possible. At an applied level, the pioneering Hawthorne experiments of the 1920s and early 1930s conducted at Western Electric confirmed the extent to which social networks between workers mattered not only in terms of the immediate process of production but in shaping and reshaping attitudes towards work, the organisation and careers. This led Mayo (1933, 1945) to conclude that if managers better understood social attitudes and ties, people could be managed more effectively. Indeed, Mayo went so far as to suggest that the bulk of conflict in the workplace was simply due to misunderstandings – both sides had an interest in the prosperity of the organisation. This led to the rise of the human relations approach to people management, centred on promoting ways of more effective communication. On the one hand, there is little doubt that many everyday grievances and issues can be resolved through a better understanding of the other side's point of view. On the other hand – as we noted earlier in the introductory chapter – the employment contract is an unclear exchange, and whereas employers have an interest in maximising profit, a main concern of employees is the maximisation of wages. By working together the proverbial pie may be bigger, but it still has to be shared out, and there will inevitably be at least some divergence of interests in the slice of the pie awarded to each party.

MECHANISMS FOR COMMUNICATION

Communication may assume a number of different forms. Firstly, there is informal day-to-day contact between managers and employees, which may primarily centre on verbal instructions. Whereas feedback may be solicited, 'bad news' or unwelcome opinions may not. Individual workers are vulnerable of being typecast as 'difficult', 'complainers' and/or 'awkward', opening themselves up to retaliation by management. Retaliation may be immediate or deferred, and assume a range of forms from outright dismissal to low-key victimisation, with subtle alterations in working conditions and career advancement possibilities. In many contexts, workers thus have incentives to err on the side of caution, filtering out bad news or presenting information in a manner that they think will be most likely to please their superiors. Although comforting, this means that managers may remain ignorant of serious organisational problems and challenges. In contrast, collective and representative voice affords workers the protection of the group; it is more difficult to victimise a large number of people than a single individual, and the collective concerns of many are likely to be taken more seriously (Wood *et al* 2004).

Given these limitations, some forms of individual communication and feedback are designed to afford the employee the comfort of anonymity. Although this does not mean that a single complaint will necessarily be taken seriously, it does mean that victimisation and retaliation is less likely – individuals can take the risk of presenting 'bad news'. Most commonly, such forms of communication take the form of staff surveys or suggestion boxes. However, individuals may be asked to give their names, those making the best suggestions for improving work organisation or other aspects of production being given a reward. The problem with such mechanisms is that they may lack legitimacy. Managers are under no obligation to act on the information that is given to them. In the end, such schemes only work if they have a reputation for being taken seriously. For example, suggestion boxes/schemes have a good track record among certain areas of Japanese manufacturing, but a poor one among more traditionally minded British firms. Meanwhile, a limitation of staff surveys is 'survey fatigue'. In contemporary society, individuals are often subject to surveys in many different forms, some of which are poorly designed and far too long, leading the respondent to lose interest early in the process.

Other forms of communication include meetings. However, many organisations battle to strike a balance between short, concise (and often top-down and inherently authoritarian) meetings and lengthy, rambling proceedings. Cynical commentators have accordingly charged that meetings often represent little more than a practical alternative to work. In the 1980s and 1990s the idea of 'team briefings' came into vogue, whereby key information would be cascaded down the organisation in a short and easily accessible form to groups or teams of employees, with representatives of management/supervisors explaining issues that were unclear, answering questions and, in some instances, soliciting feedback. A limitation of team briefings is that they can be a somewhat mechanical process, snippets of information being presented on a regular basis, rather than a forum in which really important information is disseminated as and when needed. This explains why they appear to have gone out of fashion in recent years.

Noticeboards and company newsletters represent further mechanisms for disseminating information. However, these may lack legitimacy and can either include too much superfluous material or be only irregularly updated (in the case of noticeboards) or produced (newsletters). Such forms of communication are likely to work best if employees are given space of their own. But because such forms have so public a nature, managers are likely to carefully filter what is presented and what is not. Within unionised workplaces, a good deal of communication may take place as supervisors inform shop stewards about everyday concerns, grievances and petty disputes.

Other mechanisms commonly employed include semi-autonomous/autonomous teams and quality circles. In the case of teamworking, workers are accorded responsibility in the execution of an identifiable component of the production process. This invests work with more meaning, such that workers take responsibility for a range of quality and supervisory issues. However, two problems may emerge. Firstly, this may challenge the position and authority of junior managers and supervisors, who may resent or seek to undermine this process. Ideally, their role should shift to that of facilitators, but this may require considerable retraining. Secondly, some jobs lend themselves better to such work than others – highly deskilled and repetitive jobs where the rate of production may be readily monitored electronically (for example, junk food outlets and call centres) rarely lend themselves to this kind of involvement. A further means of communication is through collective bargaining and works councils, which are often deemed to form a central part of employment relations (and are dealt with in more detail in later sections).

A limitation of all involvement mechanisms is that they concern work relations rather than the employment contract. Yet employee concerns about their employment contracts may affect how receptive they are to schemes that involve them in the process of production. Moreover, employees may differ in how they respond to communication. Such different views towards involvement mechanisms are highlighted in the *Applying theory to practice* box below.

APPLYING THEORY TO PRACTICE

Divergent views of involvement mechanisms

There may be different views about the likely effectiveness of involvement mechanisms. These differences may be influenced by an employee's position within the same organisation.

A manager within Organisation X described the effects of an employee involvement scheme as follows (Wood and Sela 2000):

> *By giving the worker more responsibility, you are actually showing that you have trust and faith in them. Trust is vitally important in any type of working relationship. They are more willing to co-operate with you.*

However, within the same enterprise, some employees complained that junior managers and supervisors often did not trust them, and were prone to disrupt production with frequent inspections. They evidently did not feel that they were empowered in their work.

Which voice mechanisms are likely to help employees to feel empowered?

What can get in the way of employee empowerment?

The following sections define key terms for voice mechanisms, and outline the ways in which they might be exhibited within organisations.

DEFINING THE TERMS 'INDUSTRIAL DEMOCRACY', 'PARTICIPATION' AND 'EMPLOYEE INVOLVEMENT'

'Industrial democracy', 'employee 'participation' and 'employee involvement' are often used interchangeably to describe the processes and institutions of employee influence on decision-making at the workplace. Moreover, employee involvement or participation is primarily a philosophy, not a particular institutional form. This means that it may assume different organisational, social, political, economic and ideological functions. It may be there to promote greater fairness and equity, to redistribute power, and/or to make organisations work more effectively in attaining predetermined strategic goals.

The impetus for greater employee influence over decision-making processes stems from demands by employees and unions for an increased say in the running of the organisation as well as a realisation by management that technological and organisational changes could be implemented more effectively with the active participation of the employees concerned. Governments may also compel management to open certain decision-making processes to employee influence in an attempt to extend democracy from the political sphere to the workplace, and/or to promote greater social harmony and industrial efficiency.

The term 'industrial democracy' refers to the introduction of democratic procedures to restructure the power and authority relationships in organisations, thereby creating a system that involves employee self-management and control over production (Salamon 1998: 353–5). An extreme form of industrial democracy is worker-controlled and managed enterprises, or co-operatives. However, not all employee-owned enterprises are inherently democratic, and more conventional organisational forms may incorporate democratic features in the interests of efficiency, of philanthropy, or in order to reduce conflict.

Employee 'participation' refers to the influence of employees over terms and conditions of employment through collective bargaining, as well as their influence on work organisation and the deployment of new technologies. Common examples of mechanisms used in participation include works councils and joint consultative committees (JCCs). Works councils are required by the law in all organisations other than the smallest in size in many continental European countries. JCCs tend to be voluntary and may be unilaterally introduced by management. Although it could be argued that they have the potential to undermine unions and collective bargaining – by subsuming issues traditionally covered by unions – research has indicated that they do not have more adverse effects on unions than works councils. In both instances, they appear to complement union activity (Brewster *et al* 2007a).

Employee 'involvement' is often associated with human resource management and the introduction of a range of techniques. Quality circles involve workers meeting in company time to discuss measures to improve the efficiency and/or quality of production. These measures have been introduced by management to optimise the utilisation of labour, increase organisational flexibility, and secure the employees' identification with and commitment to the goals of the organisation. Team briefings may allow new information to be cascaded down the organisation, but may provide scope only for limited feedback. Employees may be also involved via company newsletters, intranets, through opinion surveys and suggestion boxes. More traditional forms of involvement include general meetings and informal consultation with workers on an *ad hoc* basis. A common feature of all of these forms of involvement is that management provides mechanisms for employees to express their views. However, management is normally under no obligation to adopt these opinions or even take them seriously. The entire process may therefore be devoid of legitimacy, which may defeat the entire purpose of the exercise. In contrast, 'participation' suggests that managers have conceded some real power to workers and will at least seek a compromise with them.

The situation is further complicated in that involvement tends to be direct – in other words, managers deal directly with individual workers. Given that participation is often about negotiation, this is often conducted on a representative basis: in other words, managers engage with worker representatives, who may represent the workforce directly or, alternatively, indirectly via a trade union.

◉ REFLECTION ON PRACTICE

Voice mechanisms

Which voice mechanisms are most commonly used in the organisation where you work (or have worked)?

Why do you think that these voice mechanisms were most common? Was this related to the presence/influence of a trade union? Was it related to the degree to which managers wished to allow employees to influence higher-level decision-making?

LEGISLATION RELATING TO INVOLVEMENT AND PARTICIPATION

Various rights to consultation and bargaining are enshrined in law. It is not possible here to outline all legislation in this area. The example of the United Kingdom is used to illustrate legislation within one country, and the way in which the introduction of legislation has been impacted upon by an international institution – specifically, the European Union.

In the United Kingdom, employment legislation has often been influenced by European Union Directives, one of the most important of which is the Directive for informing and consulting employees, which gives employees the right to be informed about their business's economic situation, employment prospects, and decisions that are likely to lead to substantial changes in work organisation or contractual relations, including redundancies and transfers. However, it is possible for employers and employees to agree alternative procedures to those outlined in the Directive or use existing agreements. This Directive has been implemented in stages since 2005, but now applies to all businesses with more than 50 employees.

Secondly, employees of large multinational companies based in the UK and with a presence elsewhere in Europe have a right to ask for a European Works Council (EWC) to be set up. An EWC is a body that represents employees of the multinational in the European Economic Area (EEA) in discussions with management on transnational issues. The limitation to transnational issues is due to the prior existence of national-level consultative arrangements within multinationals in many countries. The right to be represented by an EWC was first introduced by the European Works Council Directive in 1994. This was extended to cover the UK in 1997 and was implemented in the UK via the Transnational Information and Consultation of Employees Regulations 1999. A new EWC Directive was agreed in May 2009, which retained the structure and overall approach of the earlier Directive while introducing some important changes. In the UK, the Transnational Information and Consultation of Employees (Amendment) Regulations 2010 implement the new Directive. The legislation applies to multinationals that have at least 1,000 employees in the European Economic Area and at least 150 employees in each of at least two EEA member states. (The EEA is composed of the member states of the European Union plus Norway, Iceland and Liechtenstein (Department for Business Information and Skills, 2010)). Further information on this legislation can be found from the Department for Business Information and Skills (BIS) website, www.bis.gov.uk.

Employees in the UK must also be consulted on health and safety at work. The Safety Representatives and Safety Committees Regulations 1977 require an employer to consult union safety representatives on health and safety where a trade union is recognised by the employer. Employees who are not covered by trade union safety representatives must be consulted by their employer either directly or through elected representatives under the Health and Safety (Consultation with Employees) Regulations 1996. However, where existing agreements are in line with legislation, these can be used. The Health and Safety Executive website gives further details on legal requirements for consultation in this area within the UK (hse.gov.uk). Again, the legislation will vary according to country context. That which applies within the UK is generally held to be quite comprehensive.

Other areas for consultation include redundancy and occupational pensions. Redundancy is covered in more detail in Chapter 13. However, here it is worth noting that employers in the UK are required to consult employees when considering making employees redundant for a range of reasons, including transfers of staff to other organisations. With regard to occupational pensions, the Social Security Pensions Act 1975 requires employers to consult with independent recognised trade unions on the contracting-out of an occupational pension scheme from the state scheme, while the Occupational and Personal Pension Schemes Regulations 2006 require employers to inform and consult employee representatives about planned changes to pensions. In addition, organisations with more than 250 employees are required by the Companies Act 1985 (as amended by the Companies Act 1989) to include a statement in their Director's report describing actions in relation to information, consultation and financial participation (ACAS, 2005).

This brief summary of UK legislation provides an insight into the wide scope of legislation that exists in this area, and also the way in which national legislation is influenced by international institutions. The regulations do, of course, vary in different countries. However, similar national-level legislation has been or will be enacted within all countries where EU Directives are applicable.

INVOLVEMENT AND PARTICIPATION

A TYPOLOGY OF EMPLOYEE INVOLVEMENT AND PARTICIPATION

There has been extensive debate over the levels of influence that employees can or should exercise over decision-making processes at the workplace (Farnham and Pimlott 1979: 428–34). As noted above, industrial democracy, employee participation and employee involvement represent descending levels of control by employees over work and organisations. However, participation itself may vary in terms of efficiency. In her classic work on the subject, Pateman (1970) identifies three different kinds of employee participation:

- 'pseudo' participation – management uses participation as a way of persuading workers to accept decisions that have already been made

- 'partial' participation – two or more parties are able to influence the decisions that are made but the final power rests with one of them. For example, management may negotiate, but ultimately decides on what offers are made and how much to concede

- 'full' participation – a process in which each member of a decision-making body has equal power to determine the outcome of decisions.

Marked variations are possible in:

- the extent of employee participation

- the scope of decisions subject to participation

- the form that participatory structures may assume

- the persons that are party to participatory arrangements

- the organisational levels at which participation occurs

- the purpose and outcomes of participatory actions.

The extent of employee voice may, as we have seen, range from mere information disclosure by management through consultation and negotiation to co-determination, which involves more or less equal influence in setting agendas and determining the outcome of decision-making processes. However, there are few, if any, concrete examples that would satisfy Pateman's (1970) notion of 'full' participation. The range or scope of issues usually depends on a number of interlocking variables including (Blyton and Turnbull, 1998: 226):

- the attitudes of the parties, especially management's commitment to a long-term participatory endeavour

- the extent to which participation is based on statutory compulsion or voluntary agreement

- the degree of stability in product markets

- the nature of ownership and organisational characteristics (such as size, degree of centralisation in decision-making and available resources)

- the levels of experience and skill among employees and their representatives to engage in participation.

With regard to the persons that are party to participatory arrangements, a distinction is often made between employees participating directly in decision-making structures and participation that is achieved indirectly via the election of representatives.

DIRECT AND REPRESENTATIVE VOICE

It was explained above that voice may be direct or via representatives. As Hyman (1997: 327) notes, however, the concept of 'direct' forms of employee representation assumes that 'employees can articulate their own interests effectively without collective intermediation'. Direct voice may occur when an employee's job responsibilities are extended through a process of job redesign and the delegation of certain managerial functions. Indirect participation is best exemplified by collective bargaining and refers to the processes through which employee representatives influence organisational decision-making (Farnham and Pimlott 1979: 423–6; Nel *et al* 2005: 291–4).

The level at which participation takes place also has a significant bearing on its scope and dynamics. Many of the new managerial strategies involve a third 'channel' of representation – ie employer-initiated mechanisms of direct employee participation or involvement – alongside the first (collective bargaining) and second (works councils) channels. Recognising the different levels at which participation may occur allows for the possibility of an extension of participation at one level (eg the workplace) and the restriction of it at another (eg at corporate level).

TASK- AND POWER-CENTRED PARTICIPATION AND INVOLVEMENT

Power-centred forms of employee participation are usually initiated by trade unions and involve a shift in the balance of power between management and the workers in the organisation's decision-making processes. Task-centred forms of employee involvement are usually initiated by management and involve the transfer of authority for a limited range of work-related decisions (such as the allocation of tasks and quality control) from management to the workers. Trade union militancy has almost invariably encouraged employers to seek out less adversarial and less powerful channels of employee representation. According to Kelly (1996: 60), the level of trade union interest in workers' control and industrial democracy via extended collective bargaining is normally matched by employer interest in rival schemes of employee involvement.

A continuum of possibilities – ranging from no involvement to receiving information, joint consultation, joint decision-making and worker control – can be determined. The vertical line in Figure 7.1 indicates the level at which involvement and participation takes place within the organisation. This can range from the lowest (the employee's immediate work situation) to the highest (board of directors) levels. The diagonal line indicates the objective of involvement and participation (task- or power-centred), while the horizontal line specifies the method of involvement and participation (direct or indirect).

Figure 7.1 Types of employee involvement and participation

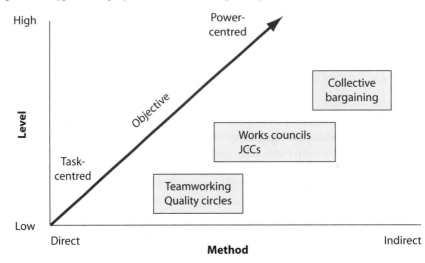

VARIATIONS IN THE DEPTH AND SCOPE OF PARTICIPATION

There is considerable variation in the depth and scope of participation, even in countries where employee involvement and participation are mandated by statute and managerial commitment. In an attempt to explain cross-national variations in employee participation, Bean (1985: 163–78) identifies four sets of determinants:

- specific cultural and ideological factors
- differences in collective bargaining structures
- the nature of power relations between the state, employers and trade unions
- the particular historical circumstances which prevailed at the time when the decision to create participatory institutions was first made.

In mapping out employee involvement and participation, it is therefore necessary to account for the constraints and opportunities associated with task-centred and power-centred institutions of labour regulation as well as their potential for dysfunctional outcomes. These constraints and opportunities are outlined in the following three sections through an examination of collective bargaining and industrial democracy, trade unions and participation, and managerial power and employee participation.

CONSTRAINTS AND OPPORTUNITIES FOR PARTICIPATION

As mentioned above, the term 'participation' refers to the influence of employees over terms and conditions of employment through collective bargaining as well as their influence on work organisation and the deployment of new technologies.

The subsections below outline the different dimensions of such participation, considering in particular the role of collective bargaining and works councils before turning to managerial power and the limits to participation.

COLLECTIVE BARGAINING, WORKS COUNCILS AND INDUSTRIAL DEMOCRACY

The structure of collective bargaining can be a major influence on the extent and form of employee participation within a country (Clegg 1976). Where bargaining structures are most developed at the workplace level (for example, in the USA and the UK), participation tends to occur through workplace union–management processes and procedures. Conversely, where collective bargaining is strongest at the industry or national level (as in Germany and Sweden), there may be very much weaker employee voice at the local level. In countries such as Germany, this vacuum has led to some works councils being agents of co-operation rather than confrontation. Works council members (including trade unionists) view themselves not as adversaries of management but as co-managers (Sorge 1976: 278–9), although their increased role in 'top up' bargaining may reverse this tendency. In countries with more adversarial and decentralised systems of collective bargaining, employers can seek a mutual understanding with works councils and bypass unions (Slomp 1995: 309).

In many contexts, works councils cannot function effectively without unions, while unions use the councils as an institutional framework and a major source of support for their activities at the workplace (Streeck 1992). However, works council unionism is by no means assured of continuing success. It runs the risk of 'giving the impression that employees need not join unions, and engaging more with the immediate concerns of managers than of union members' (Terry 1994: 247–8). This may lead to disputes over demarcation – in simple terms, who is responsible for what. Nonetheless, works councils may provide a forum to renegotiate or improve on an agreement between unions and employers that has been agreed at an industry or national level, making the system work better (Brewster *et al* 2007a).

TRADE UNIONS AND PARTICIPATION

The manner in which the trade unions use their power, strategic capacity and organisational resources has a crucial bearing on the nature and forms of employee participation. Marchington (1992: 136–43) distinguishes between four different models of participatory structures in terms of their relationship with collective bargaining:

- employee participation as an *alternative* to collective bargaining
- employee participation as *marginal* to collective bargaining
- employee participation *competing* with collective bargaining
- employee participation or involvement as an *adjunct* to collective bargaining, where participation and/or involvement and bargaining are complementary rather than competing processes.

It has sometimes been argued that non-union forms of voice will undermine union voice: employers will have an interest in shifting issues off the collective bargaining table towards more compliant forums. However, comparative survey evidence has revealed that this is generally not the case, and that different forms of voice may readily co-exist (Brewster *et al* 2007b).

MANAGERIAL POWER AND EMPLOYEE PARTICIPATION

Existing institutional arrangements, formal and informal rules of work behaviour, and managerial strategies can affect the form that participation is likely to assume and whether trade unions acquiesce, reject or embrace these strategies. Management commitment is vital to co-operative employment practices (Geary 1994; Grossett and Venter 1998). However, at the higher levels of decision-making, employee participation schemes initiated by management have been 'restricted in terms of the scope, level and range of issues involved' and have not implied 'any significant erosion of managerial prerogatives' (Poole 1986: 44–8).

It is often assumed that common interests in the workplace are both desirable and achievable. Much of the management-oriented literature on employee participation is silent on the structured antagonism between business and labour – in other words, on the deep-seated conflict of interest due to the employer's need to extract value from the employee yet at the same time encourage commitment and creativity. The fact that employee participation schemes are only ever partly successful is rooted in the basic contradictions underlying the employment relationship. Participation is not, however, simply a matter of managers trying to deceive employees. Support for such schemes also emanates from workers and their representatives, usually on the basis that employee participation offers an opportunity to expand labour's influence and control.

LIMITS TO EMPLOYEE PARTICIPATION

The 'success' of participatory schemes depends on their ability to legitimate what is in practice an asymmetrical reciprocity – employers and employees do not have to make equal numbers of concessions. This is often overlooked in the emphasis placed on the role of 'trust' (Rogers and Streeck 1994: 106):

> For firms to decentralise production decisions, managers must trust workers not to misuse their increased discretion. For workers to contribute to efficiency, they must trust management not to exclude them from the benefits of their effort.

There are definite limits and risks in the extent of autonomy that management can concede to any sector of the workforce. However, employers have a general interest in all their employees displaying a certain degree of willingness to co-operate, and can employ coercion to achieve it. Indeed, it has been argued that non-union forms of participation may 'owe more to the attempts of management (and the state) to exert control over labour than they do to involve or empower employees' (Blyton and Turnbull 1998: 223).

The currently fashionable emphasis on greater employee 'involvement' in the workplace must be contextualised within the framework of prevailing economic conditions, managerial strategies and government policies. The key to increased competitiveness, according to the proponents of 'new' industrial relations, is production and employment 'flexibility' (Burchill 1997: 185–98). With the shift to post-Fordist production, control through formal procedures is replaced by control through commitment. This involves a shift towards peer-group discipline based on notions of task-based participation and individual responsibility. The ideology of employee 'involvement' is therefore circumscribed by the real imperative of contemporary production – namely, getting employees to work harder.

There is often an implicit assumption that a direct, causal relationship exists between employee involvement and increased productivity and profitability. In fact, these claims ought to be treated with caution due to the effects of all other associated changes in technology, work organisation and labour markets. It cannot be assumed that firms that make use of such strategies will automatically be more effective or profitable.

In addition, a central assumption in the literature on 'involvement' is that employees stand to gain more from collaboration than they do from adversarialism. In reality, management-sponsored forms of involvement usually mean that employees are expected to adopt the interests of the enterprise (such as quality and efficiency) as their own. These initiatives can only therefore succeed insofar as workplace trade unionism is not characterised by autonomy and opposition. Trade union resistance to the introduction of involvement programmes, according to Salamon (1998: 372–3), may stem from factors such as management's introducing changes without consultation or negotiation; management's emphasis on the intrinsic rewards of increased job satisfaction in order to prevent the desire for extrinsic rewards; management's primary objective being the improvement of productivity and the reduction of costs rather than increasing the employees' role in decision making; and direct forms of participation being regarded as an attempt by management to undermine the representative functions of the shop steward.

COLLECTIVE BARGAINING

Collective bargaining refers to the process of negotiation between one or more employers and one or more trade unions in an effort to jointly regulate terms and conditions of employment. Although the terms 'negotiation' and 'consultation' are sometimes used interchangeably, in the sphere of industrial relations they have distinct meanings. *Negotiation* assumes a process of bargaining or haggling, with the objective of reaching a compromise acceptable to both sides, and *consultation* the soliciting of information or advice, with no obligation for acting upon suggestions made.

Collective bargaining constitutes the core of employment relations within unionised workplaces where the role of the union is recognised by management, and in many countries, such as the UK, managers are required to recognise and bargain with the union when it represents a significant (typically 50%) proportion of the workforce. In the UK this legal requirement was established under the Employment Relations Act 1999. Collective bargaining has been described as a right that should belong to every worker in a democratic society and as the great social invention that has institutionalised industrial conflict. This explains why many countries enshrine bargaining rights in the law (Salamon 1998). Indeed, Convention 98 of the International Labour Organisation states that

> measures appropriate to national conditions shall be taken, where necessary, to encourage and promote the full development and utilisation of machinery for voluntary negotiation between employers or employers' organisations and workers' organisations, with a view to the regulation of terms and conditions of employment by means of collective agreements.

However, this has not deterred conservative governments from attempting to eliminate collective bargaining. Most notably, right-wing governments in New Zealand and, more recently, Australia have attempted it. Significantly, in both cases, despite union weakness, this had disastrous electoral consequences for the said governments, and the reforms were subsequently rolled back.

A defining characteristic of collective bargaining is that employees do not negotiate individually and on their own behalf, but do so collectively through representatives. This affords individual employees anonymity and protection against victimisation (Wood *et al* 2004). The emphasis on the joint regulation of employment and its voluntary nature distinguishes collective bargaining from statutory regulation (in other words, regulation via legislation).

Strong trade unions and employers' organisations are necessary for effective collective bargaining. Collective bargaining can only function as a regulatory mechanism (Farnham and Pimlott 1979: 221–2) if:

- employees are prepared and allowed to identify a commonality of purpose, organise and act collectively
- management is prepared to recognise the trade union and accept a change in the employment relationship which constrains its ability to deal with employees on an individual basis.

◖◖◯◗ REFLECTION ON PRACTICE

Collective bargaining and shared objectives

Collective bargaining assumes a 'commonality of purpose'. However, do employees all think the same way? Do they have the same objectives?

In particular, you might wish to consider whether managers have the same opinions as lower-level employees, whether administrative members of staff have the same views as technical staff, and whether manual workers have the same views as white-collar workers.

If they do not have the same objectives, how might a union decide which objectives to pursue?

In the following sections further analysis is undertaken of collective bargaining, taking into account its functions, and the definitions of terms such as 'recognition agreements', a 'bargaining unit', 'collective' and 'closed shop' agreements. Trends in single and multiple employer bargaining are then outlined before there is discussion of the significance of decentralised and centralised bargaining.

THE FUNCTIONS OF COLLECTIVE BARGAINING

Collective bargaining, as Farnham and Pimlott (1979: 218–22) and Jackson (1991: 157–60) point out, fulfils many functions. The most important of these include an economic function, and a redistribution of real income between pay and profits; a social function through industrial peace, uninterrupted production, and the creation and maintenance of certain standards of workload, rewards and stability of employment; and a political function, bringing a measure of democracy to working life. In this sense, collective bargaining is essentially a power relationship. In addition, it can also fulfil an ideological function. Although collective bargaining implies fairness within organisations, particularly in relation to wages (Hyman and Brough 1975), notions of fairness can be used to ensure a continuance of the existing social order and sustained positions for those with privilege and power.

These four broad functions of collective bargaining are not exhaustive or mutually exclusive. However, an essential feature of the collective bargaining process in all these functions is its power basis and adaptability to particular conditions.

APPLYING THEORY TO PRACTICE

The functions of collective bargaining

Outlined above are four functions of collective bargaining.

Think of two countries with which you are familiar.

Is collective bargaining a frequently used voice mechanism in those countries?

If it is used frequently, what function does it appear to have – a political, economic, social or ideological function?

RECOGNITION AGREEMENTS

Before collective bargaining can take place, management and the trade union need to enter into a recognition agreement. A recognition agreement stipulates that the employer accepts the union's role as a representative of the employees, provides a set of ground rules and procedures for conducting the employment relationship, and establishes the parameters within which the parties will jointly determine terms and conditions of employment.

Organisations adopt varying approaches towards trade union recognition depending largely on factors such as the prevailing management style and structure, the size and nature of the organisation and the skill composition of the workforce. However, the acceptance of collective bargaining by employers is often entirely pragmatic in the sense that opposing it may be more costly. As Chamberlain and Kuhn (1965) argue, employers do not enter into collective bargaining with trade unions simply because they are forced to do so. Collective bargaining, they point out, satisfies two primary objectives of employers: market control and managerial control. In exchange for subjecting certain work rules to joint regulation between the employer and the trade union, as Sisson (1987: 12) points out, employers require the unions to recognise their right to make other rules unilaterally – whereby the employer takes decisions without involving the union. Collective bargaining therefore has an inherent control dimension (Blyton and Turnbull 1998).

When a collective agreement is in force, union members have committed themselves to accept their terms and conditions of employment, no matter how much they, as individuals, are unhappy with them. However, the rights that a recognition agreement confers on employees are set out in various procedures, and amount to a restraint on management's capacity for unilateral decision-making. Once management agrees to recognise the union as a bargaining agent, issues such as dismissals, retrenchment and conditions of employment, which were previously within management's sole discretion, become the subjects of collective regulation. Recognition agreements, however, generally contain a clause which reserves management's right to the overall direction and control of the firm. There is thus a tension between the idea that an employer must negotiate with a representative trade union over issues affecting its members *and* the employer's prerogative (or right) to manage the business as he or she sees fit.

Recognition agreements, as Piron (1990) notes, may take either of two different forms: *restricted* agreements that merely outline the key principles that will govern the interaction between the parties, or *comprehensive* agreements containing detailed procedures and providing for almost every eventuality. A restricted agreement has the advantage of flexibility or adaptability and is less conducive to a climate of distrust, but has the disadvantage of leading to uncertainty and conflict, and presupposes a relationship of trust. A comprehensive agreement has the advantage of minimising uncertainty in the sense that managers and shop stewards have clear guidelines to follow when implementing the agreement. Rights and obligations are also clearly spelled out so that the parties are in a position to monitor and enforce the provisions of the agreement. This type of agreement has the disadvantage of being intricate and legalistic, rigid and cumbersome to change, and prone to creating distrust between the parties.

In summary, a recognition deal may vary depending on the union, the employer, and the country context. However, it should also be noted that just because a union and employer have signed a recognition deal does not mean that there will necessarily be a long-term trust relationship between them. The example below is of a company based in the UK, and explains potential responses to union recognition.

⚙ APPLYING THEORY TO PRACTICE

Recognition agreement in the UK

In 2010, Unite – the largest union in the UK – signed a recognition deal with the holiday airline company Thomas Cook in respect of the cabin crew. The recognition deal covered pay, holidays and hours of work and was signed by the company voluntarily. The general secretary of the Unite union commented that he was 'delighted' to have signed the recognition agreement, while the management of the airline was also positive about the possibility of 'more efficient and representative lines of communication' (International Transport Workers Federation 2010).

What is the current relationship between Unite and Thomas Cook? Browse relevant websites using an appropriate search engine.

A BARGAINING UNIT

A bargaining unit can be defined as a group of employees, usually sharing a common workplace or working conditions or having a common interest, to whom a set of collective agreements are to apply. Sometimes a bargaining unit is a whole organisation, while in other cases it might be one workplace site. According to Salamon (1998), the boundaries of a bargaining unit are established by the following factors: the characteristics of the workgroup, existing trade union membership and collective bargaining arrangements, and management structure and authority. A trade union always seeks recognition for and acts on behalf of a defined group of employees. In the process of defining the boundaries of a bargaining unit, the parties must decide whether negotiations will be conducted at the workplace, at head office or with employers in the industry.

COLLECTIVE AND CLOSED SHOP AGREEMENTS

Collective agreements refer to agreements entered into between an employer or a group of employers and employees, groups of employees, or a trade union or a number of trade unions. These agreements may be reached for a specific group in the workplace, for the entire workplace, for a group of workplaces or for a whole industry. Collective agreements can be:

- *either* substantive – contain terms and conditions of employment (eg a wage agreement)
- *or* procedural – lay down procedures that the parties will use to regulate their relationship (eg a recognition agreement).

According to Farnham and Pimlott (1979), procedural agreements regulate relations between management and the trade union, and establish the processes that govern interactions between the parties. Substantive agreements regulate jobs, their remuneration, and the conditions under which they are performed. These agreements tend to be renegotiated more regularly than procedural agreements.

A closed shop agreement provides a union with exclusive bargaining rights and strengthens its bargaining position with an employer. Under a closed shop agreement, non-union employees must join the union or face dismissal. If a union expels a member or refuses to allow a new employee to become a union member and if this expulsion or refusal is in accordance with the union's constitution or is for a fair reason, the employer has to dismiss the employee. There are arguments against and in favour of closed shop agreements (Salamon 1998: 191–2). The main arguments against a closed shop are that it infringes the individual's right to freedom of association, increases union power, allows the union to take its members for granted, and employees may lose their jobs if they challenge union policy or come into conflict with union officials. The main arguments in favour of a closed shop are that it endorses the social utility of strong unions, it is an effective instrument for trade union security, it confirms the position of the union and alleviates the need for the union to act aggressively towards management in order to recruit and maintain its membership.

? CRITICAL DEBATE

Closed shop agreements

As outlined above, the main arguments for a closed shop are that it:

- endorses the social utility of strong unions

- is an effective instrument for trade union security

- confirms the position of the union, and

- alleviates the need for the union to act aggressively towards management in order to recruit and maintain its membership.

The main arguments against a closed shop are that it:

- infringes the individual's right to freedom of association

- increases union power

- allows the union to take its members for granted, and

- may cause employees to lose their jobs if they challenge union policy or come into conflict with union officials.

What is your opinion on this debate? *If you are in favour of closed shops, try to think of circumstances in which they would not be appropriate. If you are against the idea, try to think of circumstances where they might be necessary. In doing so, you might wish to consider different industrial and country contexts.*

SINGLE AND MULTIPLE-EMPLOYER BARGAINING

Trade unions can enter into bargaining relationships with individual employers or groups of employers/employers' organisations. Multi-employer bargaining can be national or regional and/or single-industry or multi-industry in scope depending on the organisational structure and resources of employers' organisations. Single-employer bargaining can be either workplace bargaining or conglomerate-level bargaining. Besides the various levels at which negotiations may take place, collective bargaining also varies in terms of its coverage, the range of topics subject to negotiation, the extent of trade union influence over negotiations, the responsibilities of the parties, and the form of collective agreements. The scope for variation in bargaining structures is therefore considerable. Within many north-western continental European countries, industry-wide bargaining is common. Within the UK, bargaining tends to be confined to the level of the individual employer, outside the public sector.

THE COVERAGE OF COLLECTIVE BARGAINING

High levels of collective bargaining coverage in many countries, despite low levels of union density, can be attributed not only to the greater use of multi-employer sectoral-level agreements but also to the existence of legal provisions that grant unions the right to bargain at industry level and/or for collective agreements to be extended to all organisations within a particular sector (Salamon 1998: 306). Although such legal provisions may extend the coverage of collective bargaining, they may also serve to discourage employees from joining trade unions because they will receive the benefits irrespective of whether they are union members. This may account for the low levels of union density in relation to collective bargaining coverage in France, Spain and the Netherlands. The low rates of collective bargaining coverage in the United Kingdom, Japan and the United States are a product of the predominance of workplace-level bargaining in their industrial relations systems.

Table 7.1 **Collective bargaining coverage and principal bargaining level, by country**

COUNTRY	BARGAINING COVERAGE (%)	PRINCIPAL BARGAINING LEVEL
Australia	60	Company
Austria	99	Industry
Belgium	96	National
Canada	32	Company
Chile	24	Company
Czech Republic	44	Company/Industry
Denmark	82	Industry/Company
Estonia	22	*None*
Finland	90	Industry (national framework)
France	95	Industry/Company
Germany	63	Industry
Greece	85	Industry
Hungary	35	Company
Iceland	88	Industry
Ireland	—	National/Company

COUNTRY	BARGAINING COVERAGE (%)	PRINCIPAL BARGAINING LEVEL
Israel	56	Industry/Company
Italy	80	Industry
Japan	16	Company
Luxembourg	60	Industry/Company
Netherlands	82	Industry
New Zealand	30	Company
Norway	72	National/Industry
Poland	35	Company
Portugal	62	Industry
Russian Federation	62	Multiple
Slovak Republic	35	Industry/Company
Slovenia	100	National/Industry
Spain	80	National/Industry/Company
Sweden	92	Industry
Switzerland	48	Company
Turkey	24	Company
United Kingdom	35	Company
United States	13	Company

Source: Based on Table 1, p. 17 from Venn, D. (2009), *Legislation, Collective Bargaining and Enforcement: Updating the OECD Employment Protection Indicators*, OECD Social, Employment and Migration Working Papers, No. 89, http://dx.doi.org/10.1787/223334316804

Perhaps the most significant variation in bargaining structures is the level at which negotiations between employers and trade unions take place. Bargaining can take place at both a decentralised level (ie the workplace) and at a bargaining institution for the industry as a whole.

DECENTRALISED AND CENTRALISED BARGAINING

Decentralisation of bargaining reflects the need of employers to gain increased control over wage and productivity levels. The nature and dynamics of trade unionism are also a key determinant of the balance between centralisation and decentralisation in industrial relations. The decentralisation of collective bargaining and the growing differentiation of interests within the labour movement have contributed to a decline in the centralised authority of unions in many countries (Hyman 1994: 112).

Centralised collective bargaining occurs when employers in a sector (such as mining or textiles) get together and bargain with one or more unions representing the employees in that sector. Macro-economic regulation is greatly facilitated by centralised industrial relations structures. Countries with more centralised bargaining institutions have tended 'to ride out shocks to the international economy with less unemployment and lower inflation than countries whose bargaining is fragmented' (Brown 1992: 298–9). Centralised bargaining can neutralise the impact of trade unionism in the workplace (Sisson 1987). It can also encourage a rupture between the leadership and membership of the unions, thereby undermining internal democracy. Or, as Olson (1982) notes, unions have to rein in their members, binding them to central agreements. However, there is little doubt that employee rights are generally stronger and terms and conditions of service more favourable in those industries and contexts where centralised collective bargaining is in place.

THE BARGAINING PROCESS

Bargaining may be undertaken by individuals or trade unions. Where bargaining takes place it is necessary to possess adequate bargaining skills. The process of bargaining generally is usually in three main stages, for which these skills need to be applied carefully.

INDIVIDUAL-LEVEL BARGAINING

In the absence of trade unions and collective bargaining, individual employees can and do bargain with their employer over terms and conditions of service. The strength of the employee's position depends on the scarcity of her/his relative skills, experience, knowledge and attributes.

Other than in very senior and/or highly skilled positions, the voice of the individual is relatively weak, and the employee runs the risk of being ignored and/or being categorised as 'difficult' or 'unreasonable'. It is hardly surprising, therefore, that individual bargaining is at its most effective at the point of entry to the organisation. Individuals may, other than in the case of menial jobs fixed to a minimum wage, readily present – within broad parameters – what they regard as a desirable wage, and the employer may present a counter offer. A deal is made when the employee formally accepts the offer of employment.

Individuals may seek to renegotiate their terms and conditions of service later on. This is most effective when they reinforce their position with the threat of exit or leaving the organisation (most convincing when she/he is in possession of an alternative offer of employment by another organisation). The organisation's response will reflect both how readily substitutable the individual is and the existing management philosophies and strategies. More conservative organisations may refuse to consider advancing a counter-offer to an alternative offer of employment as a matter of principle; this precludes the possibility of entering into 'bidding wars'. However, this strategy may lead to a 'brain drain' of talented individuals, with the organisation's staff being divided between younger incumbents seeking valuable (and externally marketable) experience and the less ambitious, incompetent or complacent, who are willing to accept lower wages than they could potentially obtain elsewhere in return for continuity, comfort or predictability. Organisations making counter-offers to retain talented individuals run risks of their own such as falling prey to the bluff of employees who have no real intention of moving, being enticed into making counter-offers that the individual in question then uses as a basis for bargaining for an even better-paid job elsewhere, and/or alienating other, more loyal and committed staff.

NEGOTIATION SKILLS INVOLVED IN COLLECTIVE BARGAINING

As noted above, bargaining involves negotiation, and the ability to persuade others of the importance or relevance of your point of view. The discussion below describes negotiation in the case of collective bargaining, but many of the points and issues are also relevant to individual bargaining.

The process of negotiation evolves through a set of three distinct phases, which must be managed effectively in order to ensure a successful outcome. Each stage poses unique challenges that require a specific set of skills (Grossett and Venter 1998; Nel *et al* 2005).

PREPARING FOR NEGOTIATIONS

This stage involves initiating the process, selecting the negotiators, obtaining a mandate, setting objectives, identifying the issues, gathering information, establishing the settlement range, strategic planning and administrative arrangements. Negotiators who have not adequately prepared for the encounter can only react to events and will not be able to act in a proactive manner.

Employers and employees possess a wide range of diverse and often competing interests. Interest representation therefore involves a difficult internal process of aggregation and the selection of priorities. Both sides need to formulate demands, tactics and strategies before and during the negotiating encounter. With union–employer bargaining, this process occurs within the trade union structure and the management hierarchy in an attempt by each party to reach internal consensus on matters such as the goals, areas of concession and non-negotiable items.

A vital part of the preparation stage is the establishment of a 'settlement range' around each issue (as outlined in a section above). However, neither party can be entirely sure of the extent to which the other party will move, under what circumstances it is likely to compromise, or which concessions will have to be made in exchange.

When the bargaining involves groups of people, it is usually advisable to keep the number of people in each negotiating team as small as possible. This will reduce the range of opinions, the time necessary for negotiations and the potential for misunderstandings. It is also important to limit the number of issues for discussion. Too many issues may prevent the parties from reaching consensus.

The chances of reaching a settlement are further enhanced when the issues are concrete and quantifiable rather than abstract and intangible.

The final step in this stage is to plan how to obtain movement in the negotiating process. At this point, as Anstey (1991) notes, attention is given to issues such as the potential sources of power and their use, possible concessions and trade-offs, the arguments that might be used, how to establish common ground, and the use of pressure tactics.

CONDUCTING THE NEGOTIATIONS

In the case of union–management negotiations, this stage includes deciding on the chairperson. It also includes determining the structure of the meeting and time-frames, establishing the positions of the parties, tabling proposals and counter-proposals, seeking and making concessions, caucusing, impasses, final offers and demands, threats and bluffs, deadlocks (neither party is willing to compromise and both are willing to risk the consequent sanctions), sanctions (temporary walk-outs, bad publicity, strikes, lock-outs – where an employer prevents employees from entering the workplace – and so on), closure, and report-back. In this stage, the parties confirm that a conflict situation exists, attempt to establish their positions, and negotiate until a settlement or impasse is reached. An effective negotiator will listen to the other party, obtaining as much information as possible, seeking clarification and exploring the concerns, assumptions and arguments.

It is possible to distinguish three distinct 'styles' of bargaining (Bendix 2000):

- distributive bargaining, common in countries such as South Africa – According to Bendix (2000), it is based on the adversarial relationship between labour and management, where their goals are in direct conflict and negotiation is a zero-sum process. Bargaining is focused mainly on wages, leave entitlement, benefits and bonuses. With this style of bargaining, the employer seeks to give as little as possible while the union tries to gain as much as possible. It also involves the use of power tactics, coercion and threats. Under these conditions, the most likely outcome is a win/lose situation

- integrative bargaining, when both parties have the same preference for a successful outcome or are equally concerned to solve a problem – It is associated with negotiation strategies – such as extensive information exchanges, a readiness to compromise and concerted efforts to maintain a climate of trust – that reflect a lack of conflict in the goals of the parties. The aim of the bargain is not to persuade one party to give up something but for both parties to take action to achieve a common goal. In these circumstances, the most likely outcome is a win/win situation. Matters that may be dealt with by integrative bargaining include health and safety, job security and promotion

- destructive bargaining, which occurs when employees would rather lose their jobs and employers would rather shut down the business than compromise on their demands – Both parties believe that a matter of principle, which neither is prepared to sacrifice, is at stake if they compromise. The inevitable outcome is a lose/lose situation.

REACHING AGREEMENT

This stage is not immediately applicable if negotiations break down and the parties resort to industrial action. If the parties reach a consensus, following negotiations or industrial action, attention then shifts to the implementation, monitoring and enforcement of the agreement. To avoid disputes at this stage, the parties must clarify the content of an agreement reached during negotiation and put the agreement in writing.

Figure 7.2 The collective bargaining process

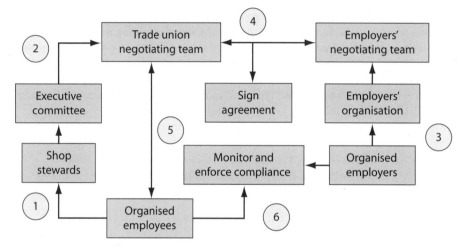

Figure 7.2 represents the collective bargaining process. Shop stewards and the trade union's executive committee formulate an initial position and obtain a mandate (1) from the membership via a ballot (or in some national or industry contexts via meetings) – essentially stating that the members allow the union to negotiate on their behalf. The initial position is translated into proposals (2) to be presented at the bargaining table. In a similar, though less demanding, process, an employers' organisation (in the case of industry-wide bargaining) obtains and converts directives from its members into proposals (3) that can be tabled during negotiations. The negotiating encounter involves a process of give-and-take (4). Throughout this encounter, the union's negotiating team reports back to the members on its progress (5). Once an agreement is concluded, it should be referred back to membership for approval, and then signed by the parties, who are then responsible for monitoring its implementation and enforcing compliance with its provisions (6).

THE NATURE OF VOICE IN NON-UNION FIRMS

The global decline of unions has meant that non-union firms are the norm in a wide range of contexts. As noted earlier, it can be argued that a complete disregard of the voice and concerns of employees may not only be detrimental to the latter's well-being but also be inefficient and potentially dangerous for the organisation as well. Apparent harmony and silence may mask deep-seated resentments, low-key but damaging resistance by employees, or indeed, terminal organisational decay. (More detail on forms of resistance is provided in Chapter 12.) There has accordingly been a growing recognition of the need for alternative mechanisms for representing employees in contexts where unions are absent (Taras and Kaufman 2006: 3). However, such arrangements are typically confined to a single firm/organisation that is averse to collective bargaining which may encompass entire industries.

Employee voice may be expressed formally via specialised structures (eg works councils) or informally during day-to-day interchanges between managers, supervisors and the rank and file. Within non-union forms, informal voice mechanisms are likely to be relatively more important, in that firms have few incentives to have collective, representative voice mechanisms unless obliged by the law (Webster and Wood 2005).

A second difference between union and non-union voice is that the former involves a third party (ie the union itself) as well as employees and managers, and so has an external dimension. In contrast, non-union voice is largely internal (Gollan 2009: 213; Taras and Kaufman 2006). In non-union firms, therefore, employees cannot count on the availability of external resources or support. In contrast, managers can bring the accumulated financial and logistical resources of the organisation to bear, and are more likely to be more able to afford external advice.

A third distinction is that because non-union voice is likely to be weaker, it is likely to be less efficient in terms of discouraging exit (Budd *et al* 2009: 3). In other words, because they have fewer opportunities and incur more risks in expressing their concerns, employees are more likely to leave should they be unhappy with their terms and conditions of employment. And because voice mechanisms are weaker, employers are less likely to be able to find out why employees are leaving. It could further be argued that managers will be able to make more informed decisions if they can draw on the accumulated knowledge and experience of employees – better and more effective voice mechanisms make for better information flows (Gollan 2009: 220).

From a union perspective, it can be argued that non-union forms of representation in non-union firms may provide a foothold that could be exploited, and, indeed, not preclude a later, more overt union role (Gollan 2009). For example, individual workers who are elected to representative bodies could be union members or at least sympathetic to the union project. However, conservative managers may be more sympathetic to voice mechanisms that are ostensibly non-union to those that are explicitly union (Bryson 2004). From a management point of view, allowing workers some form of representation may allow for better flows of information and knowledge, and encourage workers to take greater responsibility in their work (Gollan 2009: 220). It may also be seen as less risky than dealing with a union (Gollan 2009: 229), but of course holds the risk that proceedings may be less effective or lack legitimacy.

THE ROLE OF HR SPECIALISTS AND LINE MANAGERS IN ESTABLISHING VOICE MECHANISMS

A final issue is the relationship between the employment relations practitioner/ HR manager and line management. Although the former may play a central role in the drafting of employment contracts and the collective bargaining process (where it exists), her/his role vis-à-vis many other forms of participation and involvement will probably be more indirect, providing line managers with advice and support as and when needed. This may lead to some tensions, involving problems associated with demarcating authority. Line managers may resent interference from HR managers, whereas the latter may be disparaging about the former's understanding of the complexity of the employment relationship and its regulation. Further difficulties may arise owing to information imbalances. The HR manager/employment relations practitioner may possess a lot more information about the precise nature of relations with the union, the legal rights of employees, and the legal obligations of the firm. On the other hand, line managers are likely to know much more about the process of production and the specific nature of work organisation, and are likely to have forged considerably closer relations with individual employees. This can be difficult when the headquarters of an organisation is based in a country different from the sites of operation.

CASE STUDY

HR SPECIALISTS AND LINE MANAGERS IN NGOS BASED IN NAMIBIA

Non-governmental organisations have an important role to play in emerging economies. For example, NGOs can assist in the development of infrastructure such as roads, schools and hospitals, providing training programmes or establishing systems for micro-finance. The headquarters of an NGO might be in an advanced economy, while the sites for delivery might be in a range of areas within the target country. In this context, workplace participation in decision-making can be quite complex. HR will have to establish clear lines of authority and policies, but those dealing with problems

'on the ground' will be aware of changes to situations.

Questions

Consider the case of a charity that seeks to address the needs of those suffering from HIV/AIDs in Namibia, a country in south-west Africa.

What would be the most appropriate mechanisms for communication?

How might these lines of communication be affected by tensions between HR managers in the home country and line managers operating in Namibia?

SUMMARY

This chapter has examined a range of dimensions of individual and collective voice, and investigated in some detail the process of collective bargaining. No employment relationship solely operates through the power and authority of, and one-way communication from, the employer to the employee. The simplest of production processes require some form of two-way communication, and information flows in both directions. In many small and medium-sized enterprises, such communication flows may remain informal and *ad hoc*, their duration and scope being at the behest of the employer. Within more complex organisations, and where employees are in a stronger bargaining position and/or are collectively represented, such interchanges are likely to assume a more formal and rule-bound dimension. However, the range and scope of participation may still vary greatly from effective collective bargaining and/or co-decision-making in key areas of the production process through to limited communication and consultation.

While individual voice mechanisms might present a limited opportunity for employees to voice their opinions, collective mechanisms are likely to present a clearer voice and prevent discrimination against individuals. In examining negotiation, attention has been given to the way in which this might be effectively conducted in order to obtain gains for both parties – relevant to both individual–employer and management–union negotiations.

EXPLORE FURTHER

Reading

- ACAS (2005) Advisory booklet: *Employee Communications and Consultation*. Available online at http://www.acas.org.uk/index.aspx?articleid=675 [accessed 29 June 2010]

- Brewster, C., Wood, G., Croucher, R. and Brookes, M. (2007a) 'Are works councils and joint consultative committees a threat to trade unions? A comparative analysis', *Economic and Industrial Democracy*, Vol.28: 49–77

- Gollan, P. (2009) 'Employer strategies towards non-union collective voice', in A. Wilkinson, P. Gollan, M. Marchington and D. Lewin (eds) *The Oxford Handbook of Participation in Organizations*. Oxford: Oxford University Press

Websites

- Advisory, Conciliation and Arbitration Service www.acas.org.uk

- Chartered Institute of Personnel and Development www.cipd.co.uk

- Organisation for Economic Co-operation and Development www.oecd.org.uk

- International Labour Organisation www.ilo.org.uk

CHAPTER 8

Employee Engagement

CHAPTER OVERVIEW

Employee engagement is a topical subject, but one that is multi-faceted and contested. Engagement can be regarded as an important way of reinforcing the employment relationship. The concept variously incorporates emotions, attitudes, behaviours and performance outcomes. In some ways, employee engagement could be regarded as a prescriptive toolbox for managing employment relations since it has been assumed that it will lead to increased productivity and thus contribute towards the 'bottom line'. However, to what extent is employee engagement a tool for increasing performance or an outcome in itself? Moreover, to what extent can we ever say that employees are totally 'engaged'?

This chapter begins by defining the term 'employee engagement' and outlining how it has been measured. It then outlines, in turn, the constituent elements associated with employee engagement, commencing with the initial influence of employer branding and the value of high-performance work practices, thereafter turning to examine intermediate outcomes in terms of organisational commitment, job satisfaction, employee health and well-being, and emotional labour. The chapter finally evaluates the assumed benefits of employee engagement in terms of improved performance.

LEARNING OUTCOMES

After studying this chapter you should be able to:

- define employee engagement
- evaluate the potential contribution of employer branding and high-performance work practices to employee engagement
- assess the intermediate outcomes in terms of organisational commitment, job satisfaction, employee health and well-being
- critically evaluate the concept of employee engagement and its relationship to emotional labour
- assess the relationship between employee engagement and performance

DEFINING EMPLOYEE ENGAGEMENT

Employee engagement is a relatively new topic, in that the term has not been in use for many years. At the same time it is a buzz word that has been 'heavily marketed by human resource consulting firms that offer advice on how it can be created and leveraged' (Macey and Schneider 2008: 3). As Woodruffe suggests, it has become 'something of a vogue word, eclipsing commitment and motivation in the management literature' (CIPD 2006a: 9), or as Saks comments, 'a fad with little basis in theory and research' (Saks 2005). It is therefore important to assess carefully the ways in which it has been used before examining its implications for practice.

In simple terms, employee engagement can be regarded as the combination of a positive psychological contract and the willingness to offer 'discretionary behaviour' (CIPD 2009a: 1). For Macey and Schneider (2008: 24), employee engagement includes traits, the state of being engaged, behaviour, and the work and organisational conditions that facilitate this.

CRITICAL DEBATE

Employee engagement: fad or fact?

'Employee engagement' is a new term to many people. For some, it offers a new way of ensuring commitment from employees. To others, it is simply another term for the range of strategies that are used to entice employees to work harder.

Prior to reading the rest of this chapter, what is your opinion on the concept of 'employee engagement'?

THE ORIGINS OF EMPLOYEE ENGAGEMENT

The term 'employee engagement' has been used to incorporate many aspects of the employment relationship that have, in themselves, been subject to greater levels of investigation (MacLeod and Clarke 2009). For example, it has been associated with psychology (and individual attitudes) such as organisational commitment and job satisfaction (Purcell 2010). These aspects have been tested through a range of surveys and are themselves rooted in motivational theory (a concept from organisational behaviour). In this sense, the term has been used to capture the ways in which employees feel about their organisation and the managers to whom they report. In addition, employee engagement is generally regarded as a two-way process, in many ways echoing the assumptions of a positive psychological contract (Purcell 2010). Saks (2005) suggests that the reciprocal relationship between the employer and the employee implied within employee engagement can be conceptualised within the framework of social exchange theory, implying that the relationship will 'evolve over time into trusting, loyal commitments' (Saks 2005: 603).

The term also incorporates high-performance work practices such as employee involvement (covered in depth in Chapter 7), teamworking (Purcell 2010), and HR practices relating to employee health and well-being (Robinson *et al* 2004), work–life balance, and (even before the employee starts working within the organisation) employer branding. These HR practices can be used to improve working conditions for employees but also, in doing so, enhance employee engagement and consequently performance. Indeed, an Institute for Employment Studies report (Robinson *et al* 2004) includes the following definition of 'employee engagement':

> a positive attitude held by the employee towards the organisation and its values. An engaged employee is aware of business context, and works with colleagues to improve performance within the job for the benefit of the organisation. The organisation must work to develop and nurture engagement, which requires a two-way relationship between the employer and the employee.

Fourthly, and more critically, employee engagement can be seen as a more subtle way of ensuring emotional labour. Robinson *et al* (2004) argue that employee engagement implies that employees will be willing to go beyond the requirements of the job. In addition to providing extra discretionary effort, employee engagement surveys might be used to encourage employees to express positive feelings towards the organisation and their work – even though they may not feel this way in reality.

The various components can be conceived of separately, and also as interlinked, as suggested in Figure 8.1.

Figure 8.1 The multiple components of employee engagement

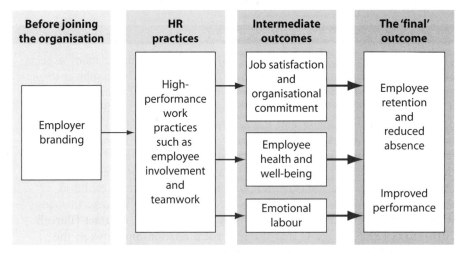

Effective employer branding is necessary in order to recruit 'engaged' people to the organisation. This positive attitude towards the organisation might then be reinforced by high-performance work practices once the employee has begun work within the organisation in question. These might then lead to intermediate outcomes (either positive or negative), contributing in turn to positive outcomes. The positive outcomes will benefit the employer, and where an employee is not being exploited, they will also be to the benefit of the employee.

A pertinent question at this stage is: what is the available evidence on levels of employee engagement?

MEASURING EMPLOYEE ENGAGEMENT

The measurement of employee engagement has been undertaken by a range of organisations. One of the most widely quoted is a survey by the CIPD of employees in British workplaces (2006b). This survey sought to measure engagement according to three dimensions:

- emotional engagement – being highly involved emotionally with the work

- cognitive engagement – concentrating hard on doing the work

- physical engagement – being willing to 'go the extra mile' for the employer.

The findings of the survey indicated that around 60% of employees were emotionally engaged, 60% cognitively engaged, and 40% physically engaged (CIPD 2009a: 3). The survey showed, however, that levels of engagement varied according to different worker characteristics. Levels of engagement were higher for older workers than for younger workers (under-35s), and higher for women than for men (CIPD 2006b). However, contrasting findings regarding the age of workers emerged in a survey of 10,000 employees in 14 NHS organisations, where it was found that engagement levels declined over age up until the age of 60 (Robinson *et al* 2004). The latter survey also found that engagement levels were higher for ethnic minority workers and for managers and professionals, and for those with personal development plans and yearly appraisals. Perhaps not surprisingly, however, they were lower for those who had experienced an accident or injury at work or were currently suffering from harassment. The working conditions and organisational context were also relevant in the CIPD survey (2006b), which showed that levels were higher for part-timers than for full-time workers, for those on flexible contracts (including flexitime and homeworking), and for those working in small compared to large organisations. Two illustrations of employee engagement within small organisations are provided in the *Applying theory to practice* box below.

APPLYING THEORY TO PRACTICE

Engagement in small charitable organisations

MacLeod and Clarke produced a much-cited report in 2009 on employee engagement. Within the report they drew attention to various examples of employee engagement in practice. One of the organisations described was Broadway, a London-based charity providing services and support for homeless people. The organisation employs 180 staff and finds that it needs to compete for talented employees by offering good HR practices. The charity aims to recruit people who are 'willing to be engaged', although the charity's exact interpretation of this expression is not defined in the report. In terms of HR practices, the charity offers flexible working, communication mechanisms, and a degree of autonomy to staff. However, at the same time, members of staff are expected to buy in to the organisation's values and standards. The engagement of staff reportedly leads to 'quality services that are rated highly by clients', and to its rating as an 'employer of choice' (MacLeod and Clarke 2009: 20).

A second organisation, also highlighted as an example of best practice within the report, is School Trends, a company that supplies uniforms directly to schools. This company employs 130 members of staff and is somewhat unusual in that it is employee-owned. In common with the Broadway charity, it seeks to engage the workforce through strong HR practices, in this case including involvement mechanisms, fair reward, shared profits, employment protection, and development opportunities. Employee engagement is regarded as a way of securing 'customer service and improved efficiency that lead to greater profitability' (MacLeod and Clarke 2009: 106).

The examples provided above are of a charity and an employee-owned organisation. Is it easier or more difficult to secure employee engagement in these types of organisation as opposed to large private sector corporations? Give reasons for your answer.

Are there any HR practices missing from those detailed above that might also help to secure employee engagement?

The two organisations described are successful because of employee buy-in and active support for the participative initiatives embarked on. However, such employee buy-in does not automatically take place – both organisations have invested considerable effort in making things work. Organisations all too often attempt to develop participation 'on the cheap', involving little more than downward communication combined with an unwillingness to hear bad news. Genuine participation involves a sharing not just of responsibility but also of power.

The sections below now examine in turn each of the features of the model outlined in the first part of this chapter.

EMPLOYER BRANDING

An employer brand can be defined (CIPD 2010a: 1) as:

> a set of attributes and qualities – often intangible – that makes an organisation distinctive, promises a particular kind of employment experience, and appeals to those people who will thrive and perform best in its culture.

All organisations have an employer brand, whether or not they have sought to develop one, and it will be a factor that determines the behaviour and attitudes of new recruits, current employees and those leaving the organisation (CIPD 2010: 2). An employer brand can assist competition within the labour market and encourage employee loyalty. However, it is possible to damage the employer brand through, for example, making employees redundant. Employers should ensure equity during the process and consider the impact on 'survivors'. (See Chapter 13 for more details on how to manage 'survivor syndrome'.) Perceptions of an organisation can relate to broader concepts of social responsibility (MacLeod and Clarke 2009: 115). Component parts of social responsibility might include 'green' practices – taking care of the environment and recycling – or community engagement – giving money to charities, employee secondment to the voluntary sector, and investing in charitable causes. However, they might also include ethical employment practices – including for those directly employed by an organisation and for those employed throughout the supply chain.

Some organisations choose to take a segmented approach to employer branding, to promote benefits packages to particular target groups, whether this is by age or job type. Moreover, multinationals can seek to adapt their brand depending on the culture of the location. However, it is important not to make assumptions about people based on their grouping, because stereotypes can be incorrect (CIPD 2010a: 2).

According to the CIPD (2009a: 1) there is a strong link between employee engagement and employer branding:

> Organisations increasingly recognise the importance of their 'brand'. Engaged employees will help promote the brand and protect the employer from the risks associated with poor service levels or product quality. Similarly, a strong employer brand will help in attracting and retaining employees.

Employer branding might lead to employee engagement. A positive employer brand can impact on the attitudes of the public to an organisation, including potential employees, resulting in employee engagement even before people join an organisation. Moreover, it can influence decisions on whether to apply to work for a company. Conversely, it could also be the case that employee engagement improves employer branding. Where employees are engaged, they may feel better able to undertake staff advocacy, speaking highly about the organisation to others outside the organisation (MacLeod and Clarke 2009).

HIGH-PERFORMANCE WORK PRACTICES AND EMPLOYEE ENGAGEMENT

Often related to the achievement of employee engagement are the bundle of 'modern' HR practices that are variously referred to as high-performance work practices (HPWPs), high-performance practices (HPPs), high-involvement work systems (HIWSs) or high-commitment management practices (HCMPs). The terms for the bundles of practices have more often been applied to studies in the UK and the United States (Edwards and Wright 2001), although they can be relevant to other countries. There has been some questioning of the ability of such practices to transform attitudes into improved performance, one criticism being the need to incorporate into the analysis the impact of state policies and legislation (Godard 2004). However, others (Edwards and Wright 2001: 569) have argued that:

> the ties between HIWSs and outcomes are variable, reciprocal and contingent, but the remaining weak ties still have a strong and simple message – that managing people well rather than badly affects productivity.

The bundle of HR practices often includes those such as merit- or performance-related pay, job security and training, although employee involvement and teamworking are generally regarded as key elements (Edwards and Wright 2001). Guest (1997, cited in Edwards and Wright 2001: 570) outlines how such practices can lead to improved performance:

> systems such as teamwork are established; they influence workplace practice; employee attitudes change, with increased satisfaction or commitment; there is a consequent effect on behaviour; and this in turn feeds through to the performance of the work unit and eventually the company.

EMPLOYEE INVOLVEMENT

In Chapter 7 we examined a range of aspects of voice, including collective means of representation and individualised forms of communication. Employee involvement is often considered to be a key aspect of employee engagement. Firstly, voice mechanisms can improve communication between managers and employees and therefore contribute towards a more open and trusting relationship. This in turn can improve the psychological contract (see Chapter 1). At the same time, employee involvement mechanisms can be used to avoid conflict, particularly where employees might have genuine concerns about management behaviour. Thirdly, employees may be consulted on potential improvements to tasks, organisational culture or strategy, and might thereafter feel more valued and better engaged in the decision-making processes of the organisation. Where decisions are taken on board and feedback to employees is achieved, this might lead to increased job satisfaction. If employees feel that their concerns are treated with respect, the result might be improved organisational commitment and, in turn, improved retention and improved performance. The CIPD survey mentioned above revealed that voice mechanisms were of central importance in employee engagement, and in particular the communication to employees of organisational strategy and mission (CIPD 2006b: 4).

Management and supervisors interact with employees at both informal and formal levels, with a view to enhancing the extent to which employees are aware of and concerned with the organisation's objectives. Informal interaction includes day-to-day conversations surrounding operational tasks and planning, but also may provide opportunities for voice (see Chapter 7 for more detail on voice mechanisms). Such interactions may improve operations and employee morale. However, within many organisations there is a culture of intolerance of negative feedback. On a formal level, engagement may be facilitated through a wide range of mechanisms for voice, involvement and participation. An example of indirect contact is via surveys, which may provide insights into how to improve motivational techniques for employees (MacLeod and Clarke, 2009). Formal mechanisms do have the advantage in that their parameters can be predetermined. From an employee perspective, this may provide guidance on what is acceptable, and provide some protection against victimisation. Moreover, the organisation is formally committed to taking such processes seriously. Informal interactions are open-ended, flexible and dynamic – but they can be either overly restrictive or lacking in structure and continuity. In practice, both formal and informal practices have a vital role to play not only in enhancing performance but, indeed, in making an organisation's activities possible.

TEAMWORKING

Effective teamwork is another commonly cited high-performance work practice, contributing towards employee commitment and the well-being of the organisation. Within the literature, attention has variously been paid to self-managed work teams, self-directed work teams, and self-maintaining, self-leading and self-regulating work teams (Brewster *et al* 2003: 9). The teams have responsibility for what they do, how and when they do it, and participate in decisions regarding equipment and training (Brewster *et al* 2003).

In team-building, it is necessary to achieve a good balance between being supportive and being challenging, which will then extend the creative potential of the team, leading to increased productivity (CIPD 2006b: 5). Moreover, it is important to consider the context for the development of team-based working. It has been suggested that the costs associated with building teams can lead to increased performance pressures and stress, leading to a lack of sustainability (Godard 2004). Where team-building is effective, it might lead to increased employee engagement.

WORK–LIFE BALANCE

An appropriate work–life balance might also be a contributory factor towards employee engagement. Where employees are either forced or encouraged to work long hours, at the expense of leisure or family, they might be less engaged with the organisation. Indeed, the CIPD survey showed that employees who are satisfied with their work–life balance were more engaged with their work than others (CIPD survey 2006b).

There is considerable variation between countries in terms of the working hours culture. Britain and the United States are well known for their long working hours. In Britain the working week is officially limited to 48 hours, as established within the European Directive on working hours. However, the CIPD survey (2006b) showed that in Britain one in ten employees works more than 50 hours per week. Indeed, employees can choose to work longer than 48 hours in one week. The element of choice is an interesting matter of debate – if an employee chooses not to work beyond 48 hours, does it imply that he or she is not committed to the organisation? Management is responsible for setting expectations on working culture – but might also work long hours. Moreover, in times of recession, employees might be expected to work beyond their normal hours to cover for those who have been made redundant, and also to work harder during their time at work – a concept referred to elsewhere as 'work intensification' (see Chapter 13).

Another factor affecting working hours and work–life balance is childcare. There is country variation in relation to gendered responsibilities. In countries within Scandinavia (Finland, Sweden, Denmark and Norway), childcare is generally seen as the responsibility of women, but good childcare provision is in place. Moreover, in countries such as Norway, jobs within the caring profession are rewarded well, compared to other jobs. In contrast, in countries such as South Africa childcare tends to be less reliable and there can be ineffective monitoring of childcare provision.

ORGANISATIONAL COMMITMENT AND JOB SATISFACTION

Organisational commitment and job satisfaction are concepts that have been around for a number of years, and are generally perceived to be closely related to employee engagement – so much so that as terms they are sometimes used interchangeably with 'employee engagement'.

ORGANISATIONAL COMMITMENT

Organisational commitment has been regarded as closely related to behaviour that affects productivity, such as absence and turnover. Defining organisational commitment tends to be reasonably uncontentious. According to Mowday et al (1982: 27, cited in Gallie et al 1999), organisational commitment can be defined as 'the relative strength of the individual's identification with and involvement in the particular organisation', and can be linked to three factors: strong belief in and acceptance of organisational values, a willingness to exert considerable effort on behalf of the organisation, and a strong desire to maintain membership in the organisation. Meanwhile, Meyer and Allen (1991, cited in Muthuveloo and Rose 2005) refer to 'affective', 'continuance' and 'normative' commitment. Affective commitment means the way in which an employee identifies with and is involved in the organisation; continuance commitment refers to the costs that the employee perceives to be related to leaving the organisation; and normative commitment refers to the employee's feeling of obligation to remain within the organisation.

Employee engagement can be seen as closely related to organisational commitment, but 'one step up' from it (Robinson *et al* 2004). More specifically, Macey and Schneider (2008) argue that although organisational commitment captures both psychological attachment to an organisation and the willingness to exert energy in support of it, it is only one of the states that comprise engagement.

JOB SATISFACTION

Job satisfaction can be defined as the extent to which an employee expresses a positive affective (emotional) orientation towards a job (Curry *et al* 1986). It has less scientifically been defined in terms of overall satisfaction, and also in relation to a number of facets of work such as pay, supervision and workload (Curry *et al* 1986). Job satisfaction tends to be measured according to overall job satisfaction, intrinsic job satisfaction and extrinsic job satisfaction (Rose 2003; Stride *et al* 2007). Extrinsic factors include job security, pay and promotion prospects, while intrinsic factors include the actual work, using initiative and good relations with managers (British Household Survey, cited in Rose 2003: 507).

Reported levels of job satisfaction can be high. Over half of the employees who responded to the CIPD survey of workers mentioned above replied that they were 'very satisfied' or 'satisfied' with their jobs (CIPD 2006b). Similarly, a cross-national study of job satisfaction in 21 countries showed that workers in all countries were quite satisfied (13.6% stated that they were completely satisfied, 26.5% very satisfied, and 38.6% fairly satisfied). However, levels of satisfaction varied between countries so that, for example, Denmark had the highest job-satisfaction level, the United States came 7th, Great Britain 15th and Japan 19th (Sousa-Poza and Sousa-Poza 2000). However, not all workers express high levels of satisfaction. There can be differences according to the type of occupation. In the British Household Survey 1999, there was occupational variation. When examining the rankings of occupations in terms of the proportion of scores away from the median score (50), childcare assistants scored 75% and bus drivers scored 23% (British Household Survey findings in Rose 2003: 514).

The role of managers can be an important predictor of job satisfaction. In the cross-national study, an important predictor of job satisfaction was the relationship with managers. Similarly, in the CIPD survey, while most stated that they were satisfied with their relationships with their co-workers, only 20% were satisfied with the relations between workers and managers (CIPD 2006b). Thirdly, a study of public sector agencies in the United States has shown that managers with a participative style and effective supervisory communication are predictors of higher levels of job satisfaction (Soonhee Kim 2002).

In common with organisational commitment, job satisfaction can be seen as synonymous with employee engagement. In the case of job satisfaction, this is particularly the case when the measures used include those that relate to emotions as well as the conditions of work (Macey and Schneider 2008). However, Macey and Schneider argue that employee engagement incorporates these aspects of job satisfaction but goes beyond this to include the propensity to actively engage in different behaviours. Similarly, 'job involvement' or 'job engagement' (willingness to invest effort towards the attainment of tasks) is regarded by the same authors as a partial but not full measure of employee engagement (Macey and Schneider 2008).

EMPLOYEE HEALTH AND WELL-BEING

Employee engagement might also rely on adequate protection through health and safety policies and practices and be positively associated with employee perceptions of well-being.

HEALTH AND SAFETY

In many countries, there is clear guidance on health and safety within the workplace. For example, within the European Union occupational health and safety is covered by a substantial body of European law (see James 2009). As James (2009) explains, the first European Directive on health and safety at work was adopted in 1959. However, more emphasis on health and safety occurred in the late 1980s, and 20 Directives were adopted between 1988 and the 1990s. Arguably the most important was the 'framework' Directive 89/391/EEC, which applied to all sectors and set out a series of principles concerning 'the prevention of occupational risks, the protection of safety and health, the elimination of risk and accident factors, the informing, consultation, balanced participation in accordance with national laws and/ or practices and training of workers and their representatives' in addition to guidelines on their implementation (James 2009).

However, member states have differed in their legal frameworks on health and safety and how they have been enforced. In the UK, European Directives have resulted in new legal requirements since the early 1980s regarding asbestos, visual display equipment, personal protective equipment, manual handling, vibration, working at height, construction work, and hazardous substances. These complemented the provisions established under the Health and Safety at Work Act (1974). The Act arose after the Royal Commission on Safety and Health at Work resulted in the Robens report, published in 1972, which showed that in Britain every year 1,000 people were killed at work and 500,000 injured, that approximately 23 million working days were lost as a result of industrial accidents and disease, and that annual costs in terms of lost production were about £200 million.

The Health and Safety at Work Act (HASAWA) 1974 brought in a criminally enforceable duty on employers to take reasonable care of employees and all others who work on or visit their premises. Employees also have responsibility for co-operating with the employer on health and safety matters and taking reasonable care of their own health. The Act included codes of practices and enforcement, and the setting up of a Health and Safety Commission and Executive responsible for the administering of the legislation. Moreover, trade unions could appoint safety representatives at the place of work. However, although HASAWA covers a range of areas, the European Commission has disagreed with the way in which it allows employers to avoid responsibility owing to the phrase within it that states that action should be taken 'so far as reasonably practicable'. This phrase has, however, been retained (James 2009). Additional legislation has subsequently been introduced covering areas such as control of substances and work equipment.

In order to comply with the law in Britain, employers should at least carry out the duties pertaining to the responsibilities listed in the *Legislation in practice* box below.

⚷ LEGISLATION IN PRACTICE

Employer duties in relation to health and safety

In the UK, legislation regarding health and safety includes stipulations that the employer must:

- publish a health and safety policy
- arrange for the appointment of health and safety representatives and consult with them
- establish a health and safety committee if requested by a recognised trade union
- appoint a competent person to evaluate risks and hazards
- prevent risks, arrange periodic risk assessments, inform staff of risks, combat risks at source, and arrange protection from unavoidable risks
- provide health risk surveillance
- comply with provisions concerning health and safety posters and leaflets and provide comprehensible health and safety information
- adapt work to the individual, especially with respect to the design of workplaces
- alleviate monotonous work
- establish procedures against the occurrence of serious and imminent danger
- provide adequate health and safety training during working hours.

Source: CIPD (2010b)

Within Britain there has been a concerted campaign in the some areas of the media against health and safety legislation. It is argued that health and safety criteria are used by workers to shirk their duties, and that 'busybodies' interfere in the lives of others. One example of exaggeration concerns the banning of children from playing with conkers unless they wear safety goggles. Although the original story turned out to be a hoax, the tabloids have repeated it so often that it has become a widely accepted 'fact'. This and other, equally endlessly recycled, myths have had some effect in undermining public confidence in health and safety legislation. Rather less attention is accorded to the wholesale flouting of health and safety legislation by organisations employing large numbers of illegal workers, in areas ranging from food processing to construction, and to the thought that any further relaxing of the law and its enforcement may open the floodgates to a new torrent of bad practices. Legislation plays a vital role in protecting the bulk of the workforce.

EMPLOYEE WELL-BEING

It has been argued (MacDonald 2005: 1) that

> promoting employees' health and well-being is rapidly becoming the single most powerful way of enhancing performance and productivity in order to gain a competitive edge.

Health and well-being are a matter of key importance to management, not least because of their coverage under health and safety legislation (as outlined above) and also under more general legislative stipulations such as the 'duty of care'. In Britain, this latter duty for employers reportedly dates back to 1932 and the case of a person who found a snail in a glass of ginger beer, which resulted in 'considerable psychological trauma'! It was subsequently established in law that 'everyone has a duty of care not to injure, by act or omission, any other person who might reasonably foreseeably suffer an injury as a result of their act or omission' (MacDonald 2005: 5). In order to further improve well-being, employers may engage in a number of practices including employing an in-house occupational health service, providing health insurance, and promoting health and well-being initiatives (MacDonald 2005). However, the costs of such practices may prove to be more manageable for large than for small organisations.

The specific responsibilities associated with employee well-being are less clearly defined than those for health and safety. As with the term 'employee engagement', the term 'employee well-being' has come into fashion in recent years but has been defined and measured in different ways. To some extent the concept relies on actual physical and mental health. However, it also refers to perceptions of health and happiness. Research on call centres examined the relationship between factors that might contribute towards well-being (job design, performance monitoring, HR practices and team leader support) and four measures of well-being: anxiety, depression, and intrinsic and extrinsic job satisfaction. It was found that the factors most associated with well-being were high control over work methods and procedures, a low level of monitoring and a supportive team leader (Holman 2002).

There has been some evidence of a link between employee engagement and employee health and well-being. According to the CIPD (2009a: 2):

> Engagement is wholly consistent with an emphasis on employee well-being: arguably, it is an essential element in contributing to that well-being.

The CIPD (2006b) survey on employee engagement included a set of 12 questions on people's emotions at work. Six possible responses were positive (enthusiastic, optimistic, cheerful, contented, calm and relaxed) while six were negative (tense, miserable, depressed, worried, uneasy and gloomy) (CIPD 2006b: 6). The questions were based on Warr's (1990) scales of anxiety–contentment (tense, calm, relaxed, worried, uneasy and contented) and depression–enthusiasm (miserable, depressed, optimistic, enthusiastic, gloomy and cheerful). It was found that emotions are significantly related to the following performance indicators: job satisfaction, meaningfulness of work, cognitive engagement (being absorbed in tasks at work), physical engagement (being committed to completing work tasks), loyalty, and self-reported performance. Whereas negative emotions undermined these relationships, positive ones supported them (CIPD 2006b).

Levels of engagement can be related to the health characteristics of workers. The CIPD survey (2006b: 12) showed that workers with a disability felt less listened to, were less satisfied with their work, less in control of their work and more anxious, stressed and pressurised than able-bodied colleagues. They also rated their performance lower and reported higher absence levels, were less likely to be rated highly in appraisals, and were more likely to leave their job. In addition, they were more likely to have experienced bullying and harassment than others (CIPD 2006b: 12). Other factors influencing levels of engagement included employee experiences of bullying and harassment. Those who have experienced bullying or harassment were more likely to be depressed and anxious, to be less satisfied with their work, to have a low opinion of their managers and senior managers, and to want to leave the organisation (CIPD survey 2006b). Additional discussion on bullying and harassment is included within Chapter 11.

The case study below tackles the issue of stress in the workplace, and considers its relationship to a range of attitudes and behaviours.

CASE STUDY

WELL-BEING AND WORKPLACE STRESS

A report by Bevan (2010) outlines how employee well-being is vital in sustaining productivity. It details how too much stress can lead to a range of symptoms such as heart disease, hypertension, depression and absenteeism. At the same time, those who have a degree of control over their job content and workload and are supported effectively may not suffer from such conditions. In order to support those who are struggling with work pressure, employers might refer employees to employee assistance programmes or provide training for line managers so that they can detect problems and refer sufferers to an occupational health specialist, where appropriate.

Questions

Why has stress become more of an issue in today's workplace?

In which jobs is stress likely to be more prevalent?

What practical steps, in addition to those outlined above, can organisations adopt to alleviate stress in the workplace?

A common feature in liberal market economies (eg the USA, the UK, Australia) has been that secure jobs have become less common. From an employer perspective it could be argued that weak job security allows the firm to readily weed out shirkers, whereas genuinely productive staff have little to fear. In practice, regular dismissals are likely to engender a climate of insecurity and make working life more stressful for all employees, with knock-on effects in terms of productivity and well-being. Indeed, it should be noted that although employees in the USA typically work longer hours and have more insecure jobs, and less leave, than their West European counterparts, they are no more productive – and the incidence of mental illnesses is generally higher.

PERFORMANCE AND EMPLOYEE ENGAGEMENT

As already explained, employee engagement has been viewed as a way to improve performance (Robinson *et al* 2004; MacLeod and Clarke 2009). Indeed, MacLeod and Clarke go so far as to state (2009: 3) that:

> We believe that if employee engagement and the principles that lie behind it were more widely understood, if good practice was more widely shared, if the potential that resides in the country's workforce was more fully unleashed, we could see a step change in workplace performance and in employee well-being …

The findings of the CIPD survey suggested that engaged employees performed better than others, were more likely to recommend their organisation to other people, were less likely to take sick leave, and were less likely to leave the organisation (CIPD 2006b). However, if we take into account the different aspects of employee engagement, it could be the case that particular attitudes contribute towards particular measures of performance. Shore and Martin (1989), for example, assessed the relationship between both job satisfaction and organisational commitment and different measures of performance. They found that job satisfaction seemed to be a predictor of performance (as rated by supervisors), while organisational commitment was a better predictor of the intention to remain within the organisation. In summarising their findings they acknowledge weaknesses in these conclusions. For example, the employee–supervisor relationship could influence both job satisfaction and performance ratings. Nevertheless, these findings do suggest that a more detailed investigation of causal links is necessary. Indeed, even if there is a causal relationship, it is possible that the causality might be in the other direction. In other words, it is possible that higher levels of performance improve the way in which employees engage with the organisation since they feel proud to belong to the organisation and identify more closely with it. A further complication relates to the aspect of employee engagement of undertaking discretionary effort beyond any required by the employment contract. This is assessed within employee engagement surveys as one of the aspects determining engagement, but also as one that indicates improved employee performance. Yet 'going the extra mile' might not be due to engagement with the organisation but may instead be prompted by intense work pressures or the expectation that employees should appear to be engaged, as discussed in the following section.

EMPLOYEE ENGAGEMENT AND EMOTIONAL LABOUR

Employee engagement appears to be, on the face of it, a very positive strategy. However, there are two main problems with it. The first is the need for employees to show engagement through extra effort. The three dimensions referred to above also explicitly refer to physical engagement:

- emotional engagement – being highly involved emotionally with the work
- cognitive engagement – concentrating hard on doing the work
- physical engagement – being willing to 'go the extra mile' for the employer.

However, trade unions have expressed concern about the 'discretionary effort' that is referred to within discussions of employee engagement, which implies that employees should work hours additional to those that are covered in the employment contract and effectively work unpaid overtime (MacLeod and Clarke 2009: 99; Purcell 2010).

Secondly, employees should not just feel engaged but also *show* that they feel engaged. For example, while positively extolling the virtues and benefits of employee engagement, MacLeod and Clarke (2009: 4) implicitly refer to the need for employees to demonstrate positive attitudes at work when referring to the different types of job where employee engagement is of value:

> Nor is employee engagement only relevant in retail, where customers expect a cheerful face on the till rather than a languid hand waving them to a far-off aisle in response to a query about the availability of marmalade, and where employees' attitudes demonstrably and immediately impact on customer satisfaction.

Employee engagement thus implies the use of 'emotional labour'. Emotional labour has been generally defined as 'the effort, planning and control needed to express organisationally-desired emotion during interpersonal transactions'. More specifically, it can be related to the following four dimensions (Morris and Feldman, 1996: 987):

a) frequency of appropriate emotional display
b) attentiveness to required display rules
c) the variety of emotions required to be displayed, and
d) the emotional dissonance generated as the result of having to express organisationally desired emotions not genuinely felt.

Even where employees feel a sense of happiness while smiling, the way in which they smile may be determined by how the organisation wishes them to perform, and hence requires an effort beyond that which they would normally use in interacting with people (Morris and Feldman 1996). As Hochschild (1983, cited in Morris and Feldman 1996) has argued, the expression of emotion was formerly privately determined but is now a market commodity, involving either surface acting (simulating emotions that are not actually felt) or deep acting (attempting to feel the appropriate emotions). Emotional labour will vary according to a number of factors such as the gender of the worker (women having a greater frequency of emotional display than men) and type of job, and may result in negative consequences such as a lack of well-being and job dissatisfaction. However, these consequences may not be uniformly experienced (Morris and Feldman 1996).

To take the idea of emotional labour further, it can be argued that it requires employees to be 'living the brand'. In other words, workers are required to manage 'their appearance, demeanour and feelings during any interaction with customers' (Blyton and Turnbull 2004: 91–2). This was apparently the case within British Airways during the 1980s and 1990s. In common with staff in other airlines such as the US carrier Delta Airlines, female cabin crew were required to be caring, to present themselves as 'feminine' and aesthetically pleasing, and appear to be submissive. This attention to customer service appeared to be a positive attribute of the company. British Airways were reported as having high worker job satisfaction levels at the same time as they increased profits. However, the situation was completely different by the late 1990s, when the company showed a dramatic fall in profits and difficult relations with staff. A quote from one of the cabin crew ran thus (Turnbull *et al* 2001, cited in Blyton and Turnbull 2004: 93):

> Customer service and good employee relations go hand-in-hand. But all BA want is the customer service – they've dismissed the idea of good employee relations.

Emotional labour has therefore been used as a tool to increase profits. As such, it has been linked with labour process theory (see Chapter 3), which (Bolton 2010: 205):

> highlights the context of a capitalist economy, the tensions and contradictions inherent in the emotional labour process, along with the realities of it as hard and productive work.

Using the lens of labour process theory facilitates a better understanding of the actual conditions of work, recognises the tensions inherent in the way in which employers can tend to use employees as a commodity, and acknowledges the active role of employees (Bolton 2010).

It could thus be argued that emotional labour is present in all lines of work where employees are expected to display a particular set of emotions (either positive or negative, as in the case of debt collectors) when they do not feel that way in reality. If this is the case, then do surveys of 'employee engagement' capture how employees are really feeling, or are they instead capturing the emotions and attitudes that employees have become used to expressing while at work?

REFLECTION ON PRACTICE

Employee engagement and emotional labour

Bolton (2010) refers to how emotional labour can be used in many different sectors, but draws attention to workers in the entertainment industry who must laugh and pretend to be well at all times.

Think of an organisation where you are working, or where you have worked in the past. To what extent were you expected to seem happy when you were not happy in reality?

If you were expected to show different feelings from those you really felt, how did it affect you?

EMPLOYEE ENGAGEMENT IN SMALL AND MEDIUM-SIZED ENTERPRISES AND VOLUNTARY SECTOR ORGANISATIONS

A central factor of employee engagement seems to be the use of a survey to assess employee attitudes prior to embarking on 'employee engagement' practices. However, small and medium-sized enterprises (SMEs) might find that conducting a survey is an unnecessary cost. Moreover, where there are a small number of employees (for example, fewer than 20), it would be difficult to draw any firm conclusions based on the evidence accumulated. There might also be difficulties in delegating further responsibility to employees. The whole issue of employee engagement surveys also relies on the necessary resources being available to conduct this work. In emerging economies, a large proportion of work is conducted within SMEs, but these may be both formal sector and informal sector organisations. Although employee engagement might be just as important in those organisations, the feasibility of conducting a survey might be minimal.

A further issue to consider is the managerial style present within the organisation. As discussed in Chapter 2, in SMEs the dominant style might be patriarchal or authoritarian. If patriarchal, employers might feel that employees are 'part of the family' and do not need to be 'engaged', and if an authoritarian style is prevalent, employers may be unwilling to involve employees in decision-making.

In voluntary, non-profit-making or third-sector organisations (referred to as non-governmental organisations in emerging economies) employee engagement may similarly be seen as a valuable tool. However, in such organisations employee engagement might be low in reality since – although it is often assumed that employees are well treated, highly motivated and dedicated to their jobs – work pressures can arise due to funding pressures and the performance targets set by funders (Cunningham 2008).

THE IMPLEMENTATION OF EMPLOYEE ENGAGEMENT SURVEYS AND PRACTICES

Assuming that employee engagement is not used to exploit workers but instead to improve working conditions and empower them, the establishment of employee engagement mechanisms within the workplace will require the support of a range of stakeholders in addition to the employees themselves.

The role of organisational leaders in employee engagement has been referred to as 'crucial' (MacLeod and Clarke 2009: 5). However, many chief executives and senior managers are unaware of employee engagement or are not convinced of its benefits. Many regard it as 'soft and fluffy' and do not see it as contributing towards 'the bottom line'. They may also see it as the role of HR (MacLeod and Clarke 2009: 32). Yet a clear shared vision of the organisation is arguably 'at the heart of employee engagement'. Also important is visible leadership, involving CEOs who 'walk the floor' on a regular basis (MacLeod and Clarke 2009: 76). Trust of senior management appears to be vital, together with perceptions of fairness (CIPD 2006a: 4).

Line managers also have an important role to play. One of the drivers of employee engagement is (MacLeod and Clarke 2009: 33):

> Engaging managers who offer clarity, appreciation of employees' effort and contribution, who treat people as individuals and who ensure that work is organised efficiently and effectively so that employees feel they are valued, and equipped and supported to do their job.

However, managers can be a barrier to effective employee engagement due to an unwillingness to delegate, an obsession with targets rather than people, a lack of listening skills, and/or a lack of training (MacLeod and Clarke 2009). Their engagement might also depend on their own self-efficacy (their belief in their ability to complete specific tasks) (Luthans and Peterson 2001). In addition, in order to take responsibility line managers need (Purcell 2010: 9):

> a positive and supportive relationship with their senior manager, providing career opportunities, achieving a good work–life balance, the opportunity to raise matters of concern with their manager and the belief that their job is secure.

HR managers also have a vital role to play, both in acknowledging the importance of engagement and in facilitating access to an appropriate range of tools and techniques that might be used to help line managers to implement engagement practices. They will also be responsible for adapting and administering a survey and the analysis of results (MacLeod and Clarke 2009). However, surveys of employee engagement can sometimes reveal areas that would normally be beyond the scope of HR managers – since responses to survey results often reveal the importance of relationships within the workplace and the need for greater trust of senior managers. This may imply the need for changes to management style and leadership (CIPD 2006b: 3) – which may not be a palatable conclusion. Results can also show the need for additional voice mechanisms, job redesign, and more attention paid to anti-discrimination measures with respect to age, gender, disability (CIPD 2006a: 11). The costs of implementing all of the necessary changes might be prohibitive.

Trade unions and employee representatives have also been acknowledged to be vital in employee engagement (MacLeod and Clarke, 2009: 5), playing a role in the dissemination of information and the implementation of employee engagement: 'Trade union and employee representative involvement in programmes to boost employee engagement will help ensure that such gains are maximised and shared' (Purcell 2010: 9). However, trade unions will also argue for independent collective representation, and emphasise the need for trade union representatives to sustain their role as intermediaries (MacLeod and Clarke 2009).

The *Applying theory to practice* box below outlines the way in which employee engagement might be implemented in practice.

APPLYING THEORY TO PRACTICE

An effective employee engagement survey

Purcell (2010: 6–8) identifies a number of steps that might be followed in order to conduct an effective employee engagement survey. These include:

- securing the support of senior management

- aligning the survey with the existing business strategy

- involving employees (and/or trade unions) in the design of the survey

- ensuring confidentiality

- attitudinal questions on the nature of work (autonomy, discretion, responsibility, control), on the nature of the job (workload, pace, monitoring, skills), on management and unions (communication, involvement, representation, trust), and on the company (advocacy, pride, loyalty)

- benchmarking the results over time and across sectors

- reporting back and taking action to address problems and concerns.

However, conducting a survey is not enough to ensure long-term commitment. As Blyton and Turnbull (2004: 365) suggest,

Long-term commitment and motivation on the part of workers will be more likely to be secured if management are prepared to offer jobs that are stable, well paid, interesting, and in which employees' views are adequately represented. Considerable lip-service has been paid by management to the importance of building long-term relationships grounded on partnership, trust and commitment, but in reality the reciprocity required to build a genuine improvement in employee relations has often been more notable by its absence.

EMPLOYEE ENGAGEMENT IN NON-UNION FIRMS

On the one hand, it could be argued that collective bargaining may 'crowd out' other more bottom-line-oriented forms of employee engagement. In addition, unions may be hostile to anything likely to undermine the collective bargaining process. On the other hand, there is little research evidence to suggest that one form of participation will marginalise other forms of engagement (Brewster *et al* 2007). Indeed, collective bargaining may ensure that terms and conditions of service enjoy a greater legitimacy, making employees more willing to give management 'the benefit of the doubt' in other areas. In other words, employees may be more willing to trust management if they feel that the terms and conditions they work under are fair, and/or that they will have the support of the union in the event of management systematically abusing the trust of workers.

SUMMARY

This chapter has considered various aspects of employee engagement, including its potential for improving workplace performance, and has outlined the way in which employee engagement practices and surveys might be used.

'Employee engagement' is a fashionable term that has been used fairly frequently by management consultants. The means used to secure 'employee engagement' and the measures used to address any shortfalls may lead to positive benefits for both workers and employers. However, it is important to be aware of the ways in which it could be used to exploit workers. Workers ought to be *really* engaged through appropriate workplace practices and employment relationships built on trust, rather than simply encouraged to *show* that they are engaged through positive responses to a series of surveys. If employee engagement is not used appropriately, it could simply be another way in which employees are encouraged to be 'emotional labourers'.

EXPLORE FURTHER

Reading

- Bolton, S. (2010) 'Old ambiguities and new developments: exploring the emotional labour process', in P. Thompson and C. Smith (eds) *Working Life: Renewing labour process analysis*. London: Palgrave

- Purcell, J. (2010) *Building Employee Engagement*. ACAS Policy Discussion Paper, January. Available online at www.acas.org.uk

Websites

- Advisory, Conciliation and Arbitration Service www.acas.org.uk

- Department for Business, Innovation and Skills www.bis.gov.uk

- Chartered Institute of Personnel and Development www.cipd.co.uk

- The Institute for Employment Studies (IES) www.employment-studies.co.uk

CHAPTER 9

Pay and Reward

CHAPTER OVERVIEW

In earlier chapters we saw that the employment relationship represented an 'indeterminate exchange' whereby a readily quantifiable wage is exchanged for an inherently uncertain amount of labour power. Yet the manner in which wage rates are themselves determined is a complex business, reflecting custom, institutions, internal and external markets for labour, social relations and strategic choice. Most organisations will naturally seek to optimise their output (in terms of goods manufactured or services offered), giving greater rewards to the most productive, skilled and/or capable employees. However, too much emphasis on closely controlling the work of employees and/or the distribution of rewards in a manner that is perceived to be unfair or overly punitive will result in the most competent staff members migrating to other organisations, leaving behind discontented, less capable, and less mobile staff. The operation of reward systems may thus have effects opposite of those intended. Moreover, the close monitoring of employee performance may encourage dishonesty. Reward systems aim to control costs and increase staff morale. Many countries prohibit pay discrimination on the grounds of gender and race: the operation of a reward system has legal implications. Reward is therefore one of the key policy-making areas within the workplace.

In this chapter we review the basis under which pay is calculated, the role of incentives and rewards, individual- and collective-based pay systems, and the role of employment relations practitioners and line managers in this regard. Although the chapter includes reference to a range of countries, greater attention is drawn to OECD countries due to the possibilities for useful comparison.

LEARNING OUTCOMES

After studying this chapter you should be able to:

- understand the processes linked to pay determination

- determine a range of approaches to reaching pay awards/settlements

- explain a variety of incentives and rewards that might be offered to an employee, and critique these methods

- compare individual and collective pay systems

- critically evaluate the role of employment relations specialists and line managers in the reward process

PAY DETERMINATION

There are a number of basic ways in which firms may seek to determine wage rates. Each has implications for productivity and equity.

MINIMUM WAGES

The first is to seek to pay the bare minimum that will be necessary to secure the desired quantity and quality of labour. A limitation of this approach is that firms never possess perfect information about the state of the external labour market. This means that, at best, a decision to pay as little as possible will result in at least some guesswork in making wage offers, possibly leading to shortages of labour and/or excessively high staff turnover rates. Moreover, whereas it is easy to quantify the physical size of a workforce, it is more difficult to quantify its capabilities – low pay may attract the desperate, but it will be unlikely to attract suitably qualified or motivated individuals. In many instances, firms have chosen to respond by resorting to more vulnerable categories of labour: children and women. Interestingly, there is some evidence that single establishments employing relatively small numbers of workers tend to pay less (McNabb and Whitfield 2000).

A second possibility is to set pay rates for the lowest-ranked jobs in line with the legal minimum wage. Many countries, ranging from the United Kingdom to the United States, have minimum wage legislation in force, which may help to determine the minimum acceptable rate. Firms may choose to pay as little as is legally possible for the lowest-ranked jobs, in the expectation that many other firms will adopt a similar position, giving those with the least marketable skills little option but to accept it. A problem with this approach is that in many contexts, minimum wages are extremely low, leading to the same problems as encountered with the first possibility: low staff morale, and low productivity. Despite this, conservative critics of national minimum wages have persistently argued that they reduce the demand for labour and encourage shirking. However, in a 2005 study, Morris *et al* (2005) found that among smaller employers it was the more effective and successful enterprises that were strongly supportive of minimum wages, on the basis that they discouraged more short-termist competitors from undercutting them through extreme labour repression.

There is a very large body of literature on national minimum wages. It is generally the case that the harshest critics of national minimum wages legislation come from the ranks of neo-liberal economists, while, on the whole, writers within the broad field of industrial and employment relations are more sympathetic (see Metcalf 1999a and 1999b; Neumark and Wascher 2001; Williams and Mills 2001; Stewart 2002). In a definitive study, Card and Krueger (1995) found that the imposition of minimum wages only had negligible effects on employment.

Within different contexts, minimum wage rates vary greatly. In Mozambique, minimum wage rates are so low, and enforcement so weak, as to have only limited effect on what firms actually do. Within the United States, certain jobs are subject to federal minimum wage law under the Fair Labor Standards Act. Others are subject to state, city or local laws. A few states, mostly located in the 'deep south' (eg Texas), have no minimum wage laws at all. In 2009 the US federal minimum wage stood at $6.55 per hour.

In Canada, general minimum wages (rather than confined to specific jobs) are set at state level. In 2009 the lowest minimum wages were encountered in New Brunswick at 8.80 Canadian dollars per hour (US $8.45), and the highest in Ontario at 10.25 Canadian dollars per hour.

In the United Kingdom, minimum wages are linked to age. In 2009 the rates were GB£5.80 per hour for the main body of workers, which included those of 22 years of age or older. Meanwhile, workers aged between 18 and 21 must be paid at least GB£4.83 per hour, and those aged 16 to 17 GB£3.57 per hour (Direct Government UK 2010).

In contrast, a number of continental European countries – most notably Germany and Denmark – have no national minimum wages. Instead, minimum wages for entire occupations and industries are set through national collective bargaining, which are then compulsory for particular sectors. In practice, this means that pay rates for the lowest-ranked jobs are higher than in countries where there is little or no centralised bargaining, but where national minimum wages are in force. Does this mean that employers in such countries are less likely to hire labour? Although the job creation record of Germany may indeed appear superficially worse than that of the United States, a closer scrutiny reveals the converse. Large numbers of the employed in the United States are in part-time contingent jobs owing to a lack of alternatives (some 7 to 8 million people); there are some 2.3 million people in prison (by far the highest national proportion of prisoners per capita – and in terms of sheer numbers – in the world) and around 1.5 million people in the armed forces. If these numbers are taken into account, the USA has the worst job creation record in the developed world, despite – or perhaps because of – weak labour market regulation. Table 9.1 compares national minimum wage rates across the OECD in those contexts where minimum wages are in force; it will be seen that there is considerable variation from context to context, but rates are generally low.

Table 9.1 National minimum wages in national currency units per year

Country	National currency unit	2005	2006	2007	2008	2009	2010 GB£*
Australia	Australian dollar	24820	25309	26757	27432	28277	17,466
Belgium	Euro	15224	15451	15933	16732	17288	15,128
Canada	Canadian dollar	15184	15808	16182	17305	18429	11,455
Chile	Chilean peso	1485000	1575000	1674000	1818000	1944000	2,545
Czech Rep	Czech koruna	86220	93150	96000	96000	96000	3,479
France	Euro	14232	14833	15206	15664	15952	13,959
Hungary	Forint	684000	750000	786000	828000	858000	2,777
Ireland	Euro	12168	12521	13873	14164	14164	12,602
Korea	Won	7937120	8407200	9437760	10224240	10848000	615
Lithuania	Litas	6300	6900	7800	9600	9600	2,474
Luxembourg	Euro	17711	18078	18843	19235	20045	17,835
Mexico	Mexican peso	11762	12233	12709	13218	13829	715
Netherlands	Euro	16392	16570	16964	17442	18013	16,026
Portugal	Euro	5245.8	5402.6	5642	5964	6300	5,605
Slovak Rep	Euro	2629	2818	3077	3226	3546	3,155
Spain	Euro	7181	7573	7988	8400	8736	7,772
Turkey	Turkish lira	5864	6372	6885	7483	8154	3,649
Utd Kingdom	Pound sterling	8606	8944	9334	9656	9953	9,953
United States	US dollar	10712	10712	11350	12806	14262	9,094

Data from Minimum Wages at Current Prices in NCU under Earnings under Labour from OECD.Stat Extracts, http://stats.oecd.org [accessed on 31 October 2010].

*The pound sterling equivalent (2010) facilitates a rough comparison of amounts. However, this does not take account of the costs of living in each country.

In some cases, organisations have paid the required minimum wage rates to their core employees but have neglected to enforce appropriate wage rates for suppliers. The case study below illustrates this situation.

WAGE RATES – A SWEATSHOP SCANDAL IN INDIA

An investigation carried out by the *Observer* newspaper (2010) revealed that the suppliers of three large retail companies – Marks & Spencers, Next and Gap – were consistently paying low wages to workers and employing them under 'sweatshop' conditions. In some cases, factories in India used middlemen to employ workers who were then paid as little as 25p an hour, and required to work up to eight hours a day in overtime, while some worked seven days a week. In one case, it was reported that those who objected to working overtime had been beaten. The corporations were seeking to address the situation through ordering suppliers to pay workers any amounts that were owed to them, and to reduce working hours to legal limits.

Questions

Do you think that large corporations have any responsibility for the industrial relations policies (and wage rates) of their subcontractors? Give reasons for your answer.

What are the consequences of the use of cheap outsourced labour in India for wage rates within advanced economies such as Britain and the United States?

NEGOTIATING WAGES THROUGH COLLECTIVE BARGAINING

A third possibility is to set wage rates through a negotiated agreement with one or more representative trade unions via the collective bargaining process. An advantage of this mechanism is that wage rates enjoy legitimacy; it is the union's responsibility to sell any deal to its members. Moreover, in between annual rounds of collective bargaining, it is administratively easy – all the firm has to do is pay what has been agreed upon. Also, although collective bargaining may result in higher wages than would otherwise be the case, the determination of wages through collective bargaining encourages firms to take labour and the concerns of labour more seriously (which, in turn, is good for productivity). More generally, higher average wages boost consumer demand across an economy. However, although the agreement is a collective one (in other words, it covers a pre-agreed component – generally, the bulk – of a workforce), not all workers covered by the agreement will be paid the same. Rather, pay within particular job bands is typically linked to seniority, but within the parameters of agreed pay rates. More detail is given on collective bargaining in Chapter 7. Within non-union firms, this entire dimension of pay-setting is absent; pay is therefore set through one of the other mechanisms outlined in this chapter.

LINKING PAY TO PERFORMANCE

As Heery (1996: 57) notes, criticisms of the above three possibilities centre on the fact that they reward job categories, not the productivity or actual operational capabilities of a particular worker. Central to the rise of human resource management in the 1980s was the argument that pay should be linked to actual performance – in other words, that the risks borne by the firm are shared by the workers, with pay and upward movement on pay scales being closely linked to performance (Heery 1996). There was thus a renewed emphasis not only on bonuses but on the linking of base pay to the quality and quantity of labour power delivered (*ibid*). This philosophy is often referred to in the literature as 'New pay', a fourth possibility.

In practice, in common with many 'new-style' HRM policies, New pay represented 'old wine in new bottles' (Guest 1987) rather than genuine innovation. During the Industrial Revolution – and, indeed, before it – many employers adopted piecework-based pay systems, simply paying a worker according to how much he or she produced. Although the physical amount produced is easy to quantify, quality is often rather harder. Those employed under this basis are often remarkably adept at concealing low-quality goods and waste in order to maximise their pay. In turn, employers that profess to practise piecework are often more arbitrary than systematic in quantifying real value generated by employees.

There are a number of reasons why the piecework system was gradually replaced by standardised pay systems. Firstly, not all types of output are readily quantifiable and it is significantly easier to measure quantity of output than quality. Secondly, as we saw in Chapter 2, the rise of trade unions was characterised by struggles for procedures and equity. In response, employers increasingly chose to adopt standardised systems based on a fixed rate for a job within parameters set by experience and the length of tenure (Brown 1996). However, the decline of unions in many industrialised societies has made output-based pay more attractive again (see Brown 1996). New pay is not, however, simply a product of union weakness; its proponents argue that it also allows for a closer integration between the different functional areas of HRM and a more strategic perspective (see Richbell and Wood 2009). New pay is inherently flexible, in that pay can be adjusted according to output – indeed, through subtly 'moving the goalposts', firms may, in fact, cut real wages in a manner that is not immediately visible. As Twomey and Quazi (1994) note, in order to function properly, pay must genuinely be adjusted upward and downward according to the circumstances the firm finds itself in and how well employees perform. Keeping the fixed component of pay low means that, should an individual employee under-achieve, he or she will bear some of the indirect costs borne by the firm (Twomey and Quazi 1994: 567).

New pay is based on the assumption that remuneration should reflect not just external labour markets but also the real contribution of the individual employee to the firm. The operation of more flexible pay systems forces staff to take more responsibility for their work. Those who excel can do extremely well, potentially resulting in a win/win situation for both the firm and the employee. In practice, many firms have been reluctant to abandon more traditional systems owing to fears of employee resistance and because of the administrative complexities associated with quantifying and duly rewarding the output of every single employee. New pay-type reward systems are more commonly encountered within more senior jobs bands than those at the base of the organisation. However, within all job categories, a further problem that can be encountered is in terms of employment equity legislation. For very good reason it may be difficult for an organisation to prove that imbalances in perceived performance and pay on gender, age and/or ethnicity are wholly coincidental. Given this, it may be attractive to reduce the risk through the use of more standardised reward systems (Richbell and Wood 2009). A further limitation of New pay systems is that the adoption of a reward system linked to performance assumes that pay is the primary motivator – most psychological theories of motivation assume that a range of other factors are at work.

 APPLYING THEORY TO PRACTICE

Performance-related pay in China

Research conducted by Baruch *et al* (2004) focused on payment systems in China. Since China is often identified as a collectivist country, it could be considered that performance-related pay (PRP) is not appropriate for Chinese organisations. However, the modernisation process in China has involved a range of changes, including the introduction of new HR practices such as performance-related pay. A key argument for introducing this type of reward system is that it acts as a motivator by providing incentives and recognising achievements. It might therefore be appropriate for industries such as professional sports, where both individual and team-based achievements can be measured in an objective manner. In China, performance-related pay has been used in sports organisations such as the Shanghai Sports Technical Institute (SSTI) since 1985 following Chinese participation in the Los Angeles Olympic Games (*ibid*).

Surveys conducted by the same authors (Baruch *et al* 2004) showed that team sports players regarded the PRP system to be more effective for improving performance than did individual sports players. In addition, they also found that females who played individual sports viewed PRP more favourably than males. This was because they viewed the payment system as being more likely to provide them with rewards that matched their abilities (*ibid*: 257). However, women did not view PRP as favourably when used for team sports.

Do you think that PRP is more appropriate for measuring individual than for measuring team-based performance? Give reasons for your answer.

Would you anticipate that PRP for individual performance would be viewed more favourably by females than males in countries other than China? Again, give reasons for your answer,

A HYBRID APPROACH

Given the problems identified in the previous sections, a fifth possibility for payment systems emerges – that firms adopt a mixed or hybrid approach. Indeed, in the real world, this is often the chosen path. Firstly, if New pay is indeed about the alignment of HR with general organisational strategic objectives, then the relative contingency of actual pay rates may vary greatly according to the overall goals of the organisation. An organisation may, for example, seek to simplify administration as part of a general desire to cut costs to the bare minimum, or seek to engender the long-term commitment of the workforce through equity. Mixed or hybrid approaches may involve the use of New pay only within certain job categories and/or the retention of a basic pay rate for a job that is only marginally supplemented through performance bonuses. As Heery (1996) notes, employees generally desire an income that is stable and secure, and may feel extremely unhappy that the organisation has the capacity to cut pay at will. Moreover, any form of linking pay with performance may have unexpected consequences – employees may, for example, avoid or defer more difficult tasks in order to be rewarded for performing a large number of simple ones, or conceal quality defects in order to be rewarded for a high output (Cacciope 1999). Thus, as Twomey and Quazi (1994) note, pay systems must link the needs of the firm and the individual with the social and technological context. More highly paid professionals may be more sensitive to non-pay factors, whereas those working for low wages are likely to be more immediately concerned with securing a basic income for subsistence (*ibid*). Meanwhile, in industries where the external and technological environments change rapidly, firms are more likely to adopt highly flexible systems – but even then may be left behind by events.

TEAM-BASED PAY SYSTEMS

A sixth possibility is to set pay according to the performance of a group of employees or a team. The increased popularity of teamwork in many countries in the 1980s led to an increased use of team-based pay. However, here again, finding objective measures of group performance may be difficult, meaning that organisations may often opt for superficial gestures rather than properly linking performance with pay (Cacciope 1999). In addition, team-based pay systems may undermine individual pay rather than being complementary (*ibid*). In practice, Kerrin and Oliver (2002: 323) argue that teamwork is often incompatible with individual pay systems – the former may encourage free-riding whereas the latter may discourage information-sharing and undermine team efforts (Kerrin and Oliver 2002: 323). As Cacciope (1999) notes, there are always difficulties in reconciling team solidarities and in effectively measuring actual performance. Finally, the relationship between individual effort and group-based rewards may seem tenuous in practice (*ibid*). At the same time, team-based pay may represent a viable alternative in those cases where the individual performance or contribution of employees is hard to measure, and where technology more readily lends itself to group work (Ichniowski and Shaw 2003). Examples of team-based pay systems include rewards according to the physical output generated by a team. Not all group-based pay needs to be team-based. For example, profit-sharing represents a form of group incentive that transcends the efforts of a single grouping performing a set range of tasks. However, profit-sharing may be associated with even more pronounced problems of free-riding, the links between what an individual does and firm-level outcomes often appearing tenuous (*ibid*). Training and the promotion of specific value sets may mitigate this, with performance being promoted via peer pressure (*ibid*). However, where objective circumstances are poor, no amount of training or indoctrination is likely to work.

PAY AND INEQUALITY

The uncertainties inherent in any contingent pay system, and the inevitable discretion given to supervisors and managers, means that existing inequalities may be perpetuated – for example, women may be paid less than men (Heery

1996). As noted earlier, this may open the organisation to legal challenges in those circumstances where employment equity legislation is in force. In addition, because contingent performance-based pay is predicated on the absence or complicity of a union, it means that employees may lack genuine representation, which, again, may mean that the system is lacking in legitimacy (*ibid*).

There are also issues regarding distributive justice. Such models transfer risks on to the shoulders of employees and away from managers – it is employees who share the costs of poor overall organisational performance. Chronic failings in corporate governance mean that senior managers are often relatively free to set their own pay, meaning that they are insulated from the costs of organisational failure (*ibid*). The 2008 financial crisis underscored the extent to which senior managers are often able to continue to reap exceptional rewards even when their incompetence is clearly visible.

A further point worth observing is that within liberal market economies such as Britain and the United States (see Chapter 5) the gaps between top- and lower-ranked jobs have grown wider since the 1970s. There is, however, little objective evidence that senior managers have become progressively better at their jobs – indeed, some of the best-rewarded managers often seem to be among the most incompetent. Moreover, as Baron and Cooke (1992) comment, there is significant evidence that smaller gaps between the senior managers and ordinary workers are associated with higher product quality. The reasons for this are simple: greater equity promotes trust and commitment, and therefore a greater willingness of employees to excel. It is worth noting that in some of the most unequal mature economies – such as the United States and the United Kingdom – rising social inequality has been associated with declining competitiveness in manufacturing and, indeed, a host of social ills. There is little doubt that there is a contradiction between increased inequality within both firms and society at large, and rhetoric about teamwork, gain-sharing and partnership (Baron and Cooke 1992: 193). Employees are unlikely to be deceived by rhetoric about commitment in the absence of material evidence.

APPROACHES TO REACHING PAY AWARDS/SETTLEMENTS

This leads us on to the practical approaches for determining pay. Where collective bargaining is in force (see Chapter 7), a collective agreement results in staff being placed on specific pay scales that, in turn, are subject to renegotiation, typically on an annual basis. What an individual is paid is thus subject to the specific job and where he or she finds himself or herself on the pay scale. Although an individual's position on the scale is generally related to seniority, there may be some room for upward adjustment on the scale in the case of exceptional performance (within the broad parameters of the collective agreement), whereas new employees with previous work experience or some or other desirable attribute may be able to negotiate a favourable point of entry. Such approaches are founded on attempts to quantify what a specific job is worth, rather than to measure the performance of individuals or groups. This may be problematic in that there are considerable variations in the performance of individuals and groups, but it does leave considerably less room for personal prejudices and for the possibilities of discrimination.

MARKET TRENDS

Pay may reflect market trends. For example, in 2010 a commitment by the UK government to freezing pay in the public sector led to employers in other areas seeking to follow suit, and, indeed, to moves to withdraw previously tabled pay offers. Moreover, more generally, the exponential increase in senior managerial pay in the early 2000s led to mutually supporting rounds of leapfrogging. Proponents of very high managerial pay argued that this was necessary to retain high talent in the face of increased competition for much-needed skills. However, as noted above, there often appears to be little connection between high managerial pay and real and sustainable performance.

It is also worth noting that downturns strengthen the relative power of employers, and so mean downward pressures on pay. In liberal market economies (see Chapter 5), wages have stagnated for those in the lower job bands for many years, contributing to a chronic crisis of consumer demand only resolved through excessive borrowing. Calls for pay restraint or cuts during a recession may make things worse, and exacerbate existing systemic distortions. For example, within the United States, as much as 17% of the population may be considered to be objectively poor (US Census Bureau 2009) and lack the capacity to meaningfully consume goods and services. Increasing poverty means that fewer people can consume, leading to reduced demand for goods and services, leading to further wage squeezes and business failures, resulting in turn in worsening poverty – a vicious cycle that is difficult to overcome. So although cutting wages might mean that a firm can, in the short term, make more money, if all or most firms do it, then all lose – and stagnant wages for most workers make it difficult to sustain growth.

PAY AS A MECHANISM FOR DISCIPLINE OR GAIN-SHARING

The determination of pay in practice may also reflect how a firm understands the operation of reward systems: as a mechanism for disciplining the workforce, as genuinely sharing in any gains, or, as something to be grudgingly dispensed to workers, with as little being paid out – as noted earlier – as the external labour market and/or the law will tolerate. In a particularly influential paper, Kochan and Osterman (2000) argued that if firms wish to actively promote their competitiveness in terms of quality, flexibility and innovation, they need to be willing to share gains with employees. This includes equitable reward systems, the employees being given a fair share of any new profits generated through employee endeavour, resulting in a self-reinforcing virtuous circle. However, firms can, and do compete through paying very low wages – which makes it difficult to promote fairness in pay on profitability grounds.

Despite the rhetoric of gains-sharing, therefore, it has been argued that HRM is concerned with control and discipline and promoting individual self-interest, rather than collective identity (Storey 1995). Indeed, there has been an increased move away from secure employment contracts characterised by wage stability, to greater contingency and flexibility, with increasing risks downloaded on to employees, even if there is, at least, in theory, the possibility of greater rewards accruing to exceptional achievement (Kato and Morishima 2002: 488). However, employment relations cannot operate where trust is completely absent. The employment relationship is one that is based on reciprocity, framed by norms and unwritten expectations (Akerlof 1982). Management may seek to enhance notions of fairness via financial participation, linking reward to overall organisational outcomes – in effect sharing in gains (MacInnes *et al* 1985). In other words, rather than piecework – which primarily aims to discipline workers – financial participation may be seen as a positive incentive … although in reality it may not always be seen as such by workers.

REFLECTION ON PRACTICE

Financial participation – a positive incentive?

Have you worked in an organisation where employees were given shares in the firm?

Do you think that being given shares, and consequently benefiting from the firm's profits, will motivate workers to increase productivity? Give reasons for your answer.

FINANCIAL PARTICIPATION

Financial participation policies may be adopted by the firm for a wide range of reasons, from a genuine commitment to fairness through to coercing workers to act in a particular way. It is fair to say that in the 1990s and 2000s, the latter has become more prominent than the former. As Poutsma and de Nijs (2003) note, financial participation may be broadly based on the entire workforce, or narrowly focused on a specific component. The most prominent example of the latter constitutes financial participation schemes aimed at managers, with the specific aim of more closely aligning them to the interests of shareholders, and on distributing returns to those who own the firm. However, this practice may have perverse effects. It may weaken the ties that exist between the manager in the firm in a way that is not necessarily good for shareholders. It may, for example, encourage excessively instrumental views towards the firm – that it is an immediate source of personal enrichment rather than something to be nurtured or sustained. In other words, it may encourage excessive managerial 'irresponsibility' (Boyer 2010). Secondly, not all shareholders have an interest in prioritising short-term returns. Although short-term gains may be in the interests of fund managers (whose pay is often linked to short-term performance), many shareholders are concerned with long-term stability in earnings. The 2008 financial crisis highlighted the limitations of excessive short-termism. However, the dominance of neo-liberal ideologies and powerful vested interests has meant that narrowly based financial participation remains popular in liberal market economies.

Why do firms adopt financial participation schemes aimed at non-managerial employees? There are three reasons for it (Croucher *et al* 2010). Firstly, there is the legitimating role that such schemes can play (*ibid*). The managerial agenda may be a lot more acceptable to workers if they have a material interest in its success. Secondly, it may be argued that increasing workers' involvement in the financial affairs of the enterprise may incentivise workers to maximise their potential and to share their 'insider' knowledge with managers (Croucher *et al* 2010). It may therefore be part of a broader commitment to involvement and participation with a view to maximising productivity and co-operation. Thirdly – albeit increasingly less common – there may be a commitment towards fairer working (Croucher *et al* 2010). Co-operatives and employee-owned enterprises share profits among their members/employees. Although this may incentivise employees to work harder, it also reflects a commitment to a fairer and more democratic working life.

Clearly, there are a number of different rationales for financial participation. It may be part of a general 'hard' or instrumental HR strategy, aimed at maximising value to shareholders and avoiding unnecessary waste or 'excessive' diversion of resources towards rank-and-file employees (Croucher *et al* 2010). Alternatively, it may transcend 'soft' or co-operative HRM, as part of a broader framework of workplace democracy. As noted earlier, a single pure HR strategy is rarely encountered, firms often mixing and matching policies and strategies. Financial participation may indeed reflect a combination of motives, especially given that different schemes may be directed at different categories of employee – for example, managers versus non-managers.

WAGE RATES AND INFLATION

Before we conclude this section it is necessary to consider two further issues pertinent to pay rates. Firstly, wages rates may vary according to inflation. Although inflation has been generally low in advanced societies for many years, it should be noted that this has not always been the case. Official indices of inflation may mask differential increases within the notional baskets of goods that are used to calculate official inflation rates. For example, in recent years, food prices have increased significantly more than the cost of manufactured goods. Those on very low incomes will necessarily spend a far higher proportion of their income on the former, so those on low incomes may immediately feel increases in the cost of living even if increases in the overall inflation rate are slight. Firms are, of course, under no obligation to increase wages in line with inflation, but inflation is likely to have effects on overall wage rates.

WAGE RATES AND INEQUALITY

Secondly, we noted a tendency towards rising inequality in liberal market economies. Table 9.2 compares increases in inequality rates within the OECD economies since the mid-1970s (the higher the figure, the more inequality). Liberal market economies such as the United Kingdom and the United States are more unequal, and inequality has worsened over the past 30 years.

Table 9.2 Inequality in the OECD – general trends

Age	Working age population: 18–65					
Period Country	mid- 1970s	mid- 1980s	around 1990	mid- 1990s	around 2000	mid- 2000s
Australia	..	..	..	0.30	0.29	0.31
Austria	..	0.23	..	0.23	0.25	0.27
Belgium	..	..	..	0.28	0.28	0.27
Canada	0.28	0.29	..	0.29	0.31	0.32
Czech Republic	..	..	0.23	0.25	0.26	0.27
Denmark	..	0.21	0.21	0.21	0.22	0.23
Finland	0.23	0.20	..	0.23	0.26	0.27
France	..	0.31	0.30	0.28	0.29	0.28
Germany	..	0.25	0.25	0.27	0.27	0.30
Greece	0.41	0.33	..	0.32	0.34	0.31
Hungary	..	..	0.27	0.30	0.30	0.30
Ireland	..	0.34	..	0.32	0.29	0.32
Italy	..	0.31	0.29	0.35	0.34	0.35
Japan	..	0.30	..	0.32	0.33	0.31
Luxembourg	..	0.24	..	0.26	0.26	0.26
Mexico	..	0.45	..	0.52	0.50	0.47
Netherlands	0.25	0.26	0.28	0.28	0.28	0.27
New Zealand	..	0.26	0.31	0.33	0.33	0.33
Norway	..	0.22	..	0.25	0.26	0.28
Poland	..	..	..	..	0.32	0.38
Portugal	..	..	0.32	0.34	0.35	0.38
Slovak Republic	..	..	..	..	..	0.27
Spain	..	0.30	0.27	0.28	0.27	0.31
Sweden	0.20	0.20	0.20	0.22	0.24	0.24
Switzerland	..	..	..	..	0.28	0.27
Turkey	..	0.43	..	0.51	..	0.42
United Kingdom	0.28	0.32	0.36	0.35	0.37	0.34
United States	0.30	0.33	0.34	0.35	0.35	0.37
OECD Total	..	..	..	..	..	**0.31**

Data from Income Distribution – Inequality under Social Protection under Social and Welfare Statistics from OECD.Stat Extracts, http://stats.oecd.org [accessed on 31 October 2010].

What does this means in terms of employment relations? Firstly, in highly unequal societies, psychological well-being is generally speaking worse; there is a higher incidence of mental and stress-related illnesses. Secondly, the gap between senior managers and the rank and file is much greater. This means that managers have a diminishing understanding of the material conditions of employees, which is likely to weaken internal solidarity and cohesion within the organisation. For similar reasons, the worldview of employees is likely to be completely different from that of senior managers, reducing the common ground on which consensus may be reached. Highly opaque managerial pay systems, from which senior managers visibly live a lifestyle that is totally unreachable for employees, is further likely to diminish the latter's trust in, and commitment to, the firm. Thirdly, although firms can seize short-term competitiveness by reducing or freezing wages, if all firms do so, the capacity for consumption across a society will decline. In turn, firms will be under greater pressure to cut costs, resulting in a vicious downward circle that is extremely difficult to break out of. Equity thus matters, not only in terms of fairness and morals but also potentially in terms of competitiveness and in ensuring overall economic growth. However, in exercising pay restraint on themselves, and in ensuring decent pay for employees, costs are incurred for managers up front, without necessarily reaping immediately recognisable benefits.

CRITICAL DEBATE

Pay and inequality

Are you aware of inequality of income in the country that you are most familiar with (either Britain or another country)? If you are, how have you been made aware of it?

Some people would argue that inequality of income is not a problem as long as there are 'trickle-down' effects from the rich to the poor. If the rich invest their money in business, it will help those who are poorer in the long run. Others argue that it is not morally right for there to be a great deal of inequality of income in society. What is your opinion on this issue?

INCENTIVES AND REWARD

What forms can incentive-related reward systems take? The simplest – as we saw when we were linking pay and performance, above – is piecework, where employees are paid according to how much output they generate. A variation of this is commission-based pay. For example, estate agents receive an income that directly relates to the number of properties they can sell. Profit-related pay involves cash handouts to employees according to annual returns. On some occasions this may be deferred in order to encourage employees to take a somewhat longer-term view. In the case of share ownership schemes, employees have the option of purchasing shares at a preferential rate via pay deductions.

Alternatively, employees may receive shares as part of their overall pay (Poutsma and de Nijs 2003: 866). In theory, because employees own shares, they have a say in the overall governance of the firm (Cin *et al* 2002: 922), although in practice it may be the case that employee shares are held in a trust. This may preclude employees from immediately selling on their shares and/or limit their voting power at shareholders' meetings. Within the UK, employee share ownership schemes were used as a means of making privatisations more palatable to workers. A further issue is that specific managerial agendas – for example, encouraging employee buy-in without necessarily increasing the say that employees enjoy in the running of the firm – may mean that such schemes are extremely complex, and so are incomprehensible to the average worker and, more specifically, those in the lower job bands (Morris *et al* 2005). Moreover, as Poutsma and de Nijs (2003) note, share ownership schemes rarely form part of the contract of employment, which in turn limits the rights employees enjoy in that regard. This is sometimes due to the difficulties in incorporating share ownership schemes into collective agreements (*ibid*), but may also be due to a desire to impart a greater flexibility and contingency into pay. Studies by Jones (1997) and Kato and Morishima (2002) have found that financial participation works best when there are effective forums for employee participation in other areas. In this event employees can obtain a clearer picture of managerial intentions, facilitating legitimacy. The *Applying theory to practice* box below gives an example of where employees might have doubted the legitimacy of payment systems.

 APPLYING THEORY TO PRACTICE

Executive pay in the United States

A number of banks in the United States have been bailed out by the US government – some more than once. In effect, the government has sometimes become a major shareholder. However, at the same time there have been various news reports of chief executives and senior managers receiving huge payments, either in salaries or through bonuses.

What is the relationship between the problems experienced by large US banks and the operation of the reward system enjoyed by senior managers?

What should be done about this situation, and by whom?

Can the financial crisis, in any respect, be considered caused by the failures of HR practitioners?

Is the case of the USA unique, or is the situation similar in other countries?

INDIVIDUAL AND COLLECTIVE PAY SYSTEMS

A review of the nature of collective- versus individual-based reward systems is provided above. However, there is a further issue worth considering. The decline of trade unions in liberal market economies, and the general weakening of the position of ordinary employees, have led to increasing pay dispersion within firms. As collective-based pay systems have become less common, increasing organisational resources have been directed away from ordinary employees, and managers have benefited from this process. Agency theory suggests that as agents of owners, managers should be reined in from unnecessary extravagance or empire-building (Pendleton 2006: 754). In attempting to solve this problem, managerial pay has increasingly become incentive-based, linked to the performance of the firm on the stock market. Yet even prior to the 2008 economic crisis there were growing concerns over whether these changes had really led to more competent or effective management (see, for example, Bebchuck and Fried 2006). Significantly, Core *et al* (2008) found that executive pay appeared to be immune to negative press coverage. The financial crisis appears, to date, to have done little to dent this excess. Indeed, as noted earlier, Boyer (2010) argues that share price-linked executive reward systems contributed directly to the financial crisis.

THE CRITICAL ROLE OF EMPLOYMENT RELATIONS SPECIALISTS AND LINE MANAGERS

In devising and running reward systems, employment relations practitioners not only have to fall into line with overall organisational strategy and policy (even if they may be in a position to lobby for specific sets of practices) but also have to ensure that they abide by current legislation. This includes ensuring that pay is in line with the legal minimum, the firm's contractual commitments are maintained, and workers within particular job categories are treated equitably. Meanwhile, line managers also face the challenge of ensuring that employees are treated fairly and equitably. In practice, in the case of individual performance-based pay, it may be very difficult to be totally objective. Operationalising accurate measures of value generated by workers remains an open-ended challenge for line management. This can lead to tensions in the workplace that may be resolved through union involvement where there are co-operative relations.

As noted elsewhere, gender, age and ethnicity often coincide with pay inequalities. Although there may be structural reasons for this across society at large, it is likely that they will be mirrored in the actions of managers. For example, if society expects men to be the principal breadwinners, lower pay for women can be justified – in other words, women can 'afford' to have lower pay because men will be the main source of household income. However illogical this may be (especially in the light of the large numbers of woman-headed single-parent households), such attitudes are widespread. Social inequality can often thus be reconstituted through the day-to-day decisions of managers and supervisors.

◀◉▶ REFLECTION ON PRACTICE

Gender gaps in pay

Are you aware of any gender gaps in pay in the organisation where you are currently working, or where you have worked before?

In Britain, the Equality Act 2010 established that all workers should have the right to see the pay of other workers – so that both women and men can compare pay rates. What effect, if any, do you think that this will have on equal pay claims in Britain over the next five years?

Are you aware of similar legislation in other countries?

SUMMARY

This chapter has examined the determination of pay systems, and included coverage of both individual and collective pay. Complementing other chapters that have drawn attention to fairness and equity issues, this chapter has addressed the issue of minimum pay, and pay and equity.

Pay and reward represent one side of the operationalisation of the employment contract, the other being the physical delivery of labour power. The amount of pay and rewards and the manner in which they are delivered are thus central to understanding employment relationships. The amounts given to employees will depend on the relative power of each party (determined by relationships within the organisation and external labour market conditions) and the role of external regulating bodies. They will also reflect the relative commitment of the employer to fairness and equity, and the ability of employees to promote this. Within liberal market economies there has been increasing inequality in earnings since the 1970s between those in the highest-paying jobs and the majority of the workforce. In many cases, the latter have had to contend with wages that are stagnant or have declined. Although this may have helped to boost the profit rates of individual firms, it has also contributed to a chronic crisis of consumer demand, leading to growth being fuelled by debt, and attempts to rekindle demand via cost-cutting (which again places downward pressures on wages, worsening the cycle). In short, whereas it may be good for an organisation's short-term profits to constrain the amount that it spends on its workforce, if all organisations operate in the same way, it can create structural economic problems. Moreover, there is no evidence that the emergence of a highly paid managerial super-elite has made organisations any more effective – rather, it appears in many cases to have contributed to a climate of excessive short-termism and irresponsibility (Boyer 2010).

EXPLORE FURTHER

Reading

- Gerhart, B. and Trevor, C. O. (2008) 'Merit pay', in A. Verma, P. S. Budhwar and A. DeNisi (eds) *Performance Management Systems: A global perspective.* London: Routledge

- Kato, T. and Morishima, M. (2002) 'The productivity effects of participatory employment practices', *Industrial Relations Journal*, Vol.41, No.4: 487–520

- McNabb, R. and Whitfield, K. (2007) 'The impact of varying types of performance-related pay and employee participation on earnings', *International Journal of Human Resource Management*, Vol.18, No.6: 1004–25

Website

- Chartered Institute of Personnel and Development www.cipd.co.uk

CHAPTER 10

Discrimination, Difference and Diversity

CHAPTER OVERVIEW

Discrimination takes many different forms, and may, for example, be on the lines of age, gender, ethnic, religious affiliation or disability. Although some forms of discrimination are highly visible, a good deal of discrimination is subtle, contributing to persistent inequality both within the organisation and wider society. This chapter explores the nature of discrimination, the forms it may assume, the relative efficacy of legislation in overcoming discrimination, and the role of different players in promoting greater equity.

The chapter begins by outlining the concepts of justice and fairness, since these underpin attitudes toward discrimination. It then moves on to explore the different forms of discrimination, and examines different theoretical explanations for their continuance. Subsequently, the focus turns to the legislative provisions that have been made to attempt to remove workplace discrimination, and then evaluates the extent to which legislation has been able to prevent discrimination in practice. The next section examines the management of diversity, and scrutinises policies and practices that might be established. The final sections assess the role of trade unions in relation to discrimination and equity, and consider the situation in non-union firms.

LEARNING OUTCOMES

After studying this chapter you should be able to:

- understand the concepts of justice and fairness

- identify the principal forms that discrimination may take

- compare and contrast different explanations for the emergence and persistence of discrimination within organisations

- assess the importance of complying with employment law in order to mitigate risk

- evaluate policies and practices associated with diversity management, and both moral and business case arguments for addressing discrimination

- critically discuss ways in which organisations may reduce discrimination and manage diversity, considering the role of HR and line managers

- assess the contribution of trade unions towards reducing discrimination and improving equity in the workplace

JUSTICE AND FAIRNESS

From a theoretical starting point, discrimination may be seen in terms of different conceptualisations of justice. From a *distributive justice* point of view, it can be argued that the benefits, risks and challenges of specific job categories should be distributed equally between those of different backgrounds (O'Boyle 2001: 962). In other words, justice is about the outcomes of allocating jobs, roles and responsibilities, fairness in human resource planning, and the outcomes of this process. *Procedural justice* concerns the processes and procedures that are put in place to ensure fairness (Bratton and Gold 2007). In other words, whereas distributional justice concerns actual allocations and outcomes, procedural justice concerns itself with processes. So, from a procedural justice starting point, if a recruitment process is fair and equitable, justice concerns are met, even if the outcomes do not appear equitable; a distributional justice perspective would see this as evidence of persistent unfairness. This distinction has important practical implications. Is it enough if firms have equal opportunities policies and procedures in places, or should they be concerned about what the outcomes are, and should they take active steps to reduce or eliminate any persistent imbalances? Meanwhile, *interactional justice* concerns itself with social processes, interpersonal dynamics and the treatment of people in everyday organisational life (Bratton and Gold 2007). How do people interact? Why are some people treated differently from others? In addition, what can be done to promote greater fairness and equity in such interactions?

REFLECTION ON PRACTICE

Compliance with legislation and conceptualisations of fairness

Although different conceptualisations of justice may seem to be far removed from the real world of employment relations, an important issue is whether firms seek simply to comply with the bare minimum of legal standards or to take a more proactive view in promoting fairness at the workplace.

Think of an organisation that you are familiar with. Which category do you think it falls into, and why?

FORMS OF DISCRIMINATION

Discrimination may be direct or indirect. *Direct discrimination* takes place when a particular group is treated less favourably than another. For example, an organisation may avoid hiring women of childbearing age in order to avoid providing maternity leave, or, for similar reasons, may not promote women. Alternatively, an organisation may choose not to hire members of a particular ethnic minority, or favour applicants from another. *Indirect discrimination* occurs when an action applied to the whole workforce is discriminatory in its effect on one particular group. For example, a firm may choose – where it is not prohibited by the law – not to give maternity leave; this will have the effect of discouraging female job applicants and/or reducing the number of female employees. Similarly, a firm may give preference to job applicants that are related to existing staff members – a common practice in many emerging economies. This may have the effect of reproducing the existing composition of the labour force.

Anybody can be a victim of discrimination. As mentioned above, discrimination may take place on the lines of gender, age, ethnicity, disability, religion, caste and/or class. In terms of age, it is not just the elderly that may be discriminated against – for example, younger job applicants are often discriminated against on the basis of a lack of maturity. In terms of religion, there is considerable evidence of discrimination against Muslims in the United States following the onset of the 'war on terror'. Caste discrimination (that is, discrimination because of assigned status in society) is historically most associated with India; despite equity legislation, the vast majority of lower castes – and above all the 'untouchables' – continue to be impoverished and overwhelmingly carry out poor and demeaning jobs. However, caste discrimination has also been noted in Latin America and parts of West Africa (eg São Tomé e Príncipe).

CLASS, INEQUALITY AND OCCUPATIONS

Class discrimination may be extremely subtle. Within the United Kingdom, many of the most prestigious jobs and occupations are dominated by individuals who have received private (non-state) education and attended Oxbridge (Oxford or Cambridge) colleges. Subtle barriers are erected against outsiders, with insiders benefiting through the operation of extensive informal networks. Class-based inequality is an extremely complex phenomenon. Confusingly, members of this elite grouping like to refer to themselves as part of the 'middle classes', whereas most people in the middle classes are in fact state-educated and earn incomes that are less than £30,000 per annum. The difference between classes has worsened in recent years, in line with diminishing social equality.

Both within Britain and in many former British colonies (for example, Nigeria and India), a further visible form of inequality is the divide between manual 'blue-collar' workers and their 'white-collar' counterparts. Traditionally, the latter were accorded a far higher status, with higher job security, better pay and perceived greater reliability. Meanwhile, manual workers were subject to considerably greater control and standardisation. This status divide between blue-collar and white-collar work has eroded to some extent, for both positive and negative reasons. Positive reasons for the erosion include the process of multi-skilling, and more functionally flexible working practices within areas of manufacturing. Negative reasons include the rise of new low-end white-collar jobs in areas such as call centres, fast food, and outsourced administrative functions that are subject to a similar degree of discipline and control as earlier assembly-line work. So although there have been some changes, a new divide has emerged in the workforce between those in well-paid skilled jobs in areas such as IT and financial services, and those in low-end service sector jobs ('McJobs') (Wright and Dwyer 2006). There is only limited mobility between these two areas. In short, in many advanced economies the divide is not so much between manual and non-manual jobs but between 'better' white-collar jobs and the rest, whether they are manual or office-bound (*ibid*). This does not mean that manual jobs have become more desirable. Not only is there the issue of prestige, but there is also the fact that the decline in manufacturing has made many trades obsolete. Other trades – such as plumbing and construction work – are highly cyclical, the members of such trades facing very lean times indeed in times of recession. In contrast, although many office-bound jobs are low-paid and demeaning, few are as vulnerable to the effects of downturn as are industries such as construction.

⌇ CRITICAL DEBATE

Evidence of a class divide?

Some people would argue that the class divide in Britain has disappeared. Others would argue that it is still present, but now more subtle.

What is your opinion on this issue?

Also, are you aware of a class divide in any other countries?

WHY DOES DISCRIMINATION OCCUR?

There is little doubt as to the persistence and durability of discrimination on gender, age, ethnic, caste, and class lines: there are no social contexts where discrimination is totally absent. But why does discrimination occur? There are many different perspectives, but debates have been dominated by two different strands of thinking: neo-liberalism and political economy approaches.

NEO-LIBERAL ACCOUNTS

The neo-liberal camp is a very broad one. Two broad explanations have been advanced: lifestyle choices and imperfect information/market distortions.

Lifestyle choice

It has been argued that inequality in terms of representation in jobs is simply a response of poor lifestyle choices on behalf of those occupying menial and insecure positions. So, for example, women 'choose' to have children, and because they often opt for career breaks as a result, they have only themselves to blame if their careers advance more slowly than those of men. Moreover, it has been argued that older workers are often simply less proactive and dynamic in marketing themselves and their 'youthful qualities' (Shen and Kleiner 2001: 25). Those from poor backgrounds and other disadvantaged individuals should be more responsible in terms of developing their skills, and be more willing to move regions and switch industries, in line with changes in the economy (see Shen and Kleiner 2001). Those who remain poor have chosen to do so, through laziness and/or moral failure.

It has also been argued that poor choices may be prompted through overly generous social security or pensions (McVittie *et al* 2003: 596; Palmore *et al* 1985). The logical conclusion is to reduce the scope of the welfare state in order to 'solve' the problem. These arguments are deeply entrenched in the right-wing media, an example being the anti-poor rhetoric on Fox News, the Murdoch-owned US cable television network (see http://www.newshounds.us/). In practice, such arguments are only a variation on notions of 'the undeserving poor' and/or of feminine incapability and weakness. Indeed, it can be argued that inequality might be due more to the proponents of market distortion than to the 'poor' choices of those stuck in menial and poorly paid work. Behavioural economists have suggested that people can be 'nudged' or given incentives to make the 'right' choices (Piore 2010). However, in practice, conservative policy prescriptions have centred on paring back meagre welfare benefits and on devising coercive punishments for the poor and vulnerable (with the increased use of imprisonment for petty offences and the withdrawing of welfare benefits for those who do not take up low-grade job offers or who have otherwise fallen foul of the system), which is likely only to exacerbate the situation.

But why do the poor and/or members of disadvantaged groupings supposedly make more 'wrong' choices than those from wealthier backgrounds? Behavioural economics seeks to explain why individuals may make sub-optimal choices, and, as we have seen, explores ways in which individuals may be enticed into the right direction (Piore 2010: 385). A more extreme variation on this is neuro-economics, which seeks to understand the psychological underpinnings of incorrect decisions (*ibid*). Critics have charged that this amounts to social

Darwinism, centring on devices and tools for identifying the unfit, who are seen as incapable of being anything other than a drain on society (Piore 2010: 385).

A variation on the lifestyle-choice argument is that certain historically disadvantaged groupings – most notably women and the elderly – often opt for temporary or part-time work because it allows individuals to combine family obligations and/or greater leisure while still enjoying an income stream (Chou and Chow 2005: 243). For example, it has been suggested that older workers may enjoy a 'third age' of greater leisure while still being able to enjoy an income (Branine and Glover 1997: 241). Similarly, younger workers may gain valued skills and experience while being able to balance work and study. Indeed, it has been argued that this represents a win/win situation: firms can use their workforce more flexibly, and workers can reconcile working with other interests and obligations (Arrowsmith and McGoldrick 1997: 260). Such arguments ignore the point that most of those employed in temporary and part-time jobs perform very menial work for very low wages, under tight control, with often unpleasant or demeaning working conditions, carrying out jobs that are so lacking in prestige as to hold little positive experiential value. Those who opt for poorly paid and insecure jobs may be forced to do so by circumstances and owing to a lack of meaningful alternatives, because they desperately need income, rather than through a genuine choice of lifestyle (see Branine and Glover 1997: 240). Although flexible working may be attractive to some, most flexible jobs are located in particularly low value-added areas of the service sector (Sargeant 2001). Low-paid unskilled jobs represent more of a last resort than a positive choice (Urwin 2004).

Imperfect information

Alternatively, it could be argued that members of disadvantaged groupings do not wilfully make wrong choices but are lacking in accurate information in order to make better ones. It could also be argued that companies may choose to discriminate for similar reasons: because of the persistence of negative stereotypes. Better flows of information should thus eliminate such problems. Such thinking has informed campaigns to promote best practice regarding the utilisation of people (McDonald and Potton 1997: 298). In time, firms will become aware of the advantages of best practice, and this will alleviate discrimination. This line of argument can be extended to suggest that individuals may have unrealistic expectations as to what they are worth, or be unaware of how times have changed. For example, older workers may expect higher pay, when organisations have increasingly discarded linear approaches to careers. Job seekers must therefore be 'realistic' in their pay expectations and career plans.

Neo-liberals have argued that insecure tenure may be beneficial in keeping workers alert, while sourcing new staff from the external labour market may cut labour costs and impart greater flexibility. Such arguments assume, however, that the accumulated wisdom, knowledge and experience of existing staff matter little. Moreover, high staff turnover rates impose additional costs on organisations in terms of formal and informal induction training. Finally, workers may choose to put up with inferior pay or working conditions on the assumption of career advancement – the firm may tacitly hold out the prospect of career advancement and more pay in the future, as organisation-relevant skills and experience accumulate. This also may be used as a mechanism for discouraging shirking because benefits are loaded towards the close of the job cycle (Hutchens 1986: 439). However, if a firm reneges on the implicit contract by dispensing with employees who are due to become more expensive, it is likely to have consequences for staff morale and for commitment.

In what other ways might markets be distorted? It could be argued that any form of employee rights or social welfare precludes markets from operating efficiently. For example, if legislation guarantees maternity leave, rational profit-maximising individuals may carefully time events such as pregnancy in order to gain the maximum benefits and return. Minimum wages may mean that very young workers – who have little marketable experience – are no longer cheap, and so are less attractive than older workers to employers. A problem with these arguments is that it assumes that the state is the primary source of market inefficiency, and that state action to deter excessive short-termism is detrimental. Yet a lack of regulation in the nineteenth century led to the value of large components of the labour force being simply discounted, which itself was grossly inefficient. In addition, excessive short-termism that results from light regulation may be hugely destructive – as borne out by the 2008 financial crisis.

A third strand of neo-liberal thinking suggests that age discrimination reflects poor judgement of, and misinformation regarding, the skills and abilities of older and minority workers (cf Branine and Glover 1997). In other words, if markets operate properly, such discrimination would be 'driven out'. Conlin and Emerson (2006: 115) suggest that employers are more likely to discriminate during hiring than on redundancy. In a redundancy situation, employers have more knowledge about the actual performance of the individuals concerned. It follows that if firms were freer to eject newly hired poor performers, they would take more 'chances' in hiring so-called 'high-risk' workers (McDonald and Potton 1997: 298). Employment protection legislation thus acts as a 'market distortion'. However, in reality, lightly regulated labour markets (such as those in Britain or the United States) appear to be worse at creating 'good' secure jobs than more heavily regulated ones (such as Germany).

POLITICAL ECONOMY APPROACHES

Political economy approaches tend to be dominated by arguments about a 'reserve army of labour' or the impact of economic and industrial change. However, a further strand of thinking highlights the multiple and interlinked facets that can lead to discrimination and inequality.

Reserve armies of labour

Political economy approaches have a fundamentally different starting point from those associated with neoliberalism. They assume that, under capitalism, it is functional in many instances to discriminate. Capitalism is characterised by periods of growth and recession, otherwise known as cycles of 'boom' and 'bust'. This means that the demand for labour will fluctuate over time. However, the laying off of large numbers of young men without alternative means of subsistence is likely to be highly destabilising, and can, indeed, threaten the existing order. In contrast, women can be readily reabsorbed into the household, and can be occupied with domestic duties. Patriarchal ideologies reinforce the notion that full-time domestic employment for women is an ideal, and that men, as principal breadwinners, should have priority in respect of jobs. In periods of economic growth, women can then be enticed back into the labour market through financial necessity and/or even coercion. Women thus constitute a 'reserve army of labour'. Within the developing world, an impoverished peasantry (sometimes composed of subordinate castes or ethnicities) may also serve such a function, supplying labour as and when needed, and returning to rural subsistence when not (Hirson 1989).

Patriarchy (male domination) may also be used to justify paying women inferior wages and/or consigning them to particularly poor jobs. Working-class men can be co-opted into this repression, because it reduces the competition for marginally better-paying and more secure work. The same argument can be applied to racial discrimination. In South Africa in the *apartheid* era, the system co-opted white working-class men, reserving particular jobs and occupations for them. They traded off militancy for the benefits accruing from preferential treatment on the basis of race (Webster 1986). In both instances the marginally better-off category of labour can draw comfort from the fact that others are visibly worse off than them.

Economic and industrial change

It can be argued that persistent crises since the 1970s have resulted in liberal market economies becoming ever more reliant on flexible and insecure labour, and on the increasing use of part-time and temporary work (Jessop 2001). Cut-throat competition has had the effect of forcing down labour standards, while the adoption of new technologies has opened up possibilities for increased surveillance and control, and in this way reduced the need to secure the co-operation of labour. Moreover, an emphasis on leaner, more flexible organisations is likely to affect the most vulnerable the worst – some groups will inevitably shoulder a disproportionate burden of the costs imposed by systemic crisis. As noted above, it is socially more acceptable for female workers to return to full-time domestic duties than men. Similarly, older workers who are made redundant can be seen as 'retired'. In contrast, young men would be simply unemployed. Older workers are more likely to be concentrated in declining industries (for the simple reason that in the past they were a relatively larger sector of the economy) and in individual firms having to contend with market decline – meaning that older workers are more likely to lose their jobs (Urwin 2004).

Culture, job status and discrimination

Discrimination is not simply about tenure but also about job status. Many low-paid and demeaning jobs are badged 'women's work': cleaning, catering and low-grade administrative jobs. Women are socialised into being more accepting of performing such jobs. Again, working-class men are co-opted into supporting this ideology as other better-paying jobs are defined as 'men's work'. Interestingly, ideologies of race have also been used to enforce workforce compliance. Traditionally, British shipping companies employed martial tribal peoples such as Zulus and Pathans in physically demanding and dangerous jobs, most notably stoking (in steamships) (Bonnin *et al* 2004). Members of such tribes could reconcile the difficulties of such work with the mistaken pride that only they were capable of performing it, and the fact that employers would give them preference for such jobs. The colonial technique of 'divide and rule' meant that such racially based employment policies allowed other groupings each to have its own constructed notions of superiority (intelligence, versatility, honesty, etc), and be unlikely to forge alliances with their fellow-workers of different ethnic origin, no matter how bad working conditions and pay were for all groups of workers.

Different groupings may therefore undermine each other to protect themselves (Darity 2001: 980), and in doing so perpetuate general social injustice. This tendency continues to the present day, some elements of the media attempting to mobilise the 'decent' working class, and above all, white males in regular employment, against the more vulnerable – members of ethnic minorities, foreigners, and the jobless. This serves both as an outlet for frustration against a general worsening of conditions and poor prospects for upward mobility, and as a mechanism for promoting a greater willingness to accept an objectively inferior social status. Social struggles become concentrated at a horizontal level, between members of the working classes, rather than vertically, challenging elites for systemic reform.

◀◉▶ REFLECTION ON PRACTICE

The media and reinforcement of difference

Do you regularly read a particular newspaper or news websites?

To what extent have you been aware of the reinforcement of difference between groups of more vulnerable people? Which groups are regularly attacked in the media?

How might the reinforcement of difference result in certain workplace practices within organisations?

As an HR practitioner, how can you challenge attitudes towards certain groups of workers (or the unemployed)?

In the advanced economies, members of specific ethnic minorities and the elderly are particularly likely to be poor (Walker 2005: 825), and single women are more likely to be poor than single men. It is a truism that poverty breeds poverty. Poor job opportunities and roles represent part and parcel of wider social exclusion –

the most marginalised are likely to have low skills and incomes, and poor accommodation. Highly unequal societies are characterised by a high degree of unhappiness and mental illness, with a lack of social progress being blamed on the individual's failings rather than those of the system. Those who work long hours for low incomes are also particularly likely to fall victim to vendors of junk foods, adding problems of obesity, poor nutrition and poor health to their woes. The most marginalised are also more likely to be more reliant on public transport – and where the public transport infrastructure is poor, this will have the effect of reducing the range of feasible job options.

It is possible for individuals to be doubly or triply disadvantaged. For example, time off for childbearing means that women are likely to have smaller occupational pensions than men. An older woman will not only have less money but face all of the challenges besetting an older worker in seeking meaningful employment. Moreover, there are particularly negative stereotypes to being an older woman (Schuman and Kleiner 2001: 48), and an older woman from an ethnic minority may find life even more difficult, since she may also have to overcome racist stereotypes.

APPLYING THEORY TO PRACTICE

Explanations for discrimination

Which of the above-mentioned theoretical explanations do you think is of most practical value in explaining the persistence of discrimination and inequality in most contemporary firms?

Give reasons for your answer.

EMPLOYMENT LAW AND MITIGATING RISK

Discrimination can arguably be reduced through legislation. There has therefore been a burgeoning of anti-discrimination legislation in many countries. Employers must be attentive to legislative changes in order to avoid challenges for compensation from employees.

EXAMPLES OF ANTI-DISCRIMINATION LEGISLATION

Many countries have bodies of legislation aimed at reducing discrimination and, in some instances, at reversing the effects of previous discrimination.

Within the UK, the Sex Discrimination Act (1975, amended in 1999) made it illegal to practise direct or indirect discrimination on the basis of gender, marital status or gender reassignment. Examples of direct discrimination include the reservation of jobs for men only, while indirect discrimination includes the imposition of physical height requirements that exclude most women. The 1970 Equal Pay Act required that employers pay the same for work of equal value. Meanwhile, the Race Relations Act (1976) made it illegal to discriminate directly or indirectly against a person on the grounds of race. This was followed by the

Racial and Religious Hatred Act 2006, which now extends protection to multi-ethnic faith groups, such as Muslims, as well as mono-ethnic groups such as Jews and Sikhs; and the Equality Act 2006, which prohibits religious or faith discrimination and victimisation in relation to employment, education, housing and the provision of goods, services and facilities.

The Age Discrimination Act (2006) prohibits discrimination on the basis of age. However, the Act did not explicitly prohibit firms from making use of compulsory retirement ages. The Disability Discrimination Act (1995) made it illegal to discriminate against those with disabilities 'without justification' and/or to fail to make 'reasonable adjustment to premises, policies, practices and procedures' accordingly. Subsequently, in 2006, under the Disability Discrimination Act 2005, exemptions for specific professions were removed, and the coverage was extended to encompass sufferers of HIV/AIDs, cancer and multiple sclerosis. In 2010, the Equality Act was introduced to streamline existing discrimination law by consolidating it into a single Act and extend the scope of protection. It also referred to a number of protected characteristics: age, disability, gender reassignment, marriage and civil partnership, pregnancy and maternity, race, religion or belief, sex, and sexual orientation. Changes to legislation include protection for both disabled people and their carers; protection for those who associate with someone who has a protected characteristic; allowing a tribunal claim for a discrimination against combined characteristics; allowing employers to take positive action in recruitment and promotion and requiring them to report on the gender pay gap; and enabling employment tribunals to make recommendations for changes where discrimination has occurred (TUC 2010).

Other countries have introduced similar legislation. In Canada, the 1977 Human Rights Act requires that employers practise equal opportunities, with discrimination being prohibited on the lines of race, age, religion, gender or disability. The Act covers federally regulated activities and is supplemented by provincial anti-discrimination legislation. The Employment Equity Act 1996 requires and encourages certain categories of employer to practise affirmative action in respect of certain historically disadvantaged groupings, most notably indigenous peoples and women. In addition, contractors to the national government are required to have an employment equity programme operating.

In Australia, the 1975 Racial Discrimination Act prohibits racial discrimination in respect of jobs and work organisation. The 1984 Sex Discrimination Act outlaws gender discrimination, discrimination in terms of marital status, and against women who are pregnant or of childbearing age in respect of employment. The 1992 Disability Discrimination Act prohibits discrimination on the basis of physical disability.

In South Africa, the 1996 Constitution incorporates a Human Rights Charter. This constitutionally prohibits discrimination in terms of work and employment on the lines of ethnicity, gender, disability or sexual orientation. The 1998 Employment Equity Act explicitly protects both employees and job seekers from discrimination, but also sets out requirements for promoting affirmative action. Designated employers have to have affirmative action plans in place that incorporate mechanisms for identifying barriers to equity, the implementation of measures to promote diversity, and priority for certain groupings. However, the Act excludes quotas, and does not allow jobs and job applications to be closed to all but the designated targets of affirmative action. The Promotion of Equality and Prevention of Unfair Discrimination Act 2000 prohibits unfair discrimination on the grounds of race, social origin, marital status, sexual orientation, disability, religion, belief, language, birth, pregnancy or marital status. The judiciary of the South African Constitutional Court has a track record of being highly progressive in interpreting legislation.

DOES ANTI-DISCRIMINATION LEGISLATION WORK?

There is little doubt that in terms of gender and racial discrimination, what was accepted practice some 40 years ago is now seen as socially unacceptable in the advanced societies. However, age discrimination remains prevalent. In many countries it is still legal to compulsorily retire workers of a certain age, and jobs are often still targeted for 'dynamic applicants' seeking to work in 'young industries', suggesting that older applicants are less welcome. Moreover, women remain concentrated in specific jobs, and are often paid less than men. This reflects the costs of taking a career break for having children, the entrenched view that somehow women are more responsible for household duties than men, and ingrained prejudices. Men are still perceived as primary breadwinners, making their jobs and responsibilities 'more important'. Within some jobs there is an ingrained culture of sexism, the dominance of young single men within areas of the financial services industry being a notorious example. Moreover, ethnic minority workers still face difficulties: discrimination is particularly pronounced against ethnic groups depicted in the popular media as 'outsiders' and particularly prone to illegal conduct or extremism. The same issue is present for religious persuasion – although there are extremists within every religious grouping, how they are perceived varies greatly. There are also deeply rooted prejudices against older workers, who are often depicted as less adaptable or dynamic, inflexible and/or likely to be mentally impaired. This means that many older workers simply call themselves retired, rather than having to face a hostile labour market. In terms of disabled workers, the definition of what constitutes 'reasonable adjustments' remains contentious.

Discrimination thus remains deeply rooted. Why is the law often ineffective? Discrimination may be very difficult to prove. It can be extremely subtle. Unsuccessful job applicants are unlikely to possess complete information about the field of candidates, making any litigation difficult. In addition, having a record of engaging in unsuccessful litigation against prospective employers is likely to make future job applications even more difficult. An organisation is likely to have far greater resources at its disposal than an individual worker, making any legal battle lop-sided at least. When an employee takes legal action against the employer, it is likely to permanently damage the future employment relationship, even if the action is successful (Harcourt et al 2004). In short, seeking to enforce the law governing discrimination is highly risky for both employees and job seekers. This is particularly so given that anti-discrimination legislation in countries with common law systems (for example, the UK, the USA, Australia, New Zealand, etc) tends to be very general, meaning that specific rights are only clear through decisions made by the courts. The result is that litigation against employers on the grounds of discrimination is relatively uncommon, the most successful instances being action taken by highly skilled employees who have accumulated significant financial resources, or where discrimination is particularly blatant and grossly visible. Trade unions are often reluctant to resort to litigation on behalf of individual members. Quite simply, their resources are limited and they cannot spend all their capabilities on a host of individual disputes. Nonetheless, they may become involved if the dispute has a collective dimension – where victory for a single employee is likely to improve the conditions for many (Harcourt *et al* 2004).

A related issue is affirmative (or positive) action. On the one hand, there is little doubt that in some contexts, a history of particularly severe discrimination can only be redressed by positive remedial action. As noted earlier, disadvantage tends to beget further disadvantage. On the other hand, some affirmative action programmes have had the effect of supporting the progress of a highly mobile and skilled elite among the target grouping, leaving the bulk of the latter as disadvantaged as before. Moreover, promoting one disadvantaged grouping may prejudice other disadvantaged groupings. In short, although often desirable, affirmative action is unlikely to work in the absence of wider societal change.

⚷ LEGISLATION IN PRACTICE

Anti-discrimination legislation in Australia

Bennington and Wein (2000) conducted research examining the effectiveness of anti-discrimination legislation in Australia. Telephone surveys of randomly selected employers and job applicants revealed that discrimination in recruitment and selection appeared to be still evident, despite the existence of legislation that had been designed to prevent its occurring. Although around half of the respondents thought that the legislation was fair, this still left a large proportion of people who did not. Meanwhile, employer respondents' comments included the following statements: 'If you have a position which requires heavy lifting, I think it's ludicrous that you can't advertise for a male' and 'There's lots of holes in the Equal Opportunity Act and you can normally find a way around it' (*ibid*: 27).

The authors argue that 'a more proactive approach is needed', including the active monitoring of human resource practices (*ibid*: 21).

Do you agree with the use of legislation to prevent discrimination?

Many countries have adopted legislation outlawing discrimination, and in a number of instances have made positive remedial action compulsory. Yet there is considerable evidence that indirect and direct discriminatory practices often persist, despite such legislation. Why does labour legislation does not always achieve its desired outcomes?

Are you aware of any loopholes in anti-discrimination legislation in other countries? Give examples from your working experience, if possible.

POLICIES AND PRACTICES OF DIVERSITY MANAGEMENT

Irrespective of legislation, organisations may choose to actively promote greater diversity through written equal opportunities or diversity policies. Employment equity is a strategy that seeks to overcome the legacy of past discrimination, opening up specific categories of employment to members of groupings that were previously excluded from them (Bratton and Gold 2007). In other words, an organisation may formally commit itself to actively promoting greater equity in employment practices through a policy that is disseminated across the organisation, making clear what is acceptable and desirable, and what is not. Diversity policies aim to ensure that care is taken to address individual needs.

Within the UK there has been an increase in the proportion of workplaces with formal written equal opportunities or diversity policies over recent years, from 64% in 1998 to 73% in 2004 (Kersley *et al* 2004), and in workplaces with recognised unions 95% had equal opportunities policies. However, there are some limitations with such policies. First, they may just be statements of intent, noting what is desirable rather than what is actually practised. Second, the focus may be overly narrow, focusing on relatively few issues (for example, recruitment) rather than encompassing the full range of people management policies and issues. Third, such policies may be ignored by line managers. And even if the formal letter of the policy is adhered to, informal discrimination may persist. Fourth, the use of such policies within the workplace does not challenge social inequality within society at large. For example, members of disadvantaged groupings may lack the same access to educational opportunities as the more privileged, meaning that even if organisations practise equality in recruitment, there will be proportionately fewer candidates from some groupings than from others. In addition, if they have childcare commitments, women may be restricted in terms of the timing and hours they are available to work, in line with the availability of other childcare arrangements.

Even if it is not compulsory under the law, organisations may choose to undertake affirmative action. This might include short-listing only members of disadvantaged groupings or targeting recruitment. For example, for many years the US military has run recruitment campaigns focusing on students in community colleges in areas that are both predominantly black and poor – this is part of a very much more ambitious equal opportunities policy. It has meant that Afro-Americans are particularly well represented within the US Army. Optimistic accounts have suggested that this is an example of best practice in affirmative action that has erased past racism in the military. There is little doubt that the US Army, in particular, takes diversity very seriously, and has well-developed diversity policies and practices that have led to blacks gaining the highest ranks (US Army 2008). However, more cynical commentators have suggested that in recent years such targeted recruitment has sought to fill the ranks with the most vulnerable, to be used as cannon fodder in that country's endless wars, while those with better options increasingly shun military careers (see Wood 2004: 73–5).

An ostensible commitment to diversity may serve a range of different purposes. For example, employers in theme parks and restaurants often recruit women on the basis of their physical appearance, with a view to attracting those male customers who experience difficulties in socialising with women in everyday situations. An example of recruitment that targets young women on the basis of appearance is that practised by the Hooters Restaurant chain. The imposition of dress codes can range from telling employees to dress in a 'feminine' way (see Redman and Wilkinson 2002) to forcing staff to wear particularly revealing outfits. As noted earlier, certain jobs are still cast as women's work. This includes work in the hospitality industry that involves caring for the comfort of others, preparing and serving food, emotional labour (see Chapter 8) and jobs which involve an extension of what is seen as women's 'normal' household duties, such as cleaning.

DIVERSITY, MORAL AND BUSINESS CASE ARGUMENTS FOR ADDRESSING DISCRIMINATION IN THE WORKPLACE

Diversity in organisations means acknowledging differences between working individuals according to factors such as gender, ethnicity and disability. Diversity management is based on managing the needs of different groupings within the workforce, and promoting fairness and equity (Cassell 2006). Governments throughout Europe have introduced measures aimed at enticing organisations to promote the diversity of their workforces. However, to many organisations, managing diversity issues does not have an immediate payback in terms of enhanced business performance, but instead implies upfront costs. Business case arguments include a more motivated workforce, and one that is more representative of local communities (the latter in turn would make what the organisation does more legitimate in the eyes of the community, with resulting benefits in areas such as marketing and recruitment) (Daniels and MacDonald, 2005). Other benefits include a better public image both with potential customers and with other stakeholders, attracting new investors that have an ethical investment agenda, and new ideas, fresh thinking, and insights and synergies that will emerge from greater workforce diversity (Cassell 2006; Daniels and MacDonald 2005). Finally, promoting fairness and diversity has value for its own sake – it is the 'right' thing to do. Indeed, should the firm be solely enticed to embracing diversity due to bottom-line considerations, it could be argued that the decision is devoid of moral worth (see Mellahi and Wood 2003). Moreover, bottom-line considerations may mean that policies are shallowly rooted and are likely to be abandoned should expected benefits not be visibly forthcoming.

Barriers to promoting diversity include organisational culture. Men can numerically dominate powerful positions in organisations, and then the culture can reflect 'male' ways of thinking and behaving. As noted earlier, it has frequently been alleged that areas of the UK financial services industry have an ingrained culture of sexism. The same may be said for certain trades. For example, mining and construction jobs remain male-dominated, involving common expectations that this is 'men's work'. A further barrier is that many women still have dual commitments, being often positioned as primary caregivers which may disadvantage them in employment. It is frequently argued that persistent inequality is simply due to a lack of credible applications from members of disadvantaged groupings. However, this does not take account of persistent differences in access to decent education in many contexts, and the extent to which socialisation may discourage applicants ('Women don't do men's work'). The company image may itself discourage people from diverse backgrounds applying for positions.

THE CRITICAL ROLE OF EMPLOYMENT RELATIONS SPECIALISTS AND LINE MANAGERS IN MANAGING DIVERSITY AND AVOIDING DISCRIMINATION

The persistence of discrimination means that organisations do not always make effective use of the full range of talent available, and it is likely that discrimination will prove a barrier to fresh thinking and open-mindedness. Yet discrimination may also pay, in terms of ensuring supplies of cheap and vulnerable – and numerically flexible – workers, and in 'dividing and ruling' a diverse but generally poorly paid and poorly treated workforce. Given these immediate benefits, an employment relations manager may experience considerable difficulty in selling active diversity policies and practices, especially as it may pose increased administrative costs in the short term. Indeed, the implementation of a diversity policy is likely to increase the role of employment relations specialists and the HR department at large – a process that may be resented by line managers because it involves a reallocation of prestige and the altered relative importance of different functional areas of management. Yet line managers have a crucial role in promoting diversity and in eliminating obvious and subtle forms of discrimination. For example, should the firm fall foul of equity legislation, it is likely that line managers will end up in the firing line in any costly litigation, which at best is likely to undermine their own careers. Moreover, leadership on the front line is in the end about persuading others to support one in one's endeavours and those of the organisation. Having to resort to coercion, the exploitation of the vulnerable and 'divide and rule' represents a failure of leadership.

TRADE UNIONS AND EQUITY

In most national contexts, unions have been historically dominated by men, and thus geared to serving the interests of men and male-dominated occupations. Indeed, it has been argued that unions often serve a 'labour aristocracy' – those occupying better jobs, and holding skills and capabilities that place them in a strong bargaining position vis-à-vis employers – that is overwhelmingly composed of men (Maree 1986). Even within occupations where employment is more equitable, men often dominate unions. This is because many female workers have to balance work and childcare commitments, and have little spare time to attend union meetings. Where men constitute the overwhelming majority of those who attend union meetings, this may lead to an excessively masculine culture, and sexual harassment or overly sexist behaviour directed against the few women who are brave enough to attend (Baskin 1991). However, in many national contexts there is growing recognition of the extent of this problem, and an increased willingness by unions to take equality concerns on board. In some cases, it has led to a specific proportion of leadership positions being reserved for women and members of ethnic minorities. This appears to be conducive to increasing participation by historically disadvantaged groupings. However, critics have charged that separate sections for women or ethnic minorities, and quotas for leadership positions, may have the effect of further marginalising or ghettoising such groupings.

Increasingly, unions have lobbied government and employers on equality issues and actively promoted best practices. Moreover, issues such as pay equality and family-friendly policies and working practices are increasingly appearing on the bargaining table. In the context of ongoing debates in the media about the 'undeserving poor'– single mothers, the unemployed, people on incapacity benefit who are unable to work, migrants and asylum seekers – unions may have an important role to play in counteracting such prejudices and fighting for equality in the workplace.

CASE STUDY

WOMEN IN MINING: INVESTIGATING THE BARRIERS

Mining has tended to be an industry dominated by men. Women have been prevented from working in mines for cultural, legislative and practical reasons. However, AngloGold Ashanti is a large mining corporation that has, in recent years, sought to increase the participation of women in its workforce (AngloGold Ashanti 2010). In 2005 the company conducted research within its South African operations, investigating the barriers facing women who wished to progress within the industry. The findings from the research study showed that barriers included poor knowledge of the industry, working in inappropriate positions, physical and health and safety constraints, discrimination by men, exclusion from male networks, and a lack of appropriate facilities and equipment (*ibid*).

As a result of the research, the company implemented a number of changes

including demonstrating senior management support for diversity initiatives and diversity training, targeted recruitment, setting up women's networking groups and mentors, assigning women to senior positions, extending assistance to all employees in balancing work and personal responsibility, and holding management accountable for progress on diversity (*ibid*).

Questions

What are the principal lessons – both positive and negative – of the AngloGold Ashanti experience in promoting equity?

What can unions and NGOs do to help to promote greater equity in the mining industry?

Are the barriers common to other industries and other countries?

To what extent are the recommendations relevant to other industries?

The mining industry is only one of many industries traditionally dominated by men. Such gender discrimination cuts across national boundaries and cultures. It could, of course, be argued that it requires considerable physical strength to operate certain machinery, but this is really an issue of design – such machinery is designed to be manipulated by people, not elephants.

DISCRIMINATION AND NON-UNION FIRMS

It could be argued that because unions have to represent all workers, they cannot afford to spend limited resources on supporting individual workers who are victims of discrimination. Yet although discrimination disputes often involve individual employees taking action in response to perceived inferior treatment or victimisation, such disputes can assume a collective dimension (Harcourt *et al* 2004). Should the individual be successful in getting her/his grievance resolved and/or receive compensation, supervisors and managers will be deterred from discriminating in the future. In other words, if one employee has presented a grievance, anybody in the workforce who is potentially a victim of discrimination may benefit in the future. It may therefore be in the interests of unions to support individual victims of discrimination. By the same token, in non-union firms there are less likely to be the same checks against discrimination. In the absence of union resources, the power imbalance between the individual employee and the firm is very much greater and he or she may be more open to victimisation in the future.

SUMMARY

This chapter has examined a range of issues related to discrimination, diversity and difference, drawing on evidence from a range of international contexts. Earlier sections included an examination of theoretical explanations of discrimination, outlining the difficulty of addressing discrimination when it is reinforced by ongoing discussions in the media. Later sections examined legislative changes, policies and practices.

Although in many national contexts legislation has been put in place to protect more vulnerable groups of workers, prejudice is more difficult to eliminate, and certain forms of inequality have proved highly durable. Often firms can seize short-term benefits from discriminatory practices, whereas the benefits of promoting greater equity may be more long-term and subtle. In many different national settings, enforcement of anti-discrimination has, at best, been uneven. Trade unions have a crucial role to play in promoting greater workplace equity, even if the labour movement itself has had to deal with the legacies of past and present discrimination. In short, although equity matters, progress has been slow, and much remains to be done.

EXPLORE FURTHER

Reading

- Cassell, C. (2006) 'Managing diversity', in T. Redman and A. Wilkinson (eds) *Contemporary Human Resource Management: Text and cases*. London: FT/ Prentice Hall

- Daniels, K. and MacDonald, L. (2005) *Equality, Diversity and Discrimination: A student text*. London: CIPD

- Trades Union Congress (2010) *Equality Act 2010: TUC briefing for affiliates*. July. London: TUC

Websites

- Statistics Office www.statistics.gov.uk

- Trades Union Congress www.tuc.org

- Organisation for Economic Co-operation and Development www.oecd.org.uk

- International Labour Organisation www.ilo.org.uk

CHAPTER 11

Discipline and Grievance

CHAPTER OVERVIEW

The appropriate use of discipline and grievance policies and procedures is essential in order to achieve an efficient workplace, and one in which employees feel that they are treated fairly. Moreover, the adherence to legislation and codes of conduct in these areas is necessary in order to avoid costly legal action and collective action. The coverage of this chapter is very closely related – and complementary – to other chapters such as Chapter 12 and Chapter 10, with respect in particular to the causes of grievance and discipline, the legislative frameworks, and how issues may be dealt with in practice.

The chapter begins by defining grievance, outlining the main causes and detailing relevant procedures. It then moves on to address discipline, critically evaluating the use of the term, and explaining how disciplinary proceedings should be conducted. Key aspects of legislation are considered, drawing particularly on British legislation since although other legislative frameworks may differ, the British guidance is quite comprehensive (drawing on the ACAS code of conduct) and therefore forms a useful benchmark.

LEARNING OUTCOMES

After studying this chapter you should be able to:

- explain the uses of grievance and discipline procedures, and outline when a failure in discipline might result in dismissal
- list potential causes of grievance
- understand the importance of handling grievances properly
- outline grievance and discipline policies and procedures
- describe the factors that influence effective discipline- and grievance-handling
- deal with bullying and harassment
- summarise legal aspects of discipline and grievance, and explain how conforming with legislation may help to mitigate organisational risk
- highlight the importance of HR and line managers in the areas of grievance and discipline

A BRIEF EXPLANATION OF DISCIPLINE, GRIEVANCE AND DISMISSAL

The use of grievance procedures acknowledges the existence of conflict and institutionalises it by the use of peaceful means of settlement (Nurse and Devonish 2007). Grievance procedures also provide a means for employees to voice concerns, and remain in the organisation rather than choosing the alternative strategy of exit (Nurse and Devonish 2007). A grievance is an allegation by an employee that he or she has been treated unjustly by either a manager or a co-worker. Grievances can consist of 'concerns, problems or complaints' (ACAS 2009a: 3). The cause may be genuine or the result of a misunderstanding. Organisations are required to fully investigate the causes and nature of the complaint and take appropriate action. Grievances that are not dealt with quickly are damaging to both the firm and the individual. Whereas in Britain grievances tend to be dealt with on an individual basis, in countries such as the United States they tend to be covered within collective bargaining arrangements (Mills and Dalton 1994). Very little research has been conducted on grievances, which is surprising given its importance to employment relations and centrality to the function of individual representation by trade unions (Ewing 2005: 8).

A disciplinary procedure is used in the event of an employee's lack of capability or performance, when the employee is incapable of performing the job, shows inappropriate conduct or breaks the rules or expectations of behaviour. The final stage of disciplinary action is dismissal. There are potentially fair reasons for dismissal. However, these vary between countries. In Britain, a fair reason includes a lack of capability or qualifications. It could in some cases nonetheless be argued that the employer should have taken action to help the employee to improve the standard of performance. A second potentially fair reason is poor conduct. Misconduct is usually dealt with through disciplinary warnings. Types of misconduct include bad language, poor time-keeping and the improper wearing of a uniform. In situations of gross misconduct it can be appropriate to dismiss the employee without notice. Gross misconduct might include theft, assault, vandalism or the falsification of records.

Other countries have different definitions of what is fair dismissal. For example, in Norway there can be fair dismissal for personal reasons (for example, disloyalty or persistent absenteeism) and economic reasons, and in India a fair reason could include theft, habitual neglect of duty, disorderly behaviour, bribery, lack of capability, financial irregularities or subordination (OECD 2008).

CAUSES OF GRIEVANCE

Grievances can involve issues surrounding:

- the working environment (eg health, safety, cleanliness, pleasant working conditions)
- the employment contract (eg pay, leave)

- career planning (eg promotion, access to training)
- interpersonal relations (eg harassment or bullying)
- discrimination (eg being dealt with differently from those of a different gender, religion, age or ethnic grouping)
- job grading, evaluation and performance appraisal
- pay
- non-pay terms and conditions
- health and safety
- new working practices
- discipline
- work allocation/staffing levels.

There can be some difficulty in detecting the causes of grievances, and formal grievances may constitute only a small part of the actual grievances that are dealt with. There may be underlying conflict within an organisation that is either ignored or dealt with informally, as explained in more detail in Chapter 12. The existence of latent conflict reinforces the need to deal effectively with potential sources of conflict that have been expressed. Further difficulties in detecting the causes of grievance arise from those placing grievances perceiving multiple sources of conflict – including those that are substantive (as defined above) or relational (Salipante and Bouwen 2007). Thirdly, in some cases grievances might be misrepresented by claimants because they do not want to identify the real source of the problem, especially where employees already consider themselves to be more vulnerable in terms of tenure, or are victims of discrimination.

❓ CRITICAL DEBATE

The expression of grievances in the United States

Research in the United States has demonstrated that females and ethnic minority groupings such as Hispanics are more prone to raise grievances. This might be partly because they have experienced injustice, and partly due to their fear that they are at greater risk of additional or greater injury if they do not file a formal grievance. A further reason is that they may feel that they are not able to achieve a change through informal means (Bamberger *et al* 2008).

Based on your knowledge and experience, which reason do you think is the most important?

THE IMPORTANCE OF HANDLING GRIEVANCES PROPERLY

Grievances may be felt by an individual or a group, or have a combined dimension. In other words, others may feel that they will suffer from similar treatment under the same situation. It is best to deal with grievances speedily because many grievances can be resolved quickly and effectively before they reach the formal stage.

There can be reasons for grievances not being handled effectively. Grievances may not be expressed formally by employees because they may fear victimisation or reprisals, especially in a time of high unemployment. It is also possible that immediate superiors may be the cause of the grievance. Moreover, managers may not possess the necessary skills to tackle issues appropriately.

Not dealing with grievances can result in individualised or collective conflict. If not dealt with, grievances may lead to costly legal action, or even a strike. Unresolved grievances can also lead to:

- frustration, low morale and poor interpersonal relations
- a lack of co-operation
- poor performance
- disciplinary problems
- high staff turnover
- a rise in damage to company property or petty theft
- absenteeism
- resistance to change.

As mentioned above, a lack of complaints does not mean that workers are necessarily satisfied with their jobs or committed to their organisations.

◀◉▶ REFLECTION ON PRACTICE

The outcomes of unresolved grievances

Have you been aware of any of the above behaviours in the organisation where you are working, or one in which you have previously worked? If so, do you think that any of these behaviours were due to unresolved grievances? If you felt that a grievance against a manager or colleague had not been dealt with properly, would you be likely to resort to any of the above behaviours?

GRIEVANCE POLICIES AND PROCEDURES

A grievance policy provides a formal means for processing and evaluating complaints. It ensures fairness and consistency and helps to ensure predictability. Moreover, it clarifies procedures, helps to promote good relations within the firm, and can avoid costly legal or collective action. Grievances are best dealt with on a one-to-one basis and unlike collective bargaining, grievances should not involve trade-offs such as dropping a complaint about bullying in return for promotion.

A formal grievance procedure may contain a fixed number of stages. In both Canada and the United States almost all unionised workplaces use multi-step grievance procedures (Colvin 2004). There should be a sufficient number of stages to ensure some impartiality, but not so many as to be unwieldy. The grievance procedure might also include time-limits, but with longer time-limits accorded to the higher stages of the process. Another important feature is the accompanying of an employer representative (referred to in more detail in a section below). Finally, it should include directions for keeping grievance records and for monitoring and review. Keeping grievance records can help to clarify the nature of the complaint, enable HR managers to keep in touch with work processes, identify delays, ensure that there is less room for later misunderstandings, and provide protection in the case of legal action.

The stages of a grievance procedure might include the following, although all stages must adhere to legislation within the relevant country:

- The employee may raise the concern orally or in written form with the immediate supervisor or manager, or the concern may be expressed by an employee representative in the case of a collective dispute. The issue should be raised with someone who is not the subject of the grievance (ACAS 2009a).

- Many grievances can be dealt with informally, prior to the formal meeting stage. Unfounded grievances may be the result of a personality clash or misunderstanding. It is wise to investigate reasons, and explain clearly (when appropriate) why a grievance merits no action. (Often a shop steward will perform this role, prior to reaching the formal stages.)

- If not resolved, after a fixed time period, the concern may be taken up with the next level of management and/or the personnel department.

- The employee should be offered a meeting/interview.

- The employer should prepare to meet the employee, collecting all relevant information and checking if rules and practices and collective or individual agreements are valid. The employer should also decide on how, ideally, the grievance might be resolved, and the least that management will settle for (a fall-back position). Additionally, the employer should decide on who will speak for management, how the management team will communicate during the meeting (eg via notes), the arguments likely to be presented, and how they may be countered/defended.

- The meeting will then be held to investigate the concern. During the grievance interview/meeting, the individual should state her or his complaint. This may be a difficult process if the plaintiff or the line manager defending her or his actions is angry. The employer representative should gather information, listen and hear. Managers must ensure that they are in full possession of all the facts. At the same time, the history of issues should be considered. Ideally, both parties should agree on common ground. The manager should then seek to resolve the grievance and report the outcome

- If unresolved in a fixed time period, the concern may be taken up with the next level of management.

- If an employee considers that his or her grievance has not been resolved satisfactorily, he or she should have the right to appeal. The appeal should be heard by someone of sufficient authority not involved in the case.

Finally, where the grievance is against a supervisor, the supervisor may need:

- counselling
- informal advice
- training
- redeployment in the case of personality clashes
- dismissal.

DISCIPLINARY POLICIES AND PROCEDURES

Disciplinary procedures are necessary because employees need to be aware of the organisation's expectations in terms of their standards of performance or conduct, and they also need to know what will happen to them if they consistently fail to meet those set standards. In addition, the disciplinary process may identify why employees fail to meet required standards, and their training needs. The employee and employer must agree on how to address any failure in standards and on an appropriate time-scale for change in performance or conduct. The use of a disciplinary procedure might mean that a problem does not go as far as an employment tribunal. If an employment tribunal does take place, the employer will have to explain how the disciplinary procedure has been used to try to avert dismissal (CIPD 2010a).

The *Applying theory to practice* box below illustrates how a simple issue can be resolved before it culminates in a disciplinary hearing.

APPLYING THEORY TO PRACTICE

Dealing with a disciplinary issue informally

A valued and generally reliable employee is late for work on a number of occasions, causing difficulties for other staff who have to provide cover. You talk to the employee on his own and he reveals that he has recently split up with his wife and he now has to take the children to school on the way to work. You agree a temporary adjustment to his start and finish times and he undertakes to make arrangements for 'school run' cover which solves the problem. You decide that formal disciplinary action is not appropriate' (ACAS 2009b: 10).

What will you do if the employee arrives at work an hour later than the agreed time on the following Monday?

Although an informal meeting can be very helpful in averting the need for further action, it is important that it does not inadvertently turn into a formal meeting for which the employee should have the right to be accompanied by a trade union representative or colleague. If a formal warning might be necessary, the meeting should be adjourned, and the employee should be informed that there will be a further meeting. It is also important to take notes at an informal meeting (ACAS 2009b).

A disciplinary procedure may be used for issues of either capability/performance or conduct. Issues of capability/performance should ideally be dealt with informally, and disciplinary procedures used only when other means have been exhausted (CIPD 2010a). The organisation should possess policies and procedures on issues likely to impact on performance, such as timekeeping, absence, health and safety, the use of facilities, discrimination, bullying and harassment, and personal appearance (ACAS 2009b).

In situations of ill health it might be necessary to use disciplinary procedures where absence levels are unacceptable. Nevertheless, employees who suffer from ill health should be offered support and dealt with sympathetically, and disciplinary procedures avoided if at all possible. The employer must also avoid discriminating against employees with disabilities (see Dibben *et al* 2001; Cunningham *et al* 2004).

⚷ LEGISLATION IN PRACTICE

Discipline, absence and disability

Tunga has recently been diagnosed with ME, and has been taking a lot of time off work during the past month. Feng, her manager, has decided that the situation cannot continue. She has decided to use disciplinary measures. However, she thinks that it might be helpful to consult Carlos, the trade union representative, before she does so, because she is aware of the Disability Discrimination Act 1996, and is not sure if it applies to her dealing with Tunga. After speaking with Carlos, she decides that it might be best to sit down with Tunga and find out if there are any adjustments that she can make to the workplace or to working time so that Tunga has no need to take time off work. During the meeting Tunga reveals that she is finding it difficult to travel in to work during rush hour, because it then takes her a long time to get into work. As a result Feng decides to allow Tunga to start work at 10am in the morning and to finish at 4pm for the next six months, and then to review the situation again.

Where the issue relates to conduct, this could include persistent late attendance at work, inappropriate use of the Internet or bullying behaviour. More serious offences might involve gross misconduct, which should be outlined in the policy, together with examples of acts that the employer would consider to be gross misconduct, including 'theft or fraud, physical violence, gross negligence or serious insubordination' (ACAS 2009a: 8). If an employee has been charged or convicted of a criminal offence, it is not in itself justification for disciplinary action – it depends on the effect that the conviction has on the employee's ability to carry out the job (eg a ban on driving would be a problem for a taxi driver).

The disciplinary procedure might include the following stages:

1 informal feedback

2 verbal warning (although this is no longer recommended in some codes of conduct, such as that provided in the UK by ACAS)

3 investigatory meeting

4 disciplinary hearing

5 written warning

6 meeting

7 final written warning

8 appeal.

THE FORMAL DISCIPLINARY HEARING

The investigation prior to the formal hearing should be as thorough as possible, and in some cases might involve the holding of an investigatory meeting. Where possible, different people should conduct the investigation and the disciplinary hearing (ACAS 2009a). The investigatory meeting should not result in disciplinary action. In some cases it might be deemed necessary to suspend an employee with pay while the investigation is being carried out. This period should be as short as possible.

As with handling grievances, the employer should keep meticulous records because these may be vital if the employee later takes the employer to an employment tribunal. These records should include minutes of meetings, emails, notes of telephone calls and copies of letters (CIPD 2010a). Disciplinary interviews should also be handled carefully, and include a series of actions as outlined below (ACAS 2009a, 2009b; CIPD 2010a).

Before a formal hearing:

- Investigate all facts (including whether there are personal issues that may have impacted on performance) and plan the structure of the meeting.
- Send a letter to the employee clearly stating the time, date and venue of the meeting, and the reason for the meeting – including the possible consequences. The employee should also be informed of the right to be accompanied by a work colleague or trade union official, and the letter should be sent at least 72 hours before the meeting.
- Gather appropriate statements from relevant people, but ensure anonymity if they wish it.
- Consider any necessity for inviting an interpreter and making reasonable adjustments where an employee has a disability.
- Ensure that another member of the management team is present at the meeting to write detailed notes and assist during the meeting.

During the meeting:

- The employee should be allowed the support of someone to accompany them where the meeting might result in a formal warning, other disciplinary action, or the confirmation of a warning or disciplinary action.
- Start by stating the complaint to the employee, referring to relevant evidence.
- Give the employee the opportunity to reply and to draw on statements from relevant witnesses and ask questions.
- The employee's companion/trade union representative should be allowed to

address the hearing, sum up the employee's case, and confer with the employee during the meeting.

- Use adjournments where necessary to collate evidence or to cool down.
- Find out whether the employee accepts that he or she has acted incorrectly or is not performing adequately, and seek agreement on action that can be taken to improve matters.
- Deliver the decision, giving reasons for the decision and taking any mitigating circumstances into account.
- Explain review periods and provide details on how to appeal.

After the meeting:

- Confirm the decision in writing. If no warning is given, an employee may simply need extra support or counselling. Other options might include a first written warning/improvement notice or a final written warning. Consider any written organisational rules that suggest which action is appropriate in a particular case, and penalties imposed on other employees in the past for a similar offence.
- Where misconduct or unsatisfactory performance has been confirmed, an employee would usually be given a written warning.
- If a warning is given, a time should be specified for when the warning is 'spent' (first written warning, six months; final written warning, twelve months). Further misconduct or unsatisfactory progress would usually result in a final written warning or demotion. However, if the first misconduct or unsatisfactory performance is serious and has had or is likely to have a 'serious or harmful impact on the organisation' (ACAS 2009a: 7), it could result in a final written warning.
- A decision to dismiss the employee should be taken by a manager with the authority to do it. In cases of dismissal, the employee should be informed of the date at which the contract will be terminated and of the right of appeal.
- Any appeal should be heard by someone who was not previously involved in the case, and the employee should again be aware of the right to be accompanied.

As Edwards (1979: 33) points out, discipline should be corrective rather than coercive in purpose, and consistent rather than arbitrary in application. It should also be noted that in some cases a grievance might be raised during a disciplinary meeting, and it may be possible for the two issues to be tackled at the same time (ACAS 2009a).

FAIRNESS AND CONSISTENCY

Fairness and consistency in the use of grievance and disciplinary procedures is vital in maintaining an efficient workplace and one in which there is a culture of mutual respect. The inconsistent use of discipline can cause a loss in productivity and can also reduce employee morale (Franklin and Pagan 2006). However, even where formal disciplinary and grievance procedures are in place there can be a lack of consistency in application (see, for example, Saundry and Antcliff 2006). As Edwards (1994: 568) warns, it should not be inferred that the existence of written disciplinary rules necessarily alters actual practice in a significant manner. There is greater variability in disciplinary practice than the widespread adoption of similar procedures would suggest. Several reasons account for this variability. Firstly, it is not possible to be comprehensive in specifying the precise type of conduct that triggers disciplinary action. There will always be contingencies that cannot be foreseen or predicted. There are also significant differences between organisations and over time as to the levels of management with the authority to administer discipline.

By accompanying individual members, negotiating the form of disciplinary procedures and challenging the application of disciplinary measures, trade unions and shop stewards act as an important influence on the operation of disciplinary procedures. In practice, however, management sets the broad parameters of the disciplinary process unilaterally and union involvement in the content is through consultation and accompaniment. Unions rarely challenge management's disciplinary decisions directly.

The impact on disciplinary procedures by agencies external to the workplace is an additional source of variability. There are significant differences in the degree of third-party involvement in disciplinary procedures that is permissible or tolerated, which are principally due to differences in the power to question the substance of managerial decisions.

Fairness and transparency can be helped by developing and using appropriate rules and procedures for grievance and discipline, as outlined above. However these rules should be both specific and clearly explained, and both employees and their representatives should be involved, where possible, in their development (ACAS 2009a: 3). Managers should not be able simply to dismiss complaints out of hand. An area in which there appears to be a particular lack of consistency regarding discipline and grievance is that of discrimination (for example, in relation to gender or race). Those who have been discriminated against may find it difficult to complain when they already feel victimised. Indeed, evidence from the United States suggests that taking a complaint through a formal procedure can lead to employees feeling doubly victimised. One reason for this may be the victim's lack of awareness of procedures (Bumiller 1988, cited in Kritzer *et al* 1991). Moreover, disciplinary sanctions against groups of people seem to vary. For example, the rates of disciplinary action and dismissal in workplaces employing a large proportion of younger workers (under 50) or females can be higher than those employing a higher proportion over older workers, and disciplinary rates have been higher in organisations employing a large proportion of ethnic minority workers, and these groups are also more likely to be dismissed than other groups of workers (Knight and Latreille 2000). However, it is possible that the cause could be the type of industry rather than differences between types of workers.

EMPLOYEE REPRESENTATION

Employees should have the right to be accompanied by a colleague, shop steward or employee representative in grievance hearings and disciplinary meetings, because the individual concerned may lack the skills or education to properly express his or her case. In Britain, the 1999 Employment Relations Act gives employees the legal right to be accompanied by a fellow worker or union official. If the employee chooses the latter, the union can be any union, not necessarily one that is recognised by management. Sometimes external representatives may be involved, such as lawyers or full-time union officials. However, although legislation permits accompaniment, it does not often appear to happen in practice. A survey of British workplaces found that 22.7% of managers had permitted a full-time officer to accompany an employee in a grievance hearing, and 35.1% had allowed the presence of a union representative. In disciplinary hearings, the proportions were lower, at 19.9% for full-time union officers and 30.4% for union representatives (Saundry and Antcliff 2006). This is somewhat surprising, in view of the legislation described above.

In terms of formal grievance procedures, provision may be made for being accompanied at the second and higher stages of the process. However, in the real world, many managers prefer shop stewards or employee representatives to be involved as soon as possible because they may act as a filter, advising employees (for example) not to go ahead with complaints that are spurious, and are more likely to be able to find out what the complaint really is about.

Although shop stewards or employee representatives are also employees of the firm, in the case of grievance procedures they are accorded the status of equal partners, and should be treated with the appropriate degree of courtesy by management. Supervisors may, of course, resent this aspect, and it may require a great degree of diplomacy.

DISCIPLINE IN SMALL ORGANISATIONS

The use of formal disciplinary action in small organisations (fewer than 50 employees) can be proportionately less than in larger organisations, if measured by assessing the average number of disciplinary cases per year (CIPD 2007). Part of the reason for this might be the tendency to use informality in smaller organisations as the usual means of discipline, whereas for managers in small organisations, moving towards formal measures implies that they have already decided to dismiss the employee (Earnshaw *et al* 2000; CIPD 2007). Nevertheless, smaller organisations do tend to have some form of disciplinary procedures in place, even where this has not yet been the subject of legislation, implying that they recognise the importance of dealing with discipline effectively. For example, in Britain, 70% of workplaces with fewer than 50 employees had formal disciplinary and grievance procedures in place six years before they were legally required (Culley *et al* 1999, cited in Saundry and Antcliff 2006). By 2004, 83% of managers within small organisations (fewer than 50 employees) reported the existence of formal grievance procedures, and 85% stated that disciplinary procedures were present within the organisation (Saundry and Antcliff 2006).

Discipline in very small organisations (with fewer than 20 employees) may involve a slightly different approach from that in large organisations. Small organisations are arguably disproportionately affected by the costs associated with unfair dismissal, and may struggle to pay the administrative costs associated with keeping records (Earnshaw *et al* 2000). Moreover, because smaller organisations more often tend to be non-unionised, the only recourse for employees who are treated unfairly may be through the law, and smaller organisations may therefore face a higher number of legal cases than might otherwise be expected (Tremlett and Banerji 1994, cited in Earnshaw *et al* 2000).

In some countries, acknowledgement of the different situation for small organisations has resulted in a lower requirement for compliance with legislation. For example, in Britain, ACAS (2009b: 54) outlines the ways in which disciplinary rules should be applied in small organisations. The rules should:

- be simple, clear and in writing
- be displayed prominently in the workplace
- be known and understood by all employees
- cover issues such as absences, time-keeping, health and safety, and the use of organisational facilities and equipment (add any other items relevant to your organisation)
- indicate examples of the type of conduct which will normally lead to disciplinary action other than dismissal – for instance, lateness or unauthorised absence
- indicate examples of the type of conduct which will normally lead to dismissal without notice – examples may include working dangerously, stealing or fighting – although much will depend on the circumstances of each offence.

DISMISSAL

Under UK legislation, dismissal is normally fair if the employer has a good reason for the dismissal and has acted 'reasonably'. However, there are cases where an employee should not have been dismissed – known as wrongful dismissal or breach of contract (CIPD 2010b). Wrongful dismissal is a claim for a breach of the employment contract, whereas unfair dismissal is dismissal for a reason other than:

- deficient capability
- lack of qualifications
- poor conduct
- illegality or contravention of statutory duty
- 'some other substantial reason'

- redundancy, or
- planned retirement.

The employer must also follow its own policy and procedures or customary disciplinary process. According to the CIPD (2010b), in the UK unfair dismissal can result from dismissing an employee for:

- trade union membership or activities
- pregnancy or childbirth
- taking (perfectly legitimate) maternity, adoption, paternity or parental leave
- asserting a statutory right
- claiming the national minimum wage
- asserting rights under the Working Time Regulations.

Other reasons for why a dismissal may be unfair under UK legislation include discrimination, bullying and harassment. A further way in which an employee is deemed to have been dismissed unfairly is referred to as 'constructive dismissal', which occurs when an employee leaves the job of his or her own volition, but after leaving the job states that he/she was forced to leave the organisation because the employer was responsible for a breach of contract (CIPD 2010b).

The award given to an employee who has been unfairly or wrongly dismissed varies depending on the country context. In the UK, an employee who has been wrongly dismissed is entitled to his or her full net salary for the notice period that is stated in the employment contract in addition to compensation for the loss of any additional benefits that he/she would have accrued. On the other hand, in cases of unfair dismissal the employee is given compensation for loss of job security and compensation for both the immediate and future loss of earnings (CIPD 2010b).

There are three steps that should be taken in relation to a dismissal, although in general the procedure for a dismissal follows from the disciplinary procedures outlined above:

- Step 1: The employer writes down the nature of employee's conduct, capability or other circumstances and sends a copy to the employee.
- Step 2: The employer invites the employee to a hearing, and the employee must take all reasonable steps to attend. After the meeting, the employer should inform the employee of any decision and offer the employee the right of appeal.
- Step 3: If the employee wishes to appeal, he or she must inform the employer. If this happens, the employer must invite the employee to another hearing, attended, where possible, by a more senior manager. The final decision must be communicated to the employee.

The fact that some organisations are more prone to dismissals than others may not reflect inherent differences between employees but rather the policies of the organisations themselves. In progressive organisations, dismissal is a relatively rare sanction, employed only when other means have failed. In others, such as small firms or firms with a high proportion of less-skilled workers, dismissal or the threat of it remains an important form of control. It is therefore misleading to draw a sharp distinction between punitive and corrective forms of discipline. Employers are likely to use a mixture of both forms.

THE 'NEW' SELF-DISCIPLINE

Rules and the sanctions that accompany their breach, as we noted above, are part of wider relations of conflict and control within the workplace. Research by Edwards (1994: 574) shows that

> the conduct of discipline cannot be separated from the overall patterns of workplace relations, and that the niceties of corrective discipline and proceduralism are not necessarily followed on the shop floor.

Because the day-to-day operation of the workplace depends on a negotiation of order, discipline is only one element in the continuous efforts to regulate the balance between control and resistance in the workplace.

The 'new' self-discipline involves the creation of expectations and understandings in order that employees govern themselves. Formal rules and procedures are thus not necessary. One way of disciplining employees is to emphasise the need to maintain 'professionalism'. Employees should behave in way that conforms to an unwritten code of conduct, and in this way, professionalism is used as a disciplinary mechanism.

The extension of managerial control can be associated with a 'panopticon' effect (Foucault 1988). According to Foucault, self-discipline can be likened to the analogy of a prison in which the guards are based in a central tower and able to see all of the prisoners in the surrounding area. The central tower has one-way windows, and the prisoners cannot see inside the tower. Consequently, they cannot tell when they are being watched. The prisoners behave in a way that the prison guards would approve of, just in case they are being watched. The guards do not need to exert any discipline because the prisoners discipline their own behaviour. In a similar way, employees in today's workplaces discipline their own behaviour.

In the modern workplace, the use of technology can be used as a tool for surveillance (Friedman and Reed 2007; Bélanger and Thuderoz 2010). For example, it is possible to check on the websites that employees access, track their phone calls, observe when they clock in and clock out, and use CCTV cameras to watch movements. As Bélanger and Thuderoz explain (*ibid*: 142):

> The proportion of employees whose work can be monitored through information collected throughout their daily routine is much higher than usually suggested ... It is by no means specific to customer service representatives in call centres or routinised assembly work that have received so much attention – it also prevails broadly in continuous-process

technology, among the huge majority of clerical workers, those working in design and engineering, and indeed most professional employees in the civil service, universities, and so on.

Employees may not always be aware of the amount of surveillance used, but various surveys have pointed towards concerns with the invasion of privacy. As Friedman and Reed (2007: 76) suggest, 'When citizens take on the role of employees, their right to privacy is increasingly subjugated to employers' interests.'

DEALING WITH BULLYING AND HARASSMENT

Bullying and harassment in the workplace can result in significant harm to employees.

Bullying can be defined (Gennard and Judge 2010: 485) as:

> offensive, intimidating, malicious or insulting behaviour, an abuse of power through means intended to humiliate, denigrate or injure the recipient.

It is generally taken to mean negative behaviours that are both repeated and persistent (CIPD 2005). Harassment is essentially unwanted conduct affecting a person's dignity. In other countries, the terms used include 'mobbing', 'employee abuse', 'workplace aggression', 'victimisation', 'interpersonal deviance', 'social undermining', and 'workplace incivility' (see Salin 2003).

It is only recently that the effects of bullying and harassment have been acknowledged within the legislative statute books of some countries. In the European Union the effects are, however, becoming increasingly acknowledged, harassment being referred to within the context of equal rights legislation. The European Framework Directive of 2000 states that harassment of a person related to their sexual orientation, religion, disability or age is contrary to the principle of equal treatment. Countries such as Sweden have legislation that deals with victimisation at work (Unison 2003). Moreover, under the British Equality Act 2010, harassment is defined (CIPD 2010c) as:

> unwanted conduct related to a relevant protected characteristic, which has the purpose or effect of violating an individual's dignity or creating an intimidating, hostile, degrading, humiliating or offensive environment for that individual.

The protected characteristics defined by the Equality Act 2010 are those usually associated with discrimination: age, disability, gender reassignment, race, religion or belief, sex and sexual orientation, pregnancy and maternity, marriage and civil partnership. However, the last four are excluded from the liability for harassment. Under the Act, employees can complain about harassment even if they do not possess the protected characteristic or if it is not directed against them. In addition, employers are liable for harassment if their employees are subjected to harassment from customers (CIPD 2010c).

Both bullying and harassment can be causes of grievances and also disciplinary action, but are often very difficult to detect and deal with effectively. It is difficult to measure the extent of workplace bullying due to the lack of reporting of bullying and the difficulty in measuring the extent of it (Cowie *et al* 2002). However, it is generally acknowledged that bullying can have many negative effects on employees' health, such as insomnia, nervous symptoms, memory loss, gastric problems, anxiety, stress and depression, and it can have similar effects to those identified with post-traumatic stress disorder (Unison 2003; Hoel, Faragher and Cooper 2004). Negative psychological and behavioural effects can also be experienced by witnesses to the bullying behaviour (Hoel, Faragher and Cooper 2004). The employer might also suffer, incurring costs that include 'time, money, staff turnover, absence, damaged employer brand, disturbed working relationships, low morale and commitment' (CIPD 2005: 3). It can also result in industrial action or unrest.

The causes of bullying are varied. Bullying may be related to worker characteristics such as age, race, disability, religion, nationality or personal disposition, and may be persistent or an isolated incident (Gennard and Judge 2005). It can also be related to changes to workplace structures or processes including restructuring, downsizing, changes in the work group or management changes (Salin 2003). The culture of the organisation can also contribute towards bullying where there is 'strong management', or a focus on efficiency at all costs (Cowie *et al* 2002; Unison 2003).

Bullying and harassment can include personal insults, intimidation through threats of violence or misuse of power, work-related harassment such as withholding information or work overload, and social exclusion through isolation (CIPD 2005). It could also involve rumours, memos, setting someone up to fail, unwelcome advances or constant criticism. The *Reflection on practice* box below gives some examples of the types of bullying behaviour that can occur.

◉ REFLECTION ON PRACTICE

Examples of bullying behaviour at work

Unison (2003:4) provides some interesting examples of types of bullying behaviour:

- Public verbal abuse: 'I was blamed for my own mistakes in front of the entire office. I was shouted at and told to do the work that *should* have been done and not to do what I *had* done again. Everyone was listening as the manager shouted at me.'

- Contract manipulation: 'I was threatened with job loss because I wanted the Bank Holiday off with my family.'

- Undermining actions: 'The manager totally undermined me in front of clients, giving them the impression I was not capable of helping them and advising them to come another day.'

Have you either experienced or seen behaviour similar to that illustrated above?

If so, what did you do when it happened?

Why is it difficult to deal with these types of behaviour?

There is limited evidence of the levels of bullying, although some research has been carried out in Britain to attempt to determine the scale of the problem. A CIPD survey (CIPD 2006) showed that 19% of employees had experienced some form of bullying or harassment within the previous two years, and that this figure rose to 30% of black and Asian employees. In addition, a survey of trade union safety representatives revealed that around 25% of workers had been bullied in the previous four years, and that 47% of workers had witnessed bullying at work (Unison 2003). These figures are somewhat surprising in view of the fact that around 83% of organisations in Britain have anti-bullying policies (CIPD 2004).

There are various measures that can be taken to try to prevent bullying and harassment. In addition to ensuring that organisations have anti-bullying policies, other strategies include a self-assessment questionnaire intended to assess the degree to which an organisation has a culture of dignity and respect, including questions that relate to areas such as personal integrity, promoting standards and challenging the status quo, terms and conditions, and appraisal procedures. Alternatively, organisations can use a risk assessment questionnaire testing issues such as autonomy, variety, pay, performance targets, fair allocation of work, plus specific questions on bullying and harassment and levels of managerial support (CIPD 2005). Further measures include the training of line managers in identifying, managing and dealing with bullying behaviours, and in mediating and counselling skills (CIPD 2005). Moreover, trade union representatives such as safety representatives should be trained in dealing with bullying and harassment, and be able to educate employees and receive complaints (Unison 2003). Beyond this, employers should consider the environment where any workplace activities take place, including social gatherings and the virtual environment, since some employees have been subject to 'cyber-bullying' through texts or emails (CIPD 2010d).

LEGAL ASPECTS OF GRIEVANCE AND DISCIPLINE

The comprehensiveness of legislation in the area of grievance and discipline tends to be associated with the attention paid to individual rights within the workplace. Although there can be collective elements involved (in other words, the representation by union officials in disciplinary and grievance cases), the emphasis tends to be on individual rights. Moreover, the scope of legislation in this area can also be related to the degree to which the government takes a voluntarist or interventionist approach towards employment relations (see Chapter 2).

LEGISLATION RELATING TO GRIEVANCE

The law on grievances has evolved over time. For example, in Britain, until the beginning of the 1970s employers had almost unlimited power to discipline and dismiss individual employees. It was possible for a dismissed employee to sue for wrongful dismissal, but this was rarely practical because of the time and costs involved. Employer power was restricted only where trade unions were present in the workplace and dismissal procedures were established through the collective bargaining process. Later, under the Industrial Relations Act 1971, employees had the right to complain to an industrial tribunal (renamed employment tribunal after 1998) that they had been unfairly dismissed. In 1972 the Act also introduced the Industrial Relations Code of Practice, outlining the correct way to deal with discipline. This has now been superseded by the Code of Practice on Disciplinary and Grievance Procedures. ACAS (the Advisory, Conciliation and Arbitration Service) is an organisation devoted to preventing and resolving employment disputes, and provides a code of practice. This is not legally binding, although a failure to follow it may be tabled as evidence to an employment tribunal. The code outlines what constitutes reasonableness in dealing with grievances and gives guidelines regarding the nature and role of the employee's representative. The Employment Relations Act (1999) now gives employees the right of representation by a trade union or employee representative. The slightly more recent Employment Act 2002 provides for two procedures – a standard procedure and a modified procedure – in the event of grievances. The standard procedure, used where a dismissal has not occurred, is as follows:

- The employee sets out a grievance or the basis of a grievance in writing, and sends it to the employer (a statement of grievance).

- After considering a response, the employer must have a meeting with the employee.

- Following the meeting, the employer makes a decision and notifies the employee of her or his right to appeal.

- If the employee intends to appeal, she or he must inform the employer, who must then hold a further meeting

Where a dismissal has occurred, the modified procedure applies.

- The employee should send a statement of grievance or a copy to the employer.

- The employer must respond to the employee in writing.

After either procedure, or 28 days after the initial complaint was tabled, the employee can take the matter to an employment tribunal.

Further statutory procedures for handling both grievance and discipline were established in 2004 but then repealed in 2009. From 6 April 2009, the most important provisions are within the Employment Act 2008 and the Employment Tribunals (Constitution and Rules of Procedure) (Amendment) Regulations 2008. Two of the changes relating to grievances are that, firstly, there should be written notification given to an employee including the details of the time and location of the grievance meeting and their right to be accompanied. Secondly, where an employee persistently does not attend a meeting without good cause, an employer can make a decision based on the available evidence (although 'good cause' is not defined). Thirdly, organisations should follow the ACAS code of conduct, and also their own procedures.

The legislation in other countries varies to a greater or smaller extent from that outlined above. In the United States, for example, grievance procedures are outlined within the collective bargaining agreement. Employees are allowed to appeal against any disciplinary action or obtain a hearing for treatment that they consider to be unjust. Where the dispute is not easily resolved within the workplace, the final stage is arbitration. This is the system also existing in, for example, Australia and New Zealand. In other countries such as Austria, Germany, Luxembourg, Switzerland and Scandinavian countries, use is made of a similar system within labour courts. Although most cases are resolved before arbitration or the labour courts, this system is important because cases set precedents, providing guidance for employees who might subsequently take a grievance to that level (Mills and Dalton 1994).

LEGISLATION RELATING TO DISCIPLINE

Modern labour laws which constrain management's power to administer discipline are part of a broader policy of intervention by the government that is based on the belief that formalised and standardised procedures reduce the number of workplace grievances and industrial action. As mentioned above, in Britain the most important provisions are within the Employment Act 2008 and the Employment Tribunals (Constitution and Rules of Procedure) (Amendment) Regulations 2008. Former Statutory Dispute Resolution Procedures have recently been abolished and replaced by the ACAS code of practice on disciplinary and grievance procedures (see www.acas.org.uk). However, there is no automatically unfair dismissal if the employer does not follow the new code (CIPD 2010a). This is a key change in law, and could be regarded as a real attack on workers' rights.

MITIGATING ORGANISATIONAL RISK

HR managers should avoid falling foul of the legislation that applies in the country in which they are operating. In the case of multinationals, employers should ensure that they comply with the host country or home country legislation, as appropriate. Some general points are (CIPD 2010a):

- Organisational norms can develop over time, and it is easy to assume that they conform to procedures. However, HR practitioners should ensure that they have up-to-date knowledge of their own company's procedures, and also that these procedures conform to relevant legislation and/or codes of practice.
- Include employees or their representatives in the development or revision of procedures.
- Ensure that line managers possess the necessary skills and competence to follow procedures.
- Include time-scales within procedures, even where legislation or codes of practice do not include them.
- Deal with issues raised by ex-employees even where this is not covered within legislation or codes of practice.

As stated in the ACAS guide to discipline and grievances at work (2009b: 4):

> Good employment relations practices – including recruitment, induction, training, communications and consultation – can prevent many discipline and grievance problems arising. Organisations are also more likely to have positive relationships if they make efforts to gain their employees' commitment through:
>
> - showing them clear leadership and letting them know how they can contribute
>
> - engaging them in their work and giving them the power to make some decisions themselves rather than trying to control and restrict them
>
> - showing them respect and appreciation
>
> - giving them ways to voice their views and concerns.

Research from the United States also supports the importance of employee involvement schemes in preventing grievances. Higher involvement practices, the use of problem-solving work groups and the involvement of work groups in decision-making have all been associated with a lower rate of grievances (Colvin 2004).

THE ROLE OF HR, LINE MANAGERS AND TRADE UNIONS IN GRIEVANCE AND DISCIPLINE

In order to achieve effective grievance resolution, the HR manager should:

- develop training where necessary for line managers
- ensure that line managers have a clear idea of how grievance procedures are intended to operate
- devise a clear grievance procedure
- promote good practice
- ensure that employees know their rights
- promote a constructive approach to grievances across the firm.

Line managers should have the power to settle grievances, should ensure that they are properly informed on the process and outcome of grievance procedures, should know the nature and limits of their authority, and should apply procedures consistently. However, there may be a tendency for supervisors to take an inconsistent approach. In terms of discipline, the tendency to use informal strategies, although positive in some cases when used to prevent the need for formal disciplinary procedures, can be marked by inconsistency in approach (Franklin and Pagan 2006). The inconsistency in the use of discipline can sometimes be related to the severity of the misdemeanour, the approach used varying to a greater extent in more serious cases (Rollinson *et al* 1996). One explanation for this could be the concern felt by line managers to explore cases more fully before taking them through formal procedures. However, another could be the lack of training in this area. Some research has indicated a lack of supervisor awareness of the content and even the existence of disciplinary procedures within the organisation (Rollinson *et al* 1996).

Trade unions can play an important role within the workplace in relation to discipline and grievance. Survey evidence from Britain has suggested that workplaces where trade unions are present were more likely to possess comprehensive disciplinary and grievance procedures and to implement them more thoroughly (Saundry and Antcliff 2006). With regard to discipline, other evidence has suggested that the number of disciplinary sanctions and dismissals can be lower in workplaces where trade union density is higher, implying that unions can be a positive force within the workplace in protecting workers rights and in maintaining order (Knight and Latreille 2000). The union also has an important role in relation to grievances. Evidence from the United States has suggested that shop stewards can act as a filtering mechanism for grievances, influencing whether an employee decides to take out a formal grievance. They might counsel individual employees not to take out grievances or attempt to resolve them informally with supervisors prior to taking them through formal procedures. The willingness of shop stewards to encourage employees to take out formal grievances seems to vary, to some extent, on the degree of commitment of the shop stewards towards the organisation, emphasising the importance of relationships between managers and unions within the workplace (Dalton and Todor 1982).

Another contribution of trade unions is towards the development of procedures. Unionised workplaces in the United States and Canada, for example, employ detailed and standardised grievance procedures, whereas in non-unionised workplaces there is considerable variation in both the type of grievance procedure and whether they exist at all. Managers are able to choose whether to use formal or informal procedures (Colvin 2004). Similar findings have emerged from Australia where non-unionised workplaces have been less likely to provide formal disciplinary and grievance procedures (Deery *et al* 2001).

The role of trade unions can vary significantly between countries. The case study below examines the role of trade unions in China in respect of representing employees in the workplace. In China the role of trade unions is very different from that in Britain, and they have traditionally been seen as an arm of management. The case study thus provides an interesting contrast to the British system as described above.

CASE STUDY

INDUSTRIAL RELATIONS AND GRIEVANCES IN CHINA

A study by Clarke *et al* (2004) examines changes to industrial relations in China. Firstly, they draw attention to a new institutional framework which includes tripartite resolution of labour disputes, consultation between trade unions and employers, and changes to legislation, including a trade union law that requires trade unions to provide support for an employee who 'believes that the enterprise infringes upon his labour rights and interests' (Art.21, *ibid* 2004: 250).

However, questions have been raised about the extent to which these changes bring China closer to countries in the West, or are merely evidence of adjustments to new economic conditions which do not translate into real changes in the power and influence of trade unions (*ibid*). One argument which supports the latter position is that 'For most trade union cadres at the workplace, the idea of representing and protecting the legitimate rights and interest

of their members in opposition to those of the employer is something unfamiliar' (*ibid*: 242). Moreover, trade unions apparently tend to filter complaints and suggestions, only dealing with those that are seen as acceptable by management. Workers have therefore tended not to use trade unions as a means of solving problems either formally or informally (*ibid*: 244).

Questions

How does the role of trade unions in China appear to be similar to or different from that in Western countries such as Britain and/or the United States?

Do you think that trade unions should maintain their current role in the workplace in China, or attempt to change their role?

Do you anticipate that the role of trade unions in Chinese workplaces will have remained the same or changed in ten years' time? Give reasons for your answer.

SUMMARY

The focus of this chapter has been on the procedures to be undertaken in order to resolve grievance and hold disciplinary meetings. In particular, use has been made of CIPD and ACAS advice, since this offers useful, practical assistance to HR and line managers. However, the chapter has also considered issues of fairness and discrimination, and the potentially valuable role of trade union representatives. Moreover, in critiquing the notion of discipline, reference has been made to the possibility that workers increasingly engaging in self-discipline, preventing the need for formal measures.

Although the operation of discipline and grievance procedures may seem to be purely a matter of established methodology, in the real world it is rarely the case. Firstly, any procedures may be modified to reach a conclusion favourable to the stronger party, or, indeed, totally absent. Secondly, it is possible for disputes to be apparently 'solved' only to reappear in a different or modified form. The operation of discipline in grievances can therefore only be understood from a perspective that takes account of power, conflict and equity.

EXPLORE FURTHER

Reading

- ACAS (2009a) Code of Practice: *Disciplinary and Grievance Procedures*. London: ACAS

- ACAS (2009a) Guidance booklet: *Discipline and Grievances at Work*. London: ACAS

- CIPD (2010b) *Dismissal*. Factsheet. Available online at http://www/cipd.co.uk/ subjects/emplaw/dismissal.htm?IsSrchRes=1 [accessed 4 August 2010].

- CIPD (2010c) *Equality Act 2010*. Factsheet. Available online at http://www/ cipd. co.uk/subjects/dvsequl/general/equality-act-2010.htm?wa_src=email [acessed 4 August 2010].

- CIPD (2010d) *Harassment and Bullying at Work*. Factsheet. Available online at http://www/cipd.co.uk/subjects/dvsequl/harassmt/harrass.htm?IsSrchRes=1 [accessed 4 August 2010].

Websites

- Advisory, Conciliation and Arbitration Service www.acas.org.uk

- Chartered Institute of Personnel and Development www.cipd.co.uk

- Organisation for Economic Co-operation and Development www.oecd.org.uk

- Unison www.unison.org.uk

CHAPTER 12

Conflict and Dispute Resolution

CHAPTER OVERVIEW

Conflict arises in a range of forms, and these forms have to be recognised and effectively dealt with in order to manage employment relations successfully. No workplace is conflict-free, and it is sometimes the workplaces with the lowest levels of visible conflict that have very high levels of less visible or 'hidden' conflict. Seeking resolutions to disputes thus remains a core area of employment relations practice.

This chapter begins by outlining the main forms of conflict, including those that are individual and those that are collectively organised. Although a focus often tends to be placed on strikes, there are a multitude of other forms that can cause a significant amount of harm to organisations. The subsequent sections then turn to strikes, examining causes and trends in strike patterns, before examining dispute resolution and legislation governing industrial disputes. Legislative aspects draw heavily on the British context because it provides a useful framework for explaining such features as employment tribunals. The final sections in this chapter cover sources of tension and forms of conflict in non-union firms, and refer to practical dimensions of managing conflict.

LEARNING OUTCOMES

After studying this chapter you should be able to:

- describe the main forms of individual and collective action and industrial sanctions

- critically evaluate the causes of strikes and trends in strike patterns

- understand the nature of unofficial and official dispute resolution and dispute-handling, and identify methods of third-party conciliation, mediation and arbitration

- describe legislation governing industrial disputes, and explain the purpose and process followed within employment tribunals, through reference to the UK case

- outline issues relevant to managing conflict in non-union firms and describe the role of employment relations specialists and line managers in managing conflict

CONFLICT BEHAVIOURS AND INDUSTRIAL SANCTIONS

Conflict can assume a variety of different forms that vary in terms of their scale, duration and impact. Writers on employment relations regularly distinguish between 'unorganised' forms of action (such as absenteeism and turnover) and 'organised' forms of action (such as a strike or work-to-rule). Both forms of action express discontent, and their primary difference resides in the intention behind them. As Hyman (1984: 56) explains, with unorganised conflict,

> workers typically respond to the oppressive situation in the only way open to them as *individuals*: by withdrawing from the source of the discontent, or, in the case of certain forms of sabotage or indiscipline, by reacting against the immediate manifestation of oppression.

Whereas unorganised conflict is usually spontaneous and reactive, organised conflict is 'far more likely to form part of a conscious strategy to change the situation which is identified as the source of the discontent' (Hyman 1984: 56).

On the one hand, there are studies which suggest that if organised forms of industrial action are suppressed or otherwise made unavailable, employees will inevitably resort to unorganised forms of action (Eldridge 1968). Other studies suggest that a high incidence of organised forms of action is invariably associated with a high incidence of unorganised forms (see Knowles 1952). Either way, the relations between these two forms of industrial action are exceedingly complex.

The idea that there is a single source of discontent that pervades all forms of industrial action diverts attention from the more important and demanding task of understanding the ways in which social structures in the workplace and beyond constrain and/or enable different forms of industrial action. If sabotage, for example, is regarded as any form of action that results in a loss of production or lower-quality service and output, it may be active or passive, offensive or defensive, individual or collective, overt or covert, and spontaneous or organised, depending on the circumstances (Blyton and Turnbull 1998: 313). Similarly, ostensibly unplanned, reactive and individual acts such as absence and pilfering, or petty destruction of company property, may in fact have a collective dimension, with informal agreements and understandings between workers coordinating, or at least making possible, seemingly random incidents (Cohen 1994). In addition, absenteeism and pilfering are arguably more costly and more difficult for management to control than strikes.

The various forms of industrial action are best viewed along a continuum. At the collective end of the spectrum, strikes are the most notable form of action organised by employees through their trade unions. At the individual end of the spectrum, turnover is the most notable form of action by employees. The middle area accentuates the difficulties in locating the dividing line between organised and unorganised, formal and informal industrial action. However, as Blyton and Turnbull (1998: 316–17) point out, with unorganised conflict it is the individual who will be disciplined and group support for him or her is likely to be implicit rather than explicit.

In an attempt to differentiate the many possible patterns of conflict, Edwards (1986: 226–7) classifies workplaces according to three characteristics of employees' approaches and organisation:

- militant – the extent to which workers perceive themselves as having interests that are opposed to or inconsistent with the interests of management, and act accordingly
- collective – the degree to which an individual or collective orientation exists
- organised – the extent to which a collective orientation is translated into collective organisation.

Using these characteristics, Edwards (1986: 227–34) identifies four possible types of workplace relations, outlined in Table 12.1. Type 1 is common, particularly in organisations in competitive industries that employ female labour and have a strict system of supervision. The key feature is the absence of resources among employees to make their demands effective against those of employers. Also included in this group, however, are organisations where sophisticated paternalism is the dominant management style (see Chapter 2). Type 2 workplaces are often characterised by militant individualism, where employees negotiate with employers over wage rates and assert their right to plan their own work, thereby exercising significant influence over effort norms. In Type 3 workplaces there is collective negotiation over the wage–effort bargain, but controls are often informal or limited to exploiting managerial leniency. In Type 4 workplaces, in which employees exercise substantial control over the wage–effort bargain, sustained through extensive union organisation, control is exercised against employers and over employees as well.

Table 12.1 A classification of the characteristics of workplace relations

	MILITANT	COLLECTIVE	ORGANISED
Type 1	O	O	O
Type 2	✓	O	O
Type 3	✓	✓	O
Type 4	✓	✓	✓

It is important to appreciate that this typology consists of idealised and simplified types. Some cases will therefore fall between types, and there is variation within each type.

◀◉▶ REFLECTION ON PRACTICE

Workplace conflict

Table 12.1 shows different types of workplace relations. Think of an organisation that you are familiar with, either from your work experience or from news reports in the media. The organisation can be based in any country.

How would you classify workplace relations in that organisation? Provide reasons for your answer.

FORMS OF INDUSTRIAL ACTION

Strikes are often regarded as the foremost and preferred form of collective action in that, by stopping work and leaving the workplace, employees visibly express their unwillingness to compromise, their solidarity and their support for the union. In common with other forms of industrial action, strikes can vary in terms of their objectives:

- Offensive economic strikes back up demands for better wages, hours of work, annual leave and working conditions than the employer is willing to grant at the bargaining table. Although such strikes may lead to a protracted battle, they are more likely to adhere to statutory requirements than defensive strikes.

- Defensive frictional strikes often occur in response to perceived unfair management practice such as dismissals, a unilateral change to employment conditions, problems of supervision, and a failure to deal with employee grievances. Such strikes are frequently 'wildcat' or unauthorised, unlawful stoppages, and are generally of short duration.

- Solidarity-building strikes may arise from a union's attempting to achieve recognition from the employer or to extend collective bargaining. It has been argued that unless the weapon of striking is sometimes used, it grows 'rusty', and it may be in the interests of unions to periodically engage in collective action in order to maintain organisational abilities and mobilisation (Hyman 1981).

- Sympathy or secondary strikes occur where employees who are not party to the original or primary dispute strike in support of the union that initiated action. The employees undertaking sympathy action may be employees of companies that are customers, suppliers or close associates of the primary company. For example, employees at an automobile factory may refuse to fit the tyres produced by a company whose employees are on strike. A variation on this is a rolling strike or strike waves. This is where a strike in a particular district spreads to adjoining firms (Maree 1986). Employees are encouraged to engage in collective action by successful action in an adjoining enterprise or are incensed by botched responses by employers or the authorities and are thereby driven to undertake further strikes.

- General strikes involve a protest from large numbers of employees from various industries. Although they may be triggered by disputes in the workplace, they invariably assume a political character and role. An example was the British general strike of 1926, which was in response to the progressive 'squeezing' of workers as employers in the coal industry sought to raise falling profits and cut costs through increasing working hours and cutting wages. A strike in the coal industry spread to other sectors, from steel workers to printers. Eventually the strike was defeated owing to the growing hardship faced by strikers and the increasingly hardline actions of the government (Renshaw 1975). However, the extension of the legal rights enjoyed by employees in subsequent years was prompted at least in part by a desire to avoid such ruinous disputes in the future.

- Trials of strength are where one side aims to inflict a major defeat on the other, and so recast employment relations. Examples are the 1984 British coal miners' strike, the 1987 gold miners' strike in South Africa, and the South African rail workers' strike in the same year. Of those, the first two resulted in a defeat for employees, and the last in a victory.

- Political strikes, unlike general strikes, are aimed at the government rather than at employers, usually involving broad political rather than narrow economic demands and goals. Nevertheless, politically oriented strikes also have employment relations objectives in the sense that they are concerned with the manner in which the employment relationship is regulated. Such strikes were relatively common in Mugabe's Zimbabwe and late *apartheid* South Africa. They can be a powerful means of mobilising opposition and revealing the illegitimacy of the status quo. At the same time, a self-seeking ruling elite may be little deterred by such action, regardless of the macro-economic consequences, as long as they can continue to engage in their own rent-extracting behaviour.

In addition to overt, collective forms of expressing discontent such as strikes and lock-outs, there are numerous other forms of industrial action, and attempts to suppress strikes without removing the underlying causes may simply lead to other forms of conflict (Hyman 1981).

Other forms such as those below may be preferred to strike action because they involve lower costs for employees while still exerting a significant cost on management (Salamon 1998):

- Work stoppage involves a refusal to work that is normally unofficial (in that it is not supported by the union), unprotected (failing to meet the requirements of a lawful strike) and not premeditated (the decision to stop working was taken abruptly and on the spot). Work stoppages are typically of short duration and the result of dissatisfaction with an issue such as exasperation with a supervisor, the dismissal of a shop steward or an increase in the pace of production.

- Overtime bans are a collective refusal to work outside ordinary hours of work in an effort to decrease the volume of production. If the overtime ban fails to elicit an acceptable response from the employer, the union may resort to other, more drastic forms of industrial action (Eldridge 1968).

- Work-to-rule involves an inflexible adherence to the letter (rather than the spirit) of employment contracts, collective agreements and organisational rules. When engaging in this form of action, employees may demand detailed instructions from supervisors regarding the execution of tasks, and use formal job descriptions to define the limits of their work. This form of action may also be accompanied by the withdrawal of co-operation, a refusal to show initiative, excessive use of formal procedures, and the absence of flexibility on the part of employees and their representatives. This form can and does lead to considerable disorder in the workplace.

- Go-slow is aimed at reducing performance and output levels and may be either a preliminary type of protest or an alternative to strike action.

- Sit-in or work-in entails an occupation of the workplace which is sometimes associated with a continuation of production, but denies management access to, or control of, the output.

- 'Labelling' or consumer boycotts are undertaken where a union feels that it is not gaining through direct action but may gain through exerting indirect pressure via the marketplace.

- Partial withdrawal of labour may involve employees in fulfilling only part of their obligations under the employment contract. For example, in 2006, in attempting to remedy a protracted period of declining incomes in relative terms, British academics refused to mark student work. Students supported the lecturers and engaged in protests. Employers generally responded through threats of partial or total withholding of pay. The dispute ultimately resulted in a negotiated settlement.

- An unusual form of collective action is where employees return their paypackets (when they are paid a cash wage) to the employer, refusing to accept the existing terms of employment. As they are not striking, the normal legal restrictions governing strikes no longer apply, but, as is the case with strikes, employees are indicating a willingness to go without pay until the dispute is solved. Strangely, although uncommon, this form of action appears to peculiarly incense employers (Horrell 1969). However, the attendant risks may make it unattractive for employees (employees bear an immediate financial cost, whereas the employer faces only reputational costs).

The above are all official, collective forms of retaliation. In addition, employees may retaliate against employers through a wide range of hidden forms of protest, either on a collective or individual basis (Cohen 1994). The following represent some possible examples:

- Unofficial absence or misuse of sick leave for petty or vague ailments can be very effective because it is difficult for the employer to police. In some national contexts, certain larger employers have resorted to employing company doctors to better police sick leave.

- Industrial sabotage can include literally putting a 'spanner in the works' or deliberately reducing the quality of finished goods. An example is the quality of customer service sometimes given within call centres. Other well-known examples include inappropriate messages in Christmas crackers. Thirdly, employees may deliberately feign stupidity or a lack of understanding.

- Destruction of company property may involve arson, breakages of crockery in company canteens, or the placing of viruses on computer networks.

- Desertion is where employees simply leave the job without bothering to tender a formal resignation. Some of the high staff turnover rate in areas of the fast food industry can be ascribed to this (Cohen 1994).

- Theft of office stationery represents a clear message from employees that they believe that they are entitled to be better-paid, and are taking the opportunities open to them to recover value.

Employers can also use a variety of tactics to bring pressure to bear on employees (Hyman 1981). These include obtaining a court interdict. Employers may even provoke strikes, taking the opportunity to perform essential maintenance or to run down excessive stockpiles of finished goods in order to save money (because they are generally under no obligation to pay strikers). In addition to these tactics, the employer's equivalent of a strike is to lock employees out of the workplace, either in response to industrial action by the employees or when the employer wishes to impose a demand on, or gain a concession from, the employees. Employers may also seek to victimise specific employees. Subtle forms of victimisation may be difficult to prove in subsequent legal action. Employers may also seek to relocate or close the organisation. In view of the permanence of a dismissal or a plant relocation or closure, these sanctions are much more powerful than the temporary stoppage of work through strike action by employees.

APPLYING THEORY TO PRACTICE

Forms of industrial action

Scan the newspapers for the previous week or scan the web pages of newspapers online.

How many forms of industrial action can you see mentioned?

Which forms of conflict appear to be the most common?

THE CAUSES OF STRIKES, AND TRENDS IN STRIKE PATTERNS

The tendency to equate industrial action with strikes is understandable, given their (often exaggerated) impact and (often sensationalised) coverage by the media. The law on industrial action has also become increasingly concerned with controlling strikes. The need to institutionalise rising levels of conflict and integrate an increasingly powerful union movement compelled governments to protect the right to strike as an essential component of the processes of collective bargaining.

Several modern human rights charters endorse the right to strike. A strike is a deliberate and concerted withdrawal of labour aimed at inflicting losses on the employer. There has historically been some reluctance to describe the 'freedom' to strike as a 'right' because of its coercive nature. No other human right exists for the explicit purpose of forcing someone to do something. However, when employees embark on a lawful strike they do not commit a crime, cannot be held liable for losses suffered by the employer because of the strike, and are not guilty of a breach of contract. Nevertheless, the right to strike – like any other right – is not without limitations. For example, public interest may require a limitation on the rights of employees in essential services such as hospitals to engage in strike action.

Despite numerous attempts at explaining strike variations over time and across occupations, industries and countries, there is no generally accepted theory of what causes strikes. Those who take a unitarist view (see Chapter 3) are likely to stress failures of communication, personality clashes and the role of agitators. Those who take a pluralist view tend to emphasise the effects of change and the differing interests of employers and employees. Those who take a conflict perspective regard strikes as a symptom of the exploitative relationship between capital and labour. The proponents of these three perspectives differ not only with regard to the causes of strikes but also in terms of the manner in which strike activity should be controlled (Burchill 1997: 158). Whereas unitarists would call for punitive labour laws and austere management, pluralists would underline the need for institutional arrangements designed to minimise conflict and maximise output. In the conflict model, the attempts by employers to control the work process and the efforts of employees to resist the imposition of managerial authority tend to reveal the balance of power between the parties.

Hostility to strike action is normally founded on three untested assumptions: it is unnecessary and 'irrational' and causes 'unacceptable' economic disruption; it takes wealth away from the rightful owners of the firm; and it is a symptom of 'excessive' trade union power and 'opportunistic' union officials. The costs of strike activity are particularly controversial (Keenoy 1985: 176–81). It is clearly in the interests of the employer to exaggerate the economic consequences of a strike. Since it is difficult, if not impossible, to determine the actual costs of any strike, the figures cited by the employers affected by strikes must be treated with extreme caution (Salamon 1998: 408). The loss of production time, for instance, is not always necessarily proportional to the loss of output or profits. Losses of output and pay are often made up by increased production and overtime after the strike. Stocks in hand may also be sufficient to maintain adequate supplies to the market despite strike action by the employees. Other sources of economic loss, such as occupational injuries and absenteeism, often account for considerably more working days lost than strikes do. Likewise, the various costs associated with strikes may be far less detrimental than those resulting from other forms of industrial action such as output restriction and labour turnover.

Outlawing industrial action by statutory and/or repressive means entails substantial costs in terms of enforcement and damage to the social fabric of a democratic country. It is also worth noting that few highly labour-repressive countries have any reputation for good-quality manufactured goods. Prohibiting strike action is therefore likely to be more costly than attempting to regulate it. Strikes may also provide for a release of tension, facilitate agreement between the parties and generate beneficial changes to workplace relations. They may therefore benefit both employees and employers. The case study below outlines the example of the British Steel Corporation, and is followed by questions based on who benefited most from the strike. Similar situations might occur in other countries where there are mining industries, including emerging economies where large multinationals seek to exploit natural resources.

CASE STUDY

WHO BENEFITS MOST FROM STRIKES?

In the mid-1980s Britain was marked by industrial unrest due to the anticipated closure of companies in the mining and steel industry. Keenoy (1985) describes the results of a strike at the British Steel Corporation. Perhaps unexpectedly, managers gained from reduced expenditure on wages, raw materials and the storage of steel. In addition, the strike provided managers with a useful justification for undertaking further redundancies, and meant that unions were less able to protest against them. In summary, Keenoy (1985: 186) suggests that, 'in the circumstances it was good management to allow the strike to go ahead [since] the longer-term benefits were greater than the short-term costs'.

Questions

Who benefited most from this strike – the employer or the employees?

How might the trade union defend the outcomes of the strike to its members?

As noted above, strikes and other forms of industrial action may be perceived as either rational or irrational acts. Hyman (1984: 110–44) argues that apart from those who deny the existence of conflict in organisations, the view of industrial action as an irrational act stems from two main beliefs: that any conflict of interest can, and should, be resolved within the recognised procedures and institutions of the employment relations system; and that the costs to employees of undertaking industrial action far exceed any gain that may result from its use. Both of these beliefs are open to doubt. The first assumes that there is a logical and objective solution to any problem, and ignores the role played by real or perceived relative power in determining the outcome of negotiations. The second belief overlooks the fact that most striking employees initially expect the dispute to be of short duration, assumes that the assessment by either party of its position can be judged solely in economic terms, and regards a strike as a single, isolated incident. Hyman (1984: 136) points out that industrial action can also be viewed as a rational social action with both economic and political purposes and consequences.

There is significant variation in the forms, levels and trends of strike activity over time and space, and across occupations and industries. Even among employees such as miners and dockers who have a reputation for militancy, strike propensity varies significantly both within and between countries and over time. A number of general explanations of the historically and geographically differentiated patterns of strike activity have been put forward, some of which are outlined in the following section.

EXPLANATIONS IN TERMS OF ORGANISATIONAL DYNAMICS

Firstly, there are institutional approaches that relate particularly to collective bargaining arrangements. High levels of industrial conflict may be explained in terms of low levels of unionisation, extensive divisions within the labour movement, the absence of strong employers' organisations, a lack of comprehensive procedural arrangements, the non-existence of effective dispute resolution mechanisms, and in particular, the level of collective bargaining (Bean 1985: 132). In industries and regions where centralised bargaining predominates, industrial action is generally less extensive compared to decentralised bargaining systems. However, institutional approaches have been criticised for exaggerating the amount of control over wage determination exercised by centralised bargaining forums, ignoring the frequency of unofficial strikes, and assuming a mechanistic relationship between economic structures and the incidence of industrial action without considering the processes that may mediate the effect of institutional factors on actual behaviour (Bean 1985).

Alternatively, it could be argued that technology may affect the propensity to strike (Blauner 1966). Blauner (1966) argues that industries associated with difficult and unpleasant working conditions, and technologies requiring high physical exertion are associated with higher levels of industrial conflict. Indeed, miners and steelworkers tend to be among the most militant workers.

Finally, it could be simply argued that strikes are due to misunderstandings and poor communication (Mayo 2003). Although misunderstandings can and do arise in any social setting, this approach assumes that the material demands of employees (no matter how poor their pay) are unjustified. Such very simplistic communication-centred approaches remain popular among strands of the HRM literature that emanate from the USA.

EXPLANATIONS IN TERMS OF THE ECONOMY AND THE LABOUR MARKET

A further set of explanations focuses on prevailing economic conditions. It has been argued that high inflation may encourage strikes, because real wages are eroded and employees in firms who lag behind others in increasing wages try to catch up (Cronin 1979; Eldridge 1968). Unemployment has ambiguous effects: employees may be reluctant to risk their jobs in a time of high joblessness, yet if social protection is weak, the lack of a job means that the average worker has a large pool of dependants and is thus under great pressure to increase her or his earnings.

Cronin (1979) links strikes to changes in the business cycle. Although the business cycle may have some bearing on whether employees adopt a defensive or offensive stance, we should not overlook mediating factors such as the influence of employment relations institutions, the efficacy of political exchange in distributing the costs of economic restructuring, and the impact of labour market status. This does not mean that we should simply dismiss theories that focus on the impact of the economic cycle. In a landmark study, Kelly (1998) links the occurrence of strikes to economic long waves (Kondratieff waves). Strikes correspond to the downturn of the Kondratieff cycle when employees' expectations are still rising and employers are confronted by deteriorating profit margins and the threat of economic failure (Kelly 1998). In these circumstances strikes are really about an aspirations gap (see Davies 1978).

EXPLANATIONS IN TERMS OF COMMUNITY DYNAMICS

An alternative explanation is that strikes are more likely to be encountered among workforces from small closed communities (Kerr 1964). In these situations, employees close ranks, the community imposes sanctions on blacklegs (those not striking), and community networks of support provide subsistence for the families of striking workers. There are many examples of this, ranging from the mining communities of West Virginia to the miners' compounds in South Africa, to the mining villages within Wales and England. Indeed, such was the militancy of British miners that the Thatcher government was prepared to destroy almost the entire coal industry in order to break a major source of industrial resistance.

Of course, the above explanations only relate to how strikes become more likely or feasible. In the end, most strikes are about material conditions, and more specifically, wages and wage-related factors.

TRENDS IN STRIKE PATTERNS

Because strikes are a highly complex social phenomenon, there are not only problems in effectively explaining their causes but also in quantifying their scale and distribution (Bean 1985). Three main indices are routinely used to reveal strike patterns: the number of strikes, the number of employees involved, and the number of working days lost. The number of workdays lost is calculated by multiplying the number of employees involved in industrial action by the duration of the strikes. As with all statistics, however, the actual figures are subject to many qualifications and the interpretation of their meaning is more important than the distributions. It is also imperative to note that these indices reveal the *extent* rather than the *effects* of strike activity. As Blyton and Turnbull (1998: 319) warn:

> [although] much analysis focuses on strike statistics that provide a ready 'index' of conflict, these data can offer a misleading picture. In recent years, for example, there has been a tendency to equate the decline in officially recorded strikes with a decline (or even the demise) of industrial conflict. Not only does this ignore the intensity of conflict and bitterness of feelings invoked in many strike situations, it ignores the diverse nature of both strikes and other forms of industrial conflict.

In addition, it is important to consider trends in strikes, but also to take time to consider the causes of these trends. In the *Applying theory to practice* box below, the example is given of strike patterns in South Africa, since this is a country in which there have been a significant number of strikes over a long period of time.

APPLYING THEORY TO PRACTICE

Strikes in South Africa

Strike patterns in South Africa from 1956 to 2005 need careful interpretation, drawing on a knowledge of broader contextual factors.

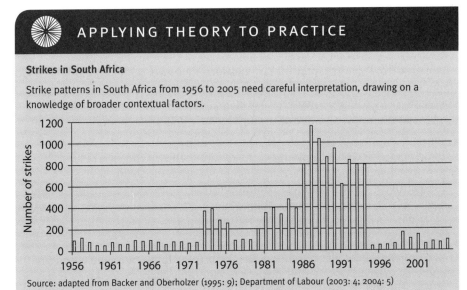

Source: adapted from Backer and Oberholzer (1995: 9); Department of Labour (2003: 4; 2004: 5)

The overall picture is one of extended periods of relative industrial peace followed by equally extensive periods of intense industrial action which occurred largely during periods of economic and political crises. The strike waves of the early to mid-1970s and mid- to late 1980s represent an exceptional spread of industrial action across industries and regions, and their timing coincided with significant political upheaval. They were a form of protest directed at the *apartheid* government rather than at individual employers.

There were almost twice as many strikes during the run-up to the elections in 1994 as there were after the elections. These strikes were still intimately related to the struggle against *apartheid*. Strike activity experienced a sharp decline in the years immediately following the 1994 election, only to increase considerably in the year of the 1999 elections due largely to a wage dispute in the public services. In the period between 2000 and 2005, strike action continued on its downward spiral. However, there have been a series of strikes, particularly within the public sector, over recent years.

MANAGING CONFLICT IN THE WORKPLACE

Negotiation is the process through which the parties involved in a dispute seek a mutually acceptable solution to their differences. For negotiation to be effective, the participants require relevant skills and must perceive that the benefits of negotiation outweigh those of other means of handling conflict. A history of confrontational and low-trust relations between the parties may reduce the perceived benefits of negotiation, and a lack of negotiating skills may constrain their capacity to utilise the process to best effect. This often leads to a vicious cycle in which confrontational and low-trust relations are reinforced by a lack of the skills necessary to conduct successful negotiations. In general, as Nel *et al* (2005: 174) suggest, there are two basic ways for resolving conflict in the workplace:

- *either* establishing a person-to-person relationship based on mutual trust and interdependence in which the causes of conflict can be identified, avoided or removed by interpersonal interaction and by effective communication

- *or* the use of mediators or arbitrators in an effort to resolve conflict, thereby avoiding the subjective component of conflict situations and facilitating interaction and compromise.

Although there is always some overlap between them, we can distinguish between competitive and co-operative dispute resolution processes in terms of which is dominant in a particular situation (Nel *et al* 2005: 174–5). These two types of dispute resolution may be contrasted as follows:

- communication
  In co-operative conflict resolution, interaction between the parties tends to be open and honest, and the level of information disclosure is high. In competitive dispute resolution, communication is either absent or misleading, and emphasis is placed on obtaining as much information as possible from the other party while providing as little information as possible.

- perception
  In co-operative conflict resolution, the focus is on similarities and common interests, whereas competitive dispute resolution is characterised by a focus on differences and conflicting interests.

- attitudes towards one another
  In the co-operative conflict resolution process, the attitudes of the parties are characterised by trust and co-operation, while in the competitive dispute resolution process they are marked by hostility and confrontation.

- task orientation
  In co-operative conflict resolution, the parties view the task as a mutual problem that requires a combined effort to reach a solution, whereas the parties in a competitive dispute resolution process view it as an opportunity to enhance one's own power and status at the expense of the other party.

Several factors may facilitate co-operative conflict resolution processes, including the extent to which the parties assign each other legitimacy in the relationship, the absence of internal factions or the degree of internal coherence of each party, and the existence of mutually acceptable rules, institutions and procedures.

Employers are interested not only in resolving disputes as successfully and expeditiously as possible but also in preventing conflict from arising in the first place. Although there can be no guarantee of success, management may adopt a wide range of conflict avoidance strategies:

- developing integrative problem-solving techniques geared towards finding mutually beneficial solutions

- introducing job-evaluation schemes aimed at making the payment system more equitable and less prone to disputes

- promoting a participative management style that involves employees in the decision-making processes, thereby removing some of the barriers between the parties

- implementing a system of job redesign to make jobs more intrinsically satisfying and to increase the autonomy of employees

- encouraging greater information-sharing, ensuring that employees are regularly informed about the short- and long-term plans of the organisation. Employees may then make informed and factually substantiated demands, and negotiations are less prone to shows of strength.

The choice of a dispute resolution procedure depends on a range of factors which include the employment relations climate in the workplace (and issues such as the levels of trust, co-operation, control and conflict); the formalities, costs and delays associated with the process; the degree of influence exercised by the parties involved and third parties; the nature of the issue in dispute; the provisions of labour legislation; and the personality dynamics of the parties.

NON-STATUTORY DISPUTE RESOLUTION

A negotiated dispute procedure acts as a deadlock-breaking mechanism when the parties fail to reach an agreement. It is normally part of a recognition agreement (outlined in more detail in Chapter 7) and regulates disagreements between collectives such as management and a trade union. These alternative dispute resolution procedures are more common in large firms with effective human resource management functions and an established trade union presence. The following steps form part of a typical dispute procedure:

- a dispute is declared in writing
  If negotiations break down, a dispute must be declared in writing to the employer. The letter is usually sent from the union office. The union must state the nature of the dispute and may indicate what is needed to settle the dispute. There is normally a time limit for management to reply to the union's claims.

- a dispute meeting is held
  Management convenes a meeting with the employees or their representatives in an effort to settle the dispute. If the dispute is not resolved within a specified period, additional meetings may be convened. If meetings do not result in a settlement within the agreed time, the parties may have recourse to other (usually external) measures.

- outside methods may then be referred to
  Depending on the issue in dispute, the union and the employer may agree to try to settle the dispute through a method such as conciliation or arbitration. The parties may develop and utilise their own dispute resolution procedures or they may refer the dispute to a mediator.

- a strike or lock-out may occur
  If the parties do not agree, the employees may go on strike or be locked out.

Figure 12.1 sets out a typical dispute procedure, and is an example of the steps that the parties may agree should form a part of an organisation's dispute procedure. The overriding objective is to promote further negotiations with the aim of reaching a settlement. Although the parties have to carry the costs of private dispute resolution procedures, the advantages of such arrangements include the ability to choose a conciliator or arbitrator, to stipulate his or her terms of reference, and to conduct the process in a speedy and purposeful

Figure 12.1 A typical dispute procedure

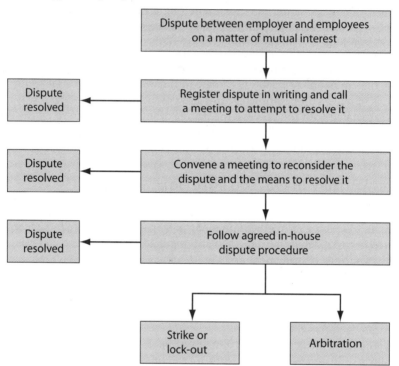

manner. As Salamon (1998: 443–5) points out, there are numerous advantages to having well-established and effective dispute resolution procedures, including the avoidance of strikes, limiting the duration and consequences of industrial action, a re-evaluation of positions and a clarification of the issues that gave rise to the dispute.

VOLUNTARISM AND COMPULSION

There is some controversy regarding the extent to which the government should intervene in the resolution of industrial disputes. In this context, the term 'voluntarism' implies that employers and employees have complete discretion in the design and implementation of dispute resolution procedures. The term 'compulsion' implies the absence of discretion on the part of employers and employees to establish their own arrangements, and the imposition of a statutory dispute resolution process. In practice, most dispute resolution systems are neither entirely voluntary nor totally compulsory, but rather contain a combination of voluntarism and compulsion. The voluntary or compulsory nature of the processes can apply at any phase or all three phases of their operation:

- the establishment of the institutions
- the use of processes
- the implementation of the outcome.

The tension between the demands for active government involvement and the need to allow the parties to conduct their own affairs may be resolved in numerous different ways. For instance, a government may allow the parties to voluntarily establish and utilise the various dispute resolution mechanisms while providing criminal or civil sanctions for non-implementation of a settlement. Government policy towards the resolution of labour disputes can be influenced by the government's desire to maintain industrial peace and prevent damage to the economy in order to ensure political success and to prevent rising inflation (Salamon 1998).

The government may be compelled to intervene in collective bargaining to realise its objectives, but excessive intervention may serve to discredit the mechanisms of dispute resolution. A precarious balance between voluntary and compulsory dispute resolution must therefore be maintained. The level of intervention varies between countries and over time, depending on a range of factors such as the economic context and the nature of government (democratic, socialist, totalitarian, etc). In some countries the government would wish to intervene in order to preserve social stability.

THIRD-PARTY CONCILIATION, MEDIATION AND ARBITRATION

All dispute resolution mechanisms have a common feature: the services of an independent third party are utilised in order to resolve, or attempt to resolve, a dispute that cannot be settled through normal bargaining procedures. The different forms of dispute resolution can be distinguished in terms of:

- the powers of the third party
- its method of operation
- whether the referral of a dispute is voluntary or compulsory.

Referring a dispute to a third party for resolution cannot be regarded as automatic evidence of the failure or breakdown of collective bargaining (Salamon 1998). Their use is indicative only of an inability of the direct negotiation process, in a specific set of circumstances, to resolve the differences between the parties and the desire of the parties to pursue alternative strategies to secure a settlement. Three main means of third party intervention are referred to below: conciliation, mediation and arbitration.

CONCILIATION

Conciliation occurs when the parties in dispute get together with a neutral third party after exhausting all internal dispute resolution procedures. According to Salamon (1998: 439), conciliation is a strategy whereby the third party supports the direct bipartite (two-party) negotiating process by assisting the parties to identify the cause and extent of their differences, to establish alternative solutions and their various implications, and to develop and agree a mutually acceptable settlement. The responsibility for reaching an agreement remains with the parties to the dispute. The conciliator simply provides an atmosphere conducive for the continuation of negotiations and the reaching of an agreement, but does not have the power to demand compromises or to impose an agreement on the parties.

Figure 12.2 Lines of communication during conciliation

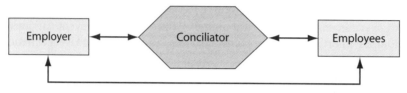

Where the internal resolution of disputes is not possible, settlement at the conciliation stage is the preferred option. The conciliation process is not complicated and does not require legal representation. Conciliation not only effectively resolves current disputes, but also is an important learning process for the reduction of future disputes.

Figure 12.3 Positive and negative settlement range

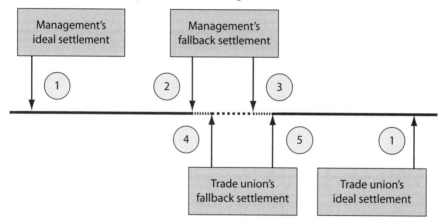

An important part of the third party's role is to establish a *settlement range*. This involves acquiring information on the fallback positions of the parties – ie the lowest possible offer that the union is willing to accept and the highest possible demand that management is willing to concede. A positive settlement range refers to the situation where there is some overlap between management and the union's fallback positions, while a negative settlement range refers to the situation where there is no overlap between their fallback positions. Figure 12.3 indicates the ideal settlement (1) of each party as well as two possible fallback positions for each party (2–3 and 4–5). While the ideal settlement may constitute an opening offer from management or an opening demand by the union, neither party will normally stick with this offer or demand. A positive settlement range exists between management's fallback position (3) and the union's fallback position (4), whereas a negative settlement range exists between management's fallback position (2) and the union's fallback position (5). A settlement is therefore much more likely in the former scenario.

MEDIATION

Mediation falls in between conciliation and arbitration. As Salamon (1998: 441) points out, mediation can be viewed as a stronger form of conciliation, allowing for a greater degree of third-party intervention. Although the mediator may suggest a possible solution to the dispute, the outcome is still dependent on an agreement between the parties themselves. In contrast to arbitration, the mediator does not possess the authority to impose an agreement on the parties to a dispute. According to Kochan (cited in Bendix 2000: 486–7), the mediation process may be divided into three stages:

- introduction and establishment of credibility – the mediator endeavours to gain the trust and acceptance of the disputing parties, discover the causes of the dispute, identify the obstacles to a possible settlement, and gain an insight into the attitudes and power of the parties

- steering the negotiations – the mediator offers advice, determines the scope for compromise, encourages the formulation of proposals and counter-proposals, and persuades the parties to identity and accept a solution

- movement towards final settlement – the mediator suggests proposals for a settlement, exerts pressure towards settlement of the dispute, and assists the parties in the drafting and implementation of an agreement.

The mediator acts as an intermediary and advises both parties. As an independent and impartial outsider, the mediator is more likely to acquire the confidence of the parties and gain access to their fallback positions. This allows the mediator to establish the distance between the opposing positions and encourage the parties to make the necessary concessions.

Figure 12.4 Lines of communication during mediation

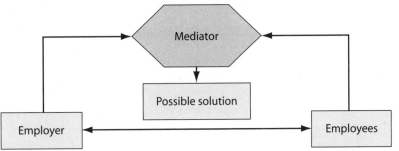

As with conciliation, mediation is an integral part of collective bargaining. It provides an alternative to more costly options such as strikes, lock-outs or litigation without ruling those choices out. However, it can only succeed if the parties are willing to settle. It also leaves the parties in control of the settlement. Unlike conciliation, mediation allows the third party to play an active part in the process of dispute resolution and to formulate possible solutions.

ARBITRATION

Attempts must be made to resolve a dispute through conciliation or mediation before it may be referred to arbitration. There are essentially two types of arbitration: rights arbitration involving disputes of right, and interest arbitration involving disputes of interest. The latter, unlike the former, is usually voluntary and concerns issues (such as wages) that are raised during the collective bargaining process. At an arbitration hearing, an arbitrator gives both parties the opportunity to state their cases fully. The arbitrator then has the authority to grant an arbitration award that is legally binding on both parties and disposes of the dispute. Arbitration therefore differs from conciliation and mediation in the sense that it does not promote the continuation of collective bargaining and it imposes a decision on the parties.

Because an arbitrator is not rigidly bound by a legal framework or judicial procedures, he or she is able to take a wider view in the interests both of an equitable settlement of the issues and of future good employment relations practices. The relative bargaining power of management and the union has little bearing on the final settlement. The arbitrator is also under no compulsion to seek conciliation between the parties. Consequently, compelling reasons must normally be shown before arbitration is made compulsory or granted at the behest of only one party to a dispute.

Figure 12.5 The arbitration process

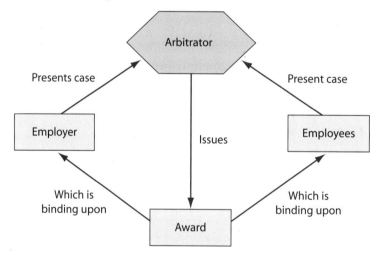

Conciliation, mediation and arbitration differ not only in the degree of intervention by the third party but also in terms of their consequences for employment relations (Bendix 2000; Salamon 1998). Arbitration, in particular, has the potential to shift the power balance between management and the trade union. Employers are often reluctant to allow an outside party, with no long-term commitment to the enterprise, to make decisions that could have a profound impact on workplace employment relations. Similarly, unions may perceive arbitration as a ploy by management to weaken their resolve to take industrial action if their demands are not met. Where the consent of both parties is necessary for a referral to arbitration, the more powerful party is likely to refuse since it can potentially secure a more beneficial agreement by resorting to industrial action. A request for arbitration is likely to arise where the referring party believes that its case is strong on logical or equity grounds but it lacks the necessary organisational muscle to achieve an acceptable settlement. In effect, a request for arbitration amounts to an appeal to the stronger party to forgo its bargaining advantage.

Within different countries, the bodies responsible for dealing with conciliation, mediation and arbitration vary, as do the procedures that are enshrined in law or in codes of practice. A useful example of third-party intervention is evident in the UK, where the body responsible for independent conciliation, mediation and arbitration is ACAS (the Advisory, Conciliation and Arbitration Service). Although given statutory powers to play an arbitration role, ACAS is primarily a service, with a strong element of voluntarism. Further details may be found at www.acas.org.uk.

LEGISLATION GOVERNING INDUSTRIAL DISPUTES

The legislation governing industrial disputes varies from country to country, although in this section the focus is on legislation within the UK. For a multinational corporation it may be necessary to consider legislation in both the home country and the host country.

In a range of European countries there is a legal right to strike, although this is not the case in the UK. However, even in the UK where there is no legal right to strike, legislation outlines the nature of rights for those involved in strikes. Under the Employment Relations Act 1999 it is illegal to dismiss a striker during the first 12 weeks of a strike, as long as the action is official and has been organised within the law. However, there are also restrictions on striking. The Employment Act 1980 prevented employees from engaging in secondary strikes in support of colleagues and associates, while the Employment Act 1982 required a strike to be directly related to the employees' relationship with the employer rather than based on a more general cause or government policy such as privatisation. The Employment Act 1990 subsequently outlawed all forms of secondary and unofficial action. There have also been stricter rules imposed on balloting under legislation such as the Trade Union Act 1984, the Trade Union Reform and Employment Rights Act 1993 and the Employment Act 1990 (Rollinson and Dundon 2007: 329–30). Meanwhile, picketing is allowed at a person's place of work, assuming that the purpose is to peacefully obtain or communicate information or to peacefully persuade workers to abstain from working, as specified in the Trade Union and Labour Relations (Consolidation) Act 1992. To better understand the way in which strikes have been conducted in recent years, against this legislative background, we can usefully consider the case study below. The case is interesting since it draws attention to issues such as immigration and the displacement of workers, which is a topical area of debate in many countries across the world. The broader issue of immigration is discussed in more detail in Chapter 5.

CASE STUDY

STRIKES IN UK CONSTRUCTION

In 2009, a series of wildcat strikes occurred in UK construction over the use of foreign labour. The strikes were in response to an Italian company that had obtained a £200 million contract at the Lindsey oil refinery, and was using a permanent workforce that primarily consisted of Italian and Portuguese workers. A spokesperson from the GMB union argued that the action was taken in order to defend the construction industry national agreement against the undercutting of wages (*Guardian* 2009). British legislation allows employers to employ workers on minimum standards rather than according to national agreements, meaning that employing foreign workers was perceived as unfair competition for British workers. However,

John Monks, the General Secretary of the European Trade Union Confederation, commented that the problem mirrored the situation in other countries across the EU where work was conducted outside an employee's home country. According to European law, if unions tried to establish the same conditions, they would breach Directives on the free movement of labour (*ibid*).

Questions

What was the apparent cause of this strike?

What were the real causes of the strike action?

How could similar conflicts be resolved in the future?

Returning to the issue of legislation governing industrial disputes, an interesting feature which varies depending on country context is the attitude taken towards essential services. Essential services are defined by the International Labour Organisation as services 'the interruption of which would endanger the life, personal safety or health of the whole or part of the population' (ILO 1983, para 24). Many countries forbid workers involved in 'essential services' (as defined by the national government) to strike, and some define 'essential services' very broadly. For example, in Mozambique – a country in southern Africa that was formerly governed by a socialist government – 'essential' services include medical, hospital and medicinal services; water, power and fuel supplies; postal and telecommunication services; funeral services; loading and unloading of animals and perishable foodstuffs; air space and meteorological control; the fire service; cleansing services; and private security; while

> public enterprises and any other public corporate entity whose employment relationships are governed by this law shall be considered as services directed at meeting essential needs of the purposes of the regime in this article.
>
> (Labour Law, Section vii, Article 205)

Regardless of the legislation on striking in essential services within a country, the ILO does suggest that in all countries a minimum service would be justified to ensure that users' basic needs are met.

EMPLOYMENT TRIBUNALS

Where employment tribunals exist, they vary depending on country context. In this section the focus is on the UK system. However, even where systems broadly follow the UK model for historical reasons, they may vary slightly within different countries.

Employment tribunals are a form of minor judicial courts at which employees bring claims against their employers. Claims can relate to an employee's ongoing employment or to its termination. There are many potential reasons for taking an employer to an employment tribunal, including unfair dismissal, discrimination relating to gender, race, disability, age, religion, or sexual orientation, and equal pay. In 2009/10, most claims that were accepted by employment tribunals in the UK related to unauthorised deductions, unfair dismissal (including following the transfer of an undertaking), equal pay, breach of contract, the Working Time Directive, sex discrimination, and redundancy (failure to inform and consult, or redundancy pay) (Tribunal Services 2010). The provisions for employment tribunals in the UK are established under the Employment Tribunals Act 1996, the Employment Tribunals (Constitution and Rules of Procedure) Regulations 2004 and the Employment Act 2008 (CIPD 2010).

THE EMPLOYMENT TRIBUNALS PROCESS

Prior to an employment tribunal claim employers and employees should have already tried to resolve their disagreement by following the ACAS Code of Practice on disciplinary and grievance procedures and by using the employer's own procedures. Where no attempt has been made to do this, the employer may be subject to financial penalties (CIPD 2010). If it has been done but has not resulted in a resolution of the situation, an employee should submit a claim to an employment tribunal within three months of the date of termination or the act that has caused the complaint. An employee should at that point submit an ET1 form to the employment tribunal. The tribunal then sends a copy to ACAS and the employer, together with an ET3 form. The employer should return the form to the tribunal within 28 days. ACAS will then contact both the employee (complainant) and the employer (respondent) to try to settle the claim before the hearing (CIPD 2010).

Three people preside over an employment tribunal: a legally qualified chairman or employment judge, and two lay people such as an HR professional or trade unionist. At the hearing, both sides present their cases, using witnesses if appropriate, and can cross-examine the witnesses of the other side. The tribunal will then adjourn for a short period so that the three people presiding can discuss the case, and they then reach a decision (judgment). If the tribunal's decision is in the favour of the complainant, the tribunal then has four main options that would go towards compensating the employee: reinstatement, re-engagement, financial compensation, or payment of wages.

Decisions of employment tribunals can be challenged, but only on limited grounds, including the following: the decision was incorrect due to an error by tribunal staff; one of the sides did not receive notice of the proceedings; new evidence has emerged since the tribunal; or the interests of justice require a review (Lewis and Sargeant 2010: 8).

EMPLOYMENT TRIBUNALS: NUMBER OF AWARDS AND COSTS AWARDED

Relatively few claims by employees have been successful within the UK. In 2009/10 the most successful were claims for redundancy pay (24% of cases), breach of contract (18%) and working time (18%). Only 2% of race and disability claims were successful, and 1% of equal pay claims (Tribunals Service 2010). The awards given also vary. For example, in 2008/9 the maximum claim for unfair dismissal was £84,005, compared to £1,353,432 for race discrimination (Tribunals Service 2010).

Employers should try to avoid a number of possible legal pitfalls. A common reason for claims in employment tribunals is breach of contract, where an employer imposes changes in contractual terms without seeking the agreement of the employee. If an employee continues to work without objection, in due course he or she may then be regarded as having agreed to the changes. However, this is not the case where there is a significant change such as a reduction in pay or a change to working hours (ACAS 2009). Many employment tribunal cases are lost by employers because of a lack of adherence to company policies and procedures. They can also be lost due to inadequate policies and procedures. The *Reflection on practice* below relates to the issue of employment tribunals and the current status of policies and procedures within organisations.

REFLECTION ON PRACTICE

Employment tribunals and HR policies and procedures

If you are currently working within an organisation in an HR position, how comprehensive are the policies and procedures?

Do line managers in your organisation try to 'get round' any of the policies and procedures that are currently in place? If this is the case, what can be done to ensure that they adhere to them more carefully in the future?

MANAGING CONFLICT IN NON-UNION FIRMS

The lack of union voice mechanisms in non-union forms means that employees cannot rely on the external involvement, advice and resources of a union (Gollan 2009: 213; Taras and Kaufman 2006). Managers may introduce employee representative structures into non-union firms in the hope that it may alleviate unhappiness or friction, and workers may choose to become involved in such structures in the expectation that it will give them a greater say over the terms of their employment and their working conditions (Taras and Kaufman 2006: 5). Pessimistic accounts have suggested that non-union voice mechanisms are likely to be ineffectual (Gollan 2009). Moreover, Kaufman and Taras (2000: 10) argue that any agreements between employers and employees in non-union firms cannot 'standardise or stabilise labour relations across firms'. Although non-union forms of representation may be safer or less threatening to managers in seeking to redress an expectation–satisfaction gap, the weaker nature of such representation may mean that disputes go unresolved (Gollan 2009: 229). The result could be that there is underlying tension within the firm, and that employee performance is less productive than might otherwise be the case. In addition, subtle forms of protest might take place where employees are not satisfied with employment relations but have no recourse to a trade union to voice their concerns.

Formal strike action around clearly expressed demands is more likely in unionised firms since in collective bargaining, unions often back up their demands with the implicit and explicit threat of striking. As long as specific formally defined processes are adhered to, employees engaging in such action are more likely to be able to count on a degree of legal protection in many national contexts (cf Gollan 2009). This means that hidden forms of workplace protest are very much more likely in non-union firms. Moreover, because management has fewer formal opportunities for engaging with workers, it is likely that managers will have less information on the underlying causes of such action, and, indeed, may struggle to identify coherent patterns in seemingly isolated protests (cf Wood and Glaister 2008).

THE ROLE OF EMPLOYMENT RELATIONS SPECIALISTS AND LINE MANAGERS IN MANAGING CONFLICT

Many workplace disputes are relatively minor and are quickly resolved – indeed, line managers should aim to resolve disputes before they assume larger dimensions. In this process they may be aided by shop stewards, who have an interest in ensuring that union resources are concentrated in dealing with serious issues rather than being frittered away in easily resolved misunderstandings. The role of the shop steward has therefore been referred to as a filter or a lubricant (Hyman 1981). However, disputes are likely to be referred to the HR department when there are potentially legal implications and/or where they threaten to draw in a significant component of the workforce. The challenge facing employment relations specialists in such cases is in reconciling the need for flexibility and expediency with the possible wider legal and power implications of any intervention.

CRITICAL DEBATE

Trade unions and conflict

In your experience, or to the best of your knowledge, are trade unions more likely to cause conflict or attempt to resolve conflict?

There are a number of possible ways in which managers may seek to resolve conflict; these strategies may overlap, and none is likely to be encountered alone. The first is to adopt a broadly pluralist approach, actively engaging with the union so as to resolve disputes before they start, and to be committed to negotiating when they do. Although it is not possible to negotiate with unions on every single individual grievance, shop stewards can play an important role in alerting management to potential problems and filtering out unjustified complaints (Hyman 1989). A second strategy, specific to individual disputes, is to have as formal as possible procedures for resolving grievances. This will reduce the discretionary power of individual supervisors, allowing for as objective a ruling as possible. A third strategy, more specific to collective disputes, is to make use of outside conciliation, mediation or arbitration, either through the use of statutory dispute resolution machinery or through independent dispute resolution services. Even if the outcome may involve compromise, it ensures that a more objective perspective is imparted to proceedings (cf Budd *et al* 2009). And even if a third party is not involved, management may seek to be as objective as possible in the event of disputes. A final strategy is a more hardline one. Here, any grievance by individual workers or collective action by a group is seen as representing an attempt to challenge managerial power and authority. Whether justified or not, the firm seeks to uphold managerial power, and in such cases employee(s) are opposed with all the legal, knowledge and financial resources that the firm has at its disposal.

SUMMARY

The study of conflict is a central feature of employment relations. The focus within this chapter has been on the causes of conflict, forms of conflict and mechanisms for dispute resolution. In common with other chapters in this text, it has drawn on theoretical explanations and empirical evidence.

No workplace is conflict-free. Indeed, many firms that claim to be harmonious may be hotbeds of hidden conflict. As noted in the opening sections of this volume, the indeterminate nature of the exchange between a readily quantifiable wage and an indeterminate amount of labour power means that disputes are inevitable. Although the incidence of formal strike action has declined over the past two decades in many countries, there is little doubt that large amounts of less visible conflict persist. In confronting conflict, HR managers must be realistic. On the one hand, constraints on organisational resources and the demands of shareholders may make it difficult to accede too much. On the other hand, employees are not going to be any happier by being talked at. Most strikes are, in the end, about resources and, more specifically, wages. And even if lacking the ability to engage in collective action, employees may retaliate in a wide range of ways that may be difficult to prevent.

Reading

- Aminzade, R. (1984) 'Capitalist industrialization and patterns of industrial protest', *American Sociological Review*, Vol.49, No.4: 437–53
- Hyman, R. (2009) *Strikes*, 3rd edition. Glasgow: Fontana
- Lewis, D. and Sargeant, M. (2010) *Essentials of Employment Law*, 10th edition. London: CIPD
- Émile Zola's classic novel *Germinal* (1885) provides a particularly searing account of a strike in a nineteenth-century French coal mine, and disturbingly accurate descriptions of general working conditions underground at that time

Websites

- Advisory, Conciliation and Arbitration Service www.acas.org.uk
- Chartered Institute of Personnel and Development www.cipd.co.uk
- International Labour Organisation www.ilo.org.uk

EXPLORE FURTHER

CHAPTER 13

Downsizing and Redundancy

CHAPTER OVERVIEW

Downsizing and redundancy are topical issues. After a recession, private sector employers may make redundancies as a matter of either necessity or choice. In better times, they may seek to downsize operations in certain areas in order to gain competitive advantage, resulting in the transfer of employees to other departments or sites, or redundancy for those who are no longer needed. In the public sector, government cuts can lead to an outcry over a potential loss of services, and job loss for public servants. Against this background, the effective management of downsizing and redundancy has significant implications for employment relations.

This chapter elucidates practical ways of dealing with dismissal and redundancy, and critically assesses potential strategies. Also included within the chapter is legislation on redundancy and dismissal, with a particular focus on European Directives and the British case – of interest due to the interaction between national- and international-level regulations. Legislation in other countries varies to a greater or lesser degree. In some areas it broadly corresponds to British legislation. However, in others it may be more or less comprehensive, depending on the political, economic and historical context. Consulting the government websites of individual countries should provide further details of legislation within different contexts.

LEARNING OUTCOMES

After studying this chapter you should be able to:

- define the terms 'downsizing' and 'redundancy'
- critically evaluate the concepts of flexibility, job security and 'flexicurity'
- outline the legal dimensions of dismissal and redundancy and the mitigation of risk
- explain dismissal and redundancy policies

- describe legislation relating to collective redundancy consultation

- discuss the negotiation of redundancy agreements

- assess how to manage 'survivor syndrome'

- evaluate the relationship between redundancy, downsizing and the role of trade unions

DEFINITIONS OF DOWNSIZING AND REDUNDANCY

In simple terms, 'downsizing' can be defined as reducing the size of the firm and the number of workers (Nieto 2006). It was a term that was frequently heard in the late 1980s and early 1990s, when many large firms engaged in large-scale redundancies. Downsizing was seen as the solution to problems encountered, and as a necessary accompaniment to 'lean production', involving the adoption of techniques such as total quality management, just-in-time production and teamworking, which made it possible to produce a higher quantity of goods within a smaller amount of time and with fewer resources.

There are a number of ways in which downsizing can take place. The strategy most commonly referred to is the use of multiple redundancy (or collective dismissal). Other strategies include de-layering – simplifying the structure of the organisation by removing hierarchical layers – in order to reduce costs and bureaucracy. This in turn might lead to better communication within the organisation and an increased responsiveness to customers. A further term used is 'decentralisation', which can entail the devolving of power to individual units and also reducing the number of workers employed within the head office. Yet other terms that have been used include 'rightsizing' – a euphemistic term for cutting jobs – and the less positive-sounding 'reduction in headcount'. The latter term is used mostly when there is to be a reduction in the number of permanent employees, their jobs undertaken instead by subcontractors who are not listed on the payroll (Kinnie *et al* 1998).

There is some evidence, mainly from the United States and Britain, to suggest that downsizing fails to result in expected benefits, the reasons given being the lack of strategic foresight, the loss of key competencies, and the negative impact on the remaining workforce (see Kinnie *et al* 1998). Alternative explanations for the non-appearance of the desired effects include the way in which downsizing is undertaken, especially when it has been used as a reactive response to environmental factors rather than as a proactive measure aiming to achieve increased competitiveness (Thornhill and Saunders 1998).

Redundancy is often seen as closely related to downsizing and, indeed, downsizing generally relies on the use of redundancy. There is a difference, however. The term 'downsizing' tends to imply a strategic issue, whereas 'redundancy' may be used to describe operational-level activity (Thornhill and Saunders 1998). An alternative term for redundancy in the North American literature is 'layoffs', while in southern Africa the more commonly used term is 'retrenchment'.

Redundancy can be viewed as a potentially 'fair' reason for dismissal (Daniels 2006). However, this perception may depend on whether redundancy is voluntary or compulsory, in theory as well as in practice. Where a firm is relocating a workplace to another geographical area, employees might be offered jobs at the new plant. But some employees with family responsibilities might find it very difficult to change routines and move location. They will therefore, in effect, have been made redundant against their will. More importantly, the degree of 'fairness' depends not only on whether redundancy is conducted within legislative requirements but also on how redundancy is implemented, and whether the management of the process is perceived to be fair, equitable and justified by those employees who are made redundant and by those who remain within the organisation.

REFLECTION ON PRACTICE

Redundancy

What is your experience of redundancy?

In reflecting on these experiences, you might wish to consider

- your own experience
- the experience of friends or family members
- how it felt to be made redundant (or unemployed)
- how you think you would feel if you were at risk of being made redundant
- what your feelings would depend upon.

FLEXIBILITY, JOB SECURITY AND 'FLEXICURITY'

'Flexibility' can be seen as a positive dimension of a firm's strategy and of employee behaviour. However, there has been some confusion around what is meant by flexibility, and the term has been applied in different ways in different contexts. Where flexibility is described as 'numerical', implying a variability in the number of people employed within an organisation, this might cause job insecurity. In recent years, debates have taken place regarding the relationship between flexibility and job security, and some have recommended the use of the term 'flexicurity'. These issues are explored in more detail in the sections below.

FLEXIBILITY

Flexibility within the labour market can relate to (Standing *et al* 1996: 6–7):

- employment flexibility – the ability to change employment levels quickly and easily

- wage flexibility – rapidly changing absolute and relative wage levels, with the possibility of wide wage gaps between sectors and occupations

- work process flexibility – the easy and low-cost alteration of work tasks, times and practices.

Each form of flexibility can present advantages for the employed but can, if taken too far, undermine labour market security (Labour Market Commission 1996). For example, if hiring and firing are too easily accomplished (in other words, a case of excessive employment flexibility), it will drastically reduce stability in the workplace and discourage firms and workers from investing in firm-specific productivity-enhancing skills. In general, employees and their representatives can associate flexibility with insecurity, and this constitutes the basis of trade union opposition to labour market flexibility. To overcome this opposition, flexibility has to be accompanied by security.

The idea of flexibility can be seen as a reaction to the bureaucratic controls associated with Fordism. As Burawoy (1985: 263) points out, these controls established

> constraints on the deployment of capital, whether by tying wages to profits or by creating internal labour markets, collective bargaining and grievance machinery which hamstrung management's domination of the workplace.

Inasmuch as these constraints stem from the statutory regulation of the labour market and the power of the trade unions, they are increasingly regarded by employers as unwarranted and unacceptable under conditions of increasing global competition. Overly protective employment policies and extensive trade union controls, according to the proponents of employment flexibility, have had the effect of curbing competition in the labour market. This has prevented the downward adjustment of terms and conditions of employment, leading to employment 'rigidity'. As a result, employers have found it difficult to adjust the quantity and the quality of labour supply to rapid changes in labour demand.

In more recent years, there has been a clear trend in many countries towards greater variability in the form of the employment relationship. As Hakim (1990: 167) notes in her review of workforce restructuring, strategies have varied from one country to the next and have followed different paths,

> but all pointed in the same general direction of increasing ... segmentation of the labour market and exploring new forms of differentiating wage/ labour relations.

Thus there have been changes in the constitution of the labour market and in the employment relationship. Meanwhile, Salamon (1998: 220–2) has argued that managerial approaches increasingly

> emphasise individualism (rather than collectivism), unitarism (rather than pluralism), consultation (rather than negotiation and agreement), flexibility

(rather than uniformity), employee commitment (rather than simple compliance) and empowerment and 'responsible' autonomy (rather than direct control).

Flexibility can therefore be regarded as part of a broader change to employment relations.

Flexibility is also commonly used to describe changes to the nature of production as well as to employment. The key to increased competitiveness is arguably production *and* employment 'flexibility'. The 'flexible firm' is said to be characterised by an ability to adapt rapidly to changes in consumer demand. This is achieved, according to Atkinson (1984), by the institutionalisation of (at least) two forms of flexibility:

- *functional* flexibility, which is achieved in two main ways: internally, by fostering the development of a 'core' group of permanent employees through multi-skilling, semi-autonomous work groups, quality circles and the like; externally, by using specialist subcontractors in non-routine projects or tasks

- *numerical* flexibility, which is established internally by using overtime or part-time working to match supply and demand; and externally by employing a 'peripheral' workforce through employment contracts such as part-time or temporary work, subcontracting and self-employment.

There is some evidence to suggest that there have indeed been changes in working patterns across many parts of the world. According to the Cranfield Network of European Human Resource Management (Cranet-E) survey, which analyses work patterns across 18 countries and 6,000 organisations employing more than 200 people, aspects of numerical flexibility such as part-time work, short-term contracts and subcontracting have grown over recent years (Brewster *et al* 2003). However, contractual flexibility is more prevalent in countries such as Greece and Spain (30% of the workforce) compared to Luxembourg, Belgium and the United Kingdom (less than 7.5% of the workforce). Greater use of non-standard work has similarly been evident in countries within Asia such as Hong Kong, and countries in the Southern Hemisphere such as Australia and New Zealand (Brewster *et al* 2003).

Functionally flexible 'core' workers are responsible for the organisation's critical firm-specific activities, whereas the activities of numerically flexible 'peripheral' workers are ancillary to the primary functions of the organisation. The peripheral workforce expands and contracts in accordance with levels of market demand, while the core workforce is shielded from market fluctuations. Tasks demanding higher skill levels and necessitating greater autonomy are therefore assigned to permanent employees who are subjected to bureaucratic control, reinforced by high wages and comprehensive extra-wage benefits. Employers seeking to fill stable, well-paid primary sector jobs – in which training and induction costs are usually high – are at pains to ensure that turnover risks are minimised.

The division between 'core' and 'peripheral' workers, it is argued, gives employers an additional measure of flexibility in that they can apply different strategies to different sectors of the workforce. This 'regulatory flexibility' stems from the strategies of inclusion exercised over a functionally flexible core and the strategies of exclusion exercised over a numerically flexible periphery. From being a cause for concern, the co-existence of a high-wage, high-protection and a low-wage, low-protection workforce is now celebrated (Linder *et al* 2002: 28) as a source of renewal:

> in today's volatile business environment, executives are called on to change their operating models much more frequently than ever before. More often than not, they do not have all the skills and capabilities that they need to succeed at the new game. Companies that have fallen behind should consider using business transformation outsourcing to regain their lead.

The alleged shift from economies of scale (mass production) to economies of scope (flexible production) necessitated a greater emphasis on employee co-operation, multi-skilling, quality control, teamwork and a de-layering of the managerial hierarchy. The establishment of quality circles, just-in-time inventories, semi-autonomous work groups, and so on, are presented as a move away from the alienating and deskilled employment associated with Fordism towards new forms of employee participation and high-trust relations in the workplace. Social integration, workplace harmony and equilibrium are central components of the shift towards more flexible forms of production. In reality, however, there is little evidence to support the notion of a single successor to Fordism. Between the two extremes of Braverman's conception of the dominance of Taylorism (referred to in more detail in Chapter 3) and 'flexible' production as a complete break with past forms of production lies the reality of intermediate forms and transformations within Fordism and Taylorism.

Flexibility approaches tend to assume that employers always act strategically and have at their disposal the managerial techniques and resources necessary to obtain the required levels of performance from their workforce. This implies that employers have a unique insight into the implications of their decisions, and largely rules out the possibility of unintended and unanticipated consequences. In reality, however, the assumption that (Sisson and Marginson 2003: 173–4)

> management is capable of selecting its approach from a range of options [which] lies at the heart of many of the recipes and prescriptions for improving the management of industrial relations ... sits very uneasily with a context in which business considerations are impacting ever more sharply on industrial relations practice and the institutional context serves to emphasise short-run returns ... A major problem ... is that there are costs associated with unlearning old practices and introducing new ones. In the circumstances, there is a strong temptation for managers to prefer the incremental path to change.

Implicit in much of the thinking underlying the flexible firm and its totalising production concepts is the fallacy that there exists 'one best way' in which to manage the workplace. In contrast to the crude, dualistic conception of managerial strategy that informs the flexible firm model, the distinction between contract- and status-enhancing strategies suggests a continuum of possibilities with multiple determinations (Streeck 1992). The conceptions of managerial strategy and workplace control that inform the notion of a 'flexible firm' tend to neglect the complex and contingent ways in which order is actually negotiated under specific conditions. Changes within the workplace must be related to internal as well as external opportunities and constraints.

A key element in the flexible firm model is the claim that employers are acting more strategically in adopting fundamentally new staffing policies. However, research in different contexts shows that the use of non-standard employment contracts is very seldom part of a long-term, coherent and strategic plan on the part of employers. In fact, Hunter *et al* (1993: 401) found 'an absence of strategy for labour use, and much more concern about survival and opportunistic cost-saving'. Managerial decisions about employment contracts, staffing levels and recruitment are largely *ad hoc*, tentative and based on the perceived benefits and drawbacks of each type of employment. The standard employment relationship remains the default position in jobs where there are no clear or immediate advantages to using non-standard employees. The flexible firm model not only exaggerates the strategic dimensions of managerial practice but also hinges on a rather simplistic dichotomy (internal versus external) in management's strategies of labour control. Accordingly, it provides few insights into the many regulatory mechanisms utilised by employers to incorporate, allocate and control labour in different employment relationships.

JOB SECURITY

Related to numerical flexibility is, as we have already seen, the concept of job security. A review by the International Labour Organisation (Standing *et al* 1996: 8–9) has outlined different forms of security:

- labour market security – widespread opportunities for employment

- employment security – protection from arbitrary loss of employment

- job security – protection against arbitrary transfer between sets of work tasks and loss of job-based rights

- work security – health and safety protection in employment

- income security – protection against arbitrary reduction in incomes

- representation security – secure capacity to bargain and influence the character and terms of employment.

Often the terms 'employment' and 'job security' have been used interchangeably. However, as the above definitions imply, there is often a distinction drawn between employment security at the macro level, and job security at the micro level (Dibben 2007).

Job security can be measured in a range of ways. One means of measurement is the level of employment or unemployment within a society. Levels of unemployment vary, but there are generally higher levels of unemployment in recession years. There can also be extreme differences in the levels of unemployment between different countries. For example, in recent years, the level of unemployment has ranged between 5% and 10% in Britain. This figure can be compared to countries such as South Africa, where the unemployment rate has been around 30%. A further complication in measuring levels of unemployment is that official figures can themselves vary. In Britain, for example, in 1999 the rate varied from 4% according to government statistics (official claimants) to 13% for TUC statistics (those who wanted to work) (Ladipo and Wilkinson 2002). The figures also do not account for regional variation, ignoring the huge differences between urban and rural areas, particularly within emerging economies. Official figures in both advanced and emerging economies also tend to exclude those who are not working and not registered as unemployed, including those studying full-time, those not working for personal reasons (eg caring for family), those claiming long-term sickness benefits, and those who have taken early retirement. In emerging economies there are, moreover, vast numbers of people who are in casual work or who are employed within the informal sector (undeclared work). Both groups may be under-employed or lack a 'decent' wage.

Another way of measuring employment security is through assessing the mean length of jobs. However, a better way of measuring it is arguably through the number of employees who are in non-standard work. Yet again, the numbers vary according to country, but in most countries the proportion of workers in non-standard jobs has risen over recent years. In the European Union, the proportion of fixed-term contracts rose from 8.4% in 1985 to 14.3% in 2005 (European Commission 2006a: 259, cited in Gray 2009). Figures also vary according to the category of worker. Women often seem to take a higher proportion of insecure work, and it has been argued that in some countries, such as Britain, women are disproportionately within 'non-standard' employment (Purcell 2000). They tend to work in traditionally low-paid, low-skilled manufacturing and service industries and in public sector services (Purcell 2000). Further evidence of this trend is provided in Chapter 10. Other groups who take non-standard work include men with no formal qualifications (Purcell 2000).

A growth area of work activity in recent years has been temporary agency work. The levels of temporary work increased in most advanced economies within the 1990s (Grunberg 2002), while agency work has formed the subject of considerable debate. In the UK the Agency Workers Regulations 2010 now provide protection for agency workers. After 12 weeks of an assignment, agency workers are entitled to the same basic working and employment conditions (including salary, overtime or commission, rest breaks and holiday entitlement) as if they had been recruited directly. However, they are not entitled to company sick pay, redundancy pay, a pension, or bonuses. Employers may, however, choose to engage casual workers through an 'in-house' bank of workers or use an agency to employ workers directly (Hammerton 2010).

Stricter legislation on the terms of employment within agency work has driven some unscrupulous employers in countries such as the United States to use labour brokers who employ workers on a daily basis. These workers are obliged to turn up every day, hoping that they will be employed for that day, but not knowing if they will receive work. They are also forced to sign paperwork declaring that they will resign at the end of the day. This procedure ensures that the employer does not have to pay compensation for unfair treatment. Those who are forced to work in such circumstances include migrants who lack more general rights to security benefits (Purser 2010).

A further means of measurement is perceived job insecurity. However, this is difficult to quantify, not least because those employees who consider that they have marketable skills may report that they feel secure in their jobs (Charles and James 2003). The extent to which workers worry about job loss depends on their perception of how likely it is that they will lose their job, and also on the consequences of losing it (Burchell 2002).

BALANCING FLEXIBILITY AND SECURITY THROUGH COLLECTIVE REGULATION

A sustainable and dynamic balance between flexibility and security is best achieved through the mechanism of collective regulation – in other words, negotiated arrangements between employer and employee representatives (Labour Market Commission 1996). As a review of collective regulation by the International Labour Organisation (Standing *et al* 1996: 10) notes,

> The competing or conflicting set of concerns for employers and for workers both need to be taken into account, as do those of the more marginalised or vulnerable on each side of the spectrum. They cannot be given their due weight if one party or the other is enfeebled or fragmented. This is ultimately why 'voice' mechanisms, or representative institutions, are required, even though the neo-liberal supply side advocates of flexibility and 'de-regulation' regard institutions and regulations as rigidities and the main source of inflexibility. Those sirens of de-regulation are wrong, because unless flexibility is bargained between strong negotiators, opportunism would lead to short-term gains by one side or another – usually large-scale, powerful employers – that would have long-term adverse consequences for dynamic efficiency.

Providing a degree of labour market security is not simply a political imperative in a democratic society, it is also an effective economic strategy (Labour Market Commission 1996). For example, in a society where employers and the government demonstrate a commitment to ensuring employment security (that is to say, protection against arbitrary loss of employment), employees are far more likely to accept a high degree of work process flexibility as well as wage flexibility. The success of many of the rapidly growing East Asian economies, according to the Labour Market Commission (1996), was based on this type of combination of security with flexibility, the former being used to secure the latter.

BALANCING FLEXIBILITY AND SECURITY THROUGH 'FLEXICURITY'

It has been argued by some that job security is an outdated concept, and that concepts such as 'employability' are more relevant to today's workplace (Guest in Heery and Salmon 2000). Although increased skills and marketability may create the risk of losing talented staff, increased training for employability should increase functional flexibility and consequently contribute towards improved productivity (Guest 2000).

'Flexicurity' has been the main thrust of the employment component of the European Union's Strategy for Growth and Jobs, launched in 2005 (Casey 2009). The term is used to imply a balance between flexibility and security, and an environment where people can remain in employment, even if that does not mean within the same job, and where they have an adequate income and opportunities to re-enter work during interim periods when they may be between jobs. However, the term incorporates the notion of more adaptable forms of contract.

An implicit understanding of 'flexicurity' is that individuals, rather than governments, are responsible for improving their 'employability' (Casey 2009). However, it has been argued (Gray 2009: 45) that

> 'wage moderation', temporary contracts and working time made flexible to suit employers' demands often fly in the face of jobseekers' quests for 'good', secure jobs. Inevitably, lowering labour standards in order to create jobs affects the incentive to take work, and leads policy-makers to preserve that incentive by reducing out-of-work benefits or threatening benefit sanctions against jobseekers refusing to accept very low pay.

It has also been suggested, more contentiously, that because 'flexible' jobs have the lowest pay rates, and temporary workers tend to be un-unionised, the term should instead be 'flexploitation' (Gray 2009: 45).

In 2007, the European Commission adopted four dimensions of a 'flexicurity' approach – flexible contractual arrangements in order to reduce labour market segmentation and undeclared work, lifelong learning, active labour market policies (helping the unemployed into work), and modern social security systems – and member states were asked to produce strategies for each of these aspects. However, it was acknowledged that in order to produce 'flexicurity' effectively, there is a need for regulation of employment agencies, adequate government funding for active labour market policies, a compromise between flexibility and security being negotiated by the social partners (employers and trade unions), and regulatory coverage for migrant workers (Gray 2009). Yet these are not being achieved due to a lack of funding, weak union power in many European countries, and inadequate legal protection for migrants (Gray 2009).

CRITICAL DEBATE

Flexicurity or 'flexploitation'?

Who does 'flexicurity' primarily benefit – the employer or the employee?

Give reasons for your answer.

THE LEGAL ASPECTS OF DISMISSAL AND REDUNDANCY, AND THE MITIGATION OF RISK

EUROPEAN DIRECTIVES ON REDUNDANCY

European Directives cover a range of areas related to employment protection, including collective redundancies, transfers of undertakings and the rights of workers whose employers become insolvent. The term 'redundancy' means (Benson 2009: 97):

> dismissal for one or more reasons not related to the individual workers concerned. It does not, therefore, cover dismissals for ill health, incompetence, and misconduct ... but does cover dismissal for economic reasons ...

The 1975 and 1998 Directives cover 'collective redundancies'. These Directives apply to situations in which the number of redundancies that have been proposed is (Benson 2009: 97):

> *Either*, within a period of 30 days
>
>> At least ten in an establishment normally employing more than 30 and fewer than 100 workers
>>
>> At least 10% of the number of workers at an establishment normally employing at least 100 but fewer than 300 workers
>>
>> At least 30 in establishments normally employing 300 workers or more
>
> *Or*, over a period of 90 days
>
>> At least 20, however many workers normally work in the establishment in question.

Member states must cover these situations, but the coverage can be greater than the figures specified if member states choose to make it so. In Britain the government has chosen the second option under the Trade Union and Labour Relations (Consolidation) Act 1992. Originally, the government tried to exclude companies where a trade union was not recognised, but the European Court of Justice ruled against this, and new provisions were inserted into the Information and Consultation Regulations (1999) which required employers to consult with employee representatives (Benson 2009).

In addition to referring to the coverage of employees, as indicated above, the European Directive also refers to consultation with workers' representatives to cover 'ways and means of avoiding collective redundancies or reducing the number of workers affected, and mitigating the consequences' (Article 2, cited in Benson 2009: 99). However, in the case of Britain, this consultation is already covered to some extent by legislation on unfair dismissal (Employment Act 2002) – although the unfair dismissal legislation only refers to employees who have been continuously employed for more than one year – since employers are required to consult employees or their representatives before deciding to dismiss them. Under the Employment Act 2002, employers must inform the employees in writing of the reasons for redundancy and then invite them to meet to discuss the proposals (providing a right of appeal) (Benson 2009).

BRITISH LEGISLATION ON REDUNDANCY

In Britain, prior to the Employment Act 2002, legislation relating to redundancy included the Redundancy Payments Act (1965), the Employment Protection Act (1975), the Employment Protection (Consolidation) Act 1978, and the Employment Rights Act (1996).

The 1965 Redundancy Payments Act (RPA) was enacted on the grounds of economic efficiency and social protection. This Act and those following it – the Employment Protection Act (1975) and the Employment Protection (Consolidation) Act 1978 – provided statutory redundancy payments based on age and length of service, advance notice of impending redundancies and written information to recognised trade unions or employee representatives outlining the reasons for redundancy, the numbers of workers involved, the categories of workers affected, the methods of selection, and the procedures that would be followed (Turnbull and Wass, cited in Heery and Salmon 2000). However, Turnbull and Wass (2000) find a number of problems with the legislation:

- The law relies on managerial prerogative regarding the need for redundancies; employers must consult, not negotiate, with trade unions.

- Apart from regulations prohibiting discrimination on the basis of race, gender and trade union activities, employers can develop their own criteria.

- Where voluntary redundancy is offered, it may be in the context of pessimistic forecasts and a general mood of despondency.

- And although employers are required to give notice for redundancies, they have often 'bought out' statutory notice periods, which leads to less time for retraining; if the 'wrong' employees volunteer for voluntary redundancy, employers will refuse the application.

According to Section 139(1) of the Employment Rights Act 1996, employees are regarded as redundant if their dismissals are attributed either primarily or partly to (Daniels 2006: 264–5):

- the fact that the employer has ceased, or intends to cease, to carry on the business for the purposes for which the employee was employed (eg boats are henceforth to be made of fibreglass, not wood)

- the fact that the employer has ceased, or intends to cease, to carry on that business in the place where the employees were employed (eg the employee is not able to move due to family commitments)

- the fact that the requirement of that business for employees to carry out work of a particular kind, or for employees to carry out work of a particular kind in the place where they were employed, has ceased or diminished or is expected to cease or diminish (eg a change in job role from a petrol manager to a filling station controller).

Redundancy pay varies according to the individual country. In Britain, as in some other countries, the amount paid varies according to age. Employees under the age of 22 are paid half a week's pay for each year of service; employees between the ages of 22 and 40 are paid one week's pay for each year of service; and those over the age of 41 receive 1½ week's pay for each year of service (*People Management* 2010a).

LEGISLATION ON THE TRANSFER OF AN UNDERTAKING

The European Acquired Rights Directive (2001) covers the transfer of an undertaking (a business, or part of one) to a new employer. However, more specifically, the Directive covers changes in the legal ownership of the business and also the person responsible for running the business (in other words, the sale of a concession or a licence to run a business). It also covers the transfer of contracts (such as catering or security services) (Benson 2009).

Within Britain, the legislation on the transfer of undertakings is referred to as the 'TUPE regulations'. In full, the legislation is the Transfer of Undertakings (Protection of Employment) Regulations 2006. Although public authorities are excluded from the European Directive, the Cabinet Office (2000) has stated that the principles should be followed within the public sector, and for transfers from the public to the private sector (Benson 2009).

The regulations strengthen the rights of staff involved in transfers, providing them with continuity of employment and the same terms and conditions as they previously possessed prior to the transfer (except occupational pensions). They also cover services that are outsourced, insourced, or assigned by a client to a new contractor. In addition, the regulations contain specific provisions to protect employees from dismissal before or after a relevant transfer – neither the old nor the new employer can fairly dismiss an employee because of the transfer or for a reason connected with the transfer, unless that reason is an economic, technical or organisational reason entailing changes in the workforce (a change in the number of people employed or in the employees' particular functions). Representatives of affected employees have a right to be informed about a prospective transfer, and must be consulted about any measures that the transferor or transferee employer envisages taking concerning the affected employees.

✸ APPLYING THEORY TO PRACTICE

Risks to employers resulting from a transfer of operations

The transferee enterprise (the new business taking over) is responsible under the TUPE Regulations (2006) for any unexpected liabilities. For example, if the transferor (the old business) had previously discriminated against an employee, the transferee takes over responsibility in the event of legal complaint.

There are ways in which employers have been able to avoid treating transferred employees as fairly as the employees might have expected. Although the terms and conditions must remain the same, over time employers can seek to 'harmonise' the terms and conditions of existing employees and those transferred into the organisation. For example, employers may choose to restrict pay rises for those who are more highly paid. Moreover, employers are allowed to dismiss those who have been employed for less than a year. The transferee employer can also refuse to take on a transferor's workforce for economic, technical or organisational reasons, resulting in a fair dismissal – although this has to be the main reason for the dismissal.

Employers should, however, be careful, when seeking to circumnavigate the TUPE legislation, because if the economic reasons put forward are found by an employment tribunal to be spurious, the transferee can be liable for potential claims (Ayling 2010). Moreover, employees whose terms and conditions are detrimentally changed as a result of the transfer can choose to resign and claim compensation for unfair constructive dismissal, or can continue working for the new employers but sue them for loss of pay or benefits.

List the potential outcomes for employees who have been transferred through TUPE.

How many are positive, and how many are negative?

Outline the potential sources of tension between existing and 'transferred in' employees. How might these be resolved?

COLLECTIVE REDUNDANCY CONSULTATION

As mentioned above, collective redundancy consultation is covered within the European Directive of 1975/1998. Employers should provide workers' representatives with 'all relevant information' in writing. This information should include the reasons for the redundancy, the number of workers who are normally employed within the organisation, the number of workers who will be made redundant, and the period of time that the redundancies will take to implement (Benson 2009). Although the Directive does not state the period of consultation, in Britain it is covered under the Trade Union and Labour Relations (Consolidation) Act 1992 – and amended by the Collective Redundancies and Transfer of Undertakings (Protection of Employment) (Amendment) Regulations 1995 – as follows:

- If proposed redundancies involve more than 100 employees, consultation must take place over 90 days.

- If proposed redundancies involve more than 20, but less than 100 employees, consultation must take place over at least 30 days.

- Written information must be given to employee representatives at the start of consultation on the reasons for redundancy, the numbers of workers involved, the types of jobs, the selection of workers for redundancy, the procedures to be used, and payment.

Under the Collective Redundancies and Transfer of Undertakings (Protection of Employment) (Amendment) Regulations 1999, consultation has to be with a trade union where one is recognised, or with other elected representatives of the affected employees where no trade union is recognised. Employers also continue to have a duty to act fairly and reasonably in handling redundancies, and informing and consulting affected employees individually, regardless of the number of dismissals. The consultation should include discussion about ways of avoiding the redundancies, reducing the numbers to be dismissed and mitigating the consequences of any redundancies. Consultation should be completed before any redundancy notices are issued (ACAS 2005).

In relation to the transfer of business, the Transfer of Undertakings (Protection of Employment) Regulations 1981, as amended by the Collective Redundancies and Transfer of Undertakings (Protection of Employment) (Amendment) Regulations 1995 and 1999, 'require employers to consult representatives of an independent trade union where one is recognised or other elected representatives of the affected employees where there is no recognised trade union, where there is to be a transfer of a business to which the regulations apply' (ACAS 2005).

DISMISSAL AND REDUNDANCY POLICIES

If at all possible, it is best to avoid making redundancies. The costs of making redundancies include both direct costs of compensation to those who have been made redundant and also a wide variety of indirect costs such as future recruitment, induction and training, retraining, job search, employee assistance programmes, counselling, loss in productivity, managing absence, damage to the employer brand, and difficulties in recruiting new staff. However, the organisation should be prepared for the eventuality and should normally possess redundancy policies including those relating to selection for redundancy, counselling (and financial/welfare advice), training and strategic HR planning (Guest 2000).

As Guest (2000) argues, management should accept responsibility for managing both objective and subjective job security. He further suggests that policies on job security (such as job security guarantees or policies that emphasise avoiding compulsory redundancy) can assist in ensuring commitment from employees. The provision of appropriate training programmes can enhance employability. Some companies have gone as far as insisting that all employees should undergo a minimum number of hours per annum on training and/or education. Other organisations have put resources into establishing 'learning centres' – which have, however, been characterised by low uptake. Managers should also communicate expectations carefully to employees. Employees who trust management and believe that they are acting fairly are less likely to feel insecure and feel more loyal to the organisation. In this respect, job security can thus be linked to the psychological contract (see Chapter 1). Where managers break promises on job security, the psychological contract is bound to be damaged. Another possible avenue for policy relating to redundancy is the use of mentoring schemes. However, these schemes have suffered when managers have perceived the requirement to act as a mentor as an extension of their job role, and have not taken their responsibility seriously.

It is commonly recognised (CIPD 2010a) that redundancy is

one of the most traumatic events an employee may experience.

Announcement of redundancies will invariably have an adverse impact on morale, motivation and productivity.

Where a trade union is recognised within an organisation, a formal agreement may have been developed, negotiated and agreed between management and the union. This will aid employees to see its legitimacy. A redundancy policy usually covers the following stages (CIPD 2010a):

- planning and preventative measures – Subject to employment contracts, these measures might include the following: natural wastage, a recruitment freeze, stopping or reducing overtime, offering early retirement (but avoiding age discrimination), retraining or redeployment, offering sabbaticals and secondments, pay freezes, short-time working, pay cuts in return for taking time off work, or an alternative to redundancy (ATR) scheme whereby employees do not work for the employer for a specified time period and are able to seek work while in receipt of an allowance

- asking for volunteers for redundancy – Offering a reasonable redundancy package may avoid the need for compulsory redundancy. This may have better results in terms of morale for survivors, but could be criticised for not being a strategic tool – since those who choose to leave might be those with the necessary competences to drive the organisation forward. In addition, there may be pressure put to bear on certain employees to volunteer for redundancy, and this may have the effect of decreasing morale within the organisation

- individual and collective consultation – This should conform to legislative requirements for the country concerned. (The relevant legislation for Britain is outlined above.) In addition, in some countries, including Britain, case law adds to the requirements

- identification of a selection pool of people and the development of a list of objective criteria – The selection pool should initially usually be those who undertake a similar type of work within a particular department, or work at a specific location, whose work has either ceased or decreased or is expected to cease. Objective criteria may include length of service (but being aware of age discrimination), attendance records (but being aware of disability discrimination), disciplinary records, skills, competences and qualifications, work experience, and performance records. In the past LIFO (last in, first out) has been used as a selection method but this may now contravene age discrimination legislation in countries within Europe and others such as New Zealand, where such age discrimination legislation has been implemented. Moreover, other apparently objective criteria such as those who work part-time will have to be avoided where more women than men hold part-time jobs because, again, this could be seen as discriminatory

- compliance with all of the stages of the organisation's dismissal procedures – In many countries, reasons that are regarded as 'unfair' means for selecting employees include trade union membership, part-time status, pregnancy or maternity-related reasons, sex, sexual orientation, marital status, race or religion

- providing advance notice of an individual consultation meeting, and permitting a colleague to be present

- offering the employee an opportunity to appeal against selection for redundancy – The appeal should comply with the organisation's redundancy procedure and/or relevant disciplinary or dismissal procedures

- arranging the statutory or other redundancy payment – Payments vary, depending on the country

- providing relocation expenses

- helping redundant employees to obtain training or alternative work – Employers must consider suitable alternative work within the organisation

- counselling and support – Common faults include being too abrupt or too vague. An external provider might be used for counselling in areas such as housing and debt advice. Employees should also be offered practical assistance with interview skills, redrafting a CV and applying to advertisements effectively.

The *Applying theory to practice* box below summarises the way in which redundancy should be conducted, and probes into the types of workers who may be affected and the consideration that employers should have for legislation.

APPLYING THEORY TO PRACTICE

Redundancy and discrimination

Redundancy should be undertaken in a way that reflects organisational justice: distributive justice (whether survivors think that redundancy outcomes are fair), procedural justice (relating to the procedures used to make decisions), and interactional justice (focusing on employee perceptions of the interpersonal treatment that they have received during implementation) (Thornhill and Saunders 1998).

It is important to handle redundancy equitably. Which groups of people might potentially be treated unfairly?

In addition, it is necessary to abide by relevant legislation when making people redundant, including legislation that was not designed specifically to cover redundancy. Which discrimination legislation is relevant to redundancy? Refer here to broad areas of legislation rather than specific Acts.

NEGOTIATING REDUNDANCY AGREEMENTS

Organisations are likely to use redundancies as a means of ridding themselves of 'troublemakers' or 'dead wood' (Redman and Wilkinson 2006: 368). Even if firms stress the objective nature of the selection process, managers may still subjectively manipulate matters to shape the outcome (*ibid*), or be perceived to be doing so by workers. This means that redundancy processes may lack legitimacy and, indeed, be open to legal challenges. In turn, this means that organisations can benefit through negotiation – an agreement with a recognised trade union is more likely to be fair, will help ensure that a commitment to objectivity is upheld, be more legitimate than unilateral action, and probably reduce the chances of subsequent litigation. However, negotiations with unions will involve managers 'thinking beyond the box'. Too often organisations resort to redundancies as a magic bullet for cutting costs, without much thought to medium-term skills needs. Cost-cutting may placate investors, but it also may undermine the skills base of the organisation and its capabilities for meeting medium- and long-term strategic goals. A firm can thus genuinely benefit from a negotiated compromise. Moreover, if it is negotiating in good faith, the union has to put viable alternatives to redundancies on the table. The latter could include alternatives which management may not even have identified or properly considered but be worthy of serious consideration. Unions, of course, primarily represent members and not prospective members, so the union is likely to prioritise retention over future job creation possibilities, and this is likely to inform its negotiations strategy.

MANAGING 'SURVIVOR SYNDROME'

The reactions of 'survivors' (workers who remain employed after redundancies have taken place) will vary depending on whether they perceive that redundancies were necessary, and whether they perceive that the process used was fair. Survivors may feel a sense of betrayal, and may even feel guilty that their colleagues have been made redundant while they have kept their jobs. Some remaining employees may group together, while alternatively, rather than co-operate more fully with their remaining colleagues, others may instead become more competitive (Cooper, cited in Allen 2009). Their feelings may result in a number of behaviours including reduced productivity, lower levels of customer service, team conflict, presenteeism – being seen to work but not necessarily working hard – and conversely, absence from work (Kinnie 1998; Kinder 2009). Mediating factors can, however, include support from line managers or immediate supervisors (Armstrong-Stassen 1994).

Workers remaining in the organisation after redundancies have taken place may also feel stressed if their workload has increased (work intensification). Much has been written about the long working hours culture in countries such as Britain and the United States, especially compared to a range of countries within Europe (Burchell 2002). Attention has also been paid to work intensification, 'the effort that employees put into their jobs during the time that they are working' (Burchell 2002: 72). Work demands can be of particular concern for middle managers during and after downsizing because of the need to adapt their role to include other aspects of work and also the need to manage the implementation of change (Thornhill and Saunders 1998). However, work intensification can lead to stress, psychological ill health, employee demotivation and family tensions – as well as industrial accidents. Again, surveys on work intensification point towards workers in Britain faring less well than those in other countries within Europe (Burchell 2002).

Survivor syndrome can also impact negatively on the psychological contract. The psychological contract contains three kinds of unwritten expectations (Schein 1988, cited in Daniels 2006): the need to be treated fairly, the need for a level of security and certainty in return for giving loyalty to the employer, and a need for fulfilment, satisfaction and progression. Employees want to know that organisations place value on their contributions, successes and relationships.

REFLECTION ON PRACTICE

The impact of redundancy and downsizing on the psychological contract of survivors

What impact is redundancy and downsizing likely to have on the psychological contracts of survivors?

In what ways might the psychological contract be violated?

Managers should aim to treat survivors carefully in order to preserve their morale and commitment to the organisation. Management strategies might include the following (CIPD 2010a):

- ensuring that managers have the relevant personal skills and attitudes to be able to operate effectively during periods of traumatic change
- providing all of the workforce with a full explanation of the situation and explaining the policies and practices used for redundancy
- demonstrating the necessity for redundancies
- handling redundancies fairly and equitably
- providing a clear appraisal of future employment prospects
- detailing changes in working arrangements
- showing a forward-looking, positive attitude for the future
- conducting, where necessary, individual discussions with key workers in order to reassure them of their importance to the organisation.

In addition, it might be necessary to provide counselling through employee assistance or confidential counselling programmes, and mediation where there is a rise in conflict between employees as a result of heightened tension within the workplace (Kinder 2009).

REDUNDANCY, DOWNSIZING AND THE ROLE OF TRADE UNIONS

It has been argued that job (in)security has been a central force in shaping industrial relations. The fear of job loss can drive employees to seek membership of a trade union for protection against dismissal (Heery and Abbot 2000). In addition, job insecurity is a feature of life for workers who are already vulnerable to discrimination, such as minority groups. Indeed, unions have been referred to as 'flag bearers in the promotion of justice in the workplace and in the promotion and protection of jobs' (Guest 1997: 349, cited in Dibben 2007). However, there is a tension for unions in terms of union strategy. Should they fight to increase the pay of their core workers, or seek to protect the rights of the more marginal members of the workforce? In engaging with employers, which battles are they more likely to win? There has been some evidence of unions 'talking the talk' on job protection but in fact 'selling out' to employers in the longer run. Unions have made agreements with employers, offering flexible work practices in return for avoiding compulsory redundancy (Guest 1997, 2000). However, some employers have reneged on these deals. For example, Ward *et al* (2001) point to the case of an employer that agreed to redeploy members of staff who had lost jobs, in return for union agreement on restructuring and flexible job roles, but later cut back on the recruitment of permanent staff and increased the number of temporary jobs. Meanwhile, Bacon and Blyton (2006) cite situations of where co-operative unions have made agreements with management on a pay increase for a small number of employees at the expense of others who were victims of job cuts as a result of changes to teamworking arrangements. Other, more militant union branches were able to protect a greater number of jobs and also extract higher payment for teamworking arrangements. The authors refer to the problems associated with 'coerced co-operation' (Bacon and Blyton 2006: 215), and provide further backing for Kelly's (1996) claim that union militancy is necessary in order to share gains in productivity. The case study below explores the way in which academic unions have dealt with the issue of job security in recent years in Britain.

CASE STUDY

UNION STRATEGY: JOB SECURITY OR PAY INCREASE?

In Britain, the University and College Union (UCU) campaigned quite aggressively on pay rises during the late 2000s. Students supported lecturers in seeking pay rises, following many years of falling pay in real terms. The UCU achieved pay rises for staff.

However, during the subsequent recession, the UCU turned its attention to job protection and job security. Some universities and further education colleges threatened staff with compulsory redundancy in order to save costs, closing whole departments, and the UCU organised campaigns to fight this. In addition, the UCU sought to achieve better rights for temporary workers and lecturing staff on hourly pay.

As the recession bit harder, employers then started to threaten cuts to pensions or changes to pensions away from final-salary pensions and towards career-average pensions, particularly for new staff. The UCU changed tactics, turning its attention to meet this latest attack on employee rights which threatened the employment benefits of existing permanent staff.

Questions

In which areas are unions most likely to achieve results for their membership?

Should employment security be a trade union's main concern?

Is the UCU likely to achieve better results through militancy or co-operation?

SUMMARY

This chapter has engaged with debates around the downsizing of the workforce, and in doing so has examined common processes and legislative constraints. The chapter might usefully be read in conjunction with Chapter 12 and Chapter 10, since downsizing and redundancy can be significant causes of conflict and tension within the workplace. In addition, the selection of those who will be made redundant has to be carefully undertaken in a way that is fair and equitable.

Flexibility, downsizing, redundancy and flexicurity are all related to each other. They encompass a range of strategies that can be used by employers to cope with a decline in business or, in the case of the public sector or non-governmental organisations, respond to budget cuts. As explained above, employers can the tempted to engage in job cuts in order to prevent further organisational decline. However, they would be wise to consider the longer-term impacts of such strategies on employee welfare, productivity and future competitiveness.

EXPLORE FURTHER

Reading

- ACAS (2009) Advisory booklet: *Redundancy-Handling*, revised edition. London: ACAS. Available online at www.acas.org.uk

- Atkinson, J. (1984) 'Manpower strategies for flexible organisations', *Personnel Management*, August: 28–31

- Burchell, B. (2002) 'The prevalence and distribution of job insecurity and work intensification', in B. Burchell, D. Lapido and F. Wilkinson, *Job Insecurity and Work Intensification*. London: Routledge

- Kinnie, N., Hutchinson, S. and Purcell, J. (1998) 'Downsizing: is it always lean and mean?', *Personnel Review*, Vol.27, No.4: 296–311

Websites

- Advisory, Conciliation and Arbitration Service www.acas.org.uk

- Chartered Institute of Personnel and Development www.cipd.co.uk

Conclusion: The Relevance of Employment Relations and Comparative Employment Relations

CHAPTER OVERVIEW

The employment contract is central to modern work and, indeed, underpins economic life in all modern societies. Yet the study of employment relations has had to contend with a crisis of relevance in recent years. In this concluding chapter we reflect on this and on the importance of taking an international and comparative perspective on employment relations, explore ways of understanding employment relations on an international and comparative level, and conclude by revisiting some of the key questions and issues emerging from each of the chapters.

LEARNING OUTCOMES

After studying this chapter you should be able to:

- discuss the reasons for the crisis that currently besets the field of industrial and employment relations

- outline the practical relevance of employment relations studies

- summarise the academic relevance of employment relations studies

- appreciate the strategic importance of employment relations

- appreciate the need for the integration of employment relations processes and describe how they impact on policy, practice and organisational outcomes

- understand the importance of an international perspective in employment relations

- critically introduce and discuss comparative employment relations

THE CRISIS OF EMPLOYMENT RELATIONS

Within many national contexts, the study of employment relations has undergone something of a crisis. The number of institutions offering specialised degrees in employment relations has declined, with, in most cases, employment relations being relegated to the status of a sub-component of degrees in HRM. On the one hand, in part this reflects the professional requirements of bodies such as the CIPD, who justifiably require professional HR managers to be exposed to all of the sub-areas of people management. In this sense, this process is a welcome one, in that it represents part and parcel of the professionalisation of people management. On the other hand, much of the decline of employment relations as a discipline has little to do with professionalisation. Rather, it is due to the decline of trade unions. Within most of the developed societies, employees have been in a weaker bargaining position vis-à-vis employers since the 1970s. This reflects a long period of mediocre and episodic growth interposed with recession and, in many countries, the declining proportion of 'good', reasonably well-paid and secure jobs. Quite simply, employees increasingly have to accept the employment relationship on a 'take it or leave it' basis. Mirroring this process has been the decline of unions. However, union decline is not just a product of employee weakness. On the one hand, unions can and do make real strategic choices. Whereas some new forms of organising strategy have yielded good results in specific contexts (an example being the unionisation of cleaning and other low-paid workers in Los Angeles), in other cases they have failed to deliver the desired results. Moreover, in some cases, faced with declining membership, unions have alternated between different strategies in search of a magic solution, resulting in instability and confusion among members.

A second cause of union decline has been the rise of more instrumental attitudes to work. As noted in Chapter 2, increased leisure time and more affordable consumer goods have meant that employees have other avenues for (albeit fleeting) personal fulfilment than the securing of decent and meaningful work. This is particularly the case among younger workers, their declining social mobility in liberal market economies making career progression a remote dream for many, and immediate consumption of essentially valueless goods (plastic 'designer' products produced in Asian sweatshops) a welcome diversion.

A third cause is the more hardline approach by many governments towards unions, informed by neo-liberal ideologies and/or the threat of adverse reactions by unrestrained financial markets, themselves informed by rumour, ideology and prejudice. Notoriously, the World Bank 'Doing Business' reports depicted countries where individual and collective employment rights were relatively stronger as poor outlets for investment (Cooney *et al* 2010), despite empirical evidence to the contrary. In turn, this has led to the curtailing of the rights of employees and their collectives under the law, and tougher approaches in collective bargaining with public sector unions.

The weakening of unions, and the weakened position of employees more generally, has meant that employers are ostensibly more able to unilaterally revise the terms and conditions of employment. This represents one of the major reasons for the decline of the study of employment relations. During periods where unions were strong, there was strong demand for experts in the field – demand for whom has now greatly diminished. However, this does not mean that employment relations does not matter, even in respect of short-term organisational competitiveness. Weak unions and poor rights under the law may reduce overt industrial conflict, but they cannot ensure either active employee buy-in or, indeed, industrial peace.

THE CONTINUED ACADEMIC RELEVANCE OF EMPLOYMENT RELATIONS

Employment relations as a field of study has both practical and academic value. Unfortunately, employment relations academics have not always helped themselves, either occupying themselves with the study of fads for union revitalisation that pay little heed to structural realities, or retreating into increasingly abstract econometric modelling that is incomprehensible to the average practitioner or student. This is not to detract from the value and importance of more quantitative research at either the macro or micro level, or of devising ideas and deepening understandings as to the remaking of the union movement – problems in these areas centre on accessibility, transferability, and in drawing distinctions between the desired and the feasible. However, above all, the field of employment relations has great value for the critical insights it imparts. It cautions against the view that the employment relationship is without contradictions (Dickens 2008). Moreover, it brings together the insights from a number of distinct fields, most notably sociology, but also economics and psychology. This allows for syntheses and debates that transcend the boundaries and confines of disciplinary-based thought. A further strength is its theoretical rigour. This is particularly important given that a number of other areas of business and management studies do not always appear to be underpinned by rigorous investigation of empirical evidence. The stranglehold of motivational pseudo-theories on undergraduates reflects not only the triumph of simplicity and wilful ignorance but also limitations in terms of teaching and underlying conceptual understanding. To those who wish to pursue careers in academia, consulting or applied research, having exposure to a range of rigorous perspectives that are of value not only in understanding the employment relationship but indeed the firm as an entirety and society at large, is invaluable.

THE CONTINUED APPLIED RELEVANCE OF EMPLOYMENT RELATIONS

We saw in Chapter 12 that although the number of strikes has declined in many countries, there has been a rise in individual forms of unexpressed conflict such as employee absence. This may represent either conscious decisions by individual employees to retaliate against their employer for perceived injustices or, indeed, reflect physical and mental ailments caused by debilitating and disempowering working conditions. The fact that employers may, in many contexts, have amassed more power, does not mean that employees are devoid of the means of protest or, indeed, that excessive employer power will not damage the physical and mental capabilities of the workforce. It is further worth reflecting that some of the most repressive low-wage economies and regions may have been successful in terms of manufacturing low-cost goods, but many are also notorious for low-quality and sometimes dangerous products. Cut-throat competition means that many companies face persistent crises of competitiveness, and low consumer loyalty – sometimes even outright consumer resentment – making it difficult to plan for the long term. Within developed liberal market economies, stagnant wages for many have, as we have seen, also created a persistent crisis of sustainable consumer demand, a good deal of consumption being propped up by excessive borrowing. Firms may make some immediate competitive gains from paying low wages, but if the bulk of the workforce is devoid of the means of sustainable consumption, broad-based growth is not possible. Ironically, it may ultimately be up to employees, and their capacity to mobilise themselves in pursuit of better pay, to resolve the severe economic difficulties besetting many developed economies. It is the challenge facing employment relations specialists to understand these contradictions, and to devise methods for promoting fairness, equity, employee buy-in and better workforce well-being (all of which are potentially valuable to the firm itself) within the constraints imposed by ideology and markets.

ACKNOWLEDGING THE STRATEGIC IMPORTANCE OF THE MANAGEMENT OF EMPLOYMENT RELATIONS

As is commonly noted in the HRM literature (Collings and Wood 2009), work and employment relations are central to organisational competitiveness. Moreover, investors may be fickle and mobile, economic and political contexts may be subject to change, and changes may also occur in customers' demands and in the technologies of production and consumption. It is therefore all the more important that employment relations are managed in a strategic way, in order to impact on the broader organisational context.

Managing people has many dimensions, some of which – such as recruitment and selection – fall outside the domain of the study of the existing employment relationship. And yet, the employment relationship is an 'indeterminate' exchange whereby an immediately quantifiable cash wage is exchanged for an uncertain amount of labour power (Hyman 1989; Kelly 1998). This inherent flexibility provides firms with opportunities to operationalise the relationship in such a way as to secure maximum co-operation, but also to seek maximum output through coercion. Seeking to achieve co-operation can be seen to be strategic in that firms have to devise ways of achieving such co-operation, and meet the challenges of operationalising such ways given inevitable uncertainties and frictions (Collings and Wood 2009). Labour coercion cannot be strategic, in the same way that hammering in a nail is not. However, those who own hammers (in this instance, firms that are able to evade regulation and/or are possessed of overwhelming power in relation to employees) are likely to concentrate their efforts on looking for nails and on seeking opportunities to further coerce labour, rather than on thinking about alternative and more effective strategic options. But how can firms maximise cooperation from labour – to enhance output and/or quality? It could be argued that in order to maximise co-operation it is necessary to employ a certain set of techniques.

> ### ? CRITICAL DEBATE
>
> **An optimal set of strategic HR options for all country contexts?**
>
> There is a general consensus in the literature on employment relations and HRM that voice – giving employees a real say in how things are done in the firm – matters. However, there is considerable debate over whether there is an optimal set of strategies, or whether the specific strategic options are contingent on the setting (Collings and Wood 2009).
>
> Based on your reading of this text, can you identify a set of strategies that employers should undertake in order to maximise co-operation and minimise conflict? Try to draw up a shortlist of essential strategies.
>
> Does this set of strategies apply to all country contexts? Justify your answer.

This text acknowledges the strategic importance of the management of employment relations, and incorporates strategic understanding from a critical and international perspective.

THE INTEGRATION OF EMPLOYMENT RELATIONS PROCESSES AND HOW THEY IMPACT ON POLICY, PRACTICE AND ORGANISATIONAL OUTCOMES

Employment relations processes cut across a range of areas. For example, pay bargaining will influence the competitiveness of the organisation, and also the morale of employees. Discipline and grievance policies and procedures might be used to institutionalise and manage conflict in a way that impacts on the smooth running and sustainability of the organisation. The way in which downsizing and redundancy are managed will impact on the finances of the organisation and also on the psychological contract of 'survivors'. Employee engagement might lead to increased productivity, a reduction in absence, and the ability to attract workers with key competences needed for the organisation's future growth. However, a central feature of employment relations is the use of voice, in its broadest sense. The role of trade unions in representing workers' individual and collective concerns is vital in the functioning of organisations, both in terms of dealing with complaints and in terms of voicing ideas for future strategy and encouraging creativity.

◀◉▶ REFLECTION ON PRACTICE

The contribution of employment relations to organisational outcomes

In your experience, what has been the most significant contribution of employment relations to your workplace? Here you might consider the relevance of issues such as pay bargaining, voicing ideas or concerns, restructuring, the resolution of conflict, or defining the nature of the contract.

What has been your experience of the role of trade unions in these respects? Has it been positive or negative? How might trade unions and their representatives play a stronger role within the workplace?

THE IMPORTANCE OF AN INTERNATIONAL PERSPECTIVE IN EMPLOYMENT RELATIONS

Clearly, employment relations matters. But why is an international perspective valuable to those wishing to pursue a career of people management within a specific national context? Firstly, we belong to a joined-up world. Increasingly, production chains are global, while subcontracting and outsourcing make it vital that practitioners have real insights into the nature and dynamics of employment relations in other contexts. The reputational damage caused by the poor practices of subcontractors has severely harmed the image of a number of well-known brands. Moreover, one cannot understand issues and problems such as quality control and reliability without a broader understanding of the dynamics of the employment relationship.

Secondly, it is simply wrong to assume that one can learn nothing from other contexts. For example, many continental European countries have been much more successful than Britain and the United States – who are often perceived as leading the way in 'best practice'– in terms of high value-added manufacturing, the sustaining of good secure jobs, productivity per hour worked, and in well-being both within and beyond the workplace. Moreover, even within liberal market settings, where neo-liberal ideas have influenced many areas of reform in recent years, some countries are more equal than others (for example, Canada and New Zealand), and were less adversely affected by the 2008 economic crisis largely owing to more effective direct and indirect, formal and informal regulation of the employment relationship, and different norms and values of what is and what is not socially acceptable. It is therefore important to consider different international experiences and also to seek to compare and contrast different country experiences.

COMPARATIVE EMPLOYMENT RELATIONS

Attempts to make sense of the significant variations within and between different national employment relations systems have led to considerable debate and confusion. Union membership and the coverage of collective bargaining have declined substantially since the 1980s in most industrialised countries. This decline in the collective power of employees and the increase in managerial discretion and market forces have played an important role in facilitating variation in employment relations and human resource management. Despite some recent growth, comparative studies remain a marginal concern in the field of employment relations. For example, in their survey of more than 20,000 articles published between 1977 and 1997 in 29 journals, Clark *et al* (2000) found that less than 2% dealt with the management of human resources from a comparative perspective. As Frege (2005: 179) also observed, the bulk of employment relations research 'continues to be strongly embedded in nationally specific research traditions and cultures'. These research traditions are regarded by some as evidence that employment relations is increasingly out of touch with the reality of globalisation. As Clark (cited in Hollinshead *et al* 2003: 34) pointed out:

> The growing internationalisation of economic and political life is questioning the very basis of a sub-discipline whose conceptual and explanatory frameworks have been … overwhelmingly national.

Employment relations scholars are, belatedly, turning their focus to comparative and international studies.

The rapid growth in comparative studies in recent times owes much to the expanding significance of multinational corporations, the increased level of global completion in product markets, the development of new markets, the establishment and consolidation of powerful trading blocs, and the spread of new ways of working spurred on by developments in technology (Budhwar and Debrah 2001; Clark *et al* 2000; Morley *et al* 2006; Traxler *et al* 2001). There is a growing consensus that comparative studies have much to offer in terms of providing a deeper understanding of what is unique and what is universal in national employment relations systems. Comparative research can have several benefits. First, it contributes to the development of theory in employment relations by developing explanations for national and regional differences (Strauss 1998). The emergence of new theories in the process of comparing factors in different countries will undoubtedly enrich the field of employee relations. Second, comparative studies relativise our understanding of employment relations practices, procedures and institutions (Blanpain 2007). That is, placing a particular country in a broader perspective assists in a better understanding of that country's employment relations system. Third, it helps to establish the relative importance of particular factors in determining the dynamics of an employment relations system. For instance, compared to many developed countries, unions and centralised bargaining remain powerful determinants of employment relations in South Africa. Fourth, on a more practical level, comparative research aids in our understanding of the extent to which aspects of one employment relations system can be successfully replicated in another system. Accordingly, it brings to light alternative ways of conducting the employment relationship. Finally, comparative studies allow human resource managers of multinational corporations to understand the employment relations systems of countries in which they have operations or with which they have trade links (Budhwar and Debrah 2001). A comparative understanding of employment relations also has much to offer policy-makers and legislators.

CONVERGENCE AND DIVERGENCE

Most regulatory systems are tied to the nation-state. It is therefore possible for economic agents (particularly thinking here of multinationals) to move between different regulatory spaces in order to elude any perceived constraints associated with a particular regulatory regime. Instances of such 'regime shopping' have increased significantly in the era of globalisation as improvements in information technology have enabled firms to successfully coordinate their activities over large expanses of international space (Peck 1996). The globalisation of markets and firms has served to undermine the restraining consequences of regulatory systems.

Against this background, there are two diametrically opposed arguments: those that suggest global economic forces are leading to increasing convergence between national employment relations systems and those that emphasise the continuing divergence of these systems. The convergence and divergence debate has been a central aspect of the comparative literature for some time. Morley *et al* (2006: 2) summarise this debate as follows:

> Convergence arguments suggest that while differences in management systems have arisen as a result of the geographical isolation of businesses, the consequent development of differing beliefs and value orientations of national cultures are being suspended by the logic of technology and markets which require the adoption of universally applicable policies, approaches and management techniques … By contrast, proponents of the divergence thesis argue that industrial relations systems, far from being economically and technologically derived, reflect national institutional contexts which do not respond readily to the imperatives of technology or the market.

Thus, on the one hand it has been suggested that a range of external factors have driven employment relations to converge, while on the other hand there are those who still emphasise the importance of national context. The convergence literature suggests that employment relations practices have become more similar over time. Kerr *et al* (1974) claimed that industrialisation would lead to a common structuring of the workforce across and within countries. Their arguments were premised on a view of industrialisation as proceeding smoothly across the world and, in the process, transforming employment relations systems so that they would resemble the collective bargaining system that was consolidating in the USA's key industries in the 1950s. For Kerr *et al*, common patterns of employment relations were largely an outcome of the diffusion of modern technology. This view suggests that industry has developed in an unrelenting and entirely predictable pattern.

Convergence theorists differ in their assessment of the nature and extent of convergence between and within employment relations systems. Some suggest that there are clear trends towards employment relations converging towards some variant of human resource management, while others claim that there is a convergence towards Japanese-style employment practices or a form of flexible production. A key determinant in this convergence is the enhanced bargaining power of employers by virtue of 'collective labour's vulnerability to [capital's] national and international mobility' (Burawoy 1985: 127). In other words, the ability of multinationals to relocate sites to where employmenr regulation is low undermines the power of employees and trade unions. The net result is alleged to be a shift towards workplace-oriented employment relations (rather than employment relations being determined by national union strategy), decentralised collective bargaining (at the workplace level rather than the industry level), team-based work practices and a clear divide between core and peripheral workers. In other words, the claim is that nation-specific employment relations practices are increasingly giving way to generic, standardised practices under the pressures of globalisation. The arguments of Kerr *et al* (1974) therefore suggest that industrialisation has led to greater convergence between countries.

However, although countries may face similar pressures in the form of globalisation, the idea that they respond to them in a similar manner has been widely disputed. Regulation theorists, for example, reject the notion of a single, objective 'logic' to the evolution of capitalism that transcends all particularities (Jessop 1990). They adopt a view which stresses that the development of capitalism has always been mediated through historically and spatially specific institutional forms, regulatory institutions and norms of behaviour. These include wage relations, forms of competition, capital flows, the state, monetary forms, international commercial and financial systems and cultural aspects. In this line of thinking, the peculiarities of national capitalisms take on a new significance. Accordingly, the regulation approach stimulates interest in (Elam 1994: 57–8):

> the unequal capacities of different capitalist nations to generate and assimilate new techno-economic systems and a major concern becomes the qualitatively different impact of the same techno-economic forces in time and space. Although major structural crises are seen as inevitably taking on international dimensions, it becomes of importance to track down the historically specific conditions under which the determinants of crisis have collided – the *conjuncture* of general and particular determinants of crisis and transformation.

Thus, importance is given to studying both international trends and also the ways in which individual nations respond to those trends. According to the divergence literature, it is important to examine the economic, social, political and cultural context when attempting to understand employment relations. This will provide a better understanding of particularity (what is unique) and contingency (adaptation to change). The national context and its associated institutional framework are therefore overriding considerations. According to Poole (1986: 3),

> varied strategic choices set within heterogeneous cultures and ideologies, political and economic conditions, industrial relations institutions and power distributions have occasioned a rich variety of global outcomes.

Some divergence theorists go further still, and also question the relevance of ideas of distinct national systems of employment relations given the growing variation in employment relations within countries. Others highlight continuing divergences alongside some convergence. In their book *Converging Divergences*, Katz and Darbishire (2000) find increasing variation in the employment practices in the seven countries they studied as well as many commonalities in the nature of the variation appearing within these countries. The former is producing growing divergences in employment relations within countries, whereas the latter is leading to a convergence in employment systems across countries. That is (Katz and Darbishire 2000: 263),

> A greater variety of the work practices is being used within the various employment patterns (as in the wide variety of team systems of work organisation that are being adopted), and variation also is being produced through individualised and contingent work practices, such as contingent compensation. Nonetheless, in all seven countries we observe similar changes in labor–management interactions, including a decentralisation of bargaining structures and greater informality in labor–management interactions.

Variations in work practices such as pay are thus remaining at the same time as there has been a trend towards similarities in the relationship between management and unions and in the way in which structures of negotiation have developed. Peck and Tickell (1994) similarly draw attention to differences within countries but also explain how the regulation of employment at the local level is not simply a product of national-level institutions. Each organisation is also linked into a network of local institutions and also influenced by changes in technology. They suggest that systems have changed in a way that implies *spatially uneven development* (Peck 1996: 102). Whereas regulatory functions may be anchored at the local level, a local regulatory system is defined largely by its mode of integration into wider structures. At the same time, the wider (national) structures are also influenced by local systems. This analysis also finds some resonance in the emerging 'varieties of capitalism' (Hall and Soskice 2001), 'national business systems' (Whitley 1999) and 'production systems' (Rubery and Grimshaw 2003) literatures that highlight the significance of the social processes in which firms are embedded.

On balance, the literature suggests that many employment relations practices continue to be characterised by diversity across national borders and that the nature and extent of changes vary considerably (Morley *et al* 2006). This is sometimes known as 'path dependency'. Institutions within different countries (such as the educational and training system and the strength of trade unions) may change over time but change in a way that does not necessarily reflect the changes that occur in the institutions of other countries. According to Traxler *et al* (2001: 6–7), institutions remain on a similar path for two main reasons:

> First, institutions are indivisible in that one certain element cannot be altered easily without disrupting other elements. This creates high sunk costs of change in institutions. Second, since actors have to adapt to the

opportunity set defined by the institutions, symbiotic relationships between the institutions and actors crystallize. Therefore, change normally takes the incremental shape of path dependency, as institutions predetermine and guide the mode and direction of their own alterations.

In other words, it is not easy to change one institution without changing a host of others, and at the same time, those working within organisations tend to become used to the ways in which things are done and are therefore are reluctant to change and are, indeed, not able to change behaviour or strategies easily. Employment relations systems in different countries thus tend to continue along a similar trajectory to that which they have historically followed.

APPLYING THEORY TO PRACTICE

Trade unions in different contexts

Katz *et al* (2008) compare the United States' industrial relations system with that in Japan and Germany. The United States has 'one of the lowest rates of unionisation of any advanced democratic economy', and over the past 30 years it has fallen more rapidly than that of any other advanced economy (*ibid*: 375). In addition, attitudes of managers and the government toward unions tend to be very negative, and unions are not closely tied to political parties (*ibid*).

However, the United States has become increasingly marked by a high trade deficit and social inequality. As a result, it has been compared negatively with countries such as Japan and Germany that, at least prior to 2008, had enjoyed continuous economic growth for over 40 years. According to some, a major contributor to this success has been the latter countries' industrial relations systems. Germany, for example, has continued to be defined by co-determination, involving employee representation on company boards, works councils, and strong collective bargaining (*ibid*).

What lessons, if any, can the United States draw from Germany and Japan? In answering this question you may wish to consider the role of trade unions, government and multinationals.

Do you anticipate any convergence over time in industrial relations systems? Give reasons for your answer.

UNDERTAKING COMPARATIVE RESEARCH

A whole host of reasons have been advanced for the differences that exist between countries. These include country size, cultural factors, economic concentration, political factors, management structure and strategy, forms of employee representation, and national vocational and educational arrangements (Clark *et al* 2000; Katz and Darbishire 2000; Poole 1986; Traxler *et al* 2001). Noting the methodological weaknesses in comparative research, Budhwar and Debrah (2001) developed a contextual model of factors determining national human resource management policies and practices (such as recruitment and selection, training and development, performance appraisals, pay and benefits and communication), which is not only useful in identifying the main determinants of human resource management but also facilitates cross-national comparisons.

A particular context is viewed as an outcome of the interplay of many complex factors and variables. They distinguish between an inner and outer context.

The *outer* context is divided into: (a) national culture – common values, norms of behaviour and customs, the influence of pressure groups, and assumptions that shape managers' perceptions and match to the organisational culture; (b) institutions – labour laws, trade unions, educational and vocational training set-up, labour market, professional bodies, international institutions, industry bodies, employers' federations and consulting organisations; (c) business environment – competition, business alliances, composition of the workforce, restructuring, focus on customer satisfaction, facility of information, technological change and globalisation of business; and (d) industrial sector – common strategies, business logic and goals, regulations and standards, sector-specific knowledge, formal and informal benchmarking, cross-sector co-operation, common developments in business operations and labour or skill requirements.

The *inner* context is divided into: (a) contingent variables – age, size, nature, life-cycle stage, level of technology, presence of unions, human resource strategies, business sector and different stakeholders' interests; and (b) organisational strategies and policies – primary human resource functions, internal labour markets, level of integration and devolvement, nature of work flexibility, prospector, analyser, defender or reactor.

While acknowledging that these factors are by no means exhaustive, Budhwar and Debrah (2001: 510) argue that different configurations of cultural, institutional, sector or business dynamic alter the specific impact that individual contingency factors have. Understanding the complex interactions and causal relationships between these different sets of national factors, contingent variables and organisational strategies play a vital role in highlighting the cross-national yet context-specific nature of human resource management in different settings.

Blanpain (2007: 12–16), meanwhile, lists a number of rules to guide comparative research. First, in order to compare factors that are comparable, employment relations scholars must focus on the functions that institutions perform rather than on the institutions themselves. Similar institutions (eg works councils and labour courts) may perform very different functions in different countries (Strauss 1998). Second, comparative scholars should find out 'what is going on'. It is therefore not sufficient merely to compare the terms of collective agreements or the provisions in labour legislation of different countries – this would not shed much light on the actual conduct of the employment relationship. To gain insight into the latter, attention must be focused on the processes of collective bargaining, rules in the workplace, tacit understandings, custom and practice, the practical application of legislation and the actual behaviour of the parties. Third, a particularly useful way of obtaining the benefits of comparative research is to construct 'models' of employment relations systems. A model refers to a distinctive way of conducting the employment relationship. This allows the comparative scholar to illustrate how a given model functions in different contexts, and to note differences and similarities between a particular system and available models (Katz and Darbishire 2000). Finally, the best way to reap the full benefits of a comparative analysis is to adopt a group-based approach to research. This ensures the best use of national expertise and knowledge.

Comparative research is a very demanding exercise. Not surprisingly, therefore, Clark *et al* (2000: 10) note that of the 20,287 journal articles they surveyed, 42% fail to offer any explanation for their results. Where explanations for differences or similarities are provided, they are primarily cultural (22%), institutional (19%), or a combination of the two (10%). Moreover, even when these factors are used, their precise nature is rarely explained. The field of comparative human resource management, according to Clark *et al* (2000: 11), lacks coherence and is ill-defined, is overly descriptive and lacks analytical rigour, shows little inclination to draw on relevant debates in other disciplines such as organisational theory, incorporates *ad hoc* research design and planning, and fails to develop viable case material.

Not only is comparative research extremely complex, time-consuming and resource-intensive, but there are also a number of pitfalls to avoid (Blanpain 2007: 16–18; Clark *et al* 2000: 13–17). A key problem is language and terminology. Identical words in different languages may have different meanings, while corresponding terms may entail wholly different meanings. Theoretical concepts, in particular, are laden with values and assumptions, and are often closely tied to a particular historical context. In fact, Cronin and Schneer argue against comparison altogether and suggest (cited in Hollinshead *et al* 2003: 37) that it

> presupposes some degree of comparability and thus similarity, and it may well be a mistake to assume that the experience of workers at different times and places is similar. Similarities might, of course, emerge empirically, but the assumption of similarity may pre-empt the discovery of crucial differences.

A second pitfall to avoid relates to parochialism and ideological orientation. The former is evident when a researcher is overly influenced by the employment relations system in his or her own country, and attempts to analyse another country's system by continuously evaluating it in the light of local experiences. Such ethnocentric views are often most clearly evident in the belief that one's own system should be a model for others (Budhwar and Debrah 2001). This leads to a universalist approach to research whereby instruments and measures developed in one cultural context are believed to be equally applicable in all other contexts. As a result, these studies are incapable of specifying the impact of cultural differences on the phenomena under investigation. In their survey of journal articles over a 20-year period, Clark *et al* (2000: 10) found that almost two-thirds were 'ethnocentric' (ie studies designed and conducted in one culture by researchers from that culture and then replicated in a second culture) in their methodological approach. This is perhaps not surprising given the fact that more than 90% of the authors were from the United States and the United Kingdom. Strongly held ideological beliefs may also hamper the exchange of ideas and a willingness to learn from experiences elsewhere. Comparative employment relations is unlikely to advance as a subject if it fails to acknowledge the importance of different national values, beliefs and priorities.

EMERGING ISSUES FROM INDIVIDUAL CHAPTERS

A number of themes run through this volume. Firstly, irrespective of the decline in union membership and density across many countries, various chapters have pointed toward *a first theme – namely the important role of trade unions in challenging neo-liberal ideology and in instilling fair and equitable work practices.* Chapter 2 began by summarising the functions of trade unions, but also indicated their broader role in terms of political engagement. Nevertheless, challenges were also highlighted, including the difficulty of trying to represent diverse constituencies and balance a range of interests, and attempting to determine the most appropriate strategies, whether these are organising or servicing models. In particular, attention was drawn to the declining formal workforce in emerging economies, and the need for unions to consider how best to represent an informal workforce. A further obstacle to union sustainability and indeed renewal are the variants of management styles existing within a variety of organisations and contexts, and the degrees of government intervention characterised by liberalist or corporatist states.

In Chapter 3, the key theories of industrial relations were outlined, referring here to 'industrial relations' rather than employment relations in order to accentuate the strong traditions of the subject area. Here, it was recognised that the field is multidisciplinary and, indeed, that an interesting feature of more recent debates has been the willingness of those adhering to different perspectives to engage in dialogue and to search for new syntheses. Nevertheless, this chapter highlights *a second theme that runs through the text – namely, the importance of labour process theories in capturing the nature of the organisation of work in a range of contexts.*

Chapter 4 continued to develop theoretical debates but moved on to address the distinction between employment relations and human resource management. In contrast to some other texts on employment relations, this chapter traced the historical development from industrial relations to employment relations, and the way in which human resource management has developed. In addition, it drew attention to how the study of employment relations can help to elucidate the tensions between challenges and response, co-operation and conflict, control and autonomy within the workplace.

A third key theme – that of the need to consider the international dimensions of employment relations – was highlighted in Chapter 5, with consideration of the impact of factors such as globalisation, technology and demographics on employment relations. It also engaged with the varieties of capitalism literature in drawing attention to differences and similarities between different types of system, and the influence of international-level legislation and institutions. In analysing employment relations within multinationals, the use of expatriates was assessed, and in particular the difficulties inherent in addressing their needs. A further highlight of this chapter was the relevance of global union federations in a globalising world, but also the way in which their work is impeded by a lack of resources and the moving goalposts of workforce diversity and migration.

Power and authority are central aspects of the employment relationship. Chapter

6 returned to the nature of the employment relationship through examining in more depth how management has asserted power through a range of mechanisms, and attempted to drive through change against different forms of resistance. Here it was emphasised that where employees regard change management programmes as attempts to achieve efficiency and flexibility at the expense of equity and security, managers are unlikely to secure their co-operation and compliance. *The theme of flexibility, equity and security could be regarded as a fourth major element* of this volume, and was returned to in later chapters.

Chapter 7 examined the issue of voice, covering a range of forms of communication and the nature of collective bargaining. It was noted that the range and scope of participation varies greatly from effective collective bargaining and/or co-decision-making in key areas of the production process through to limited communication and consultation. In Chapter 8 this issue was explored through the lens of employee engagement, highlighting the links between voice mechanisms and other HR practices and their relationship to organisational outcomes. The reference to emotional labour drew attention, however, to the way in which 'employee engagement' can be used to commodify labour, returning to labour process theory arguments set out in Chapter 3. As mentioned in the chapter summary, workers must be engaged in practice through trust relationships rather than simply being persuaded to *show* that they are engaged.

In Chapter 9, pay and reward systems were assessed. As was explained, the amount of pay and rewards and the manner in which they are delivered are central to understanding employment relationships and related to the balance of power within the workplace. Returning to the issue of equity that formed a central theme in Chapter 6, it was noted that wage rates reflect the relative commitment of the employer to fairness and equity, and the ability of employees to promote it. A striking feature is that within liberal market economies there has been increasing inequality in earnings since the 1970s.

Chapter 10 continued the theme of equity through examining discrimination, difference and diversity, where it was found that certain forms of inequality have proved to be highly durable. One reason for this is the tendency of organisations to seek short-term benefits from discriminatory practices, while another is the lack of enforcement of anti-discrimination, particularly within emerging economies.

The importance of adhering to legislation was continued in Chapter 11 on discipline and grievance, although here reference was made to concerns around mitigating organisational risk. At the same time it was noted that the operation of disciplinary and grievance procedures can only be understood from a perspective that takes account of power, conflict and equity.

Chapter 12 examined conflict and dispute resolution, and reiterated the point that no workplace is conflict-free. The chapter elucidated different explanations of conflict and also pointed towards the need for appropriate mechanisms for conciliation, arbitration and mediation.

In Chapter 13 on downsizing and redundancy, the issues of flexibility, security and equity reappeared. The chapter engaged with theoretical debates and practical solutions, and reiterated the need for HR practitioners to consider the longer-term impacts of downsizing and redundancy on employee welfare, productivity and future competitiveness.

Finally, Chapter 14 has highlighted the importance of international employment relations and the challenges of conducting comparative research, at the same time indicating the need for further research that examines trends towards convergence and divergence and also in-depth exploration of work processes within nation-states.

SUMMARY

No book on employment relations is ever complete, and space constraints preclude additional detail in the areas of theory, union renewal, and the relationship between regulation, corporate governance and the employment relationship. Indeed, while we have sought to equip the reader (whether already engaged in, or in pursuit of, a planned career in HR management, unions, government or NGOs) with a broad understanding of the practices of the employment relationship and exposure to specific national dynamics, we hope above all that this book has kindled a greater intellectual curiosity, afforded more critical applied insights and inspired a commitment to advancing the field, whether in terms of ideas or of practice.

EXPLORE FURTHER

Reading

- Brewster, C., Sparrow, P. and Vernon, G. (2007) *International Human Resource Management*. London: CIPD

- Harzing, A.-W. and Van Ruysseveldt, J. (2006) *International Human Resource Management*. London: Sage

- Hollinshead, G. *et al* (2010) *International and Comparative Human Resource Management*. London: McGraw-Hill

- Morley, M., Gunnigle, P. and Collings, D. (eds) (2006) *Global Industrial Relations*. London: Routledge

Glossary

Arbitration: a process that involves third-party adjudication in a dispute. The arbitrator actively intervenes in the dispute and makes a decision (in the form of an arbitration award) on the terms of settlement of the dispute. The arbitrator's decision is final and binding on the parties concerned.

Authority: the power and responsibility to make decisions or act on behalf of others.

Bargaining level: the level at which collective bargaining takes place, which could be plant-, corporate-, sector-, industry- or national-level. Bargaining level therefore refers to the level of negotiations between employers and trade unions.

Bargaining range: the range of issues subject to joint regulation through collective bargaining. Bargaining range refers to the scope of negotiations between employers and trade unions (or other employee representatives).

Bargaining structure: the processes and mechanisms, agreed upon between the parties, through which collective bargaining takes place.

Bargaining unit: the composition of the group or type of employees who are to be covered by an agreement between the trade union and the employer. A union always seeks recognition for, and bargains on behalf of, a specified group of employees who normally share similar terms and conditions of employment.

Business unionism: a narrow and largely conservative approach to trade union functions, directed primarily at protecting and advancing the immediate economic interests of union members rather than engaging in broader struggles for economic, social and political change.

Class conflict: the various forms of struggle between social groupings that differ with regard to their command of economic resources and access to political power.

Collective agreement: an outcome of the processes of collective bargaining, which involves a formal agreement drawn up and signed by representatives of the employer and the trade union (or other employee representatives). Bargaining can be distinguished from negotiation in terms of the distinction between structure and process. Whereas bargaining is essentially concerned with the structure of the relationship between the parties, negotiation is the process through which it is achieved.

Collective bargaining: one of the primary functions of a trade union (or, at a lesser scale, other employee representatives), which involves attempts to improve the economic position of its members and to establish their terms and conditions of employment through formal negotiations with employer representatives.

Complementarities thesis: the proposition that high-performance practices complement each other, in the sense that whereas each practice may produce positive effects on its own, these effects are augmented when it is implemented in combination with other practices.

Conciliation: endeavour by the parties to an industrial dispute to settle a dispute prior to resorting to industrial action. Conciliation is an extension of the negotiating process and is an integral part of the dispute resolution procedure. The aim of conciliation is to allow the parties to settle the dispute between themselves with only minimal intervention by a third party.

Conflict: the situation when one party's pursuit of its interests, objectives and expectations clashes with that of another party.

Consultation: coming together to seek information or advice from someone without implying any kind of final agreement (whereas negotiation is geared towards the step-by-step formulation of an agreement).

Control: the degree to which various sources of influence are deployed by one party in an attempt to ensure that the behaviour and views of another party will conform to the goals or interests of the first party.

Convergence thesis: the claim that the process of industrialisation produces common and uniform political, social and cultural characteristics in societies.

Co-operation: the joint and collaborative functioning of (for example) workforce and management to produce particular goods and services, their conduct governed by an agreed system of rules to which each party expects the other to adhere.

Corporatism: national-level structures that incorporate business and labour into the policy processes of the state.

Disputes of interest: disputes in which a party has a distinct interest but no enforceable right (such as a right to improved wages and conditions of employment). Interest disputes are most often resolved through mediation or ultimately a trial of strength (ie industrial action).

Disputes of right: disputes in which established or existing rights are questionably interfered with or ignored. Such a right might accrue through a contract of employment, arbitration award, court judgment, legislation or a collective agreement. Because disputes of right concern the interpretation or application of an existing right, they are suitable for third-party adjudication. Industrial action is often ruled out on these disputes.

Dispute resolution procedure: a procedure agreed between the employer and a trade union to be followed in the event of a dispute. Such procedures are invoked if and when the negotiations between the parties reaches a deadlock. Deadlock-breaking mechanisms are normally contained in a recognition agreement or a statute, and their use is often a precondition for embarking on lawful industrial action.

Distributive bargaining: style of bargaining in which an employer seeks to give as little as possible while the union tries to gain as much as possible. Under these conditions, the most likely outcome is a win/lose situation.

Employee involvement schemes: management-instituted programmes designed to encourage employees' greater commitment to their work by allowing them to exchange ideas on how to improve working conditions and product quality.

Employers' associations: groups of employers' representatives who associate together for the primary purpose of regulating relations between their principals and employees or trade unions. The main task of an employers' organisation is to promote and protect common employer interests.

Fairness: a clear sense of balance and reciprocity between parties, in common dealings, negotiations or awards involving an equitable exchange in terms of substance, behaviour and procedure. To be 'fair', the actions of the parties should be commensurate with 'impartial judgement' and 'universal standards'. The notion of 'fairness' introduces equity-based considerations into labour law. That is, the courts go beyond merely asking whether the employer acted lawfully to enquire whether the action was fair – that is, not capricious, arbitrary or inconsistent.

Flexible employment: employment arrangements that provide employers with greater discretion in the assignment and allocation of work and pay (and sometimes provides employees with greater possibilities for work–life balance). It may, however, involve the extensive use of temporary and part-time employees, outsourcing and contingent pay systems.

Fordism: a system prevalent in developed countries during the pre- and post-war era, under which a virtuous cycle of economic growth was achieved by providing employees with wage increases tied to productivity gains, thereby ensuring demand for their output. However, the output was for the most part simultaneously linked with mass production assembly lines or similar compartmentalised work.

Freedom of association: a right which recognises that employers and employees may choose to associate or not to associate with any third-party organisation.

High-commitment management: a form of managerial practice in which the employer seeks to achieve high performance through job redesign, reformed employment practices and employee involvement aimed at maximising employee motivation and commitment.

Industrial action: the use of power by a trade union or management in an attempt to pressurise the other party into continued bargaining or the acceptance of a demand. It includes strikes and lock-outs as well as partial disruptions to the employer's operations such as go-slows and overtime bans.

Internal labour market: a job allocation system or job ladder within a workplace that provides employees with the opportunity to advance without having to seek employment elsewhere.

Intra-organisational bargaining: a critical component of the collective bargaining process for both trade unions and management, undertaken by members of the same organisation or grouping in an attempt to achieve a united and defensible approach to negotiations.

Integrative bargaining: bargaining that occurs when the aim is not to persuade one party to give up something but to get both parties to take action to achieve a common goal. In these circumstances, the most likely outcome is a win/win situation.

Just-in-time inventory: a system that allows firms to reduce inventory levels by arranging to have the required inputs delivered as and when needed. It not only minimises inventory build-ups within the production process but also facilitates the scheduling of work so that goods are completed only as they are needed by customers.

Labour process theory: a school of thought closely associated with the radical perspective on employee relations, which suggests that management's primary objective under capitalism is to minimise skill requirements and/or maximise control over employees.

Legitimation: the process by which management attempts to exercise its authority in a manner that elicits the voluntary compliance or consent of the employees over whom that authority is exercised.

Lock-out: the exclusion by an employer of employees from his or her workplace for the purpose of compelling the employees to accept a demand in respect of any matter of mutual interest between the parties. Lock-outs are designed to place pressure on employees to accept the employer's terms of settlement and represent a counter-balancing mechanism to an employee's right to engage in strike action.

Mandate: a position of authority granted to a person or group of people to act on behalf of others. In the negotiation process, a mandate is usually defined as the point beyond which representatives cannot move without going back for further authority to their constituency.

Mediation: the active intervention of a third party or parties for the purpose of achieving settlement of a dispute between the parties. The role of the mediator is to advise, act as intermediary, ensure the continuation of negotiations and suggest possible solutions to both parties. A mediator has no decision-making power and cannot impose a settlement on either party.

Multi-skilling: the training of employees in a wider variety of skills than those required for their own jobs, making them able to do different jobs and to acquire a broader understanding of the production process.

Negotiation: in employment relations, the interpersonal process used by representatives of management and employees, within the various institutional arrangements of collective bargaining, in order to resolve their differences and reach agreement. The definitions put forward in the employee relations literature have the following in common: (a) negotiation is a process (b) in which two or more parties with a direct stake in the issues under discussion (c) strive through the exchange and structuring of information to come to an effective agreement

(d) on a common problem or conflict that exists between them, (e) the outcome of which is dependent, in part, on the relative power relationships between the principals (on behalf of whom the representatives are negotiating).

Operational requirements: the requirements based on the economic, technological, structural or similar needs of an employer.

Outsourcing: the use of 'outside' workers, who are often employed by a third party, to perform work that the firm's own employees have previously carried out but that can in this way be carried out (at least temporarily) more economically.

Overtime ban: a general refusal by the employees collectively to perform overtime work, often accompanied by a demand that the employer changes or restores certain work practices and/or conditions.

Pattern bargaining: bargaining by a union in a specific sector of industry when a generally favourable agreement between an employer in the same industry and another union or unions has set a precedent for further agreements. This may influence trends in that industry and is an attempt by the unions to develop uniformity over time.

Performance-based pay system: a personnel practice that links pay to individual or group performance.

Picketing: a method by which striking workers publicise their action and encourage others to join them through the medium of moral persuasion such as the display of placards and verbal discussion. The 'picket line' refers to a formation of picketers formerly designed (but no longer permitted) to prevent the passage of persons or goods to and from the workplace. The purpose of a picket line is usually to peacefully promote the effectiveness of the strike action.

Power: the capacity effectively to direct the behaviour and/or outcomes of others.

Procedure: a written operational mechanism (generally in steps or stages) that details and regulates the manner in which a specified issue is handled. For example, a disciplinary procedure sets out the manner in which disciplinary matters are to be conducted.

Psychological contract: unwritten expectations and understandings that have evolved over time and that are additional to and implied by the written contract of employment.

Quality circles: human resource management participation schemes that involve workers discussing any problems or concerns they have in the workplace and putting forward ideas on how these may be addressed, in an effort to enhance quality.

Radical perspective: the ideological belief that, under capitalism, the interests of labour and those of capital are diametrically opposed, and that workers are at an inherent disadvantage in relation to management, irrespective of whether or not they belong to a trade union.

Recognition agreement: an agreement between an employer and a trade union whereby the former grants the right to collectively bargain to the latter. Such an agreement normally sets out the framework and parameters of the relationship between the parties. It is an acknowledgement by the firm that the union represents a significant number (usually the majority of a bargaining unit) of its employees for the purposes of collective bargaining. The form of recognition required by a union and granted by an employer can vary and is shaped by (among other things) the extent of union membership and the size of the enterprise.

Secondary strike: a strike, or action in furtherance of a strike, that takes place on the premises of an employer who already has strike action being taken against it by the same or an allied union, or on the premises of an associated but independent employer. Such action is almost inevitably illegal, especially if the primary employer is a local council authority.

Shop steward: a lay or part-time official who represents the union members who elected him or her to voice their interests on specific workplace matters.

Strategic choice theory: a model of employee relations that emphasises the role of values and beliefs in shaping managerial choices, and disputes the assumption that managerial actions are determined by the context in which they take place.

Strike: the partial or complete concerted refusal to work (including voluntary or compulsory overtime), or the retardation or obstruction of work, by persons who are employed by the same employer (or by different but associated employers) for the purpose of remedying a grievance or resolving a dispute in respect of any matter of mutual interest between employer and employee. The legal aspects – particularly on pay during strikes and on measures that may be taken by both parties in furtherance of the strike or in terminating the strike – are specific and well documented.

Suggestion scheme: an information-sharing practice under which employees may (or may not) receive some form of reward if they contribute a suggestion that enhances performance in the workplace.

Total quality management: human resource management programmes that are designed to secure improvements in all aspects of quality, and that are based on the belief that quality is the responsibility of all employees rather than specific individuals or departments.

Trade union: an association of employees whose principal purpose is to regulate relations between employees and employers (and employers' associations).

Voluntarism: the minimal state intervention in the conduct of the employment relationship beyond the establishment and maintenance of certain institutional mechanisms. Where voluntarism prevails, the state sets enabling legislation and allows the parties to the employment relationship to establish their own collective bargaining and dispute resolution mechanisms.

Wage–effort bargain: the comparative level, within a country or an organisation, that may be expected of the exchange between an employer's wages or salary offered in return for the employee's work and discretionary diligence.

Work-to-rule: a form of industrial action which involves employees doing their work only in accordance with conditions specifically stated in their contracts of employment. This can severely hamper the operations of the enterprise, especially if employees customarily perform their tasks under their own initiative and/or do more than is strictly required.

Works councils: workplace-level committees of employee representatives with information-sharing, consultation and joint decision-making rights over production issues.

References

CHAPTER 1

AFRICAN DEVELOPMENT BANK/ORGANISATION FOR ECONOMIC CO-OPERATION AND DEVELOPMENT (AfDB/OECD) (2008) *African Economic Outlook*; online at http://www.oecd.org/dataoecd/13/6/40578303.pdf [accessed 24 November 2009].

BELLACE, J. (1994) 'The role of the state in industrial relations', in J. Niland, R. Lansbury and C. Verevis (eds) *The Future of Industrial Relations: Global change and challenges*. Thousand Oaks, CA: Sage Publications.

BLYTON, P. and TURNBULL, P. (1998) *The Dynamics of Employee Relations*, 2nd edition. London: Macmillan.

BRYSON, A., GOMEZ, R. and WILLMAN, P. (2006) 'Voice at work … what do employees want?', *Socio-Economic Review*, Vol.4, No.2: 279–82.

BUDD, J., GOLLAN, P. and WILKINSON, A. (2009) 'New approaches to employee voice and participation in organizations', *Human Relations*, Vol.63, No.3: 1–8.

CHARLWOOD, A. (2006) 'What determined employer voice choice in Britain in the twentieth century?', *Socio-Economic Review*, Vol.4, No.2: 301–10.

COLLINGS, D. (2008) 'Multinational corporations and industrial relations research: a road less travelled', *International Journal of Management Reviews*, Vol.10, No.2: 173–93.

COLLINGS, D. and WOOD, G. (2009) *Human Resource Management: A critical approach*. London: Routledge.

DANIELS, K. (2006) *Employee Relations in an Organisational Context*. London: CIPD.

DIBBEN, P. (2010) 'Trade union change, development and renewal in emerging economies: the case of Mozambique', *Work, Employment and Society*, Vol.24, No.3: 468–86.

DIBBEN, P., JAMES, P., ROPER, I. and WOOD, G. (eds) (2007) *Modernising Work in Public Services*. London: Palgrave.

EDWARDS, P. (1995) *Industrial Relations: Theory and practice in Britain*. Oxford: Blackwell.

EUROPEAN FOUNDATION FOR THE IMPROVEMENT OF LIVING AND WORKING CONDITIONS (2007) 'Industrial relations in the public sector'; online at http://www.eurofound.eu.int [accessed 15 October 2010].

GOLLAN, P. (2009) 'Employer strategies towards non-union collective voice', in A. Wilkinson, P. Gollan, M. Marchington and D. Lewin (eds) *Oxford Handbook of Participation in Organizations*. Oxford: Oxford University Press.

GRIMSHAW, D., WARD, K., RUBERY, J. and BEYNON, H. (2001) 'Organisations and the transformation of the internal labour market', *Work, Employment and Society*, Vol.15, No.1: 25–54.

GUEST, D. and CONWAY, N. (2002) *Pressure at Work and the Psychological Contract*. London: CIPD.

HYMAN, R. (1989) *The Political Economy of Industrial Relations*. London: Macmillan.

HYMAN, R. (1994a) 'Theory and industrial relations', *British Journal of Industrial Relations*, Vol.32, No.2: 165–80.

HYMAN, R. (1994b) 'Changing trade union identities and strategies', in R. Hyman and A. Ferner (eds) *New Frontiers in European Industrial Relations*. Oxford: Blackwell.

LITTLER, C. (1982) *The Development of the Labour Process in Capitalist Societies*. London: Heinemann.

LONTI, Z. and VERMA, A. (2004) 'Canadian public management developments', in P. Dibben, G. Wood and I. Roper (eds) *Contesting Public Sector Reforms: Critical perspectives, international debates*. London: Palgrave.

MARSDEN, D. (1999) *A Theory of Employment Systems: Micro-foundations of societal diversity*. Oxford: Oxford University Press.

MICHON, F. (1992) 'The institutional forms of work and employment', in A. Castro, P. Méhaut and J. Rubery (eds) *International Integration and Labour Market Organisation*. London: Academic Press.

MORLEY, M., GUNNIGLE, P. and COLLINGS, D. (eds) (2006) *Global Industrial Relations*. London: Routledge.

NIETO, M. L. (2006) *An Introduction to Human Resource Management*. London: Palgrave.

PECK, J. (1996) *Work-Place: The social regulation of labor markets*. New York: Guilford Press.

PERLMUTTER, H. (1969) 'The tortuous evolution of the multinational corporation', *Columbia Journal of World Business*, Vol.4, No.1: 9–18.

PICCIOTTO, S. (2002) 'Introduction: reconceptualizing regulation in the era of globalization', in S. Picciotto and D. Campbell (eds) *New Directions in Regulation Theory*. Oxford: Blackwell.

POLANYI, K. (1957) *The Great Transformation*. Boston, MA: Beacon Press.

POOLE, M. (1986) *Towards a New Industrial Democracy: Workers' participation in industry*. London: Routledge & Kegan Paul.

SALAMON, M. (1998) *Industrial Relations: Theory and practice*, 3rd edition. Hemel Hempstead: Prentice Hall.

STANDING, G. (1999) *Global Labour Flexibility: Seeking distributive justice.* London: Macmillan.

STREECK, W. (1992) *Social Institutions and Economic Performance: Studies of industrial relations in advanced capitalist economies.* London: Sage.

TARAS, D. and KAUFMAN, B. (2006) 'Non-union employee representation in North America: diversity, controversy, and uncertain future'. Andrew Young School of Policy Studies Research Paper Series, No.06–46. Atlanta: Georgia State University.

CHAPTER 2

ADLER, G. and WEBSTER, E. (eds) (2000) *Trade Unions and Democratization in South Africa, 1985–1997.* London: Macmillan.

BASKIN, J. (1995) 'The need for centralised (but flexible) bargaining', *South African Labour Bulletin*, Vol.19, No.1: 48–56.

BEAN, R. (1985) *Comparative Industrial Relations: An introduction to cross-national perspectives.* London: Croom Helm.

BELLACE, J. (1994) 'The role of the state in industrial relations', in J. Niland, R. Lansbury and C. Verevis (eds) *The Future of Industrial Relations: Global change and challenges.* Thousand Oaks, CA: Sage Publications.

BENDIX, S. (2000) *Industrial Relations in the New South Africa*, 3rd edition. Cape Town: Juta.

BHATTACHARJEA, A. (2006) 'Labour market regulation and economic performance in India'. Working Papers 146, Indian Council for Research on International Economic Relations. New Delhi: ICRIER.

BLYTON, P. and TURNBULL, P. (1998) *The Dynamics of Employee Relations*, 2nd edition. London: Macmillan.

BROOKES, M., HINKS, T., WOOD, G., DIBBEN, P. and ROPER, I. (2004) 'Pulled apart, pushed together: diversity and unity within the Congress of South African Trade Unions', *Relations Industrielles/Industrial Relations*, Vol.59, No.4: 769–92.

BURCHILL, F. (1997) *Labour Relations*, 2nd edition. London: Macmillan.

CHEN, S.-J., KO, R. and LAWLER, J. (2003) 'Changing patterns of industrial relations in Taiwan', *Industrial Relations*, Vol.42, No.3: 315–40.

CROUCH, C. (1982) *Trade Unions: The logic of collective action.* London: Fontana.

DARLINGTON, R. (1994) *The Dynamics of Workplace Unionism: Shop stewards' organization in three Merseyside plants.* London: Mansell.

DIBBEN, P. (2004) 'Social movement unionism', in G. Wood and M. Harcourt (eds) *Trade Unions and Democracy.* Manchester: Manchester University Press.

DIBBEN, P. (2007) 'Industrial relations and employment insecurity in South Africa', in G. Wood and C. Brewster, *Industrial Relations in South Africa*. London: Palgrave.

DIBBEN, P. (2010) 'Union change, development and renewal in emerging economies: the case of Mozambique', *Work, Employment and Society*, Vol.24, No.3: 468–86.

DIBBEN, P. and NADIN, S. (2010) 'Trade unions and informal sector organisations'. Labour Movements Research Committee RC-44, International Sociological Association Congress, July 2010.

DIBBEN, P., WOOD, G., I. ROPER and JAMES, P. (2007) *Modernising Work in Public Services*. London: Palgrave.

DURKHEIM, E. (1969) *The Division of Labor in Society*. New York: Free Press.

EDWARDS, P. (ed.) (2003) *Industrial Relations: Theory and practice*, 2nd edition. Oxford: Blackwell.

FARNHAM, D. and PIMLOTT, J. (1983) *Understanding Industrial Relations*, 2nd edition. London: Cassell.

FLANDERS, A. (1968) 'Collective bargaining: a theoretical analysis', *British Journal of Industrial Relations*, Vol.6, No.2: 1–26.

FREEMAN, R. and MEDOFF, J. (1984) *What Do Unions Do?* New York: Basic Books.

GAHAN, P. (2006) 'Trade unions as regulators: theoretical and empirical perspectives', in C. Arup, C., P. Gahan, J. Howe, R. Johnstone, R. Mitchell and A. O'Donnell (eds) *Labour Law and Labour Market Regulation*. Sydney: Federation Press.

GENNARD, J. and JUDGE, G. (2010) *Managing Employment Relations*. London: CIPD.

GERTH, H. and MILLS, C. (1977) *From Max Weber: Essays in sociology*. London: Routledge & Kegan Paul.

GODARD, J. (2006) 'The US and Canadian labour movements: markets vs. states and societies', in M. Harcourt and G. Wood (eds) *Trade Unions and Democracy*. Manchester: Manchester University Press.

GOLDTHORPE, J., LOCKWOOD, D., BECHHOFER, F. and PLATT, J. (1968) *The Affluent Worker: Industrial attitudes and behaviour*. Cambridge: Cambridge University Press.

GROSSETT, M. and VENTER, R. (1998) *Labour Relations in South Africa*. Johannesburg: International Thompson.

HARCOURT, M. and WOOD, G. (eds) (2004) *Trade Unions and Democracy: Strategies and perspectives*. Manchester: Manchester University Press.

HYMAN, R. (1992) 'Trade unions and the disaggregation of the working class', in M. Regini (ed.) *The Future of Labour Movements*. London: Sage.

HYMAN, R. (1996) 'Changing union identities in Europe', in P. Leisink, J. van Leemput and J. Vilrokx (eds) *The Challenge to Trade Unions in Europe: Innovation or adaptation*. Cheltenham: Edward Elgar.

JACKSON, M. (1991) *An Introduction to Industrial Relations*. London: Routledge.

KELLY, J. (1998) *Rethinking Industrial Relations: Mobilization, collectivism and long waves*. London: Routledge.

MARX, K. (1967) *Capital: A critique of political economy*. New York: International Press.

MICHELS, R. (1966) *Political Parties*. New York: Free Press.

PECK, J. (1996) *Work-place: The social regulation of labor markets*. New York: Guilford Press.

PURCELL, J. (1987) 'Mapping management styles in employee relations', *Journal of Management Studies*, Vol.24, No.5: 533–48.

PURCELL, J. and SISSON, K. (1983) 'Strategies and practice in the management of industrial relations', in G. Bain (ed.) *Industrial Relations in Britain*. Oxford: Blackwell.

SALAMON, M. (1998) *Industrial Relations: Theory and practice*, 3rd edition. Hemel Hempstead: Prentice Hall.

SISSON, K. (1983) 'Employers' organisations', in G. Bain (ed.) *Industrial Relations in Britain*. Oxford: Blackwell.

STANDING, G. (1993) 'Labor regulation in an era of fragmented flexibility', in C. Buechtemann (ed.) *Employment Security and Labor Market Behavior*. Ithaca, NY: ILR Press.

TAYLOR, A. (1989) *Trade Unions and Politics: A comparative introduction*. London: Macmillan.

VON HOLDT, K. (1992) 'What is the future of labour?', *South African Labour Bulletin*, Vol.16, No.8: 30–7.

VON HOLDT, K. (1995) 'The dangers of corporatism', *South African Labour Bulletin*, Vol.17, No.1: 46–51.

WEBSTER, E. (1988) 'The rise of social-movement unionism: the two faces of the black trade union movement in South Africa', in P. Frankel, N. Pines and M. Swilling (eds) *State, Resistance and Change in South Africa*. Johannesburg: Southern Book Publishers.

WOOD, G. and DIBBEN, P. (2008) 'The challenges facing the South African labour movement: mobilization of diverse constituencies in a changing political and economic context', *Industrial Relations/Relations Industrielles*, Vol.63, No.4.

CHAPTER 3

ALLEN, V. (1971) *The Sociology of Industrial Relations*. London: Longman.

BATSTONE, E. (1988) *The Reform of Workplace Industrial Relations: Theory, myth and evidence*. Oxford: Clarendon Press.

BAUDRILLARD, J. (1990) *Revenge of the Crystal*. London: Pluto.

BEYNON, H. (1984) *Working for Ford*. Harmondsworth: Penguin.

BLYTON, P. and TURNBULL, P. (1998) *The Dynamics of Employee Relations*, 2nd edition. London: Macmillan.

BRANNIGAN, T. (2010) 'Ninth worker falls to death at Foxconn's Shenzhen plant in China', the *Guardian*, 25 May 2010; available online at http://www.guardian. co.uk/ world/2010/may/25/foxconn-ninth-worker-death-fall-china

BRAVERMAN, H. (1974) *Labor and Monopoly Capital: The degradation of work in the twentieth century*. New York: Monthly Review Press.

BROTHERTON, C. (2003) 'Social psychology and industrial relations', in P. Ackers and A. Wilkinson (eds) *Understanding Work and Employment: Industrial relations in transition*. Oxford: Oxford University Press.

BURAWOY, M. (1985) *The Politics of Production: Factory regimes under capitalism and socialism*. London: Verso.

CLEGG, H. (1979) *The Changing System of Industrial Relations in Great Britain*. Oxford: Blackwell.

DUNLOP, J. (1958) *Industrial Relations Systems*. New York: Holt.

DURKHEIM, E. (1957) *Professional Ethics and Civic Morals*. London: Routledge & Kegan Paul.

EDWARDS, P. (1986) *Conflict at Work: A materialist analysis of workplace relations*. Oxford: Blackwell.

EDWARDS, P. (1995) *Industrial Relations: Theory and practice in Britain*. Oxford: Blackwell.

EDWARDS, P. (ed.) (2003) *Industrial Relations: Theory and practice*, 2nd edition. Oxford: Blackwell.

ETZIONI, A. (1995) *The Spirit of Community: Rights, responsibilities, and the communitarian agenda*. London: Fontana.

FARNHAM, D. and PIMLOTT, J. (1983) *Understanding Industrial Relations*, 2nd edition. London: Cassell.

FELLS, R. (1989) 'The employment relationship: control and strategic choice in the study of industrial relations', *Labour and Industry*, Vol.2, No.3: 470–92.

FOUCAULT, M. (1988) 'On power', in L. Kritzman (ed.) *Foucault: Politics, philosophy, culture*. New York: Routledge.

FOX, A. (1966) 'Industrial sociology and industrial relations'. Royal Commission Research Paper No.3. London: HMSO.

FOX, A. (1974) *Beyond Contract: Work, power and trust relations*. London: Faber & Faber.

HARCOURT, M. and S., and WOOD, G. (2004) 'Do unions affect employer compliance with the law?', *British Journal of Industrial Relations*, Vol.42, No.3: 527–41.

HARVEY, D. (2003) *The New Imperialism*. Oxford: Oxford University Press.

HIRST, P. and ZEITLIN, J. (2001) 'Flexible specialization versus post-Fordism', in B. Jessop (ed.) *Regulationist Perspectives on Fordism and PostFordism*. Regulation Theory and the Crisis of Capitalism Vol.3. London: Edward Elgar.

HYMAN, R. (1975) *Industrial Relations: A Marxist introduction*. London: Macmillan.

HYMAN, R. (1987) 'Strategy or structure: capital, labour and control', *Work, Employment and Society*, Vol 1, No.1: 25–55.

HYMAN, R. (1989) *The Political Economy of Industrial Relations*. London: Macmillan.

HYMAN, R. (1994) 'Theory and industrial relations', *British Journal of Industrial Relations*, Vol.32, No.2: 165–80.

JAROS, S. (2010) 'The core theory: critiques, defences and advances', in P. Thompson and C. Smith (eds) *Working Life – Renewing labour process analysis*. London: Palgrave.

KALLEBERG, A. L. (2009) 'Precarious work, insecure workers: employment relations in transition', *American Sociological Review*, Vol. 74: 1–22.

KELLY, J. (1998) *Rethinking Industrial Relations: Mobilization, collectivism and long waves*. London: Routledge.

KNIGHTS, D. and WILLMOTT, H. (eds) (1988) *New Technology and the Labour Process*. London: Routledge.

KNIGHTS, D., WILLMOTT, H. and COLLINS, D. (eds) (1985) *Job Redesign*. Aldershot: Gower.

KRIPPNER, G. (2005) 'The financialization of the American economy', *Socio-Economic Review*, Vol.3, No.2: 173–208.

LA PORTA, R., LOPEZ-DE-SILANES, F., SHLEIFER, A. and VISHNY, R. (2000) 'Investor protection and corporate governance', *Journal of Financial Economics*, Vol.58: 3–27.

MACEWAN, A. (1999) *Neo-liberalism or Democracy?* London: Zed.

MARSDEN, R. (1982) 'Industrial relations: a critique of empiricism', *Sociology*, Vol.16, No.2: 232–50.

MOODY, K. (1997) *Workers in a Lean World*. London: Verso.

PAREKH, B. (1982) *Contemporary Political Thinkers*. Oxford: Martin Robertson.

POSTER, M. (1984) *Foucault, Marxism and History*. Oxford: Blackwell.

RUBERY, J. and GRIMSHAW, D. (2003) *The Organisation of Employment: An international perspective*. Basingstoke: Palgrave Macmillan.

SALAMON, M. (1998) *Industrial Relations: Theory and practice*, 3rd edition. Hemel Hempstead: Prentice Hall.

SCHIENSTOCK, G. (1981) 'Towards a theory of industrial relations', *British Journal of Industrial Relations*, Vol.19, No.2: 170–89.

SHALEV, M. (1980) 'Industrial relations theory and the comparative study of industrial relations and industrial conflict', *British Journal of Industrial Relations*, Vol.18, No.1: 26–43.

SHERIDAN, A. (1990) *Michel Foucault: The will to truth*. London: Routledge.

STURDY, A., KNIGHTS, D. and WILLMOTT, H. (eds) (1992) *Skill and Consent*. London: Routledge.

THOMPSON, P. (1989) *The Nature of Work: An introduction to debates on the labour process*, 2nd edition. London: Macmillan.

THOMPSON, P. and MCHUGH, D. (1990) *Work Organisations: A critical introduction*. London: Macmillan.

THOMPSON, P. and MCHUGH, D. (2009) *Work Organizations: A critical approach*, 4th edition. London: Palgrave.

THOMPSON, P. and SMITH, C. (2010) *Working Life – Renewing labour process analysis*. London: Palgrave.

WALTON, R. and MCKERSIE, R. (1965) *A Behavioural Theory of Labour Negotiations*. New York: McGraw-Hill.

WOOD, S., WAGNER, A., ARMSTRONG, E., GOODMAN, J. and DAVIS, J. (1975) 'The industrial relations system concept as a basis for theory in industrial relations', *British Journal of Industrial Relations*, Vol.13, No.3: 291–308.

CHAPTER 4

ACKERS, P., MARCHINGTON, M., WILKINSON, A. and GOODMAN, J. (1992) 'The use of cycles? Explaining employee involvement in the 1990s', *Industrial Relations Journal*, Vol.23, No.4: 268–83.

BACON, N. (2003) 'Human resource management and industrial relations', in P. Ackers and A. Wilkinson (eds) *Understanding Work and Employment: Industrial relations in transition*. Oxford: Oxford University Press.

BAIN, G. and CLEGG, H. (1974) 'A strategy for industrial relations research in Great Britain', *British Journal of Industrial Relations*, Vol.12, No.1: 91–113.

BARKER, K. and CHRISTENSEN (eds) *Contingent Work: American employment relations in transition*. Ithaca, NY: ILR Press.

BÉLANGER, J. (1994) 'Job controls under different labor relations regimes: a comparison of Canada and Great Britain', in J. Bélanger, P. Edwards and L. Haiven (eds) *Workplace Industrial Relations and the Global Challenge*. Ithaca, NY: ILR Press.

BLYTON, P. and TURNBULL, P. (1998) *The Dynamics of Employee Relations*, 2nd edition. London: Macmillan.

BROWN, W. and NOLAN, P. (1988) 'Wages and labour productivity', *British Journal of Industrial Relations*, Vol.26, No.3: 339–61.

BRYSON, A., GOMEZ, R. and WILLMAN, P. (2006) 'Voice at work…what do employees want?', *Socio-Economic Review*, Vol.4, No.2: 279–82.

BUDD, J., GOLLAN, P. and WILKINSON, A. (2009) 'New approaches to employee voice and participation in organizations', *Human Relations*, Vol.63, No.3: 1–8.

CRESSEY, P., ELDRIDGE, J. and MACINNES, J. (1985) *'Just Managing': Authority and democracy in industry*. Milton Keynes: Open University Press.

CROMPTON, R., GALLIE, D. and PURCELL, K. (1996) 'Work, economic restructuring and social regulation', in R. Crompton, D. Gallie and K. Purcell (eds) *Changing Forms of Employment: Organisation, skills and gender*. London: Macmillan.

DANFORD, A. (1997) 'The "new industrial relations" and class struggle in the 1990s', *Capital and Class*, Vol.61: 107–41.

DAVIES, M. and RYNER, M. (eds) (2006) *Poverty and the Production of World Politics: Unprotected workers in the global political economy*. Basingstoke: Palgrave.

DELBRIDGE, R. and TURNBULL, P. (1992) 'Human resource maximization: the management of labour under just-in-time manufacturing systems', in P. Blyton and P. Turnbull (eds) *Reassessing Human Resource Management*. London: Sage.

EDWARDS, P. (1995) *Industrial Relations: Theory and practice in Britain*. Oxford: Blackwell.

EDWARDS, P. (2003) 'The future of industrial relations', in P. Ackers and A. Wilkinson (eds) *Understanding Work and Employment: Industrial relations in transition*. Oxford: Oxford University Press.

ELGER, T. (1990) 'Technical innovation and work reorganization in British manufacturing in the 1980s: continuity, intensification or transformation?', *Work, Employment and Society*, Vol.4, No.1: 815–58.

FELSTEAD, A. and JEWSON, H. (eds) (1999) *Global Trends in Flexible Labour.* London: Macmillan.

FROST, A. (2008) 'The high performance work systems literature in industrial relations', in P. Blyton, N. Bacon, J. Fiorito and E. Heery (eds) *The Sage Handbook of Industrial Relations*. London: Sage.

FUCINI, J. and FUCINI, S. (1990) *Working for the Japanese: Inside Mazda's American auto plant*. New York: Free Press.

GALLIE, D. and WHITE, M. (1994) 'Employer policies, employee contracts, and labour-market structure', in J. Rubery and F. Wilkinson (eds) *Employer Strategy and the Labour Market*. Oxford: Oxford University Press.

GALLIE, D., WHITE, M., CHENG, Y. and TOMLINSON, M. (1998) *Restructuring the Employment Relationship*. Oxford: Clarendon Press.

GARRAHAN, P. and STEWART, P. (1992) 'Management control and a new regime of subordination', in N. Gilbert, R. Burrows and A. Pollert (eds) *Fordism and Flexibility: Divisions and change*. London: Macmillan

GEARY, J. (1994) 'Task participation: employees' participation enabled or constrained?', in K. Sisson (ed.) *Personnel Management*. Oxford: Blackwell.

GUEST, D. (1987) 'Human resource management and industrial relations', *Journal of Management Studies*, Vol.24: 503–22.

HAKIM, C. (1990) 'Core and periphery in employers' workforce strategies: evidence from the 1987 E.L.U.S. survey', *Work, Employment and Society*, Vol.4, No.2: 157–88.

HEERY, E. and SALMON, J. (2000) *The Insecure Workforce*. London: Routledge.

HUNTER, L., MCGREGOR, A., MACINNES, J. and SPROULL, A. (1993) 'The flexible firm: strategy and segmentation', *British Journal of Industrial Relations*, Vol.31, No.3: 383–408.

HYMAN, R. (1994) 'Theory and industrial relations', *British Journal of Industrial Relations*, Vol.32, No.2: 165–80.

KAUFMAN, B. (2004) *Theoretical Perspectives on Work and the Employment Relationship*. Champaign, IL: Industrial Relations Research Association.

KELLEY, M. and HARRISON, B. (1992) 'Unions, technology, and labor-management cooperation', in L. Mishel and P. Voos (eds) *Unions and Economic Competitiveness*. Armonk, NY: M. E. Sharpe.

KELLY, J. (1998) *Rethinking Industrial Relations: Mobilization, collectivism and long waves*. London: Routledge.

KELLY, J. and KELLY, C. (1991) 'Them and us: social psychology and the new industrial relations', *British Journal of Industrial Relations*, Vol.29, No.1: 25–48.

LEGGE, K. (1995) *Human Resource Management: Rhetoric and realities*. London: Macmillan.

MARCHINGTON, M., WILKINSON, A., ACKERS, P. and GOODMAN, J. (1994) 'Understanding the meaning of participation: views from the workplace', *Human Relations*, Vol.47, No.8: 867–94.

MARSDEN, D. (1999) *A Theory of Employment Systems: Micro-foundations of societal diversity*. Oxford: Oxford University Press.

MILKMAN, R. (1997) *Farewell to the Factory. Auto workers in the late twentieth century*. Los Angeles: University of California Press.

MORRIS, J., WILKINSON, B. and GAMBLE, J. (2009) 'Strategic international human resource management or the "bottom line"? The cases of electronics and garments commodity chains in China', *International Journal of Human Resource Management*, Vol.20, No.2: 348–71.

NEWELL, H. (2000) 'Training in Greenfield sites', in H. Rainbird (ed.) *Training in the Workplace*. Basingstoke: Macmillan.

NOLAN, P. and MARGINSON, P. (1990) 'Skating on thin ice? David Metcalf on trade unions and productivity', *British Journal of Industrial Relations*, Vol.28, No.2: 227–47.

PECK, J. (1996) *Work-Place: The social regulation of labor markets*. New York: Guilford Press.

POOLE, M. (1986) *Towards a New Industrial Democracy: Workers' participation in industry*. London: Routledge & Kegan Paul.

PROCTER, S. (2008) 'New forms of work and the high performance paradigm', in P. Blyton, N. Bacon, J. Fiorito and E. Heery (eds) *The Sage Handbook of Industrial Relations*. London: Sage.

PURCELL, J. (1987) 'Mapping management styles in employee relations', *Journal of Management Studies*, Vol.24, No.5: 533–48.

RUBERY, J. and GRIMSHAW, D. (2003) *The Organization of Employment: An international perspective*. Basingstoke: Palgrave Macmillan.

SALAMON, M. (1998) *Industrial Relations: Theory and practice*, 3rd edition. Hemel Hempstead: Prentice Hall.

SISSON, K. (1990) 'Introducing the human resource management journal', *Human Resource Management Journal*, Vol.1, No.1: 1–11.

SPENCER, D. (2000) 'The demise of radical political economics? An essay on the evolution of a theory of capitalist production', *Cambridge Journal of Economics*, Vol.24, No.5: 543–64.

STEWART, P. (1997) 'Striking smarter and harder at Vauxhall: the new industrial relations of lean production?', *Capital and Class*, Vol.61, No.1: 1–7.

STOREY, J. (ed.) (1989) *New Perspectives on Human Resource Management*. London: Routledge.

STOREY, J. (1992) *Developments in the Management of Human Resources*. Oxford: Blackwell.

STOREY, J. (2001) *Human Resource Management: A critical text*. London: Thomson Learning.

STOREY, J. and SISSON, K. (1993) *Managing Human Resources and Industrial Relations*. Buckingham: Open University Press.

STRAUSS, G. and WHITFIELD, K. (2008) 'Changing traditions in industrial relations research', in P. Blyton, N. Bacon, J. Fiorito and E. Heery (eds) *The Sage Handbook of Industrial Relations*. London: Sage.

STREECK, W. (1992) *Social Institutions and Economic Performance: Studies of industrial relations in advanced capitalist economies*. London: Sage.

THOMPSON, P. and MCHUGH, D. (1990) *Work Organisations: A critical introduction*. London: Macmillan.

WHITLEY, R. and KRISTENSEN, P. (eds) (1997) *Governance at Work: The social regulation of economic relations*. Oxford: Oxford University Press.

CHAPTER 5

AMABLE, B. (2003) *The Diversity of Modern Capitalism*. Oxford: Oxford University Press.

BBC (2007) 'Vietnamese strike at Nike plant 2007'; available online at http://news.bbc.co.uk/1/hi/business/7118902.stm [accessed 2 July 2010].

BISLEY, N. (2007) *Rethinking Globalisation*. London: Palgrave.

BREWSTER, C., CAREY, L., DOWLING, P., GROBLER, P., HOLLAND, P. and WARNICH, S. (2003) *Contemporary Issues in Human Resource Management: Gaining a competitive advantage*, 2nd edition. Oxford: Oxford University Press.

CHARTERED INSTITUTE OF PERSONNEL AND DEVELOPMENT (2009) *EU Employment Policy*. London: CIPD.

CHARTERED INSTITUTE OF PERSONNEL AND DEVELOPMENT (2010) *PESTLE Analysis*. Factsheet. Available online at http://www.cipd.co.uk/subjects/corpstrtgy/general/pestle-analysis.htm [accessed 2 July 2010].

CLARK, I. (2009) 'The private equity business model and associated strategies for HRM: evidence and implications?', *International Journal of Human Resource Management*, Vol.20, No.10: 2030–48.

CROUCHER, R. and COTTON, E. (2009) *Global Unions, Global Business*. London: Middlesex University Press.

DEPARTMENT FOR BUSINESS INNOVATION AND SKILLS (2010) Agency Workers Directive; available online at http://www.berr.gov.uk/Policies/employment-matters/strategies/awd

DIBBEN, P., JAMES, P., ROPER, I. and WOOD, G. (2007) *Modernising Work in Public Services: Redefining roles and relationships in Britain's changing workplace*. London: Palgrave.

DICKEN, P. (2007) *Global Shift: Mapping the contours of the world economy*, 3rd edition. London: Sage.

DORE, R. (2000) *Stock Market Capitalism: Welfare capitalism*. Cambridge: Cambridge University Press.

EDWARDS, T. and REES, C. (2006) *International Human Resource Management*. London: Pearson Education Ltd.

EURACTIV (2004) 'EU-25: Member States grapple with the free labour market'; available online at http://www.euractiv.com/en/enlargement/eu-25-member-states-grapple-free-labour-market/article-117775 [accessed 1 July 2010].

FEATHERSTONE, L. (1998) 'The Burger International', *Left Business Observer*, 86.

FUKUYAMA, F. (1992) *The End of History and the Last Man*. New York: Free Press.

GALLIN, D. 2010. Interview. Available online at: http://www.mcspotlight.org/people/interviews/gallin.html [accessed 4 January 2011].

GOERGEN, M., BREWSTER, C. and WOOD, G. (2009) 'Corporate governance regimes and employment relations in Europe', *Industrial Relations/Relations Industrielles*, Vol.64, No.6: 620–40.

HALL, P. and SOSKICE, D. (eds) (2001) *Varieties of Capitalism: The institutional basis of competitive advantage*. Oxford: Oxford University Press.

HALL, R. (2010) 'Renewing and revising the engagement between labour process theory and technology', in P. Thompson, P. and C. Smith (eds) *Working Life: Renewing labour process theory*. London: Thompson.

HARZING, A. and VAN RUYSSEVELDT, J. (2004) *International Human Resource Management*, 2nd edition. London: Sage.

LA PORTA, R., LOPEZ-DE-SILANES, F., SHLEIFER, A. and VISHNY, R. (1998) 'Law and finance', *Journal of Political Economy*, Vol.106, No.6: 1113–55.

LA PORTA, R., LOPEZ-DE-SILANES, F., SHLEIFER, A. and VISHNY, R. (2000) 'Investor protection and corporate governance', *Journal of Financial Economics*, Vol.58, No.1-2: 3–27.

LANE, C. and WOOD, G. (2009) 'Diversity in capitalism and capitalist diversity', *Economy and Society*, Vol.38, No.4: 531–51.

LEVITAS, R. (1999) *The Inclusive Society? Social exclusion and new labour*. Basingstoke: Macmillan.

MACEWAN, A. (1999) Neo-liberalism or Democracy? *Economic strategy, markets, and alternatives for the 21st century*. London: Zed.

MARSDEN, D. (1999) *A Theory of Employment Systems*. Oxford: Oxford University Press.

MEIKSINS WOOD, E. (1997) 'Labor, the state and class struggle', *Monthly Review*, July-August.

MORRISSEY, O. and FILATOTCHEV, I. (2000) 'Globalisation and trade: the implications for exports from marginalised economies', *Journal of Development Studies*, Vol.37, No.2: 1–27.

MURAKAMI, T. (1999) 'Employee relations and teamwork in a German plant', *Employee Relations*, Vol.21, No.1: 1–53.

NORTH, D. C. (1990) *Institutions, Institutional Change and Economic Performance*. Cambridge: Cambridge University Press.

PERKINS, S. and SHORTLAND, S. (2006) *Strategic International HRM: Choices and consequences in multinational people management*, 2nd edition. London: Kogan Page.

PIORE, M. and SABEL, C. (1984) *The Second Industrial Divide: Possibilities for prosperity*. New York: Basic Books.

QUACK, S. and DJELIC, M.-L. (2005) 'Adaption, recombination and reinforcement', in W. Streeck and K. Thelen (eds) *Beyond Continuity*. Oxford: Oxford University Press.

ROYLE, T. (2006) 'The dominance effect? Multinational corporations in the Italian quick-food service sector', *British Journal of Industrial Relations*, Vol.44, No.4: 757–79.

RUBERY, J. and GRIMSHAW, D. (2003) *The Organisation of Employment: An international perspective*. Basingstoke: Palgrave Macmillan.

SEGER, M. B. (2003) *Globalization: A very short introduction*. Oxford: Oxford University Press.

SOROKIN, P. (1966) *Sociological Theories of Today*. New York: Harper International.

SOUTHALL, R. (1995) *Imperialism or Solidarity? International labour and South African trade unions*. Cape Town: University of Cape Town Press.

THOMPSON, P. and SMITH, C. (2010) *Working Life: Renewing labour process theory*. London: Thompson.

VISSER, J. and EBBINGHAUS, B. (2000) *Trade Unions in Western Europe Since 1945*. London: Palgrave.

WHITLEY, R. (1999) *Divergent Capitalisms: The social structuring and change of business systems*. Oxford: Oxford University Press.

WOOD, G. and FRYNAS, G. (2006) 'The institutional basis of economic failure: anatomy of the segmented business system', *Socio-Economic Review*, Vol.4, No.2: 239–77.

WOOD, G. and WRIGHT, M. (2009) 'Private equity: a review and synthesis', *International Journal of Management Reviews*, Vol.11, No.4: 361–80.

WOOD, G., HARCOURT, M. and WILKINSON, A. (2008) 'Age discrimination and working life', *International Journal of Management Reviews*, Vol.10, No.4: 425–42.

WOOD, G., PSYCHOGIOS, A. and SZAMOSI, L. (2008) 'International HRM', in T. Redman and A. Wilkinson, *Contemporary Human Resource Management*. Harlow: Pearson.

WOOD, G., DIBBEN, P., STRIDE, C. and WEBSTER, E. (2010) 'HRM in Mozambique: homogenization, path dependence or segmented business system?', *Journal of World Business* (forthcoming).

WORTH, O. and KUHLING, C. (2004) 'Counter-hegemony, anti-globalisation and culture in international political economy', *Capital and Class*, Vol.84: 31–42.

CHAPTER 6

BEAN, R. (1985) *Comparative Industrial Relations: An introduction to cross-national perspectives*. London: Croom Helm.

BLYTON, P. and TURNBULL, P. (1998) *The Dynamics of Employee Relations*, 2nd edition. London: Macmillan.

BOYER, R. (1988) *The Search for Labour Market Flexibility. The European economies in transition*. Oxford: Clarendon Press.

BOYER, R. (2009) 'History repeating for economists'. Paper for the Annual Conference of the Society for the Advancement of Socio-Economics, Paris, July 2009.

BREWSTER, C., GOERGEN, M. and WOOD, G. (2010) 'Corporate governance systems and employment relations', in A. Wilkinson and M. Townsend (eds) *The Future of Employment Relations: New paradigms, new developments*. London: Palgrave Macmillan.

BURAWOY, M. (1978) 'Towards a Marxist theory of the labour process', *Politics and Society*, Vol.8, No.3 and 4: 247–311.

BURAWOY, M. (1985) *The Politics of Production: Factory regimes under capitalism and socialism*. London: Verso.

CHANDLER, A. (2005) *Shaping the Industrial Century*. Cambridge, MA: Harvard University Press.

CHARLWOOD, A. (2006) 'What determined employer voice choice in Britain in the twentieth century?', *Socio-Economic Review*, Vol.4, No.2: 301–10.

CROUCH, C. (1982) *Trade Unions: The logic of collective action*. London: Fontana.

DAVIES, P. and FREELAND, M. (eds) (1983) *Kahn-Freund's Labour and the Law*, 2nd edition. Oxford: Clarendon Press.

DORE, R. (2000) *Stock Market Capitalism, Welfare Capitalism: Japan and Germany versus the Anglo-Saxons*. Oxford: Oxford University Press.

DUNLOP, J. (1958) *Industrial Relations Systems*. New York: Holt.

EDWARDS, P., BÉLANGER, J. and WRIGHT, M. (2006) 'The bases of compromise in the workplace: a theoretical framework', *British Journal of Industrial Relations*, Vol.44, No.1: 125–45.

EDWARDS, R. (1979) *Contested Terrain: The transformation of the workplace in the twentieth century*. London: Heinemann.

FOX, A. (1974) *Beyond Contract: Work, power and trust relations*. London: Faber & Faber.

FREEDLAND, M. (1995) 'The role of the contract of employment in modern labour law', in L. Betten (ed.) *The Employment Contract in Transforming Labour Relations*. The Hague: Kluwer.

FROUD, H., JOHAL, S., LEAVER, A. and WILLIAMS, K. (2006) *Financialization and Strategy: Narrative and numbers*. London: Routledge.

GEARY, J. (1994) 'Task participation: employees' participation enabled or constrained?', in K. Sisson (ed.) *Personnel Management*. Oxford: Blackwell.

GERTH, H. and MILLS, C. (1977) *From Max Weber: Essays in sociology*. London: Routledge & Kegan Paul.

GUARDIAN (2007) article available online at http://www.guardian.co.uk/business/2007/may/01/usnews.supermarkets [accessed 20 August 2007].

HYMAN, R. (1975) *Industrial Relations: A Marxist introduction*. London: Macmillan.

HYMAN, R. (1987) 'Strategy or structure: capital, labour and control work', *Employment and Society*, Vol.1, No.1: 25–55.

HYMAN, R. (1996) 'Changing union identities in Europe', in P. Leisink, J. van Leemput and J. Vilrokx (eds) *The Challenge to Trade Unions in Europe: Innovation or adaptation?* Cheltenham: Edward Elgar.

KELLY, J. (1996) 'Works councils: union advance or marginalization?', in A. McColgan (ed.) *The Future of Labour Law*. London: Cassell.

LA PORTA, R., LOPEZ-DE-SILANES, F., SHLEIFER, A. and VISHNY, R. (2002) 'Investor protection and corporate valuation', *Journal of Finance*, Vol.57, No.3: 1147–70.

LAZONICK, W. and O'SULLIVAN, M. (2000) 'Maximizing shareholder value: a new ideology for corporate governance', *Economy and Society*, Vol.29, No.1: 13–35.

LEGGE, K. (1995) *Human Resource Management: Rhetoric and realities*. London: Macmillan.

SALAMON, M. (1998) *Industrial Relations: Theory and practice*, 3rd edition. Hemel Hempstead: Prentice Hall.

SISSON, K. (1987) *The Management of Collective Bargaining: An international comparison*. Oxford: Basil Blackwell.

STANDING, G. (1999) *Global Labour Flexibility: Seeking distributive justice*. London: Macmillan

STOREY, J. (1983) *Managerial Prerogative and the Question of Control*. London: Routledge & Kegan Paul.

STREECK, W. (1992) *Social Institutions and Economic Performance: Studies of industrial relations in advanced capitalist economies*. London: Sage.

THOMPSON, P. (1989) *The Nature of Work: An introduction to debates on the labour process*, 2nd edition. London: Macmillan.

WOOD, S., WAGNER, A., ARMSTRONG, E., GOODMAN, J. and DAVIS, J. (1975) 'The "industrial relations system" concept as a basis for theory in industrial relations', *British Journal of Industrial Relations*, Vol.13, No.3: 291–308.

CHAPTER 7

ACAS (2005) Advisory booklet: *Employee Communications and Consultation*; available online at http://www.acas.org.uk/index.aspx?articleid=675 [accessed 29 June 2010].

ANSTEY, M. (1991) *Negotiating Conflict*. Cape Town: Juta.

BEAN, R. (1985) *Comparative Industrial Relations: An introduction to cross-national perspectives*. London: Croom Helm.

BENDIX, S. (2000) *Industrial Relations in the New South Africa*, 3rd edition. Cape Town: Juta.

BLYTON, P. and TURNBULL, P. (1998) *The Dynamics of Employee Relations*, 2nd edition. London: Macmillan.

BREWSTER, C., WOOD, G., CROUCHER, R. and BROOKES, M. (2007a) 'Are works councils and joint consultative committees a threat to trade unions? A comparative analysis', *Economic and Industrial Democracy*, Vol.28: 49–77.

BREWSTER, C., WOOD, G., CROUCHER, R. and BROOKES, M. (2007b) 'Collective and individual voice: convergence in Europe?', *International Journal of Human Resource Management*, Vol.18, No.7: 1246–62.

BROWN, W. (1992) 'Bargaining structure and the impact of law', in W. McCarthy (ed.) *Legal Intervention in Industrial Relations: Gains and losses*. Oxford: Blackwell.

BRYSON, A. (2004) 'Management responsiveness to union and nonunion worker voice in Britain', *Industrial Relations*, Vol.43, No.1: 213–41.

BUDD, J., GOLLAN, P. and WILKINSON, A. (2009) 'New approaches to employee voice and participation in organizations', *Human Relations*, Vol.63, No.3: 1–8.

BURCHILL, F. (1997) *Labour Relations*, 2nd edition. London: Macmillan.

CHAMBERLAIN, N. and KUHN, J. (1965) *Collective Bargaining*. New York: McGraw-Hill.

CLEGG, H. (1976) *Trade Unionism Under Collective Bargaining*. Oxford: Blackwell.

FARNHAM, D. and PIMLOTT, J. (1979) *Understanding Industrial Relations*. London: Cassell.

FARNHAM, D. and PIMLOTT, J. (1983) *Understanding Industrial Relations*, 2nd edition. London: Cassell.

GEARY, J. (1994) 'Task participation: employees' participation enabled or constrained?', in K. Sisson (ed.) *Personnel Management*. Oxford: Blackwell.

GOLLAN, P. (2009) 'Employer strategies towards non-union collective voice', in A. Wilkinson, P. Gollan, M. Marchington and D. Lewin (eds) *The Oxford Handbook of Participation in Organizations*. Oxford: Oxford University Press.

GROSSETT, M. and VENTER, R. (1998) *Labour Relations in South Africa*. Johannesburg: International Thompson.

HYMAN, R. (1994) 'Changing trade union identities and strategies', in R. Hyman and A. Ferner (eds) *New Frontiers in European Industrial Relations*. Oxford: Blackwell.

HYMAN, R. (1997) 'The future of employee representation', *British Journal of Industrial Relations*, Vol.35, No.3: 309–36.

HYMAN, R. and BROUGH, I. (1975) *Social Values and Industrial Relations*. Oxford: Blackwell.

INTERNATIONAL TRANSPORT WORKERS FEDERATION (2010) 'British union signs agreement with Thomas Cook Airline – value for Ryanair crews as well'; article available online at http://www.itfglobal.org/campaigns/britishunion. cfm [accessed 5 July 2010].

JACKSON, M. (1991) *An Introduction to Industrial Relations*. London: Routledge.

KELLY, J. (1996) 'Works councils: union advance or marginalization?', in A. McColgan (ed.) *The Future of Labour Law*. London: Cassell.

MARCHINGTON, M. (1992) *Managing the Team: A guide to successful employee involvement*. Oxford: Blackwell.

MAYO, E. (1933*) The Human Problems of an Industrial Civilization*. New York: Macmillan.

MAYO, E. (1945) *The Social Problems of an Industrial Civilization*. Cambridge, MA: Harvard University Press.

NEL, P., SWANEPOEL, B., KIRSTEN, M., ERASMUS, B. and TSABADI, M. (2005) *South African Employment Relations: Theory and practice*, 5th edition. Pretoria: Van Schaik.

OLSON, M. (1982) *The Rise and Decline of Nations: Economic growth, stagflation and social rigidities*. New Haven, CT: Yale University Press.

PATEMAN, C. (1970) *Participation and Democratic Theory*. Cambridge: Cambridge University Press.

PIRON, J. (1990) *Recognising Trade Unions*. Johannesburg: Southern Book Publishers.

POOLE, M. (1986) *Towards a New Industrial Democracy: Workers' participation in industry*. London: Routledge & Kegan Paul.

ROGERS, J. and STREECK, W. (1994) 'Workplace representation overseas: the works council story', in R. Freeman (ed.) *Working Under Different Rules*. New York: Russell Sage Foundation.

SALAMON, M. (1998) *Industrial Relations: Theory and practice*, 3rd edition. Hemel Hempstead: Prentice Hall.

SISSON, K. (1987) *The Management of Collective Bargaining: An international comparison*. Oxford: Basil Blackwell.

SLOMP, H. (1995) 'National variations in worker participation', in A. Harzing and J. Ruysseveldt (eds) *International Human Resource Management*. London: Sage.

SORGE, A. (1976) 'The evolution of industrial democracy in the countries of the European community', *British Journal of Industrial Relations*, Vol.14, No.3: 274–94.

STREECK, W. (1992) *Social Institutions and Economic Performance: Studies of industrial relations in advanced capitalist economies.* London: Sage.

TARAS, D. and KAUFMAN, B. (2006) 'Non-union employee representation in North America: diversity, controversy, and uncertain future'. Andrew Young School of Policy Studies Research Paper Series, No.06-46. Atlanta, GA: Georgia State University.

TERRY, M. (1994) 'Workplace unionism: redefining structures and objectives', in R. Hyman and A. Ferner (eds) *New Frontiers in European Industrial Relations.* Oxford: Blackwell.

VENN, D. (2009) 'Legislation, collective bargaining and enforcement: updating the OECD employment protection indicators', paper available online at www.oecd.org/els/workingpapers [accessed 5 July 2010].

WEBSTER, E. and WOOD, G. (2005) 'Human resource management practice and institutional constraints', *Employee Relations*, Vol.27, No.4: 369–85.

WOOD, G. and SELA, R. (2000) 'Making human resource development work', *Human Resource Development International*, Vol.3, No.4: 451–64.

WOOD, G., HARCOURT, M. and HARCOURT, S. (2004) 'The effects of age discrimination legislation on workplace practice', *Industrial Relations Journal*, Vol.35, No.4: 359–71.

CHAPTER 8

BEVAN, S. (2010) article in the *Guardian*, 25 June; available online at http://www.guardian.co.uk/commentisfree/2010/may/29/stress-management-stephen-bevan [accessed 20 August 2010].

BLYTON, P. and TURNBULL, P. (2004) *The Dynamics of Employee Relations*, 3rd edition. London: Palgrave.

BOLTON, S. (2010) 'Old ambiguities and new developments: exploring the emotional labour process', in P. Thompson and C. Smith (eds) *Working Life: Renewing labour process analysis.* London: Palgrave.

BREWSTER, C., WOOD, G., CROUCHER, R. and BROOKES, M. (2007) 'Collective and individual voice: convergence in Europe?', *International Journal of Human Resource Management*, Vol.18, No.7: 1246–62.

BREWSTER, C., CAREY, L., DOWLING, P., GROBLER, P., HOLLAND, P. and WARNICH, S. (2003) *Contemporary Issues in Human Resource Management*, 2nd edition. Oxford: Oxford University Press.

CHARTERED INSTITUTE OF PERSONNEL AND DEVELOPMENT (2006a) *Reflections on Employee Engagement.* London: CIPD.

CHARTERED INSTITUTE OF PERSONNEL AND DEVELOPMENT (2006b) *How Engaged Are British Employees?* Annual Survey Report, 2006. London: CIPD.

CHARTERED INSTITUTE OF PERSONNEL AND DEVELOPMENT (2009a) *Employee Engagement*. Available online at http://cipd.co.uk/subjects/empreltns/general/empengmt?NRMODE=Published&. [accessed 24 March 2010].

CHARTERED INSTITUTE OF PERSONNEL AND DEVELOPMENT (2010a) *Employer Brand*. Available online at http://cipd.co.uk/subjects/corpstrtgy/empbrand/employerbrand?NRMODE=Publ. [accessed 24 March 2010].

CHARTERED INSTITUTE OF PERSONNEL AND DEVELOPMENT (2010b) *Health and Safety at Work*. Available online at http://cipd.co.uk/subjects/health/general/healthsafetywork.htm. [accessed 4 August 2010].

CUNNINGHAM, I. (2008) *Employment Relations in the Voluntary Sector*. London: Routledge.

CURRY, J. P., WAKEFIELD, D. S., PRICE, J. L. and MUELLER, C. W. (1986) 'On the causal ordering of job satisfaction and organizational commitment', *Academy of Management Journal*, Vol.29, No.4: 847–58.

EDWARDS, P. and WRIGHT, M. (2001) 'High-involvement work systems and performance outcomes: the strength of variable, contingent and context-bound relationships', *International Journal of Human Resource Management*, Vol.12, No.4: 568–85.

GALLIE, D., KOSTOVA, D. and KUCHAR, P. (1999) 'Employment experience and organisational commitment: an East–West European comparison', *Work, Employment and Society*, Vol.13, No.4: 621–41.

GODARD, J. (2004) 'A critical assessment of the high-performance paradigm', *British Journal of Industrial Relations*, Vol.42, No.2: 349–78.

HOLMAN, D. (2002) 'Employee wellbeing in call centres', *Human Resource Management Journal*, Vol.12, No.4: 35–50.

JAMES, P. (2009) 'Occupational health and safety', in M. Gold (ed.) *Employment Policy in the European Union: Origins, themes and prospects*. London: Palgrave Macmillan.

KIM, S. (2002) 'Participative management and job satisfaction: lessons for management leadership', *Public Administration Review*, Vol.62, No.2: 231–41.

LUTHANS, F. and PETERSON, S. (2001) 'Employee engagement and manager self-efficacy: implications for managerial effectiveness and development', *Journal of Management Development*, Vol.21, No.5: 376–87.

MACDONALD, L. A. (2005) *Wellness at Work: Protecting and promoting employee well-being*. London: CIPD.

MACEY, W. H. and SCHNEIDER, B. (2008) 'The meaning of employee engagement', *Industrial and Organizational Psychology*, Vol.1: 3–30.

MACLEOD, D. and CLARKE, N. (2009) *Engaging for Success: Enhancing performance through employee engagement*. London: Department for Business, Innovation and Skills (www.bis.gov.uk).

MORRIS, J. A. and FELDMAN, D. C. (1996) 'The dimensions, antecedents, and consequences of emotional labor', *Academy of Management Review*, Vol.21, No.4: 986–1010.

MOWDAY, R. T., PORTER, L. W. and STEERS, R. M. (1982) *Employee–Organization Linkages: The psychology of commitment, absenteeism and turnover.* New York: Academic Press.

MUTHUVELOO, R. and ROSE, R. (2005) 'Typology of organisational commitment', *American Journal of Applied Science*, Vol.2, No.6: 1078–81.

PURCELL, J. (2010) *Building Employee Engagement.* ACAS Policy Discussion Paper, January. Available online at http://www.acas.org.uk.

ROBINSON, D., PERRYMAN, S. and HAYDAY, S. (2004) The drivers of employee engagement. Report 408. *Institute for Employment Studies*, April 2004.

ROSE, M. (2003) 'Good deal, bad deal? Job satisfaction in occupations', *Work, Employment and Society*, Vol.17, No.3: 503–30.

SAKS, A. M. (2005) 'Antecedents and consequences of employee engagement', *Journal of Managerial Psychology*, Vol.21, No.7: 600–19.

SHORE, L. M. and MARTIN, H. J. (1989) 'Job satisfaction and organizational commitment in relation to work performance and turnover intentions', *Human Relations*, Vol.42, No.7: 625–38.

SOUSA-POZA, A. and SOUSA-POZA, A. (2000) 'Well-being at work: a cross-national analysis of the levels and determinants of job satisfaction', *Journal of Socio-economics*, Vol.29: 517–38.

STRIDE, C., WALL, T. and CATLEY, N. (2007) *Measures of Job Satisfaction, Organisational Commitment, Mental Health and Job-Related Well-Being: A benchmarking manual*, 2nd edition. Chichester: John Wiley & Sons.

WARR, P. B. (1990) 'The measurement of well-being and other aspects of mental health', *Journal of Occupational Psychology*, Vol.63: 193–210.

CHAPTER 9

AKERLOF, G. (1982) 'Labor contracts as partial gift exchange', *Quarterly Journal of Economics*, Vol.97, No.4: 543–69.

BAKAN, I., SUSENO, Y., PINNINGTON, A. and MONEY, A. (2004) 'The influence of financial participation and participation in decision-making on employee job attitudes', *International Journal of Human Resource Management*, Vol.15, No.3: 587–616.

BARON, J. and COOKE, K. (1992) 'Process and outcome: perspectives on the distribution of rewards within organizations', *Administrative Science Quarterly*, Vol.37, No.2: 191–7.

BARUCH, Y., WHEELER, K. and ZHAO, X. (2004) 'Performance-related pay in Chinese professional sports', *International Journal of Human Resource Management*, Vol.15, No.1: 245–59.

BEBCHUCK, L. and FRIED, J. (2006) *Pay Without Performance: The unfulfilled promise of executive compensation.* Cambridge, MA: Harvard University Press.

BOYER, R. (2010) 'The collapse of finance, but labour still looks weak', *Socio-Economic Review*, Vol.8, No.2: 348–53.

BROWN, D. (1996) 'Team rewards: lessons from the coal face', *Team Performance Management*, Vol.2, No.2: 12.

CACCIOPE, R. (1999) 'Using team/individual reward and recognition strategies to drive organizational success', *Leadership and Organization Development Journal*, Vol.20, No.6: 322–31.

CARD, D. and KRUEGER, A. (1995) *Myth and Measurement: The new economics of the minimum wage.* Princeton, NJ: Princeton University Press.

CIN, B., HAN, T. and SMITH, S. (2002) 'A tale of two tigers: employee financial participation in Taiwan and Korea', *International Journal of Human Resource Management*, Vol.14, No.6: 920–41.

CORE, J., GUAY, W. and LARKCER, D.(2008) 'The power of the pen and executive compensation', *Journal of Financial Economics,* Vol.88, No.1: 1–25.

CROUCHER, R., BROOKES, M., WOOD, G. and BREWSTER, C. (2010) 'Context, strategy and financial participation: a comparative analysis', *Human Relations*, Vol.63: 835–55.

DIRECTGOV UK (2010) *The National Minimum Wage.* Available online at http://www.direct.gov.uk/en/employment/employees/pay/dg_10027201.

GUEST, D. E. (1987) 'Human resource management and industrial relations', *Journal of Management Studies*, Vol.24: 503–21.

HEERY, E. (1996) 'Risk, reward and the New Pay', *Personnel Review*, Vol.25, No.6: 54–65.

ICHNIOWSKI, C. and SHAW, K. (2003) 'Beyond incentive pay', *Journal of Economic Perspectives*, Vol.17, No.1: 155–80.

ICHNIOWSKI, C., SHAW, K. and PRENNUSHI, G. (1997) 'The effects of human resource management practices on productivity: a study of steel finishing lines', *American Economic Review*, Vol.87, No.3: 291–313.

JONES, D. (1997) 'Employees as stakeholders', *Business Strategy Review*, Vol.8, No.2: 21–4.

KATO, T. and MORISHIMA, M. (2002) 'The productivity effects of participatory employment practices', *Industrial Relations Journal*, Vol.41, No.4: 487–520.

KERRIN, M. and OLIVER, N. (2002) 'Collective and individual improvement activities: the role of reward systems', *Personnel Review*, Vol.31, No.3: 320–37.

KOCHAN, T. and OSTERMAN, P. (2000) 'The mutual gains enterprise', in C. Mabey, G. Salaman and J. Storey (eds) *Strategic Human Resource Management*. London: Sage.

MACINNES, J., CRESSEY, P. and ELDRIDGE, J. (1985) *Just Managing: Authority and democracy in industry*. Milton Keynes: Open University Press.

MCNABB, R and WHITFIELD, K. (2000) 'Worth so appallingly little: a workplace-level analysis of low pay', *British Journal of Industrial Relations*, Vol.38,No.4: 585–609.

MCNABB, R. and WHITFIELD, K. (2007) 'The impact of varying types of performance related pay and employee participation on earnings', *International Journal of Human Resource Management*, Vol.18, No.6: 1004–25.

METCALF, D. (1999a) 'The British national minimum wage', *British Journal of Industrial Relations*, Vol.37, No.2: 171–201.

METCALF, D. (1999b) 'The Low Pay Commission and the national minimum wage', *Economic Journal*, Vol.109, No.453: 46–66.

MORRIS, D., BAKAN, I. and WOOD, G. (2005) 'Employee financial participation: evidence from a major UK retailer', *Employee Relations*, Vol.28, No.4: 326–41.

NEUMARK, D. (2001) 'The employment effects of minimum wages: evidence from a prespecified research design', *Industrial Relations*, Vol.40, No.1: 121–44.

NEUMARK, D. and WASCHER, W. (2001) 'Minimum wages and training revisited', *Journal of Labor Economics*, Vol.19, No.3: 563–95.

THE OBSERVER (2010) article, 8 August; available online at http://www. guardian. co.uk/world/2010/aug/08/gap-next-marks-spencer-sweatshops

OECD (2010) OECD statistics; available online at www.oecd.org [accessed 15 August 2010]

PENDLETON, A. (2006) 'Incentives, monitoring, and employee stock ownership plans: new evidence and interpretations', *Industrial Relations*, Vol.45, No.4: 753–77.

POUTSMA, E. and DE NIJS, W. (2003) 'Broad-based employee financial participation in Europe', *International Journal of Human Resource Management*, Vol.14, No.6: 863–92.

RICHBELL, S. and WOOD, G. (2009) 'Reward management', in D. Collings and G. Wood (eds) *Human Resource Management: A critical approach*. London: Routledge.

STEWART, M. B. (2002) 'The impact of the introduction of the UK minimum wage on the employment probabilities of low wage workers' (mimeo).

STOREY, J. (1995) *Human Resource Management: A critical text*. London: Thompson.

TWOMEY, D. and QUAZI, H. (1994) 'Triangular typology approach to studying performance management systems in hi-tech firms', *Journal of Organizational Behaviour*, Vol.15, No.6: 561–73.

US CENSUS BUREAU (2009) 'Income, poverty, and health insurance coverage in the United States: 2008'. September. US Census Bureau: http://www.census.gov/prod/2009pubs/p60-236.pdf.

WILLIAMS, N. and MILLS, J. A. (2001) 'The minimum wage and teenage employment: evidence from time series', *Applied Economics*, Vol.33, No.3: 285–300.

CHAPTER 10

ANGLOGOLD ASHANTI (2010) 'Labour practice – case studies: women in mining: uncovering the barriers'. Available online at http://www.anglogold.com/subwebs/ informationforinvestors/ReportToSociety05/values_bus_principles/labour/lp_cs_sa_5_4.htm [accessed 23 August 2010].

ARROWSMITH, J. and MCGOLDRICK, A. (1997) 'A flexible future for older workers?', *Personnel Review*, Vol.26, No.4: 258–73.

BASKIN, J. (1991) *Striking Back: A history of COSATU*. Johannesburg: Raven.

BBC (2002) 'Sexism in the city'. Available online at http://news.bbc.co.uk/1/hi/business/ 3086835.stm.

BENNINGTON, L. and WEIN, R. (2000) 'Anti-discrimination legislation in Australia: fair, effective, efficient or irrelevant?', *International Journal of Manpower*, Vol.21, No.1: 21–33.

BONNIN, D., LANE, T., RUGGUNAN, S. and WOOD, G. (2004) 'Training and development in the maritime industry', *Human Resource Development International*, Vol.7, No.1: 7–22.

BRANINE, M. and GLOVER, I. (1997) 'Ageism in work and employment: thinking about connections', *Personnel Review*, Vol.26, No.4: 233–44.

BRATTON, J. and GOLD, J. (2007) *Human Resource Management: Theory and practice*. London: Palgrave.

CASSELL, C. (2006) 'Managing diversity', in T. Redman and A. Wilkinson (eds) *Contemporary Human Resource Management: Text and cases*. London: FT/Prentice Hall.

CHOU, K.-L. and CHOW, N. (2005) 'To retire or not to retire: is there an option for older workers in Hong Kong?', *Social Policy and Administration*, Vol.39, No.3: 233–46.

CONLIN, M. and EMERSON, P. (2006) 'Discrimination in hiring versus retention and promotion', *Journal of Law, Economics and Organization*, Vol.22, No.1: 115–36.

DANIELS, K. and MACDONALD, L. (2005) *Equality, Diversity and Discrimination: A student text*. London: CIPD.

DARITY, W. (2001) 'The functionality of market-based discrimination', *International Journal of Social Economics*, Vol.28, No.10-12: 980–6.

HARCOURT, M. and S., and WOOD, G. (2004)' Do unions affect employer compliance with the law?', *British Journal of Industrial Relations*, Vol 42, No.3: 527–41.

HIRSON, B. (1989) *Yours for the Union*. London: Zed.

HUTCHENS, R. (1986) 'Delayed payment contracts and a firm's propensity to hire older workers', *Journal of Labour Economics*, Vol.4, No.4: 439–57.

JESSOP, B. (2001) *Regulationist Perspectives on Fordism and Post-Fordism. Regulation theory and the crisis of capitalism*, Vol.3. London: Edward Elgar.

KERSLEY, B., ALPIN, C., FORTH, J., BRYSON, A., BEWLEY, H., DIX, G. and OXENBRIDGE, S. (2006) *Inside the Workplace: Findings from the 2004 Workplace Employment Relations Survey*. London: Routledge.

MAREE, J. (1986) 'An analysis of the independent trade unions in South Africa in the 1970s'. Unpublished PhD thesis. Cape Town: University of Cape Town.

MCDONALD, F. and POTTON, M. (1997) 'The nascent European Policy towards older workers', *Personnel Review*, Vol.26, No.4: 293–306.

MCVITTIE, C., MCKINLEY, A. and WIDDICOMBE, S. (2003) 'Committed to (un)equal opportunities', *British Journal of Social Psychology*, Vol.42: 585–612.

MELLAHI, K. and WOOD, G. (2003) *The Ethical Business: Challenges and controversies*. London: Palgrave.

O'BOYLE, E. (2001) 'Salary compression and inversion in the university workplace', *International Journal of Social Economics*, Vol.28, No.10-12: 959–79.

OFFICE FOR NATIONAL STATISTICS (2010) 2009 annual survey of hours and earnings (ASHE). Available online at http://www.statistics.gov.uk/cci/nugget.asp?id=285 [accessed 23 August 2010].

PALMORE, E., BURCETT, B., FILLENBAUM, G., GEORGE, L. and WALLMAN, L. (1985) *Retirement: Causes and consequences*. New York: Springer.

PIORE, M. (2010) 'From bounded rationality to behaviourial economics', *Socio-Economic Review*, Vol.8, No.2: 383–7.

REDMAN, T. and WILKINSON, A. (2002) *Contemporary Human Resource Management*. Harlow: Prentice Hall.

SARGEANT, M. (2001) 'Lifelong learning and age discrimination in employment', *Education and the Law*, Vol.13, No.2: 141–54.

SCHUMAN, E. and KLEINER, B. (2001) 'Is age a handicap in finding employment?', *Equal Opportunities International*: Vol.20, Nos 5/6/7: 48–52.

SHEN, G. and KLEINER, B. (2001) 'Age discrimination in hiring', *Equal Opportunities International*, Vol.20, No.8: 25–32.

TAYLOR, P. and WALKER, A. (1994) 'The ageing workforce: employers' attitudes towards older people', *Work, Employment and Society*, Vol.8, No.4: 569–91.

TRADES UNION CONGRESS (2010) *Equality Act 2010: TUC briefing for affiliates.* July. London: TUC.

URWIN, P. (2004) 'Age matters: a review of existing survey evidence', *Employment Relations Research* Series 24. London: Department of Trade and Industry.

US ARMY (2008) *Information Papers: Workforce diversity.* Available online at http://www.army.mil/aps/08/information_papers/sustain/Diversity.html [accessed 23 August 2010].

WALKER, A. (2005) 'Towards an international political economy of ageing', *Ageing and Society*, Vol 25: 815–39.

WEBSTER, E. (1986) *Cast in a Racial Mould.* Johannesburg: Raven.

WOOD, N. (2004) *Tyranny in America.* London: Verso.

WRIGHT, E. and DWYER, R. (2006) 'The pattern of jobs expansion in the USA', in G. Wood and P. James (eds) *Institutions, Production and Working Life.* Oxford: Oxford University Press.

CHAPTER 11

ADVISORY, CONCILIATION AND ARBITRATION SERVICE (2009a) Code of Practice: *Disciplinary and grievance procedures.* April. London: ACAS.

ADVISORY, CONCILIATION AND ARBITRATION SERVICE (2009b) Guidance booklet: *Discipline and grievances at work.* November. London: ACAS.

BAMBERGER, P., KOHN, E. and NAHUM-SHANI, I. (2008) 'Aversive workplace conditions and employee grievance filing: the moderating effects of gender and ethnicity', *Industrial Relations*, Vol.47, No.2: 229–59.

BÉLANGER, J. and THUDEROZ, C. (2010) 'The repertoire of employee opposition', in P. Thompson and C. Smith (eds) *Working Life: Renewing labour process theory.* London: Thompson.

CHARTERED INSTITUTE OF PERSONNEL AND DEVELOPMENT (2004) *Managing Conflict at Work.* Survey Report. London: CIPD.

CHARTERED INSTITUTE OF PERSONNEL AND DEVELOPMENT (2005) *Bullying at Work: Beyond policies to a culture of respect.* London: CIPD.

CHARTERED INSTITUTE OF PERSONNEL AND DEVELOPMENT (2006) *How Engaged Are British Employees?* Annual Survey Report. London: CIPD.

CHARTERED INSTITUTE OF PERSONNEL AND DEVELOPMENT (2007) *Managing Conflict at Work.* Survey Report. February. London: CIPD.

CHARTERED INSTITUTE OF PERSONNEL AND DEVELOPMENT (2010a) *Discipline and Grievances at Work.* Factsheet. London: CIPD. Available online at http://www/cipd.co.uk/subjects/emplaw/discipline/disciplingrievprocs.htm [accessed 4 August 2010].

CHARTERED INSTITUTE OF PERSONNEL AND DEVELOPMENT (2010b) *Dismissal.* Factsheet. February 2010. London: CIPD. Available online at http://www/ cipd.co.uk/subjects/emplaw/dismissal.htm?IsSrchRes=1 [accessed 4 August 2010].

CHARTERED INSTITUTE OF PERSONNEL AND DEVELOPMENT (2010c) *Equality Act 2010.* Factsheet. London: CIPD. Available online at http://www/ cipd.co.uk/subjects/dvsequl/general/equality-act-2010.htm?wa_src=email [accessed 4 August 2010].

CHARTERED INSTITUTE OF PERSONNEL AND DEVELOPMENT (2010d) *Harassment and Bullying at Work.* Factsheet. London: CIPD. Available online at http://www/cipd.co.uk/subjects/dvsequl/harassmt/harrass.htm?IsSrchRes=1 [accessed 4 August 2010].

CLARKE, S., LEE, C.-H. and LI, Q. (2004) 'Collective consultation and industrial relations in China', *British Journal of Industrial Relations*, Vol.42, No.2: 235–54.

COLVIN, A. J. S. (2004) 'The relationship between employee involvement and workplace dispute resolution', *Relations Industrielles/Industrial Relations*, Vol.59, No.4: 681–704.

COWIE, H., NAYLOR, P., RIVERS, I., SMITH, P. K. and PEREIRA, B. (2002) 'Measuring workplace bullying', *Aggression and Violent Behavior*, Vol.7: 33–51.

CUNNINGHAM, I., JAMES, P. and DIBBEN, P. (2004) 'Bridging the gap between rhetoric and reality: line managers and the protection of job security for ill workers in the modern workplace', *British Journal of Management*, Vol.15, No.3: 273–90.

DALTON, D. R. and TODOR, W. D. (1982) 'Antecedents of grievance filing behavior: attitude/behavioral consistency and the union steward', *Academy of Management Journal*, Vol.25, No.1: 158–69.

DEERY, S., WALSH, J. and KNOX, A. (2001) 'The non-union workplace in Australia: bleak house or human resource innovator?', *International Journal of Human Resource Management*, Vol.12, No.4: 669–83.

DIBBEN, P., JAMES, P. and CUNNINGHAM, I. (2001) 'Absence management in the public sector: an integrative model?', *Public Money and Management*, Vol.21, No.4: 55–60.

EARNSHAW, J., MARCHINGTON, M. and GOODMAN, J. (2000) 'Unfair to whom? Discipline and dismissal in small establishments', *Industrial Relations Journal*, Vol.31, No.1: 62–73.

EDWARDS, P. (1994) 'Discipline and the creation of order', in K. Sisson (ed.) *Personnel Management: A comprehensive guide to theory and practice in Britain*. Oxford: Blackwell.

EDWARDS, R. (1979) *Contested Terrain: The transformation of the workplace in the twentieth century*. London: Heinemann.

EWING, K. D. (2005) 'The function of trade unions', *Industrial Law Journal*, Vol.34, No.1: 1–22.

FOUCAULT, M. (1988) 'On power', in L. Kritzman (ed) *Foucault: Politics, philosophy, culture*. New York: Routledge.

FRANKLIN, A. L. and PAGAN, J. F. (2006) 'Organization culture as an explanation for employee discipline practices', *Review of Public Personnel Administration*, Vol.26, No.1: 52–73.

FRIEDMAN, B. A. and REED, L. J. (2007) 'Workplace privacy: employee relations and legal implications of monitoring employee email use', *Employee Responsibility and Rights Journal*, Vol.19: 75–83.

GENNARD, J. and JUDGE, G. (2005) *Employee Relations*. London: CIPD.

GENNARD, J. and JUDGE, G. (2010) *Managing Employment Relations*. London: CIPD.

HOEL, H., FARAGHER, B. and COOPER, C. L. (2004) 'Bullying is detrimental to health, but all bullying behaviours are not necessarily equally damaging', *British Journal of Guidance and Counselling*, Vol.32, No.3: 367–87.

KNIGHT, K. G. and LATREILLE, P. L. (2000) 'Discipline, dismissals and complaints to employment tribunals', *British Journal of Industrial Relations*, Vol.38, No.4: 533–55.

KRITZER, H. M., VIDMAR, N. and BOGART, W. A. (1991) 'To confront or not to confront: measuring claiming rates in discrimination grievances', *Law & Society Review*, Vol.25, No. 4: 875–87.

MILLS, P. K. and DALTON, D. R. (1994) 'Arbitration outcomes in the service sector: an empirical assessment', *International Journal of Service Industry Management*, Vol.5, No.2: 57–71.

NURSE, L. and DEVONISH, D. (2007) 'Grievance management and its links to workplace justice', *Employee Relations*, Vol.29, No.1: 89–109.

OECD (2008) *Employment Protection Indicators*. Available online at www.oecd. org/employment/protection [accessed 18 August 2010].

ROLLINSON, D., HOOK, C., FOOT, M. and HANDLEY, J. (1996) 'Supervisor and manager styles in handling discipline and grievance: Part 2, Approaches to handling discipline and grievance', *Personnel Review*, Vol.25, No.4: 38–55.

SALIN, D. (2003) 'Ways of explaining workplace bullying: a review of enabling, motivating and precipitating structures and processes in the work environment', *Human Relations*, Vol.56, No.10: 1213–32.

SALIPANTE, P. F and BOUWEN, R. (2007) 'Behavioural analysis of grievances: conflict sources, complexity and transformation', *Employee Relations*, Vol.12, No.3: 17–22.

SAUNDRY, R. and ANTCLIFF, V. (2006) 'Employee representation in grievance and disciplinary matters – making a difference?', *Employment Relations* Research Series No.69. London: HMSO/Department of Trade and Industry.

UNISON (2003) *Bullying at Work: Guidelines for Unison branches, stewards and safety representatives*. London: Unison.

CHAPTER 12

ADVISORY, CONCILIATION AND ARBITRATION SERVICE (2009) *Varying a Contract of Employment*. Available online at http://www.acas.org.uk/ CHttpHandler.ashx?id=316 [accessed 5 July 2010].

BACKER, W. and OBERHOLZER, G. (1995) 'Strikes and political activity: a strike analysis of South Africa for the period 1910-1994', *South African Journal of Labour Relations*, Vol.19, No.3: 12–17.

BEAN, R. (1985) *Comparative Industrial Relations: An introduction to cross-national perspectives*. London: Croom Helm.

BENDIX, S. (2000) *Industrial Relations in the New South Africa*, 3rd edition. Cape Town: Juta.

BLAUNER, R. (1966) *Alienation and Freedom*. Chicago: University of Chicago Press.

BLYTON, P. and TURNBULL, P. (1998) *The Dynamics of Employee Relations*, 2nd edition. London: Macmillan.

BUDD, J., GOLLAN, P. and WILKINSON, A. (2009) 'New approaches to employee voice and participation in organizations', *Human Relations*, Vol.63, No.3: 1–8.

BURCHILL, F. (1997) *Labour Relations*, 2nd edition. London: Macmillan.

CHARTERED INSTITUTE OF PERSONNEL AND DEVELOPMENT (2010) *Employment Tribunals*. Available online at www.cipd.co.uk/subjects/emplaw/ tribunals/emptribs [accessed 5 July 2010].

COHEN, R. (1994) 'Resistance and hidden forms of consciousness amongst African workers', in E. Webster, L. Alfred, L. Bethlehem, A. Joffe and T. A. Selikow (eds) *Work and Industrialisation in South Africa*. Johannesburg: Raven.

CRONIN, J. (1979) *Industrial Conflict in Modern Britain*. Kent: Croom Helm.

DAVIES, J. C. (1978) 'Why do revolutions occur?', in P. Lewis, D. Potter and F. Castles (eds) *The Practice of Comparative Politics*. London: Longman.

DEPARTMENT OF LABOUR (2003) *Annual Report on Industrial Action: 2003*. Pretoria: Department of Labour.

DEPARTMENT OF LABOUR (2004) *Annual Report on Industrial Action: 2004*. Pretoria: Department of Labour.

DUNSTAN, R. (2005) *Hollow Victories: An update on the non-payment of employment tribunal awards*. London: Citizens Advice Bureau.

EDWARDS, P. (1986) *Conflict at Work: A materialist analysis of workplace relations*. Oxford: Blackwell.

ELDRIDGE, J. (1968) *Industrial Disputes*. London: Routledge & Kegan Paul.

FEDERATION OF EUROPEAN EMPLOYERS (2008) *Industrial Relations across Europe*. Available online at http://www.fedee.com/condits.html [accessed 5 July 2010].

GOLLAN, P. (2006) 'A process of transition – employer strategies and outcomes of employee voice at Eurotunnel', *Socio-Economic Review*, Vol.4, No.2: 337–51.

GOLLAN, P. (2009) 'Employer strategies towards non-union collective voice', in A. Wilkinson, P. Gollan, M. Marchington and D. Lewin (eds) *The Oxford Handbook of Participation in Organizations*. Oxford: Oxford University Press.

GUARDIAN (2009) Anti-foreign labour strikes bed in as talks continue. Available online at: http://www.guardian.co.uk/politics/2009/feb/03/wildcat-strikes-foreign-labour-talks [accessed 4 January 2011]

HORRELL, M. (1969) 'South Africa's workers' (mimeo.). Johannesburg: SAIRR.

HYMAN, R. (1981) *Strikes*. Glasgow: Fontana.

HYMAN, R. (1984) *Strikes*, 3rd edition. Glasgow: Fontana.

HYMAN, R. (1989) *The Political Economy of Industrial Relations*. London: Sage.

INTERNATIONAL LABOUR ORGANISATION (1983) *Freedom of Association and Collective Bargaining*. Report of the Committee of Experts on the Application of Conventions and Recommendations. Report III (Part 4B), International Labour Conference, 69th Session. Geneva.

KAUFMAN, B. and TARAS, D. (2000) *Non-union Employee Representation: History, contemporary practice, and policy*. Armonk, NY: M. E. Sharpe.

KEENOY, T. (1985) *Invitation to Industrial Relations*. Oxford: Blackwell.

KELLY, J. (1998) *Rethinking Industrial Relations: Mobilization, collectivism and long waves*. London: Routledge.

KERR, C. (1964) *Labour and Management in Industrial Society*. New York: Doubleday.

KNOWLES, K. G. (1952) *Strikes*. Oxford: Blackwell.

LEWIS, D. and SARGEANT, M. (2010) *Essentials of Employment Law*, 10th edition. London: CIPD.

MAREE, J. (1986) 'An analysis of the independent trade unions in South Africa in the 1970s'. Unpublished PhD thesis. Cape Town: University of Cape Town.

MAYO, E. (2003) *The Human Problems of an Industrial Civilization*. London: Routledge.

NEL, P., SWANEPOEL, B., KIRSTEN, M., ERASMUS, B. and TSABADI, M. (2005) *South African Employment Relations: Theory and practice*, 5th edition. Pretoria: Van Schaik.

RENSHAW, P. (1975) *The General Strike*. London: Eyre Methuen.

ROLLINSON, D. and DUNDON, T. (2007) *Understanding Employment Relations*. London: McGraw-Hill.

SALAMON, M. (1998) *Industrial Relations: Theory and practice*, 3rd edition. Hemel Hempstead: Prentice Hall.

TARAS, D. and KAUFMAN, B. (2006) *Non-Union* Employee *Representation in North America: Diversity, controversy,* and *uncertain future*. Andrew Young School of Policy Studies Research Paper Series, No. 06-46. Atlanta, GA: Georgia State University.

TRIBUNAL SERVICES (2010) *Annual Statistics for the Tribunals Service 2009–10*. Available at: http://www.tribunals.gov.uk/tribunals/Documents/Publications/tribs-annual-stats-2009-10c.pdf [accessed 4 January 2011].

WOOD, G. and GLAISTER, K. (2008) 'Union power and new managerial strategies', *Employee Relations*, Vol.30, No.4: 436–51.

CHAPTER 13

ADVISORY, CONCILIATION AND ARBITRATION SERVICE (2005) Advisory booklet: *Employee Communications and Consultation*. November. Available online at http://www.acas.org.uk/index.aspx?articleid=675 [accessed 29 June 2010].

ALLEN, A. (2009) 'How to make redundancies', *People Management*, May: 11.

ARMSTRONG-STASSEN, M. (1994) 'Coping with transition: a study of layoff survivors', *Journal of Organizational Behaviour*, Vol.15: 597–621.

ATKINSON, J. (1984) 'Manpower strategies for flexible organizations', *Personnel Management*, August: 28–31.

AYLING, L. (2010) *Transfer of Undertakings (TUPE)*. Factsheet. London: CIPD. Available online at http://www.cipd.co.uk/subjects/emplaw/tupe/tupe?NRMODE=Published&NRNODE [accessed 19 May 2010].

BACON, N. and BLYTON, P. (2006) 'Union co-operation in a context of job insecurity: negotiated outcomes from teamworking', *British Journal of Industrial Relations*, Vol.44, No.2: 215–37.

BENSON, E. (2009) 'Employment protection', in Gold, M. (ed.) *Employment Policy in the European Union: Origins, themes and perspectives*. London: Palgrave Macmillan.

BREWSTER, C., CAREY, L., DOWLING, P., GROBLER, P., HOLLAND, P. and WARNLICH, S. (2003) *Contemporary Issues in Human Resource Management: Gaining a competitive advantage*. Oxford: Oxford University Press.

BURAWOY, M. (1985) *The Politics of Production. Factory regimes under capitalism and socialism*. London: Verso.

BURCHELL, B. (2002) 'The prevalence and redistribution of job insecurity and work intensification', in B. Burchell, D. Lapido and F. Wilkinson, *Job Insecurity and Work Intensification*. London: Routledge.

CASEY, B. (2009) 'Employment promotion', in M. Gold (ed.) *Employment Policy in the European Union: Origins, themes and perspectives*. London: Palgrave Macmillan.

CHARLES, N. and JAMES, E. (2003) 'The gender dimensions of job security in a local labour market', *Work, Employment and Society*, Vol.17, No.3: 531–52.

CHARTERED INSTITUTE OF PERSONNEL AND DEVELOPMENT (2010) *Redundancy*. London: CIPD. Available online at http://www.cipd.co.uk/subjects/emplaw/redundancy/redundancy.htm?wa_src=email& [accessed 5 February 2010].

DANIELS, K. (2006) *Employee Relations in an Organisational Context*. London: CIPD.

DIBBEN, P. (2007) '"Employment security" and "job insecurity" in public services: two sides of the same coin?', in P. Dibben, P. James, I. Roper, and G. Wood (eds) *Modernising Work in Public Services*, London: Palgrave.

GRAY, A. (2009) 'Flexicurity: solution or illusion?', in M. Gold (ed.) *Employment Policy in the European Union: Origins, themes and perspectives*. London: Palgrave Macmillan.

GRUNBERG, I. (2002) 'Jobs for all: what have we learnt since the Social Summit?', *International Social Science Journal*, Vol.51, No.162: 483–91.

GUEST, D. (2000) 'Management and the insecure workforce: the search for a new psychological contract', in E. Heery and J. Salmon (eds) *The Insecure Workforce*. London: Routledge.

HAKIM, C. (1990) 'Core and periphery in employers' workforce strategies: evidence from the 1987 E.L.U.S. Survey', *Work, Employment and Society*, Vol.4, No.2: 157–88.

HAMMERTON, M. (2010) 'How should you respond to the agency workers challenge?', *People Management*, 25 February: 53.

HEERY, E. and ABBOTT, B. (2000) 'Trade unions and the insecure workforce', in E. Heery and J. Salmon (eds) *The Insecure Workforce*. London: Routledge.

HUNTER, L., MCGREGOR, A., MACINNES, J. and SPROULL, A. (1993) 'The "flexible firm": strategy and segmentation', *British Journal of Industrial Relations*, Vol.31, No.3: 383–408.

KELLY, J. (1996) 'Union militancy and social partnership', in P. Ackers, C. Smith and P. Smith (eds) *The New Workplace and Trade Unionism*. London: Routledge.

KINDER, A. (2009) 'How to cope with survivor syndrome', *People Management*, 21 May: 41.

KINNIE, N., HUTCHINSON, S. and PURCELL, J. (1998) 'Downsizing: is it always lean and mean?', *Personnel Review*, Vol.27, No.4: 296–311.

LABOUR MARKET COMMISSION (1996) *Restructuring the South African Labour Market: Report of the Comprehensive Labour Market Commission*. Pretoria: Department of Labour.

LADIPO, D. and WILKINSON, F. (2002) 'More pressure, less protection', in F. Burchell, D. Ladipo and F. Wilkinson, *Job Insecurity and Work Intensification*. London: Routledge.

LINDER, J., COLE, M. and JACOBSON, A. (2002) 'Business transformation through outsourcing', *Strategy and Leadership*, Vol.30, No.4: 23–8.

NIETO, M. (2006) *An Introduction to Human Resource Management: An integrated approach*. London: Palgrave.

PEOPLE MANAGEMENT (2010a) 'Indicator: legal statistics'. 25 February: 54.

PURCELL, K. (2000) 'Gendered employment insecurity', in E. Heery and J. Salmon (eds), *The Insecure Workforce*. London: Routledge.

PURSER, G. (2010) 'Broke and brokered in the day labor business'. Paper presented at the RC-44 Session on Precarious Labor at the World Congress of the International Sociological Association, Göteborg (Gothenburg), Sweden.

REDMAN, T. and WILKINSON, A. (2006) 'Downsizing', in T. Redman and A. Wilkinson (eds) *Contemporary Human Resource Management*. London: FT/ Prentice Hall.

SALAMON, M. (1998) *Industrial Relations: Theory and practice*, 3rd edition. Hemel Hempstead: Prentice Hall.

SISSON, K. and MARGINSON, P. (2003) 'Management: systems, structures and strategy', in P. Edwards (ed.) *Industrial Relations: Theory and practice*, 2nd edition. Oxford: Blackwell.

STANDING, G., SENDER, J. and WEEKS, J. (1996) *Restructuring the Labour Market: The South African challenge*. Geneva: International Labour Organisation.

STREECK, W. (1992) *Social Institutions and Economic Performance: Studies of industrial relations in advanced capitalist economies*. London: Sage.

THORNHILL, A. and SAUNDERS, M. (1998) 'The meanings, consequences and implications of the management of downsizing and redundancy: a review', *Personnel Review*, Vol.27, No.4: 271–95.

TURNBULL, P. and WASS, V. (2000) 'Redundancy and the paradox of job insecurity', in E. Heery and J. Salmon (eds), *The Insecure Workforce*. London: Routledge.

CHAPTER 14

BLANPAIN, R. (2007) *Comparative Labour Law and Industrial Relations in Industrialized Market Economies*. Alphen aan den Rijn: Kluwer Law International.

BUDHWAR, P. and DEBRAH, Y. (2001) 'Rethinking comparative and cross-national human resource management research', *International Journal of Human Resource Management*, Vol.12, No.3: 497–515.

BURAWOY, M. (1985) *The Politics of Production: Factory regimes under capitalism and socialism*. London: Verso.

CLARK, T., GRANT, D. and HEIJLTJES, M. (2000) 'Researching comparative and international human resource management', *International Studies of Management and Organizations*, Vol.29, No.4: 2–23.

COLLINGS, D. and WOOD, G. (2009) *Human Resource Management: A critical approach*. London: Routledge.

COONEY, S., GAHAN, P. and MITCHELL, R. (2010) 'Legal origins, labour law and the regulation of employment relations', in A. Wilkinson, and M. Townshend (eds) *The Future of Employment Relations: New paradigms, new developments*. London: Palgrave Macmillan.

DICKENS, L. (2008) 'The point of industrial relations: rising to the challenges', in R. Darlington (ed.) *What's the Point of Industrial Relations? In defence of critical social science*. Manchester: British Universities Industrial Relations Association.

ELAM, M. (1994) 'Puzzling out the post-Fordist debate', in A. Amin (ed.) *Post-Fordism: A reader*. Oxford: Blackwell Publishers, pp. 43–70.

FREGE, C. (2005) 'Varieties of industrial relations research: take-over, convergence or divergence?', *British Journal of Industrial Relations*, Vol.43, No.2: 179–207.

HALL, P. and SOSKICE, D. (eds) (2001) *Varieties of Capitalism: The institutional basis of competitive advantage.* Oxford: Oxford University Press.

HOLLINSHEAD, G., NICHOLLS, P. and TAILBY, S. (2003) *Employee Relations,* 2nd edition. Harlow: Pearson Education.

HYMAN, R. (1989) *The Political Economy of Industrial Relations.* London: Macmillan.

JESSOP, B. (1990) 'Regulation theories in retrospect and prospect', *Economy and Society,* Vol.19, No.2: 153–216.

KATZ, H. and DARBISHIRE, O. (2000) *Converging Divergences: Worldwide changes in employment systems.* Ithaca, NY: ILR Press/Cornell University Press.

KATZ, H., KOCHAN, T. and COLVIN, A. (2008) *An Introduction to Collective Bargaining and Industrial Relations.* New York: McGraw-Hill.

KELLY, J. (1998) *Rethinking Industrial Relations: Mobilization, collectivism and long waves.* London: Routledge.

KERR, C., DUNLOP, J. HARBISON, F. and MYERS, G. (1974) *Industrialism and Industrial Man.* Cambridge, MA: Harvard University Press.

MORLEY, M. GUNNIGLE, P. and COLLINGS, D. (eds.) (2006) *Global Industrial Relations.* London: Routledge.

PECK, J. (1996) *Work-Place: The social regulation of labor markets.* New York: Guilford Press.

PECK, J. and TICKELL, A. (1994) 'Searching for a new institutional fix: the after-Fordist crisis and the global–local disorder', in A. Amin (ed.) *Post-Fordism: A reader.* Oxford: Blackwell.

POOLE, M. (1986) *Industrial Relations: Origins and patterns of national diversity.* London: Routledge & Kegan Paul.

RUBERY, J. and GRIMSHAW, D. (2003) *The Organisation of Employment: An international perspective.* Basingstoke: Palgrave Macmillan.

STRAUSS, G. (1998) 'Comparative international industrial relations', in K. Whitfield and G. Strauss (eds) *Researching the World of Work.* Ithaca, NY: Cornell University Press.

TRAXLER, F., BLASCHKE, S. and KITTEL, B. (2001) *National Labour Relations in Internationalized Markets: A comparative study of institutions, change, and performance.* Oxford: Oxford University Press.

WHITLEY, R. (1999) *Divergent Capitalisms: The social structuring and change of business systems.* Oxford: Oxford University Press.

Index